W9-AYP-340

Growth and Distribution

Growth and Distribution

Duncan K. Foley
and
Thomas R. Michl

HARVARD UNIVERSITY PRESS
CAMBRIDGE, MASSACHUSETTS
LONDON, ENGLAND
1999

Copyright ©1999 by the President and Fellows of Harvard College

All rights reserved

Printed in the United States of America

Library of Congress Cataloging-in-Publication Data

Foley, Duncan K.

Growth and Distribution / Duncan K. Foley and Thomas R. Michl

p. cm.

Includes bibliographical references and index.

ISBN 0–674–36420–1 (alk. paper)

1. Economic development. 2. Income distribution.

I. Michl, Thomas R. II. Title

HD75.F65 1999

338.9—dc21

98–53613

For Betsy, Glyn, and Meredith

For Ruth and Gerry

Contents

Preface

These notes began as a set of notes for courses at Barnard College and Colgate University.

Inspiration for this work and a good deal of the substance of the models came from André Burgstaller, who gave us the privilege of reading the manuscript of his *Property and Prices* (Cambridge: Cambridge University Press, 1994), and with whom we have had extensive conversations on the topics covered here. In particular, Burgstaller's idea that equilibrium prices in a classical model can be viewed as the outcome of speculation in forward-looking asset markets is central to the point of view developed in Chapters 11 and 12.

Other important sources for our general approach are Stephen Marglin's *Growth, Distribution, and Prices* (Cambridge: Harvard University Press, 1984), and John Broome's *The Microeconomics of Capitalism* (London: Academic Press, 1983).

We thank Adalmir Marquetti for preparing the Extended Penn World Tables dataset, which made an indispensable contribution to our work and to this book. This data can be downloaded at *http://cepa.newschool. edu.*

We would like to thank Milind Rao, Peter Hans Matthews, Sergio Parrinello, Christophre Georges, and our students at Colgate University and Barnard College of Columbia University for their help in rectifying errors in earlier drafts.

We retain the responsibility for all the things that are wrong.

Duncan K. Foley

Thomas R. Michl

Notation

A	Scale parameter in Cobb-Douglas production function
α	Capital coefficient in Cobb-Douglas production function
β	Capitalist propensity to save out of wealth
B	Effective labor productivity
	Nominal value of government liabilities (ch 13)
b	Social Security benefit (ch 13)
c^r, c^w	Consumption of household in retired and working periods
χ	Rate of capital-saving technical progress
C, c	Consumption, social consumption per worker
c^w, c^r	Consumption of workers, retired (ch 13)
δ	Depreciation rate per unit of capital
D	Depreciation
E	Nominal primary fiscal surplus
η	Propensity to invest out of profit (ch 10)
f	Production function
	Invention possibility frontier (ch 15)
	Social security reserve fund (ch 13)
F	Cost of design process (ch 15)
G	Gold holdings
g_{variable}	Growth rate of variable. Thus:
g_K	Growth rate of capital
g_K^{max}	Maximal growth rate of capital
g_X	Growth rate of output
γ	Rate of labor-saving technical progress
I, i	Gross investment, gross investment per worker
J	Capitalist's wealth
K, k	Capital stock, capital stock per worker
λ	shadow price, Lagrange multiplier

N	Labor employed
n	Growth rate of labor force
ω	Viability threshold
p	Price of capital goods in terms of consumption (ch 3)
	Price of commodities in terms of gold (ch 14)
p_u, p_q	Price of land, oil
π	Profit share in income
$Q, \Delta Q$	Oil reserves, oil depletion
R	Profits
	Total return factor (ch 13)
rd	Proportion of capital outlays devoted to R&D
ρ	Output-capital ratio, capital productivity
r	Net profit rate
u	Utility function (ch 5)
	Capacity utilization (ch 10)
S	Saving
s	Saving as a proportion of output
s^w	Saving per worker (ch 13)
σ	Elasticity of substitution in production
t	Lump-sum tax (ch 13)
θ	Coefficient of R&D technology (ch 16)
U	Land
v	Gross profit rate
v_k, v_u	Rental on capital, land
W, w	Real wage bill, real wage per worker
$\bar{w}$	Conventional real wage
X, x	Gross output, gross output per worker
Y, y	Net output, net output per worker
Z, z	Cash flow, cash flow per worker

Growth and Distribution

Chapter 1

Introduction

Economic growth is the hallmark of our historical epoch. It finances and directs the ongoing revolution in technology that continually transforms our social and personal lives. The political preeminence of nation states and the emergence of supra-national institutions have their roots in the process of economic growth. The unprecedented growth and aging of the world's population are to a large extent the result of economic growth, as are the relative decline of agriculture and the dominance of industrial and post-industrial production centered in cities. National political and military power and influence increasingly reflect relative economic performance. Economic practices have transformed social relations and ideological beliefs. The great challenges we perceive for the future, including the protection of our environmental heritage and the preservation of social justice in a world polarized between wealth and poverty, arise from the effects of economic growth.

In this book we present *theories* that economists have devised over the last 200 years to analyze and explain various aspects of economic growth, and the movement of economies through time more generally. As a background to these theories, we review in this introductory chapter some of the *social history* of economic growth.

1.1 Economic Growth in Historical Perspective

Human history shows a slow improvement in technology and productivity from the earliest periods we know anything about. This improvement seems to have occurred in distinct waves, punctuated by such rapid leaps

1

as the adoption of settled agriculture, the emergence of cities, the establishment of long-distance sea trade, and so forth. The earth's human population grew very slowly, if at all, for the thousand years before 1500 C.E. Around the fifteenth century in Europe we see a noticeable acceleration of the pace of social and technological change, and in the rate of growth of population. This acceleration is marked by the enlargement of towns and cities, the spread of trade in goods and money, the growing importance of wealth invested in capitalist trade and production in towns in relation to traditional landed wealth, and a systematic focus on the improvement of technologies in production and transportation. By the sixteenth century the more advanced European societies have become recognizable forerunners of capitalist nation states. During this period people began to view trade and production as the central sources of national influence and power. The phenomenon of economic growth, with its problems and promises, had arrived.

Toward the end of the eighteenth century these developments underwent another sharp acceleration with the emergence, most notably in Britain, of *industrialization*. The scale of production increased dramatically and became concentrated in large towns and cities. A pattern emerged in which traditional farming, still based heavily on the needs of local subsistence, gave way to market-oriented agriculture, in the process displacing large numbers of the rural poor as common lands and forests were appropriated by large landowners and converted to the production of marketable commodities. The displaced agricultural poor moved to towns and cities, becoming both the wage-seeking labor force necessary to run rapidly expanding industries, and the mass of the urban poor. These economic developments precipitated huge migrations of people, not just from the countryside to cities, but from continent to continent. The growing economic and military power of the advanced nineteenth-century European nations led to their race to carve out colonies, empires, and spheres of influence all over the globe. In this way the phenomenon of economic growth sooner or later invaded every corner of the earth.

From its earliest stages the fostering, shaping, and taxing of economic growth was a preoccupation of the politically powerful. Economic growth confers immense political and military advantages on nations. *Political economy* arose as a discussion of the impact of national policies toward trade, labor markets, and taxation on economic growth.

Despite the evident fact that world economic growth is a unified, articulated, self-reinforcing phenomenon, political economy emphasizes national differences in policy and their impact on national economies. Thus the theories we will examine below take the national economy as their starting point, and treat each nation's economic growth as a separate experimental observation.

Adam Smith sums up the discoveries of the early political economists in his *Wealth of Nations* [Smith, 1937]. Smith argues that the fundamental character of economic growth lies in the *division of labor*, the process whereby individual producers specialize in small components of productive tasks, reaping enormous gains in their collective productivity. The division of labor is always supported in part by international trade. Economic growth from this point of view is the expression of a deep qualitative transformation of the way people organize themselves to produce.

1.2 Quality and Quantity

We experience economic growth overwhelmingly as *qualitative* change. Economic growth has moved most of us from small rural communities where individuals had lifelong personal relationships and employed simple and undifferentiated techniques of production to large urban agglomerations where most interactions are mediated by the anonymity of the market and we specialize in tiny aspects of a bewilderingly complex technology in order to produce. Economic growth means qualitatively new products and services—railroads, airplanes, and automobiles; electrical and electronic appliances; radio, television, telephones and computers; anesthesia, X-rays, and MRI scans.

But despite constant change in the commodities actually produced and the techniques through which people produce them, economic growth reproduces the same basic social relationships on an ever-increasing *quantitative scale*. Capitalist economic growth arises from the organization of production in particular firms or enterprises, which assemble human workers and the means of production they require to transform inputs available on the market into marketable outputs. Capitalist production rests on the quantitative increase in the money value of the product through the process of production, insofar as the marketed output is worth more than the inputs that were consumed to produce it. This *value added* appears as the wages of the workers who actually transform the inputs into outputs, and the profit, interest, and rent that constitute the incomes of the capitalist owners of factories and machines, money and natural resources including land. Economic growth is financed by the decisions of capitalists to reinvest some part of their incomes to allow production to take place on a larger scale.

The reinvestment of profits in the expansion of capitalist production, however, always involves a qualitative change in the technique of production and the actual commodities produced. The larger scale of production is carried out with somewhat different machines, in different locations, with differently trained and organized workers. On a larger scale, improvements and adaptations of the output are possible. In the process of economic growth the quantitative aspect of simple expansion of production through the reinvestment of profit incomes and the qualitative aspect of change in the products and the lives of the producers of the product are inextricably intertwined.

While the mathematically based theories of political economy emphasize the quantitative aspects of economic growth, it is important not to lose sight of the profound qualitative changes that ensue.

1.3   Human Relationships

The self-reinforcing cycle of capitalist economic growth cannot establish itself without deep changes in the ways people relate to each other. The constant expansion and restless change of capitalist production require a flexible labor force that can be redeployed, expanded, and contracted rapidly. Before the emergence of capitalism, these changes simply could not take place: workers were bound either to their employers as slaves or to the land they worked on as serfs. Capitalist economic growth rests on the *free worker*, who can accept or reject jobs, move from city to city and country to country in response to the incentives of wage differentials, and who takes the ultimate responsibility for her or his own survival and reproduction. The preoccupation of the free worker is to control the massive insecurity that wage labor brings with it. Thus in the capitalist world economy the great mass of the population becomes free labor which works for a wage. Because workers are free, and their wages are regulated only by the vagaries of competition, some prosper and some find themselves on the margin of existence.

On the other hand, the organization of work on a national and world scale requires the separately flexible deployment of factories, machines, and transportation facilities. This is the realm of *capital*, enormous concentrations of money available to finance production.

The owners and managers of capital have very different interests from those of workers. Wages and profit incomes divide the value added from production, so that capital and labor often find themselves on opposite sides of issues of social policy that affect the level of wages. Capital seeks a flexible and adaptable labor force, a goal that runs counter to the workers' desire for stability and security in their employment and conditions of life.

The political economic theory we survey in this book centers on the impact of the distribution of income between workers and capitalists on the quantitative aspects of economic growth, and the impact of growth on distribution.

1.4 Economic Theories of Growth

Adam Smith, whose *Inquiry into the Nature and Causes of the Wealth of Nations* [Smith, 1937] marks a key turning-point in the development of political economy, was primarily concerned with economic growth. In Smith's view the central aspects of economic growth were the *division of labor*, the separation of production processes into smaller tasks that can be assigned to specialists, and the *extent of the market*, the growth of population, income, and transportation and communication facilities that allow more output to be sold. The division of labor raises *labor productivity* as labor becomes more skilled in specialized tasks, and as machinery can be devised to take over the routine aspects of production. Smith sees technological progress as an aspect of the widening division of labor. The increasing division of labor and the widening extent of the market are mutually reinforcing tendencies in Smith's vision, since a wider market makes possible a more detailed division of labor, and a higher degree of division of labor increases productivity and incomes, encourages investment in transportation and the growth of population, and thus widens the market. The two phenomena are linked through a set of positive feedbacks into an unstable cycle of upward spiraling development. Smith thought that governments should try to foster this process by securing property, providing cheap legal services and national security, and otherwise staying out of private decisions about investment (the policy now known as *laissez-faire*). He argues that the cycle of growth is virtuous in that it benefits both workers and capitalists (a version of *trickle-down* economics): capitalists will be free to pursue maximum profitability of their investments, but the growth of capital will create a demand for labor and tend to pull up workers' wages as well. While population will grow along with capital in the process of growth, Smith thought that it would lag enough to assure a long period of higher wages. In Smith's version economic growth is spontaneous, or *endogenous*: it tends to take hold like the spread of a wildfire unless restrictive government policies repress it. We will study a simplified version of Smith's model in Chapter 6.

Thomas Malthus, whose *Essay on the Principles of Population* first appeared in 1799 [Malthus, 1986], had a distinctly gloomier view than Smith. Malthus could see that capital accumulation is a self-reinforcing feedback system, but doubted that it could do anything in the long run for the well-being of workers. Malthus reasoned that an increase in the real wage would raise workers' standards of living, encourage them to marry earlier, and reduce infant mortality among their offspring, thus producing a surge in population. The growing population would in turn crowd the labor market, driving real wages back down to the point where infant mortality and later marriage would stabilize population growth. The real wage at this *demographic equilibrium* would constitute a *natural* wage level around which actual wages could only fluctuate temporarily.

David Ricardo in his *Principles of Political Economy and Taxation*, published in 1817 [Ricardo, 1951], took up Malthus' ideas about population and the real wage and combined them with his own theory that rent arises from the limited supply of fertile land. In Ricardo's view, Smith's virtuous cycle was doomed to extinction as capital accumulation and population growth eventually used up all the fertile land, food prices rose, and profit rates declined to zero in what he called the *stationary state*. Ricardo's methods of analysis had an immense influence on later thinking about political economy. In particular, Ricardo emphasized the class divisions of early industrial capitalist society. Workers, with wages depressed to the minimum compatible with reproduction by Malthusian forces, had no surplus available to save. Landowners, the remnants of the feudal aristocracy, dissipated their incomes in the support of retainers and clients for political advantage and social status. Capitalists, on the other hand, forced by competition with each other to accumulate as much of their incomes as possible, were the engine of capital accumulation and growth. As profit rates fell as a result of rising rents and wages with population growth, however, Ricardo argued that the capitalist engine of growth would be choked off by a falling rate of profit. We work out Ricardo's reasoning in modern terms in Chapter 11.

Karl Marx published the first volume of his work *Capital* [Marx, 1977] in 1865, after spending his youth in the development of a revolutionary philosophy of *historical materialism*. Marx, along with his close associate Friedrich Engels, saw the secret of human history in the ways in which particular classes controlled the *surplus product* of their societies. In a slave-based society, for example, slaveowners controlled the whole product of the slave producers and were able to use the surplus over the required maintenance of the slaves to perpetuate the system. Feudal lords bound serfs to work a certain proportion of each week on their own fields, thus providing themselves with a surplus product (the serfs providing for their own needs by cultivating their own land the rest of the week) that allowed them to maintain armies to fight each other and repress the serfs. Each form of society has its own level of development, and its own characteristic class structure, from the point of view of Marx's historical materialism, and a clear understanding of these human relations is the key to understanding the society and its history.

Marx saw in Ricardo's picture of industrial capitalism a perfect example of a class society. Because they owned the means of production (factories, land, and so forth), landowners and capitalists were in a position to appropriate the surplus labor time of workers in the form of monetary profits and rents, which Marx called *surplus value*. Marx, however, disagreed with Ricardo's view that diminishing returns to capital and labor because of limited land would eventually bring capital accumulation to a halt through rising rents and wages. Marx took a more Smithian view, arguing that the historical genius of capitalism is its technological progressivity, enforced by the pressure on each capitalist to find cost-reducing technical innovations to keep ahead of its competitors. Thus Marx thought that capitalism could always overcome diminishing returns to limited land resources by finding cheaper technologies. What would lead to a fall in the rate of profit, Marx argued, was that these cheaper technologies would use more and more capital per worker, thus driving down the rate of profit. In the end, according to Marx and Engels, the very success of capitalism in raising labor productivity would lead to its replacement by a class-free socialist organization of production in which scarcity would have been eliminated. Some elements of Marx's theory of technical progress underlie the discussion of patterns of economic growth in Chapter 9. Marx's theory of induced technical change is the inspiration for the models of Chapters 15 and 16.

Turning away from the explosive social and political issues that the classical theory of growth seemed to lead to, marginalist economists focused their attention on the static *efficiency* of economic allocation, and the tendency for markets to equalize marginal costs and marginal benefits across society. The twentieth-century crises of the two World Wars and the Great Depression raised again the questions of the stability and long-run tendencies of economic growth. Roy Harrod [Harrod, 1939] argued that the process of economic growth was inherently unstable, because the rate of growth necessary to absorb society's saving in investment projects (which Harrod called the *warranted rate of growth*) would only by accident equal the underlying rate of growth of population adjusted for the rate of increase of labor productivity (which Harrod called the *natural rate of growth*). If the actual growth rate exceeded the warranted rate, chronic labor shortages, wage increases, and inflation would disrupt the growth process, but if the actual growth rate fell short of the warranted rate, the economy would slip into increasing unemployment, stagnation, and deflation. We look at a modernized extension of Harrod's model in Chapter 10.

Harrod's dilemma was addressed by Robert Solow's seminal *neoclassical growth model.* Solow argued that the possibility of substitution of capital for labor along the isoquant of an *aggregate production function* could adjust the warranted rate to any level of the natural rate of growth, and thus stabilize the capitalist growth process. We work through Solow's model in detail in Chapters 8 and 9.

While neoclassical economists generally accepted Solow's arguments and methods as settling the basic questions of the analysis of economic growth, economists working in the Keynesian, Marxian, and Ricardian traditions, led by Joan Robinson, strongly criticized the neoclassical model. The central point of controversy was Solow's assumption that there existed a well-behaved aggregate production function that could summarize the possibilities of substitution of capital for labor in the economy as a whole. The critics argued that capital was just the market valuation of a huge range of different *capital goods*: as the wage rate changes, the prices of all these goods can undergo any pattern of change, depending on the exact structure of their costs of production. In the end there is no guarantee, according to the critics, that a lower wage rate will lead to a lower value of capital per worker or more employment for a given stock of accumulated capital value, as the neoclassical production function analysis predicts. Since Solow and his supporter in this debate, Paul Samuelson, taught at M.I.T. in Cambridge, Massachusetts, and Joan Robinson and many of her supporters taught or were students at Cambridge University in England, this debate is known as the *Cambridge capital controversy*. While the neoclassicals conceded the theoretical possibility of the effects of changing wages on capital values pointed to by their critics, they argued that these possibilities were relatively unlikely in real economies and continued to assume that an aggregate production function would give a good approximation to the behavior of real economies.

The controversies of contemporary growth and capital theory create a dilemma for us in writing this book. Which basic approach should we use in setting forth and developing theories of growth? We have chosen to resolve this dilemma by presenting the basic framework of production and capital theory in Chapters 2 and 3 in terms of the *growth-distribution schedule*, a flexible starting point that is consistent with both neoclassical and nonneoclassical models, and that allows us to explain what is at issue in the capital controversy. Through most of this book we use production models with only a single produced good that can either serve as a consumption good or be accumulated as capital. Under that particular assumption, there can be no divergence between the conclusions of neoclassical and nonneoclassical models in the area of capital theory, and we focus attention on different theories of labor supply, saving, resource availability, demand generation, and technical change.

Our aim in presenting growth theory through the perspective of the growth-distribution schedule is to bring out the insights that both the classical and neoclassical theories of economic growth have reached, and to introduce the reader to the fascinating range of economic issues and concepts that growth theory raises.

1.5 Suggested Readings

To explore the history of economic theory, a good point of departure is the masterly treatment provided by Dobb [1973] followed by Kaldor [1956], which is devoted specifically to growth and distribution theories. Gram and Walsh [1980], a textbook exposition of the Classical versus the neoclassical approach, combines clear formal exposition with well-chosen textual passages from seminal works.

The early development of growth theory is surveyed at the professional level by Hahn and Matthews [1964]; for an accessible textbook treatment, try Jones [1976]. Many of the seminal contributions to early growth theory are contained in Stiglitz and Uzawa [1969]. The recent contributions called New Endogenous Growth Theory are allied with the neoclassical approach in some ways, such as their devotion to the full employment assumption, but differ in their view of technical change. They are described in such advanced textbooks as Romer [1996], Aghion and Howitt [1998], and Barro and Sala-i-Martin [1995], and in the undergraduate text by Jones [1998].

Two works which have deeply influenced the current text through their insightful comparative approach to the Keynesian, Classical, and neoclassical theories of growth and distribution are Harris [1978] and Marglin [1984].

Chapter 2

Measuring Growth and Distribution

Economic growth is an increase in a country's *output* of goods and services. Output is equal to the number of workers employed in production, *labor*, multiplied by the output produced by each worker, *labor productivity*. Labor productivity depends on *technology*, which also determines the amounts of other inputs to production, previously produced raw materials, tools, equipment, and buildings, *capital goods*, and natural resources, *land*, required by each worker. The number of workers employed in production, given technology, is thus limited by the accumulated stock of capital and the available land.

A country's rate of economic growth ultimately depends on the growth of its productive population, its *accumulation* of stocks of capital goods, and on *technological change*. Our aim in this book is to examine each of these sources of economic growth in detail, and to explain how their interaction results in the patterns we observe in empirical data.

Before we discuss explanations of economic growth, we need to be able to measure and to account for an economy's outputs and inputs. In this chapter we present an accounting system which will be the foundation for a series of models that attempt to explain and analyze the various aspects of the economic growth process.

2.1 Measuring Output and Inputs

The *total production* of an economy in any year consists of all its newly produced goods and services. Much of the total production serves to

10

replace goods and services used up in the process of production. *Gross production*, the difference between total production and the goods and services used up in production, is the collection of goods and services available for immediate use, *consumption*, and the accumulation of capital goods, *gross investment*. The *Gross Product* (GP)* is the value of gross production at current market prices, including consumption and gross investment. Gross investment, however, is offset by *depreciation*, the wear-and-tear and deterioration of existing long-lived capital goods. *Net Product* (NP) is equal to GP less the value attributed to depreciation, and thus includes only *net investment*. Since depreciation is not measured by actual market transactions, the measurement of net product is subject to more uncertainty than the measurement of gross product.

The use of market prices to calculate gross product reduces the large number of actual goods and services that constitute gross production to a single number, which is a great simplification. Changes in gross product, however, can arise either because gross production has changed, or because market prices have changed (for example, through inflation). Economists measure price changes by constructing a *price index*, a weighted average of the actual prices observed during a year, divided by a similar weighted average of actual prices in some base year. Different systems of weights produce somewhat different price indexes. We estimate the *real output* of an economy by dividing its gross product by a price index, thus correcting for pure price changes. We will refer to the real gross product in an economy in a period simply as its *output*, and denote it by the mathematical symbol X.

A research team at the University of Pennsylvania, under the leadership of Robert Summers and Allen Heston, has undertaken the task of compiling a consistent set of measures of Gross Domestic Product and price indexes based on purchasing power parity for most countries in the world starting in 1950 (or in later years in those countries which have no statistical sources for earlier years). This data set, often called the Penn World Tables (PWT), is available on the World Wide Web. The PWT expresses the output of each country in each year in terms of 1985 international dollars, and thus corrects for differing price levels between countries and differing rates of inflation within countries. Adalmir Marquetti has supplemented the PWT tables by calculating capital stocks, including measures of the distribution of income, and adding information on population growth in the data set used in this book, which we

---

* *Gross Domestic Product* (GDP) is the gross product produced in a given country in a year. Economists also refer to *Gross World Product* for the gross product of the entire world economy, *Gross State Product* for the product of a particular state, and so on.

will refer to as the *Extended Penn World Tables*, or EPWT. Unless we specify otherwise, we measure output in this book in terms of the Penn World Tables 1985 international dollar, and use the symbol $ as a shorthand for this unit. It is important to remember that this $ is a measure of real, inflation-corrected output.

In measuring the output of an economy it is important to keep track of the deterioration of the capital stock through wear-and-tear and the passage of time, *depreciation*, D. The net product, $Y = X - D$, measures the output of the society reduced by an estimate of depreciation.

We measure labor input as the number of employed workers (or in some cases, the number of hours of work), and denote it with the mathematical symbol N. In real economies workers vary in skills and ability, so that in principle it would be desirable to measure labor input as a weighted average of employed workers, with the weights representing the skill and ability levels of individual workers. In the theoretical parts of the book we could interpret the labor input as such a weighted average without changing the arguments. Since detailed data on the skill and ability levels of workers are not available for many countries, we simply abstract from differing skill and ability levels in presenting empirical measurements of labor input.

Capital goods in real economies represent a heterogeneous collection of stocks of raw materials and partly finished goods, plant, equipment, transportation facilities, and so forth. In principle, it would be desirable to measure capital input with a detailed list of all the different categories of capital goods. It is also possible to aggregate capital goods by measuring their value at market prices at the time of their construction, which is the procedure we use. Thus we calculate the capital input, denoted by the mathematical symbol K, as the sum of the real value of past gross investment, less the estimated sum of accumulated depreciation. Capital is measured in the same units as output, 1985 international dollars.

The measurement of capital inputs in this way has been the center of considerable theoretical debate among economists, particularly during the Cambridge capital controversy of the 1960s. The difficulty is that the same value aggregate of capital can represent completely different collections of actual capital goods, and that the same collection of actual capital goods can have a different aggregate value if the prices of individual capital goods change. In our theoretical models we assume that there is only one output, and that capital is accumulated output, thereby avoiding the problem of relative prices. The empirical measures of capital input we use, however, are subject to the limitations of the aggregate value method. As we will explain in more detail below, a further controversy over capital input arises in the context of the neoclassical production function, which assumes that the value of capital as such contributes to the level of real output. We do not agree with this position, since in our view the level of real output depends on technology, which in turn requires certain levels of capital goods, and, consequently, certain values of capital goods. The exploration of these different points of view is one of the main themes of the later chapters of this book.

In some theoretical models we consider land (conceived of broadly as natural resources and environmental quality) as an input to production. In the theoretical models we simply take the available quantity of land as the unit of land, so that the quantity of land is always 1. The measurement of natural resource and environmental inputs to production in real economies is an active but relatively underdeveloped area of economic research, so that we cannot present empirical data on land inputs.

In comparing different economies, or the same economy in different years, it is often useful to measure output and capital stock per employed worker. Output per employed worker, $x = X/N$, is a measure of average labor productivity, or, more simply, *labor productivity*: labor productivity has the units of output per worker per year, or \$/worker-year. Capital stock per worker, $k = K/N$, is a measure of *capital intensity*, and has the units \$/worker. $\rho = X/K = x/k$ (the Greek letter *rho*, pronounced "row") is the *output-capital ratio*, which has the units \$/year/\$, or 1/years, a pure number like an interest rate. By analogy to x, average labor productivity, we often refer to ρ as the average productivity of capital or *capital productivity*. As we remarked above, we do not view capital as such as directly productive, since capital goods serve to enhance the productivity of workers, but this usage is so common and convenient that we have adopted it. The ratio of depreciation to the capital stock is $\delta = D/K$ (the Greek letter *delta*, pronounced "del'-ta"). $y = Y/N$ is *net output per worker*. The ratio of the net output to the capital stock is $Y/K = (X - D)/K = \rho - \delta$.

These key ratios can be calculated on the basis of the data in the Extended Penn World Tables data set for many countries for recent years. Economic historians have made estimates of these variables for a few key countries over longer historical periods.

2.2 Time and Production

Because we are concerned with economic growth, *time* plays a key role in the analysis. We will measure variables in a sequence of discrete periods, $t = 0, 1, 2, \ldots$. Real world economic time is much more complicated, with some processes (like stock and foreign exchange markets) moving extremely rapidly, even minute by minute, and other processes (the construction of large power plants or factories, the aging of the population) moving relatively much more slowly. However, the outcomes of all these processes are always measured statistically over fixed periods (each year, or quarter of a year, or month, or week, for example), and we can easily fit these real measurements into a period framework.

When we have actual economic data we will indicate its time by writing it explicitly as a subscript: X_{1995} will indicate real (that is, inflation-adjusted) Gross Domestic Product (GDP) in 1995. In order to simplify mathematical expressions, we will assume that any variable without a subscript refers to the current year, and indicate the next year's variable with the subscript "+1". Thus X will be current year GDP (for whatever particular year we are analyzing) and X_{+1} next year's GDP.

In the analysis of economic growth the concept of *growth rates* plays an important role. We will write the change in a variable, for example, X, over one period as $\Delta X = X_{+1} - X$, and the one-period growth rate as $g_X = \Delta X / X$.[†] Economists generally refer to the growth rate of output, g_X, as the *growth rate* of the economy. In our models, the growth rate of the capital stock, g_K, plays a key role.

The *growth factor* for a variable is the ratio of the next period's value to the initial period's value. For one period, this is just the growth rate plus one. For example, the growth factor of output is $X_{+1}/X = 1 + g_X$.

2.3   A Note on Units

In using this accounting system careful attention to the units involved is required to avoid confusion. X is the GDP in a period, usually a year, and is measured in units of output per year ($\$T^{-1}$). Here $\$$ stands for the units in which capital and output are measured, real dollars, and T stands for time, so that $\$T^{-1}$ means dollars per year. U.S. X_{1991} was about $\$$ 5.7 trillion/year, for example. The capital stock K is accumulated output ($\$$), and is measured in the same units as output. For example, private nonresidential U.S. K_{1991} was about $\$$ 8.7 trillion.

Since $\rho = X/K = \$T^{-1}\$^{-1} = T^{-1}$, we can see that ρ must be measured in inverse time units, like an interest rate. The output-capital ratio, ρ, shows output as a proportion of the capital stock. $\rho_{1991} = \$5.7$ trillion/year/$\$$ 8.7 trillion/year $= .66/$ year, or 66%/year.

[†]The actual average compound growth rate of a variable X between time 0 and time T is $g_X = (\ln X_T - \ln X_0)/T$, where ln is the natural logarithm. If $T = 1$, this becomes $g_X = \ln X_1 - \ln X_0 = \ln(X_1/X_0) = \ln(1 + (\Delta X/X)) \approx \Delta X/X$, since when ϵ is small, $\ln(1 + \epsilon) \approx \epsilon$. Thus if changes in variables are small relative to their levels, the definition of the growth rate in the text is close to the actual average compound rate of growth.

Depreciation, D, is measured in the same units as output. U.S. private nonresidential D_{1991} was \$ .45 trillion/year. The depreciation rate, $\delta = D/K = \$T^{-1}\$^{-1} = T^{-1}$, also has the dimension of inverse time, like an interest rate. U.S. private nonresidential $\delta_{1991} = \$ .45$ trillion/year/\$ 8.7 trillion/year $= .05$/year or 5%/year. δ measures the proportion of the value of the capital stock that disappears through deterioration each year.

N is the number of workers employed. U.S. N_{1991} was 118 million. x is output per worker per period $(\$N^{-1}T^{-1})$. U.S. x_{1991} was \$ 5.7 trillion/year/118 million workers $= \$48,000$/worker-year.

It is very important to be sure that the time units are consistent in each problem; if you measure output per year and labor input per week, the result will be nonsense.

2.4 Technology in the Real World

The Extended Penn World Tables data set contains estimates of ρ, x, and k for many countries and many years. The EPWT reveals some broad patterns that are central to understanding the process of economic growth in the real world.

Figure 2.1 shows $\{\rho, x\}$ points for 49 countries[‡] in 1980 from the EPWT. Economic development tends to lower ρ as it raises x, as the Figure indicates. Falling capital productivity arises because economic development leads to more capital-intensive methods of production. Thus workers become more productive, but the amount of capital they work with increases even more than their productivity, so that the productivity of capital actually tends to fall.

The same information can be plotted in $\{k, x\}$ terms. Figure 2.2 plots the same data in this form. The positive relation between k and x shows that the process of economic growth tends to increase the capital stock per worker at the same time that it increases output per worker. This strong correlation is one reason some economists think that a stable *production function* links k and x.

One of the aims of different theories of economic growth and technical change is to account for these strongly marked (though not uniformly observed) patterns.

[‡]Algeria, Burundi, Egypt, Ethiopia, Ghana, Kenya, Morocco, Nigeria, South Africa, Tanzania, Uganda, Zaire, Zambia, Zimbabwe, Canada, Mexico, U.S., Argentina, Brazil, Chile, Colombia, Ecuador, Peru, Venezuela, Bangladesh, China, Hong Kong, India, Indonesia, Japan, Republic of Korea, Malaysia, Pakistan, Philippines, Singapore, Taiwan, Thailand, France, West Germany, Greece, Ireland, Italy, Netherlands, Spain, Sweden, Switzerland, Turkey, U.K., and Australia.

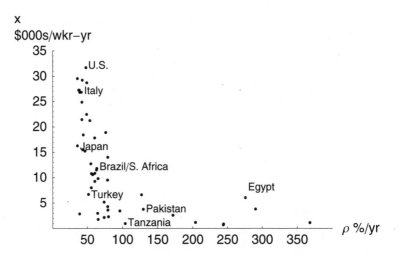

Figure 2.1: $\{\rho, x\}$ points for 49 countries at widely differing levels of economic development in 1980, from the EPWT. There is a strong inverse correlation between ρ and x: as countries develop, ρ tends to fall (due to industrialization and the adoption of capital-intensive techniques of production), as x rises.

$$\rho = \frac{x}{k} \; : \; \text{the speed of } x \ll k\text{'s}$$

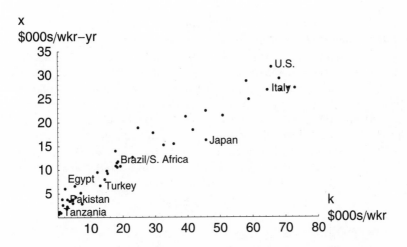

Figure 2.2: $\{k, x\}$ points for 49 countries at widely differing levels of economic development in 1980, from the EPWT. There is a strong positive correlation between k and x: as countries develop, k tends to rise (due to industrialization and the adoption of capital-intensive techniques of production) as x rises.

2.5   The Uses of Output: Investment and Consumption

Output can be used either for *consumption, C*, or *gross investment, I*.

National income accounting gives us a system for measuring the output of an economy and its uses. The basic identity of national income accounting is that GDP = Consumption + Gross Investment + Government Expenditure + Net Exports. For the analysis of economic growth we want to divide the output of an economy into two categories: consumption, output that is used up in the period, and gross investment, output that is devoted to increasing the capital stock. A significant part of government expenditure in real economies takes the form of investment in productive facilities like roads, harbors, airports, and so forth. In our theoretical models, we interpret consumption and gross investment as including the corresponding parts of government expenditure. In presenting empirical data, when detailed breakdowns of government expenditure between consumption and investment are not available we have somewhat arbitrarily allocated both government expenditure and net exports to consumption, which may distort the resulting picture of gross investment. We will accordingly write the *output identity* as:

$$X \equiv C + I \tag{2.1}$$

We can divide through both sides of this equation by N to express output per worker, x, as the sum of consumption per worker, c (which may not all be consumed by workers), and gross investment per worker, i:

$$x \equiv c + i \tag{2.2}$$

Net output, Y, is the gross product less depreciation.

$$Y \equiv X - D = X - \delta K \tag{2.3}$$

We can also express this in per-worker terms:

$$y = x - \delta k \tag{2.4}$$

Problem 2.1 *Ricardia is a corn economy, where the capital completely depreciates each year. Suppose that 20 bushels of seed corn can be planted by one worker to yield 100 bushels of harvest at the*

Table 2.1:

U.S., 1989: Output Account

Variable	Symbol	Value	Units
Output	X	4.492×10^{12}	$/year
Consumption	C	3.611×10^{12}	$/year
Gross Investment	I	$.880 \times 10^{12}$	$/year
Depreciation	D	$.663 \times 10^{12}$	$/year
Net Output	Y	3.829×10^{12}	$/year
Capital	K	6.946×10^{12}	$
Employment	N	121.863×10^{6}	workers
Labor Productivity	x	36,859	$/worker-year
Net Labor Productivity	y	31,421	$/worker-year
Consumption per worker	c	29,635	$/worker-year
Investment per worker	i	7,224	$/worker-year
Capital-Labor Ratio	k	56,997	$/worker
Capital productivity	ρ	64.7	%/year
Depreciation rate	δ	9.1	%/year

Source: Extended Penn World Tables

end of the year. Find x, k, ρ, δ, and y for Ricardia. How many workers and how much seed corn would be needed to grow a million bushels of corn?

Problem 2.2 *In Industria $50,000 worth of output requires one worker-year of labor working with $150,000 worth of capital. If 1/15 = .0666 = 6.66% of the capital depreciates in each year, what x, k, ρ, δ, and y would you choose to represent the Industrian production system? How much labor and capital would be needed to produce $8 trillion in output in this economy? What would its net output be?*

2.6 The Social Consumption-Growth Rate Schedule

The change in the capital stock from one period to the next, the *accumulation of capital*, is a key aspect of economic growth. The next period's capital stock is equal to this period's capital stock less depreciation plus gross investment:

$$K_{+1} = K - \delta K + I = (1 - \delta)K + I \tag{2.5}$$

The growth rate of the capital stock, g_K, is equal to the increase in capital divided by the initial level of capital:

$$g_K = \frac{K_{+1}}{K} - 1 \tag{2.6}$$

By dividing (2.5) by K, we can express the relation between gross investment per worker and the growth rate of the capital stock:

$$g_K = \frac{K_{+1} - K}{K} = \frac{I - D}{K} = \frac{i}{k} - \delta \tag{2.7}$$

Every economy faces a tradeoff between consuming output and investing it to provide for future consumption. This tradeoff is the *production possibilities frontier* between consumption and investment. In real economies the production possibilities frontier may be concave, reflecting rising costs as resources are shifted from producing consumption to investment. We will approximate the production possibility frontier as a straight line with slope $= -1$ and intercepts equal to X, as illustrated in Figure 2.3.

In studying economic growth, it is convenient to express this tradeoff directly in terms of consumption and the growth rate of the capital stock. To facilitate the comparison of different economies of different sizes, we measure consumption and gross investment per employed worker. Equation (2.7) allows us to construct this key relationship, the *social consumption-growth rate schedule*:

$$c = x - (g_K + \delta)k = y - g_K k \tag{2.8}$$

In words, social consumption per worker is the output left over after the replacement of depreciation and the increase in the stock of capital have been accounted for.

We can also write the social consumption-growth rate schedule in the form:

$$x = c + (g_K + \delta)k \tag{2.9}$$

The social consumption-growth rate schedule is illustrated in Figure 2.4.

Sometimes it is convenient to express the social consumption-growth rate schedule in terms of the productivity of capital, ρ, rather than the

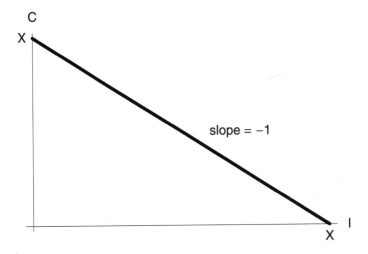

Figure 2.3: The production possibility frontier between consumption and investment is a straight line with slope equal to -1 and intercepts equal to output, if the economy can shift resources from consumption to gross investment without rising costs.

capital intensity, k. In terms of ρ, x, and δ, the social consumption-growth rate schedule is:

$$c = x(1 - \frac{g_K + \delta}{\rho})$$ (2.10)

We can also solve the social consumption-growth rate schedule for $g_K + \delta$:

$$g_K + \delta = \frac{x - c}{k} = (1 - \frac{c}{x})\rho$$ (2.11)

Problem 2.3 *Show the effect of an increase in labor productivity, holding the output-capital ratio and the depreciation rate constant, on the social consumption-growth rate schedule of an economy.*

Problem 2.4 *Show the effect of an increase in the output-capital ratio, holding labor productivity and the depreciation rate constant, on the social consumption-growth rate schedule of an economy.*

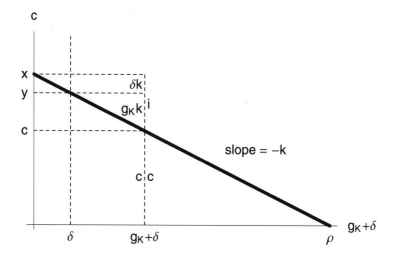

Figure 2.4: The *social consumption-growth rate schedule* expresses the tradeoff between consumption and the growth of the capital stock. For a given technology the schedule is a straight line with slope equal to $-k$, the capital-labor ratio. If the economy consumed all its output, x, $g_K + \delta = 0$, and the capital stock would shrink at the rate of depreciation $-\delta$. If the economy invested all its output, consumption would be zero, $g_K + \delta = \rho$, and the capital stock would grow at the rate $\rho - \delta$. When the growth rate of the capital stock is zero, consumption is equal to the net product, y. At the actual $g_K + \delta$, output per worker is divided into consumption per worker, c, and gross investment per worker, i, which equals net investment per worker, $g_K k$, plus depreciation per worker, δk.

Problem 2.5 *Show the effect of an increase in the depreciation rate, holding labor productivity and the output-capital ratio constant, on the social consumption-growth rate schedule of an economy.*

Problem 2.6 *Draw the social consumption-growth rate schedule for the U.S. economy in 1989, using the data presented above.*

Problem 2.7 *Draw the social consumption-growth rate schedule for Ricardia (see Problem 2.1.) If the growth rate of the capital stock is 100% per year, how large is social consumption?*

Problem 2.8 *Draw the social consumption-growth rate schedule for Industria (see Problem 2.2). If the growth rate of the capital stock is 10% per year, how large is social consumption?*

2.7 The Distribution of Income: Wages and Profit

In capitalist economies capital is owned privately by profit-seeking capitalists, and workers work for a wage. The revenue from selling the output after the costs of intermediate inputs are deducted takes the form of wages and gross profit, including depreciation. Gross profit in turn is divided into depreciation and net profit, which is distributed in a variety of ways, as interest payments on debt, rents, royalties, taxes, and dividends. We will refer to gross profit simply as "profit."

Thus in a capitalist economy we can divide the value of output, X, into wages, W, and profit, Z, and profit in turn into net profit, R, and depreciation, D. This decomposition is the *income identity*. Profit, Z, the sum of depreciation and net profit, is also called *cash flow*.

$$X \equiv W + Z = W + R + D, \text{ or} \qquad (2.12)$$

$$Y \equiv X - D = W + R$$

The ratio of the total wage bill to employment, W/N, is the *average real wage*, w. We will often refer to the average real wage simply as the *wage*.

The ratio of profit to the capital stock, Z/K, is the *profit rate*, v. The ratio of net profit to the capital, R/K, is the *net profit rate*, r. The difference between the gross and the net profit rate is the depreciation rate: $v = r + \delta$.

Table 2.2:

U.S., 1989: Income Account

Variable	Symbol	Value	Units
Output	X	4.492×10^{12}	\$/year
Wages	W	2.687×10^{12}	\$/year
(Gross) Profit	Z	1.805×10^{12}	\$/year
Depreciation	D	$.663 \times 10^{12}$	\$/year
Net Profit	R	1.142×10^{12}	\$/year
Net Output	Y	3.829×10^{12}	\$/year
Capital	K	6.946×10^{12}	\$
Employment	N	121.863×10^{6}	workers
Labor Productivity	x	36,859	\$/worker-year
Net Labor Productivity	y	31,421	\$/worker-year
Real Wage	w	22,064	\$/worker-year
Profit per Worker	z	14,795	\$/worker-year
Profit Rate	v	25.1	%/year
Depreciation Rate	δ	9.1	%/year
Net Profit Rate	r	16.4	%/year

Source: Extended Penn World Tables

2.8   The Real Wage-Profit Rate Schedule

In a capitalist economy there is a tradeoff between wages and profit, given the value of output. Just as with the social consumption-growth rate tradeoff, we can measure wages and profit per employed worker. This allows us to construct another key relationship, the *real wage-profit rate schedule*:

$$\frac{W}{N} = \frac{X}{N} - \frac{Z}{N} = \frac{X}{N} - \frac{D}{N} - \frac{R}{N}, \text{ or} \qquad (2.13)$$

$$w = x - vk = x - \delta k - rk = y - rk$$

In words, the wage can be regarded as the output left over after the capitalist has received her profit.

We can also write the real wage-profit rate relationship as:

$$x = w + vk \qquad (2.14)$$

The real wage-profit rate schedule is illustrated in Figure 2.5.

Sometimes it is convenient to express the real wage-profit rate schedule in terms of the productivity of capital, ρ, rather than the capital intensity, k. In terms of ρ, x, and δ, the real wage profit-rate schedule is:

$$w = x\left(1 - \frac{v}{\rho}\right) \qquad (2.15)$$

We can also solve the real wage-profit rate schedule for v:

$$v = \frac{x - w}{k} = \left(1 - \frac{w}{x}\right)\rho \qquad (2.16)$$

Problem 2.9 *Draw the real wage-profit rate schedule for the U.S. economy in 1989, using the data presented above.*

Problem 2.10 *Draw the real wage-profit rate schedule for Ricardia (see Problem 2.1). If the real wage is 20 bushels of corn a year, what is the profit rate, and the cash flow per worker?*

Problem 2.11 *Draw the real wage-profit rate schedule for Industria (see Problem 2.2). If the real wage is $10 per hour and workers work 2000 hours each year, what is the profit rate and the cash flow per worker?*

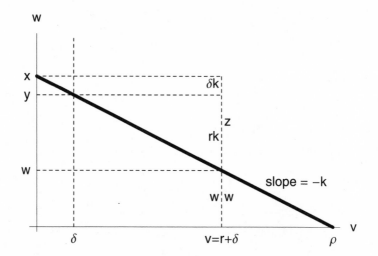

Figure 2.5: The *real wage-profit rate schedule* shows the relationship between real wages and the profit rate in a capitalist economy with given labor and capital productivity. For a given technology the schedule is a straight line with slope equal to $-k$, the capital-labor ratio. When real wages are equal to output per worker, x, the profit rate, $v = 0$, and the net profit rate, $r = -\delta$. When the real wage is zero, the profit rate, $v = \rho$, and the net profit rate $r = \rho - \delta$. When the net profit rate is zero, the real wage is equal to the net product, y. At the actual profit rate output is divided into the components of income: the wage, w, and profit per worker, z, which equals net profit per worker, rk, plus depreciation per worker, δk.

2.9 Income Shares

The value of output, which accrues to workers and capitalists as income, is divided into the part going to workers as wages (the wage bill) and the part going to the owners of capital as profit. If we want to express these two parts as shares of income, we have only to divide them by output. The *profit share* is:

$$\pi \equiv \frac{X - W}{X} = \frac{x - w}{x} = (1 - \frac{w}{x})$$

and the *wage share* is one minus the profit share, or:

$$1 - \pi \equiv \frac{W}{X} = \frac{w}{x}$$

It is sometimes helpful to use the profit or wage share instead of the wage in describing the distribution of the value of output in an economy. We can, for example, write the real wage-profit rate schedule in terms of π, using equation 2.16:

$$v = (1 - \frac{w}{x})\rho = \pi\rho \tag{2.17}$$

or:

$$\pi = \frac{v}{\rho} \tag{2.18}$$

Profit and wage shares can be calculated using national income accounts. Historical data for long periods, however, are available for only a few of the main countries. Table 2.3 shows the profit share in the U.S., the U.K., and Japan for selected years during the last century. These data show that the profit share has remained fairly stable during the twentieth century. It is usually around one-fourth to two-fifths of the GDP of these countries but because of differences in definition, we can not make comparisons between countries in Table 2.3. The profit share gives some indication of decline since the nineteenth century. This decline was not spread out evenly, but seems to occur abruptly over a few decades, depending on the country.

On close inspection, time series data show that the profit share is not very stable. One source of instability occurs at frequencies of the business cycle, or every five years or so. During recessions, profit shares tend to decline, only to recover with the return of prosperity. The data in Table 2.3 try to correct for this cyclical variation (since we are concerned

Table 2.3:

**Profit Shares in the U.S., U.K., and Japan for Selected Years
from 1956–1989**

U.S.		U.K.		Japan	
Year	Share	Year	Share	Year	Share
1869	39.7	1856	40.9	1908	42.4
1880	51.9	1873	43.1	1917	50.2
1913	38.0	1913	38.8	1924	33.7
1924	40.4	1924	29.9	1938	40.0
1937	36.6	1937	32.1	1954	24.7
1951	39.7	1951	27.1	1964	33.0
1965	41.9	1964	27.6		
1973	40.6	1973	25.5		
1989	41.1				

Sources: For the U.S., authors' calculations from [Duménil and Lévy,
1994, pp. 354–361]; U.K. from [Matthews et al., 1982, Table 6.8];
Japan from [Ohkawa and Rosovsky, 1973, pp. 316–317].

with long-term patterns) by choosing years near the peak of the business
cycle, but some cyclical variation unavoidably remains.

The advanced capitalist countries now publish national income accounts, from which it is possible to calculate the profit shares over the
last three decades. The Organization for Economic Cooperation and
Development (OECD) collects and compiles this data in standardized
form. Table 2.4 shows the average profit share over each of the last three
decades reported by the OECD for a group of six countries, at the level
of the total business sector. (Differences in coverage make it hazardous
to compare directly Tables 2.4 and 2.3.) The data reveal that the 1970s
was generally a period of shrunken profit shares among these countries,
compared to the 1960s. This historical event has been called the "profit
squeeze" by some observers. In most cases, the profit share subsequently
recovered during the 1980s and 1990s.

It would not be strictly correct to say that the profit share is constant.
Yet the profit share seems to remain near a value of one-third in the
advanced capitalist countries over long periods of time.

Table 2.4:
Profit Shares in the Business Sectors of Six Countries in Selected Periods

Country	1960–73	1974–79	1980–89	1990–95
U.S.	33.0	32.2	33.2	33.7
France	31.8	29.8	32.2	38.4
Germany	30.7	29.4	31.5	34.5
Netherlands	32.3	29.5	35.8	38.2
U.K.	30.7	29.9	30.7	29.1
Japan	40.6	30.3	31.5	33.2

Source: Authors' calculations from OECD [1997].
Notes: For the U.S., 1964-68 and 1969-79. The profit shares in the U.S. and Japan are adjusted for unpaid family members.

2.10   The Growth-Distribution Schedule

If you experienced a sense of *déjà vu* in reading section 2.8, it is not surprising, because the social consumption-growth rate schedule is exactly the same as the real wage-profit rate schedule. If you compare (2.8) to (2.13) you will see that the relations are exactly the same, except that w has been substituted for c, and v for $g_K + \delta$. The reason for this resemblance is that both the real wage-profit rate relation and the social consumption-growth rate relation depend only on k, x, and δ. The social consumption-growth rate relation represents the distribution of output between gross investment in future output and consumption. The real wage-profit rate schedule represents the distribution of the value of the output between wages and profit, including depreciation. The same technology underlies both relations. The combination of the two schedules is called the *growth-distribution schedule* for the economy, as illustrated in Figure 2.6.

Since the growth-distribution schedule describes both the distribution of output between consumption and gross investment and the distribution of the value of output between wages and profit, it shows the aggregate national income and product accounts graphically. The key income and output identities in aggregate and per worker terms are:

$$X \equiv C + I = C + (g_K + \delta)K$$

$$x \equiv c + i = c + (g_K + \delta)k \qquad (2.19)$$

$$Y \equiv X - D = C + (I - D) = C + g_K K$$

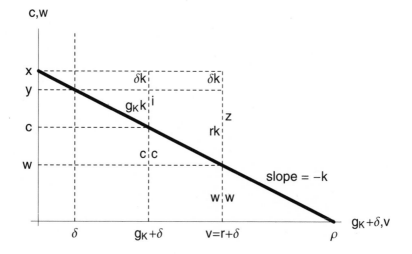

Figure 2.6: The *growth-distribution schedule* combines the social consumption-growth rate schedule and the real wage-profit rate schedule to give a complete view of the growth process in a capitalist economy. The growth rate need not equal the profit rate, because some part of the profits may be consumed. Social consumption per worker likewise exceeds the real wage because of the existence of capitalist consumption out of profits.

$$y \equiv x - \delta k = c + (i - \delta k) = c + g_K k \qquad (2.20)$$

$$X \equiv W + Z = W + vK = W + R + D = W + rK + \delta K$$

$$x \equiv w + z = w + vk = w + rk + \delta k \qquad (2.21)$$

$$Y \equiv X - D = W + R = W + rK$$

$$y \equiv x = \delta k = w + rk \qquad (2.22)$$

The product accounts show that output is social consumption plus gross investment (2.19), and that net output is social consumption plus net investment (2.20). The income accounts show that the value of output is wages plus profit (2.21), and that the value of net output is wages plus net profit (2.22).

The growth-distribution schedule is a good starting point for the empirical analysis of growth in a real-world economy. The data you need to construct it are output per worker, x, the capital-labor ratio, k, or the productivity of capital, ρ, and the depreciation rate, δ, together with income and product account measures of consumption per worker, c, gross investment per worker, i, the wage, w, and the profit rate, v. These data are available for many countries and years in the Extended Penn World Tables. You can graph the growth-distribution schedule for one country for one year, or for the same country over several years to understand the chief factors responsible for growth, or for more than one country in a single year to compare their growth patterns.

Problem 2.12 *Graph the growth-distribution schedule for the U.S. economy in 1989.*

Problem 2.13 *Graph the growth-distribution schedule for Ricardia if the wage is 20 bu/worker-year and the growth rate of capital is 100% per year.*

Problem 2.14 *Graph the growth-distribution schedule for Industria when the net profit rate is 13.33% per year and the growth rate of capital is 6.66% per year.*

2.11 Changes in Labor and Capital Productivity

A very important aspect of economic growth is changes in the productivity parameters of the economy, x, ρ (or k), and δ over time. Increases in output per worker, x, are the main source of increases in wealth and standard of living. It is useful to classify patterns of change in these parameters so that these patterns can be compared to the experience of real-world economies.

Changes in labor and capital productivity can be described in terms of shifts of the growth-distribution schedule. The growth-distribution schedule is a straight line defined by two points, for example, the point $(0, x)$ which corresponds to the minimum rate of profit and the maximum level of the real wage, and the point $(\rho, 0)$, which corresponds to the maximal profit rate and zero real wage. Since changes in δ leave output and cash flow per worker unchanged, we will classify movements of the growth-distribution schedule, and hence changes in technique, by changes in x and ρ.

An increase in x holding ρ constant corresponds to a pure increase in labor productivity (more output per worker-year) with no change in capital productivity (since the output-capital ratio ρ is unchanged). This type of technical change is called *labor-saving* since it has the effect of increasing output per unit of labor input, x. The measured rate of change in labor productivity is g_x, the percentage increase in output per worker from one period to the next:

$$g_x \equiv \frac{x_{+1}}{x} - 1 \qquad\qquad (2.23)$$

A rise in ρ holding x constant corresponds to an increase in capital productivity, since it raises the output-capital ratio. This type of technical change is called *capital-saving*. The measured rate of change in capital productivity is g_ρ, the percentage increase in output per unit of capital from one period to the next:

$$g_\rho \equiv \frac{\rho_{+1}}{\rho} - 1 \qquad\qquad (2.24)$$

Figure 2.7 illustrates an arbitrary shift of the growth-distribution schedule and shows how the rates of labor-saving and capital-saving technical progress can be calculated.

As Table 2.5 shows, the U.S. economy experienced labor-saving technical change at the rate of 2.1% per year and capital-saving technical change at the rate of .05% per year (that is, essentially 0) between 1988 and 1989.

Problem 2.15 *Graph on the same graph the new and old growth-distribution schedules for Ricardia if it experiences a 50% labor-saving and 0% capital-saving technical change.*

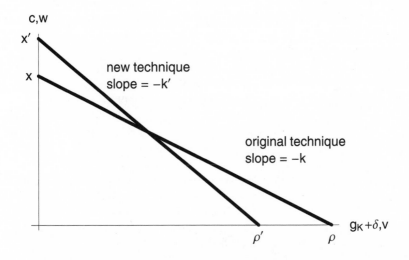

Figure 2.7: Technical change corresponds to a shift in the straight line defining the growth-distribution schedule. An upward shift in x corresponds to labor-saving technical progress, since output per worker increases. An outward shift in ρ corresponds to capital-saving technical progress, since output per unit of capital increases. The shift pictured here combines labor-saving technical progress with negative capital-saving (or capital-using) technical change.

Table 2.5:

U.S. Technical Change, 1988-89

Variable	1988	1989	Growth Rate
x	\$36,083/worker-year	\$36,859/worker-year	
g_x			2.1%/year
ρ	64.63%/year	64.66%/year	
g_ρ			.05%/year

Source: Extended Penn World Tables

Table 2.6:

Comparison of U.S. and Japan, 1989

Variable	U.S.	Japan
x	\$36,859/wkr-yr	\$21,691/wkr-yr
k	\$56,997/wkr	\$43,510/wkr-yr
ρ	64.7%/yr	49.8%/yr
δ	9.2%/yr	12.0%/yr
c	\$29,635/wkr-yr	\$13,687/wkr-yr
i	\$7,224/wkr-yr	\$8,004/wkr-yr
g_K	3.5%/yr	6.4%/yr
w	\$22,064/wkr-yr	\$11,763/wkr-yr
z	\$14,795/wkr-yr	\$9,928
v	26.0%/yr	22.8%/yr
r	16.8%/yr	10.8%/yr

Source: Extended Penn World Tables

Problem 2.16 *Graph on the same graph the new and old growth-distribution schedules for Industria if it experiences a 2% labor-saving and -2% capital-saving technical change.*

Problem 2.17 *Graph on the same graph the growth-distribution schedule for the U.S. in 1988 and 1989, using the data presented above.*

2.12   Comparing Economies

As we have seen in analyzing the U.S. economy in 1988 and 1989, the growth-distribution schedule is a good way to visualize the changes in a single economy over time. It illustrates the type of technical change that is occurring, shows how the economy allocates its product between growth and consumption, and reveals the underlying distributional relations between real wages and profits.

The growth-distribution schedule is also a good way to compare the productivity and growth patterns of two different economies. If we plot the growth-distribution schedules of the two economies on the same graph with the same units of output per worker, the relative productivities of the two economies and their relative patterns of distribution and growth can be visualized clearly.

We can use the Extended Penn World Tables Data to compare the U.S. and Japanese economies in 1989, for example, as Table 2.6 and Figure 2.8 show.

2.13 Global Economic Leadership

Modern economists have a distinct advantage over previous generations of growth theorists because much more data are now available. *Time series* data express the historical patterns of the main variables, while *cross sectional* data allow for comparisons between countries at a point in time. Often, these sorts of data are combined into *longitudinal* or *panel* data sets.

Angus Maddison has assembled an important panel data set that includes six leading advanced capitalist countries (U.S., France, Germany, Netherlands, U.K., and Japan) over nearly two centuries. Table 2.7 presents the relative levels of labor and capital productivity and relative capital intensity for these countries for selected years since 1820. The levels are measured as index numbers relative to the U.S., owing to its status as current world leader in labor productivity. Thus, productivity in the U.S. is 100 by definition, while in 1992 for example Japan's index shows that its labor productivity was 68.8 percent of the level in the U.S.

From 1820 to 1973 the global lead in labor productivity has changed hands three times. In 1820, the Netherlands was the world's most productive nation, but by 1870 the lead had passed to the U.K. By 1913, the U.S. had overtaken the U.K., and maintained leadership to the present day. This pattern is sometimes called "leapfrogging." We do not yet know if leapfrogging will continue.

Another clear possibility is that leapfrogging will make way for *convergence* in productivity levels. Between 1950 and 1992, the labor productivity lead of the U.S. has narrowed and, in some cases, vanished. Most of this "catching-up" by other advanced nations occurred between 1950 and 1973.

On the other hand, during the late nineteenth and early twentieth centuries, the other countries were "falling behind" while the U.S. surged ahead. We need to be careful not to confuse falling behind in relative terms, which the table illustrates, with falling behind in absolute terms. Since the U.S. productivity level is growing over time, countries which experience less growth will fall behind in relative terms, even though they are growing in absolute terms. During the period spanning the two world wars, the U.S. lead continued to grow, partly because of the

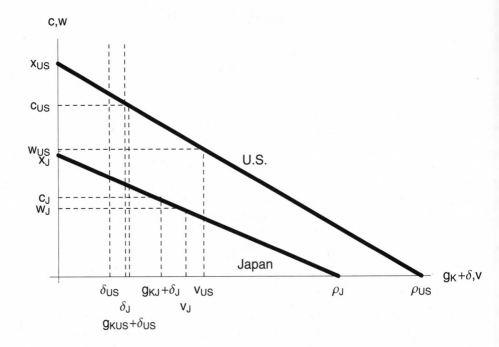

Figure 2.8: The growth-distribution schedules for the U.S. and Japan in 1989 are drawn on the same scale. The U.S. has higher productivity of both labor and capital, so its growth-distribution schedule lies above the Japanese growth-distribution schedule. The U.S. real wage of \$22,064/wkr-yr gives a profit rate of 26.0%/yr, and the Japanese real wage of \$11,763/wkr-yr a profit rate of 22.8%/yr. U.S. consumption per worker of \$29,635/wkr-yr leaves room for a growth rate of capital of 3.5%/yr, while Japanese consumption per worker of \$13,687/wkr-yr allows the Japanese capital stock to grow at 6.4%/yr.

devastations of war which were visited upon the other countries, and partly because of the dynamism of the U.S. economy.

Convergence in labor productivity levels has been associated with convergence in the capital-labor ratio, or capital intensity. Both variables have converged "from below." By contrast, capital productivity seems to converge on the world leader "from above." Nations at low levels of labor productivity have high levels of capital productivity, which then falls in the course of economic development. In 1950, all five other countries had much higher output-capital ratios than the U.S. By 1992, all but the U.K. had converged to U.S. levels.

Japan's output-capital ratio actually fell so fast that by 1992 it was below the level of the U.S. Some other sources suggest that Germany, too, now has lower capital productivity than the U.S.

The challenge presented to modern growth theory is to explain and interpret the relative growth performance of the world's nations, as well as the absolute growth performance of each individual country. Some data on absolute growth performance of the same six countries appear in the next section.

2.14 Labor Productivity Growth in Real Economies

Labor productivity has grown more or less continuously in the six advanced capitalist countries whose history we have been following. Angus Maddison divides the last one hundred and seventy-five years of history into five sub-periods. He periodizes the phases of modern growth sensibly, based on his own judgment, and we have adopted his periodization in Table 2.8.

Despite its continuity, the growth of labor productivity has not been steady. Instead, it has a stop-go quality. The two most recent phases in particular have attracted much attention. In the period from 1950-1973, labor productivity grew at unprecedented rates. By contrast, since 1973, labor productivity growth slowed everywhere; economists often refer to this event simply as the *productivity slowdown*. In the U.S., labor productivity growth was lower in the 1973-1992 period than in any previous period. In other countries, labor productivity growth remains at levels which are respectable by historical standards, but lower than in the previous phase. It is not clear if the productivity slowdown represents a true slowing in the rate of growth of global knowledge, or just a return to a more normal pace for technical progress.

Table 2.7:

**Catching-up and Falling Behind:
Productivity Relative to the U.S. for Six Countries
in Selected Years from 1820–1992**

	1820	1870	1913	1929	1938	1950	1973	1992
Labor Productivity (U.S. = 100)								
U.S.	100.0	100.0	100.0	100.0	100.0	100.0	100.0	100.0
France	94.6*	59.3	55.7	55.1	61.9	45.5	75.3	101.8
Germany	86.4*	68.6	68.3	58.0	56.0	34.4	70.5	94.7
Netherlands	121.3*	101.4	78.3	84.0	72.3	51.3	80.6	99.0
U.K.	111.0	115.0	83.6	73.6	69.6	62.0	67.5	82.4
Japan	33.1	20.2	20.2	23.6	25.4	16.0	47.2	68.8
Capital Intensity (U.S. = 100)								
U.S.	100.0	100.0	100.0	100.0	100.0	100.0	100.0	100.0
France						30.4	55.2	95.3
Germany					31.1	25.5	64.6	92.2
Netherlands						43.2	75.3	93.1
U.K.	80.1	60.6	21.3	21.1	17.5	20.5	42.0	61.6
Japan		5.0#	5.4	8.7	8.2	11.6	38.9	85.6
Capital Productivity (U.S. = 100)								
U.S.	100.0	100.0	100.0	100.0	100.0	100.0	100.0	100.0
France						149.8	136.3	106.8
Germany					179.8	134.9	109.0	102.7
Netherlands						118.7	107.1	106.4
U.K.	138.6	189.9	392.9	349.0	397.5	302.3	160.6	133.7
Japan		428.9#	372.6	270.9	308.4	138.3	121.3	80.4

Sources: [Maddison, 1995b, Tables K-1, A3a, C16a, J-2, J-4, and D1a] and
[Maddison, 1995a, pp. 148–164].
Notes: *Using GDP per person #1890

One puzzling feature of the productivity slowdown is that it has occurred during the computerization of much production technology. Some economists speculate that it may soon be reversed when the benefits of information technology begin to manifest themselves.

Capital productivity has not behaved uniformly. Since 1973, capital productivity has declined in all the countries in the table. In the U.S., capital productivity declined during the first two growth phases, but increased from 1913-1973. Over the whole expanse of time, the output-capital ratio in the U.S. declined, from 1.055 in 1820 to 0.411 in 1992. This corroborates and qualifies our earlier observation that the output-capital ratio tends to fall in the course of economic development.

The patterns of growth in Table 2.8 could reflect patterns of technical change, or they could reflect technical choices from among the existing techniques. The first case represents a shift in the production function, while the second case represents movement along the production function. Obviously, some combination of the two movements is also possible.

If we interpret the patterns as technical changes, it is clear that the rate of labor-saving technical change has been persistently positive. On the other hand, the rate of capital-saving technical change has been positive in some periods and negative in others. Negative capital-saving technical change, or capital-using technical change, is economically possible when it occurs in combination with labor-saving technical change. A new technique that uses more capital may be more profitable if it saves enough labor.

There is an important connection between Table 2.8 and Tables 2.3 and 2.4. Since the productivity of labor has grown persistently and the profit share has remained roughly constant, we can deduce that the real wage must have grown at a rate equal or close to the growth rate of labor productivity.

The pattern of rising labor productivity and declining capital productivity is common, but by no means universal in looking at real economies. Figure 2.9, for example, plots the (g_ρ, g_x) pairs for the same 49 countries plotted in Figures 2.1 and 2.2 for 1980, from the EPWT data. More countries have the pattern of positive g_x and negative g_ρ than any other pattern, though a number show positive growth in both productivities.

2.15 Stylized Facts

In this chapter we have developed a system of accounting that allows us to present the empirical facts that are the foundation of the analysis

Table 2.8:

**Growth Rates of Selected Variables (%/year)
for Six Countries in Selected Periods from 1820-1992**

	1820–1870	1870–1913	1913–1950	1950–1973	1973–1992
U.S.					
Labor Productivity, g_x	1.10	1.88	2.48	2.74	1.11
Capital Intensity, g_k	2.30	3.44	1.65	2.10	1.84
Capital Productivity, g_ρ	-1.18	-1.51	0.81	0.63	-0.72
France					
Labor Productivity, g_x		1.74	1.87	5.11	2.73
Capital Intensity, g_k				4.79	4.78
Capital Productivity, g_ρ				0.22	-1.96
Germany					
Labor Productivity, g_x		1.87	0.60	5.99	2.69
Capital Intensity, g_k				5.93	3.76
Capital Productivity, g_ρ				0.05	-1.04
Netherlands					
Labor Productivity, g_x		1.27	1.31	4.78	2.21
Capital Intensity, g_k				4.59	3.14
Capital Productivity, g_ρ				0.18	-0.90
U.K.					
Labor Productivity, g_x	1.16	1.13	1.66	3.12	2.18
Capital Intensity, g_k	1.74	0.96	1.56	5.33	3.91
Capital Productivity, g_ρ	-0.55	0.16	0.10	-2.10	-1.67
Japan					
Labor Productivity, g_x	0.09	1.89	1.85	7.69	3.13
Capital Intensity, g_k		3.03	3.75	7.63	6.16
Capital Productivity, g_ρ		-0.95	-1.85	0.06	-2.85

Source: [Maddison, 1995b, Table 2-6]

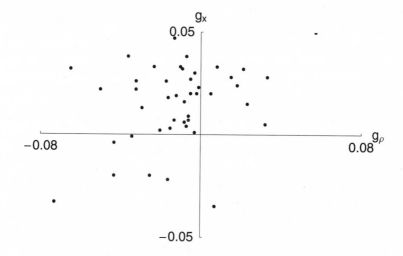

Figure 2.9: The (g_ρ, g_x) observed for 49 countries in 1980. There is a tendency for rising labor productivity to be coupled with falling capital productivity.

of economic growth. Several patterns, or *stylized facts,* emerge strongly from the data. One challenge for theories of growth is to explain these common patterns.

As capitalist economies develop, there is a strong tendency for labor productivity to increase, while capital productivity stagnates or slowly declines. As a result capital per worker rises. As labor productivity increases, the real wage also rises, at roughly the same rate. As a result, the wage and profit shares in income, despite definite fluctuations, show no strong trend.

In the next chapters, we will develop the technical concepts that are the basis of the various theories of economic growth and technical change.

2.16 Suggested Readings

The *Survey of Current Business,* published by the US Department of Commerce, regularly reports on developments in national income accounting in the U.S. through clear, well-documented articles. For a detailed discussion of the rules governing dimensions in economic analysis, see DeJong [1967] and for an introduction to the construction of price and quantity indexes, see Allen [1975]. The measurement of consumer prices in the U.S. has been the subject of considerable debate which is reviewed in a symposium published in the Winter 1998 issue of the *Journal of Economic Perspectives.* Economists in the Classical tradition have developed alternative interpretations of national income accounts, particularly by recognizing the distinction between productive and unproductive activities; see Wolff [1987] or Shaikh and Tonak [1994].

Documentation for the Penn World Tables can be found in Summers and Heston [1991]. Angus Maddison provides useful commentary along with his historical data sets in Maddison [1995a,b]. A unique and readable work that combines comprehensive macroeconomic statistics with political economy and history, Armstrong et al. [1991] is a particularly good source on the profit squeeze and its aftermath. A widely-cited source on catching-up and falling-behind is Abramovitz [1986], while Nelson and Wright [1992] focuses on the particular characteristics associated with the rise to leadership of the U.S. The McKinsey Global Institute has published several careful discussions of international comparisons of labor and capital productivity, including McKinsey Global Institute [1993, 1996]. An accessible and comprehensive treatment of productivity, the productivity slowdown, catching-up, and U.S. leadership is given in Baumol et al. [1989]. The causes and consequences of the productivity slowdown are explored in a popularly written but careful book by Madrick [1995] while Baily and Gordon [1988] consider the possibility that the slowdown is the result of mismeasurement. For a model of leapfrogging, see Brezis et al. [1993]. The idea that the computer revolution will affect productivity growth with a time lag is attributed to David [1990].

Aschauer [1989] explores the impact on growth of public investment by government, chiefly in infrastructure; his findings that the effects are quite large have generated controversy.

Finally, the original list of "stylized facts" can be found in Kaldor [1965].

Chapter 3

Models of Production

3.1 Accounting Frameworks and Explanatory Models

Description is an important step towards a complete understanding of the process of economic growth. But economists would like to go further than mere description, to explain and even to predict the consequences of historical developments and policies on the pattern of growth. In order to give explanations and make predictions, the economist needs a complete *model* of the growth process, in which the factors to be explained or predicted are *endogenous variables* determined within the model, and the factors explaining or predicting consequences are *exogenous parameters*. The model specifies enough relations among the endogenous variables and the exogenous parameters so that once we know the exogenous parameters we can calculate mathematically (or graphically) the corresponding values of the endogenous variables. *Explanation* in such a model consists of showing what change in the exogenous parameters would lead to an observed change in the endogenous variables. *Prediction* consists of calculating the effect on the endogenous variables of hypothetical changes in the exogenous variables. As a first step to developing complete models of economic growth, we need to develop a *model of production*, since so far we have only set up an accounting framework. The specification of such a model inevitably loses certain features of complex reality, so that we must consider each of the assumptions of the model carefully, to understand what real-world situations the resulting model can and cannot explain.

3.2   A Model of Production

In our model, as in the accounting framework, we will conceive of time as passing in discrete units (usually years), $t = 1990, 1991, ...$ Economic decisions, such as the decision to produce or to consume, and prices are fixed at the beginning of each period, and cannot change until the next period. The period framework forces us to conceive of all economic decisions proceeding synchronously on the same time scale, which is a drawback. More realistic modeling treatments of time, however, involve much more complicated mathematics, and we choose the period scheme as the simplest that can explicitly reflect the economic passage of time.

In the accounting framework X is GDP, the market value of all the disparate goods and services actually produced in an economy. In our model, in order to simplify as much as possible, we will assume that there is only one good produced, *output*, which we will also denote as X, and that this output can be accumulated as a single kind of capital K. (In the real world, of course, K is the value of capital goods of many different kinds.) Capital, K, and labor, N, together produce the output X. We will model the fact that production takes time by assuming that inputs must be employed at the beginning of the period, while the output becomes available at the end of the period.

A *technique of production* can be described by specifying how much capital is necessary at the beginning of a period to equip one unit of labor, how much output is produced at the end of the period, and how much of the capital stock deteriorates during the period. We will assume that techniques exhibit *constant returns to scale*, that is, that it is possible to produce exactly twice as much output with twice as much of both inputs.

A technique of production can be described by three numbers, (k, x, δ), where k is the capital stock per worker, x is the output per worker, and δ is the proportion of the value of the capital stock lost to depreciation over the period of production. In general δ will be larger than zero (some deterioration of the capital stock always takes place over the period of production) and smaller than or equal to 1 (some of the capital stock may survive to the next period). (If $\delta = 1$, the capital stock lasts only one period, like seed-corn, and the corresponding model is often called a *corn model.*) It is also possible to describe the technique as (ρ, x, δ), where $\rho = x/k$ is the productivity of capital, or as (ρ, k, δ), since if we know any two of the parameters (k, x, ρ), we can derive the other one. We can describe a single technique of production schematically as:

> 1 labor and k capital at the beginning of the period
>
> $\rightarrow$
>
> x output and $(1 - \delta)k$ capital at the end of the period

We can also describe a technique as a table of input-output coefficients:

outputs	output	x
	capital	$(1 - \delta)k$
inputs	capital	k
	labor	1

The technique of production determines the relation between output and the input of capital and labor:

$$N = \frac{X}{x}$$

$$K = \frac{kX}{x} = \frac{X}{\rho}$$

The technique in use determines the productivity of labor and capital and the capital-labor ratio in the economy. Each technique of production corresponds to a particular growth-distribution schedule, like the one in Figure 2.6.

The *technology* of an economy is the collection of all the known usable techniques. We could represent the technology as a matrix, each column of which is a technique of production. At any given real wage, different available techniques will yield different profit rates.

We assume that the technology defined by the input-output coefficients is an exogenous parameter in each period. In real-world economic growth a crucial role is played by *technological change*, which appears in the model as a change in the collection of techniques from period to period. We will study models of technical change later in this book.

3.3 Agents and Distribution

To clarify the exact mechanisms through which capitalist production functions, we will distinguish three types of agents in our model. First are *workers*, who supply labor for a wage. Second are *capitalists*, who own the capital. Third are *entrepreneurs*, who on behalf of the capitalists hire workers, organize production, sell the output, and return the residual revenue as profit to the capitalist after paying the workers their wages. In real-world capitalist economies these functions are sometimes combined in various ways. Workers may own part of the capital through pension funds, for example, or as members of producer cooperatives. Capitalists may act as entrepreneurs, both owning capital and organizing production (and, indeed, this was a common pattern in the early days of industrial capitalism). But even if the same persons sometimes act out the three roles, our analysis will be clearer if we separate them carefully.

We will always assume that there is a large number of each type of agent, even though they are all alike, so that competition rules and each agent, worker, entrepreneur, or capitalist, takes output prices and wages as given.

The entrepreneurs hire the workers for a wage measured in terms of output, w, paid at the end of the period, and organize them to produce. Entrepreneurs must choose a technique of production defined by coefficients k (or ρ), x, and δ from available technology determined by engineering and scientific knowledge and social and cultural practices that limit the possible techniques of production. For example, health and safety legislation might prevent entrepreneurs from using workers in ways that cause occupational diseases or preventable accidents.

Given the technique chosen, (ρ, x, δ), in order to produce X output in a period, the entrepreneur must hire $N = X/x$ workers for the period. The wage bill will be $W = wX/x$. The entrepreneur must also secure the services of capital equal to X/ρ from owners of capital. Competition will force the entrepreneurs to pay the residual revenue after the payment of wages, the *(gross) profit*, to the capitalists at the end of the period. Since the profit share, $\pi = (1 - (w/x))$, the profit will be:

$$Z = X - W = (1 - \frac{w}{x})X = \pi X$$

The *(gross) profit rate*, v will be:

$$v = \frac{Z}{K} = \rho(1 - \frac{w}{x}) = \pi \rho \tag{3.1}$$

The profit rate is quite different from the *price* of a unit of capital, since capital may last several periods if $\delta < 1$. The profit rate v is what the entrepreneur pays the capitalist as the result of using a unit of capital for a single period, at the end of which the depreciated capital returns to the capitalist. The price of a unit of capital is always 1, since we are reckoning prices in terms of output, and one unit of output can be invested as one unit of capital.

We assume that the entrepreneurs pay themselves a wage for whatever actual work they do in production (which is accounted for in W), and that their motivation for undertaking the entrepreneurial activity is their pure joy in bossing other people around.

Now let us consider the situation of the capitalist, who owns the capital stock. She begins the period with capital K, and receives a gross profit from the entrepreneurs of vK. At the end of the period she gets back the depreciated capital $(1 - \delta)K$ along with the profit. Thus the *net profit* consists of the profit less depreciation, $R = vK - \delta K$, and the *net profit rate*, the ratio of profit to the initial capital, is:

$$r \equiv \frac{R}{K} = \frac{vK - \delta K}{K} = v - \delta = \pi \rho - \delta$$

3.4   Choice of Technique and Production Functions

Each combination of the parameters k, x and δ define a single technique of production, one particular method of combining labor and capital to produce output, and therefore one growth-distribution schedule. Suppose there is another possible way to produce output, in which each worker is equipped with k' units of capital and produces x' units of output, assuming, for simplicity, that the depreciation rate is the same for both techniques, $\delta' = \delta$. The alternative technique has its own real wage-profit rate schedule. In Figure 3.1 we plot the real wage-profit rate schedules corresponding to both the original technique defined by k and x, and the alternative defined by k' and x'. From the entrepreneur's point of view the real wage-profit rate schedule shows how large a profit rate she can secure the capitalist at any wage. Entrepreneurs who secure a larger profit rate v will be the most popular with capitalists.

In a capitalist society entrepreneurs choose techniques of production to maximize profit. In the case illustrated, the alternative technique will pay a higher profit rate than the original when the wage is high, but a lower profit rate when the wage is low. An entrepreneur who has the option of using either technique of production, would use the alternative technique at high wage rates and the original technique at low wage rates.

A technique is *dominated* by another technique when the real wage-profit rate schedule of the first lies entirely below and to the left of the corresponding schedule of the second. The third technique illustrated in Figure 3.2 is dominated by both the original and alternative techniques.

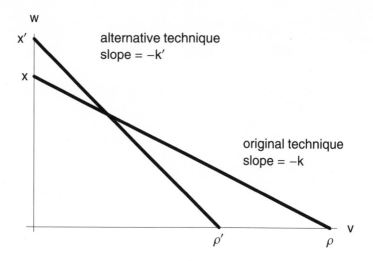

Figure 3.1: When there are two or more available techniques, each has its own real wage-profit rate schedule.

It is not profit-maximizing for an entrepreneur to use a dominated technique at any wage rate. The *efficiency frontier* for a technology is the northeast boundary of the real wage-profit rate schedules corresponding to its undominated techniques. The efficiency frontier is shown as the gray line in Figure 3.2.

(The economic definition of efficiency is not the same as the engineering definition. Engineering efficiency measures the fraction of the available energy that is turned into useful work in a system. Economic efficiency means not wasting any resources from a social point of view.)

The point A in Figure 3.2 represents a real wage at which the two undominated techniques have the same profit rate, and is called the *switchpoint* between the two techniques. Entrepreneurs will select the original technique at wages below the switchpoint, and the alternative technique at wages above the switchpoint.

This same construction works with any number of alternative techniques, even an infinite continuum. Each technique corresponds to one real wage-profit rate schedule, and the northeast boundary of the real wage-profit rate schedules of the available techniques is the efficiency frontier for the economy. Profit-maximizing entrepreneurs will choose the technique on the efficiency frontier for any level of the wage.

Neoclassical economists often assume a *production function* that shows the output, X, that can be produced by arbitrary inputs of capital, K, and labor, N:

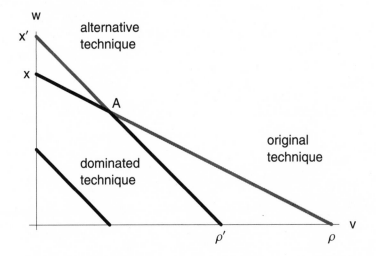

Figure 3.2: The relevant technological choices are those on the *efficiency frontier*, which is the northeast boundary of the real wage-profit rate schedules corresponding to the available techniques.

$$X = F(K, N) \qquad (3.2)$$

If the production function has constant returns to scale, which means that it is possible to increase output by any given factor, say $1/N$, by increasing both inputs by the same factor, then it can be viewed as describing a technology, that is, a collection of techniques of production. A pair of numbers (k, x) is an available technique given the production function $F(K, N)$ if

$$x = \frac{X}{N} = F(\frac{K}{N}, \frac{N}{N}) = F(k, 1) \equiv f(k)$$

This means that k units of capital and 1 unit of labor can be combined to produce x units of output. The function $f(k) \equiv F(k, 1)$ is called the *intensive production function*. If the production function is a continuous, smooth function, the corresponding technology is an infinite continuum of techniques. The efficiency frontier for a smooth production function is also smooth, and looks like Figure 3.3.

When the efficiency frontier is a smooth curve arising from a technology described by a smooth production function, every point on the efficiency frontier is a switchpoint. A small rise in the real wage will

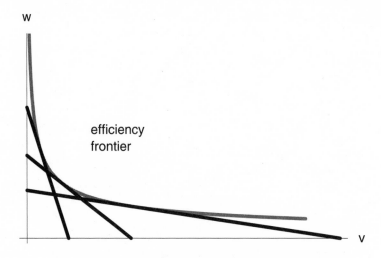

Figure 3.3: A smooth production function describes a technology with an infinite continuum of techniques. The real wage-profit rate schedules are each tangent to the efficiency frontier at one point. Only three of the individual real wage-profit rate schedules are drawn here. In fact, there is one tangent to every point on the efficiency frontier, which is the envelope of the real wage-profit rate schedules corresponding to the technology.

change the profit-maximizing technique slightly to one that employs a bit more capital per worker.

As we have seen, profit-maximizing entrepreneurs will choose the technique that has the highest profit rate for any wage. If the production function is smooth, the profit-rate maximizing technique of production at a given wage will combine labor and capital in proportions such that the marginal product of labor is equal to the wage and the marginal product of capital is equal to the profit rate. Thus the equality of the marginal products to factor prices is just another way of describing the entrepreneur's choice of the most profitable technique of production.

To see this point, consider that profit is just output less wages:

$$Z = vK = X - wN = F(K, N) - wN$$

For a given amount of capital employed, the entrepreneur will want to choose the technique of production so as to maximize this profit. Holding K constant, if the entrepreneur can continuously vary the amount of labor working with the given amount of capital, the condition for maximization is:

$$\frac{dZ}{dN} = \frac{\partial F(K, N)}{\partial N} - w = 0$$

This implies that the entrepreneur must choose a technique at which:

$$w = \frac{\partial F(K, N)}{\partial N}$$

Another way to view this situation is that a profit-maximizing entrepreneur always chooses the technique of production at a switchpoint between a slightly more- and slightly less-capital intensive technique. The equality of the marginal product of labor to the wage is just another way of defining this switchpoint.

The choice of the profit-maximizing technique at any real wage is the fundamental principle at work here, not the equalization of the marginal product of labor to the real wage. If there are only a finite number of techniques available, it may not be possible to determine a marginal product of labor, but entrepreneurs can still choose the available technique that has the highest profit rate given the real wage. The growth-distribution schedule for that technique will then determine the average productivity of labor, x, and the average productivity of capital, ρ. We would use this one particular growth-distribution schedule to analyze the relations between aggregate consumption and investment. The real

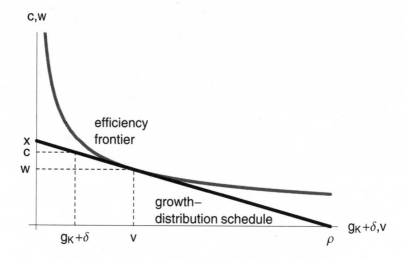

Figure 3.4: The wage determines the profit-maximizing technique, which establishes the growth-distribution schedule for an economy.

wage determines, through profit maximization, the technique in use, and the growth-distribution schedule for that technique determines the social tradeoff between gross investment and consumption.

Figure 3.4 summarizes the situation when there is a continuum of techniques represented by a smooth production function. Given the wage (or the profit rate) there is one profit rate-maximizing technique, corresponding to a point on the unit isoquant of the production function. All the entrepreneurs will adopt this technique, which will then determine the growth-distribution schedule for the economy.

3.5   Particular Production Functions

We will use two production functions in examples and problems in this book.

3.5.1   The Leontief production function

The first is called the *Leontief* or *fixed coefficients* production function. The fixed coefficients production function specifies that capital and labor can be combined in just one way to produce output, so that it corresponds to a single technique of production. The Leontief production function is written mathematically:

$$X = \min(\rho K, xN) \tag{3.3}$$

Dividing through by N, we can write the intensive fixed coefficients production function:

$$x = \min(\rho k, x) \tag{3.4}$$

The $\min(.,.)$ function of two numbers always takes the value of the smaller of the numbers. Thus this production function says that the output X is limited by either the output of the capital employed or the output of the labor employed, whichever is smaller. In other words, for each x units of output the entrepreneur has to have at least ρk units of capital and 1 unit of labor. The fixed coefficients production function exactly describes one technique of production.

With a Leontief production function technology there is only one available technique, that is, only one possible way to combine labor and capital to produce output. If there is only one way to combine labor and capital, the *marginal products* of capital and labor are not well-determined. Adding more labor without the corresponding necessary capital will give zero extra output; while subtracting labor reduces output proportionately.

The unit isoquant for the Leontief production function has the shape of the letter "L" as Figure 3.5a illustrates. The corner occurs at the input point $(1/\rho, 1/x)$. The corresponding efficiency frontier is a single straight-line real wage-profit rate schedule with horizontal intercept ρ, and vertical intercept x, as shown in 3.5b. The intensive Leontief production function is a straight line from the origin to the point (k, x), and a horizontal line at the level x for higher k as shown in 3.5c. In the first part of the intensive Leontief production function output is constrained by the capital input, and is proportional to k, and in the second part output is constrained by the labor input, and is equal to x no matter how much more capital may be available.

3.5.2 The Cobb-Douglas production function

Another widely used production function is the *Cobb-Douglas* production function, which allows for smooth substitutability between capital and labor in production. It is written mathematically:

$$X = AK^{\alpha}N^{1-\alpha} \tag{3.5}$$

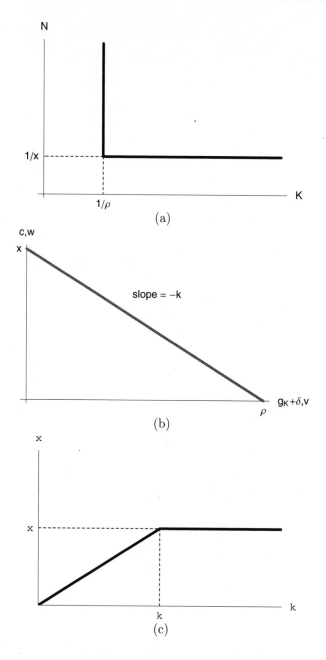

Figure 3.5: (a) The *Leontief production function* has an "L-shaped" isoquant, with a corner at the input proportions, $(1/\rho, 1/x)$. (b) The corresponding efficiency frontier is a single real wage-profit rate schedule with horizontal intercept ρ, and vertical intercept x. (c) The corresponding intensive production function consists of two lines, one from the origin to (k, x), the other a horizontal line at the level x.

Here α (the Greek letter *alpha*, pronounced "al*l*-fa") is a parameter that lies between 0 and 1, and A is a scale factor used to make the units of measurement consistent. Using (3.5) we can see that a technique (k, x) is allowed by the Cobb-Douglas production function with parameter α if:

$$x = Ak^{\alpha}(1)^{1-\alpha} \text{ or}$$

$$x = Ak^{\alpha} \tag{3.6}$$

With the Cobb-Douglas production function we can choose the capital required for one unit of labor, k, to be any number we wish, and then find the amount of output, x, the unit of labor can produce with that capital from Equation (3.6). Notice that the Cobb-Douglas production function implies a very high degree of substitutability between capital and labor, since enough labor can always make up for any reduction of capital (and vice versa).

The unit isoquant for the Cobb-Douglas production function is the modified hyperbola asymptotic to the axes shown in Figure 3.6a. Each point, such as A, B, or C on the isoquant corresponds to a particular technique of production, with its own (ρ, x), and to a particular real wage-profit rate schedule, as shown in Figure 3.6b. The efficiency frontier is the envelope of these growth-distribution functions. The intensive Cobb-Douglas production function is Ak^{α}.

With the Cobb-Douglas production function (or any production function with a smooth isoquant), it is possible to define the marginal product of labor or capital as the increase in output that could be achieved from a small increment in one factor of production, holding the other constant. In mathematical terms the marginal product of either factor is the partial derivative of the production function with respect to that factor. The marginal products of labor and capital with the Cobb-Douglas production function, for example, are:

$$MP_N = \frac{\partial X}{\partial N} = (1-\alpha)A(\frac{K}{N})^{\alpha} = (1-\alpha)Ak^{\alpha}$$

$$MP_K = \frac{\partial X}{\partial K} = \alpha A(\frac{K}{N})^{-(1-\alpha)} = \alpha Ak^{\alpha-1}$$

With the Cobb-Douglas production function, the technique that maximizes the profit rate for a wage w must satisfy the condition:

$$w = (1-\alpha)Ak^{\alpha} = (1-\alpha)x$$

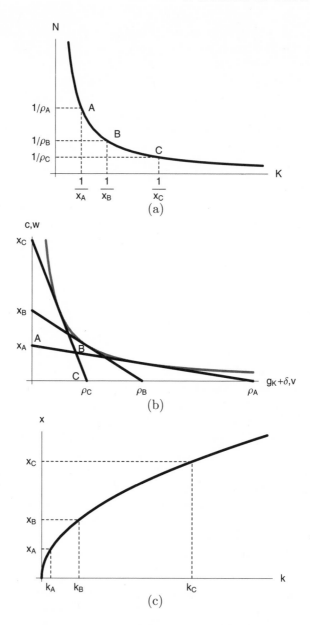

Figure 3.6: (a) The *Cobb-Douglas production function* has a smooth isoquant, representing a continuum of techniques, three of which are shown at points A, B, and C. (b) The efficiency frontier is the envelope of the growth-distribution schedules of the techniques on the isoquant. The growth-distribution schedules for points A, B, and C are shown. (c) The capital intensities and labor productivities for points A, B, and C are shown on the intensive production function.

Once we know k, we can derive x, and ρ. From the intensive Cobb-Douglas production, we see that:

$$x = Ak^\alpha$$

Dividing the Cobb-Douglas production function through by K, we see that:

$$\rho = \frac{x}{k} = Ak^{\alpha-1}$$

The profit rate will equal the marginal product of capital:

$$v = \alpha Ak^{\alpha-1} = \alpha\rho$$

The parameter α in the Cobb-Douglas production function is therefore the profit share, since:

$$\pi = \frac{vk}{x} = \frac{\alpha x}{x} = \alpha$$

Furthermore, we can see that w and v satisfy the growth-distribution schedule equation for this particular choice of k and x:

$$w + vk = (1 - \alpha)x + \alpha x = x$$

Problem 3.1 *Draw the production isoquant (the combinations of capital and labor required to produce one unit of output), the real wage-profit rate schedule, and the intensive production function for the Leontief technology with $k = \$100,000/wkr$ and $x = \$50,000/wkr$-yr. What is the marginal product of labor in the Leontief technology?*

Problem 3.2 *Draw the production isoquant (the combinations of capital and labor required to produce one unit of output), the real wage-profit rate schedule, and the intensive production function for the Cobb-Douglas technology with $A = \$10$ and $\alpha = .25$. What is the marginal product of labor in the Cobb-Douglas technology?*

Problem 3.3 *What technique of production will profit rate-maximizing entrepreneurs choose if they face a Cobb-Douglas production function and a given real wage, $\bar{w}$? What if they face a fixed coefficients production function and the same real wage?*

Problem 3.4 *Show that the efficiency frontier expressing w as a function of v for the Cobb-Douglas production function has the same mathematical form as the unit isoquant expressing $1/x$ as a function of $1/\rho$.*

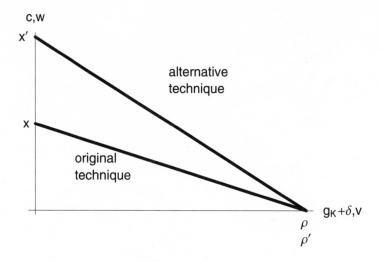

Figure 3.7: A purely labor-saving technical change corresponds to a rotation of the growth-distribution schedule around its ρ-intercept.

3.6 Classifying Technical Change

A single technique of production is determined by its capital productivity, ρ, and labor productivity, x. A change in the technique can therefore be described in terms of the change in these two parameters. For example, a purely *labor-saving* technical change corresponds to a rise in x while ρ remains unchanged. As in Chapter 2, we measure the amount of labor-saving technical change by the growth rate of the productivity of labor, g_x:

$$1 + g_x = \frac{x_{+1}}{x}$$

The growth-distribution schedule corresponding to the technique of production rotates clockwise around its ρ-axis intercept when there is pure labor-saving technical change, as in Figure 3.7.

Similarly a purely *capital-saving* technical change corresponds to a rise in ρ with x unchanged. We can measure the degree of purely capital-saving technical change by the growth rate g_ρ:

$$1 + g_\rho = \frac{\rho_{+1}}{\rho}$$

Purely capital-saving technical change rotates the growth-distribution schedule clockwise around its w-intercept, as Figure 3.8 shows.

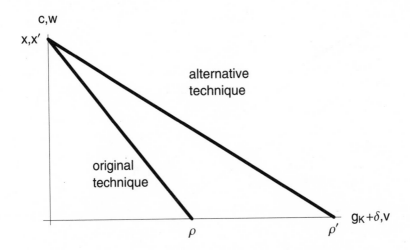

Figure 3.8: Purely capital-saving technical change rotates
the growth-distribution schedule around its w-intercept.

If technical change saves both capital and labor equally, the growth-
distribution schedule moves outward parallel to itself, as illustrated in
Figure 3.9. In this case $g_x = g_\rho$, so that both intercepts move by the
same proportion. This form of technical change is called *factor-saving*.
Factor-saving technical change can also be thought of as a rescaling
of the output itself: the same labor and capital inputs produce more
output.

A moment's thought shows that we can represent *any* pattern of
technical change for a single technique either by a combination of purely
labor-saving and purely capital-saving technical change, or by a combination of purely labor-saving and factor-saving technical change.

It is more complicated in general to describe technical change when
the technology consists of a collection of many techniques, as in the case
of a neoclassical production function. In principle, technical change
might affect each of the techniques differently, leading to a wholly new
technology. The situation is simpler if we assume that all the different techniques in the technology undergo the same pattern of technical
change.

If all the techniques in a technology undergo the *same* degree of
labor-saving technical change, the result is a *labor-augmenting* technical
change, which is also called *Harrod-neutral*. Purely labor-augmenting
technical change can be represented by multiplying the labor input in
the production function by the factor $1 + \gamma$ (the Greek letter *gamma,*
pronounced "gam*l*-ma"):

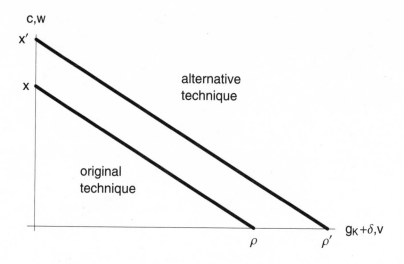

Figure 3.9: Factor-saving technical change shifts the growth-distribution schedule outward parallel to itself.

$$F'(K, N) = F(K, (1 + \gamma)N)$$

Another way to think of labor-augmenting, or Harrod-neutral technical change is as a rescaling of the measure of labor input: each worker after the technical change functions as if her efforts were magnified by a factor representing the size of the change. Economists often make this transformation and refer to *effective labor input*, which means multiplying the number of workers in any year by a factor representing the degree of labor-augmenting technical change that has taken place since the base year. Each actual worker after the Harrod-neutral technical change is the equivalent of more than one effective worker. If the wage rate increases by the same proportion as labor productivity, the profit rate will remain unchanged with purely labor-augmenting technical change, which is why Harrod called this type of technical change "neutral."

Capital-augmenting technical change is defined analogously to labor-augmenting technical change. In this case each unit of capital acts as if its productivity were multiplied by the factor $1 + \chi$ (the Greek letter *chi*, pronounced "ki").

Factor-augmenting technical change consists of equal amounts of labor- and capital-augmenting technical change, and can be represented by multiplying the whole production function by the factor $1 + \gamma = 1 + \chi$, under the assumption that the production function exhibits constant returns to scale:

$$F'(K, N) = (1 + \gamma)F(K, N) = F((1 + \gamma)K, (1 + \gamma)N)$$

Factor-augmenting technical change is often called *Hicks-neutral*. Factor-augmenting technical change can also be thought of as a rescaling of the output itself: the same labor and capital inputs produce more output, which is why Hicks regarded it as "neutral."

Notice that these various types of neutral technical change to the whole technology assume that *every* technique experiences the *same* degree and type of technical change. This need not be true in reality, since technical change might affect some techniques differently from others. In the case of a technology represented by a neoclassical production function, it might be the case that one part of the unit isoquant shifts in a different pattern from the rest, for example.

It is useful to distinguish the parameters γ and χ from the growth rates g_x and g_ρ. For the Leontief production function, which has only one technique, they will be the same, but for a more general neoclassical production function, x and ρ will change not only because of technical change, but also because of changes in the technique in use, so that g_x and g_ρ may not be equal to γ and χ.

3.7 Two-sector Growth-Distribution Schedules

We have been working under the *one-sector* assumption that there is only one produced commodity in the economy, which can be used interchangeably as a consumption good or as investment to add to the capital stock. This assumption greatly simplifies the analysis of a model economy. The production possibilities frontier for a one-sector economy is a straight line. As long as a one-sector economy is not specialized to the production of consumption or investment goods, the price of capital goods in terms of consumption goods is fixed at unity, and as a result we do not need to analyze the effect of changes in exogenous variables on the consumption goods price of capital. The output per worker, x, cannot be affected by changes in the price of capital. Under these circumstances the social consumption-growth rate schedule and the real wage-profit rate schedule are represented by the same straight line, which coincides with the growth-distribution schedule whose intercepts are the output per worker and the output per unit of capital.

In an economy with two (or more) produced outputs, relative price changes do matter, and considerably complicate the analysis. Since real economies have many different commodities, this problem is important in principle. The Cambridge capital controversy centered on the issues raised in moving from the one-sector model to the analysis of economies with more than one sector.

We can see the range of issues raised by looking briefly at a two-sector economy. In this economy, capital and labor as inputs can be combined either to produce a consumption good, c, or an investment good, i, in different techniques. We will take the consumption good as the numéraire, and denote the price of the capital good (and investment) in terms of the consumption good by p.

To describe a technique of production in the two-sector model, we must specify the capital-intensity and labor productivity in the consumption sector, k_c and x_c, and the capital-intensity and labor productivity in the investment sector, k_i and x_i.

We can calculate the real wage-profit rate frontier for a technique in the two sector model on the assumption that the economy is in a *steady state*, so that the price of investment as an output is the same as the price of capital as an input, by finding the relative price of capital, p, and real wage rate, w, consistent with the same profit rate v, in the two sectors. This requires solving the two equations:

$$x_c = vpk_c + w \tag{3.7}$$

$$px_i = vpk_i + w \tag{3.8}$$

Equations (3.7) and (3.8) express the requirement that the profit rate be the same in the two sectors. For any level of v, these two equations can be solved for p and w:

$$p = \frac{x_c}{v(k_c - k_i) + x_i}$$

$$w = x_c - pvk_c = x_c \left(1 - \frac{vk_c}{v(k_c - k_i) + x_i}\right)$$

The real wage-profit rate schedule for the technique is the graph of w as a function of v, as shown in Figure 3.10.

The real wage-profit rate schedule for a technique in the two-sector model can curve outward, as in Figure 3.11.

As in the one-sector model, the efficiency frontier is the envelope of the real wage-profit rate schedules for the available techniques. The

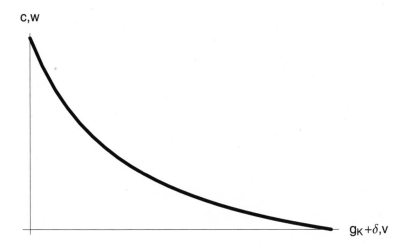

Figure 3.10: The real wage-profit rate relation for a single technique in a two-sector model is no longer a straight line, because the price of capital changes with the profit rate.

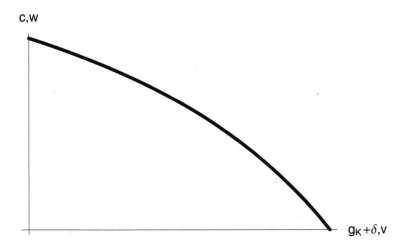

Figure 3.11: The real wage-profit rate relation for a single technique in a two-sector model can curve outward as well as inward, depending on whether k_c is larger or smaller than k_i.

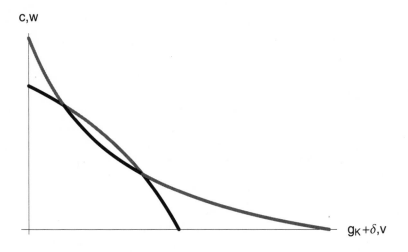

Figure 3.12: The efficiency frontier in a two-sector model is the envelope of the real wage-profit rate schedules for the available techniques. Unlike the one-sector model, the efficiency frontier in a two-sector model need not be concave toward the origin.

efficiency frontier for the two techniques illustrated in Figures 3.10–3.11 is graphed in Figure 3.12. (We assume that the consumption process of one technique cannot be operated with the investment process of the other.)

Several features of Figure 3.12 are of fundamental economic importance. The efficiency frontier is not necessarily concave toward the origin, so that it may have the same slope at several different points. In the one-sector model, each available technique of production contributes only one segment to the efficiency frontier (only a point, in the case of a technology defined by a smooth production function), but in the two-sector model (and in models with more than two sectors) it is possible for a technique to contribute to two or more segments of the efficiency frontier. Since there are two switchpoints in Figure 3.12, the same technique is the most profitable both at a low wage rate and at a high wage rate, a phenomenon known as *reswitching of techniques*. Thus in general there is no one-to-one correspondence between profit or wage rates and techniques of production in the two-sector model. In this case it is impossible to make sense of the idea of a marginal product of capital. These points are of fundamental importance to the theory of capital and the Cambridge capital controversy.

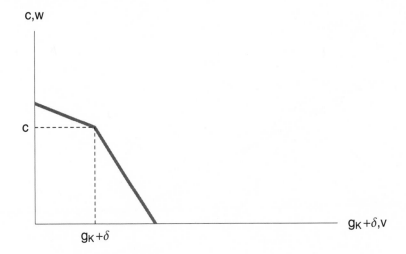

Figure 3.13: The production possibilities frontier in the two-sector economy is the minimum of the two straight lines representing the capital and labor constraints.

The production possibilities frontier for any economy depends on its endowment of factors of production. In the two-sector model we can represent this endowment by k, the amount of physical capital per worker available (since we already normalize the labor input to 1 by considering output per worker). The production possibilities for consumption per worker, c, and gross investment per worker, $i = (g_K + \delta)k$, in general are limited by the amounts of labor and capital available. We can represent these constraints as inequalities, given the technique of production:

$$\frac{c}{\rho_c} + \frac{(g_K + \delta)k}{\rho_i} \leq k \tag{3.9}$$

$$\frac{c}{x_c} + \frac{(g_K + \delta)k}{x_i} \leq 1 \tag{3.10}$$

The production possibilities frontier is the minimum of these two constraints, as illustrated in Figure 3.13, which represents the technology whose real wage-profit rate schedule is graphed in Figure 3.12.

The production possibilities frontier in the two-sector model is no longer a straight line, but is made up of two line segments.

When we draw a growth-distribution schedule for an economy, we use the value of output per worker, $x = c + p(g_K + \delta)k$, and the value

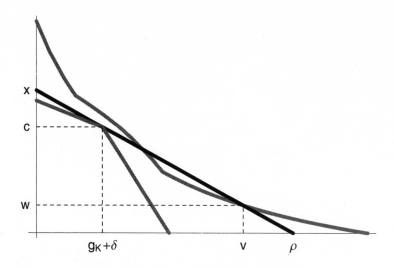

Figure 3.14: The growth-distribution schedule for the two-sector economy intersects the efficiency frontier at the profit rate, and also intersects the production possibilities frontier corresponding to the maximum profit technique.

of its capital stock per worker, pk, or the ratio of output to the value of capital, $\rho = x/pk$. For a given profit rate, v, capitalists will choose the technique of production that has the highest real wage rate, so that the growth-distribution schedule must pass through the efficiency frontier at the rental rate v, but the growth-distribution schedule need not be tangent to the efficiency frontier. The growth-distribution schedule must be tangent to the production possibilities frontier for the maximum profit technique. The situation is illustrated in Figure 3.14, which shows the efficiency frontier, the production possibilities frontier, and the growth-distribution schedule for the two-sector economy.

We can, therefore, generalize the growth-distribution schedule method to economies with two (or more sectors). But the growth-distribution schedule in these more complex economies represents neither the real wage-profit rate schedule nor the production possibilities frontier for the technique in use. It does, however, give us some information about the real wage-profit rate schedule and the production possibilities frontier. The growth-distribution schedule intersects the real wage-profit rate schedule of the profit-maximizing technique at the (v, w) point and is also tangent to the production possibilities frontier at the $(g_K + \delta, c)$ point. If the efficiency frontier is not very curved, the observed growth-distribution schedule approximates it.

3.8 Models of Production and Models of Growth

We have developed a simple model of production, in which there is only one output which can be used either for consumption or investment. A technique of production is defined by its capital intensity, k, its labor productivity, x, and its depreciation rate, δ, and corresponds to a single growth-distribution schedule. When the available technology consists of more than one technique, profit-maximizing entrepreneurs will choose the technique with the highest profit rate at the ruling real wage. The efficiency frontier is the envelope of the real wage-profit rate schedules for the technology. The point on the efficiency frontier at the ruling real wage determines the profit-maximizing technique, which in turn determines the social consumption-growth rate schedule for the economy. When the technology is described by a smooth production function, such as a Cobb-Douglas production function, the profit-maximizing technique has the marginal product of labor equal to the real wage. But there are technologies, such as the Leontief technology, in which the marginal product of capital is not well-defined.

The basic model of production can be combined with models of labor supply and of saving to create a model of economic growth.

3.9 Suggested Readings

Further detail on the mathematical properties of the Cobb-Douglas and more general neoclassical production functions can be found in Allen [1968]. Pasinetti [1977] provides a rich exposition of the fixed-coefficient model with many sectors.

For conceptually critical views of the neoclassical production function, see Nelson and Winter [1982] and Robinson [1953]. The latter began the Cambridge Capital Controversy, which is surveyed with considerable style by Harcourt [1972]. Two important summary statements of this debate are given by Samuelson [1966] and Garegnani [1970]. A particularly clear exposition of the two-commodity model developed in the text can be found in Spaventa [1970]. Samuelson [1962] first tried to show (unsuccessfully, it turned out) that the neoclassical production function and efficiency frontier could be generalized in the context of a multi-commodity world. An exhaustive treatment of the theory of production, which includes coverage of the Cambridge Controversy and other topics in the history of economic thought, is Kurz and Salvadori [1995]. Ochoa [1989] presents evidence that the wage-profit curves found in real economies are well-approximated by linear functions.

Chapter 4

The Labor Market

4.1 Models of Economic Growth

A model of economic growth is a set of mathematical assumptions that allow us to predict the behavior of an imaginary economy. In any model certain factors are taken as given *exogenous parameters* of the process. The model does not try to explain why the exogenous parameters have the values they do, but simply accepts them as determined by processes outside the model's scope. The other variables in the system are taken to be *endogenous variables*. The model is supposed to determine, and therefore explain, the endogenous variables on the basis of the values taken by the exogenous parameters. A typical analysis, for example, asks mathematically what would happen to the endogenous variables if one of the exogenous parameters were to be changed. In the real world we almost always see all the exogenous parameters changing at once, but the analytical procedure holds all of them constant except one, in order to isolate the influences of that particular exogenous parameter. If we want to use the model to explain real historical events, we have to superimpose the effects of all the changes in the exogenous parameters that have occurred.

What we take as exogenous and endogenous depends on our point of view and the type of question we want to analyze. What we take as an exogenous parameter in one model we might regard as endogenous in another model that tries to explain what determines its evolution. It is very important in studying a model (or presenting a model to others) to identify the exogenous and endogenous variables explicitly.

In general a mathematical system consists of a certain number of relations between variables expressed as equations. The number of endogenous variables that can be explained by a model is limited to the number of relations it contains. If we try to explain three endogenous variables with only two equations, for example, we will fail, because we can typically take any arbitrary value of one of the variables and solve the equations consistently for the other two. Thus a model can have any number of exogenous parameters, but the number of endogenous variables is limited to the number of relations specified in the model.

In modeling economic growth in a capitalist economy we will take as our endogenous variables the growth rate of the capital stock, the profit rate, the level of consumption and the wage: g_K, v, c and w. Among the exogenous parameters will be capital intensity, k, or the output-capital ratio, ρ, labor productivity, x, and the depreciation rate, δ. The growth-distribution schedule gives us two relations among the four endogenous variables, given the exogenous parameters:

$$w = x - vk$$

$$c = x - (g_K + \delta)k$$

A complete model of growth, however, must have two more relations expressed as equations in order to determine all four of these variables. For example, if we knew the real wage and social consumption per worker in an economy, the growth-distribution schedule would determine the profit rate and the growth rate of the capital stock. These additional relations are sometimes said to *close* the model.

Different schools of economic thought add different conditions to close the growth model. The doctrinal differences among the schools are reflected in these differences. One reason we have begun by explaining the model of production is that most of the models generated by the different major schools of thought are consistent with these core production relations. The models we will study all close the growth model by making some hypothesis about labor supply and demand and equilibrium in the labor market, which adds a third determining relation to the two expressed by the growth-distribution schedule, and some hypothesis about the behavior of households in allocating income between investment and consumption, which adds the fourth. Different hypotheses about the labor market and about household consumption patterns can lead to models that make quite different predictions about the patterns of growth.

We will begin in this chapter by discussing different models of the labor market.

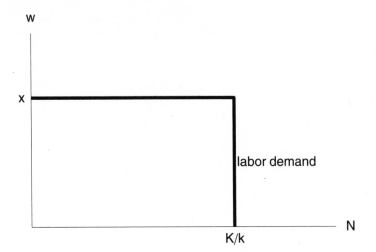

Figure 4.1: When there is only one available technique of production the demand for labor is limited by the amount of capital, which determines the level of output. At any real wage below the productivity of labor the demand for labor is equal to K/k.

4.2 Labor Supply and Demand

The real wage can be regarded as the price that equates the supply of and demand for labor. In a one-sector production model with a single given technique of production, the demand for labor is given by the amount of capital available for it to work with and the coefficient k, which determines how many jobs each unit of capital supports, since we have the relations:

$$N^d = \frac{X}{x} = \frac{K}{k}$$

This means that in any period the demand for labor is a vertical line, as illustrated in Figure 4.1.

If, on the other hand, we assume that there is a spectrum of techniques of production defined by the smooth isoquant of a production function, the demand for labor will depend on the profit rate-maximizing technique as well as on the amount of capital accumulated. We could express this by writing $x(w)$ and $k(w)$ as functions of the wage:

$$N^d(w) = \frac{X}{x(w)} = \frac{K}{k(w)}$$

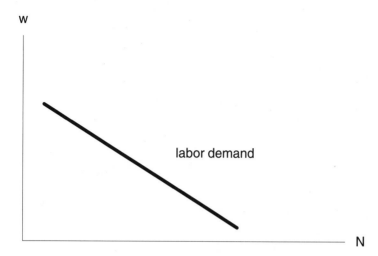

Figure 4.2: With a smooth spectrum of techniques the demand for labor given the capital stock will rise gradually as the wage falls, due to the shift to lower capital intensity techniques.

If the spectrum of techniques falls along a smooth isoquant, a fall in the wage will lower the profit rate-maximizing k, and the demand for labor will be a smoothly decreasing function of the wage, as in Figure 4.2.

With a spectrum of techniques, the elasticity of the demand for labor depends on the exact shape of the unit isoquant of the production function.

4.3 The Classical Conventional Wage Model

The Classical economists, Smith, Ricardo, Malthus, and their critic, Marx, viewed labor supply as growing or shrinking in response to the demand for labor at an exogenously given real wage. Ricardo, following Malthus, argued that the population and hence the supply of labor would rise if the real wage rose above a subsistence level, and that the population would fall if the real wage fell below this level. In the long run, at least, this theory implies that the supply curve of labor is horizontal at the subsistence wage.

The theory of a subsistence wage rests on Malthus' model of *demographic equilibrium*. Malthus argued that death and birth rates in any society would be stable functions of the standard of living, which he as-

birth rate
death rate

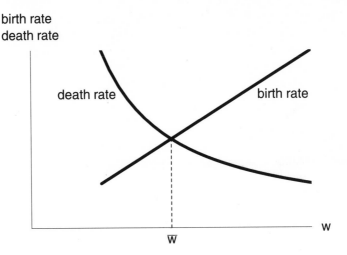

Figure 4.3: Malthus' theory of wages is based on the assumption that death rates decline and birth rates rise with increases in the wage. The intersection of the death and birth rate schedules is a demographic equilibrium that determines the subsistence level of the wage.

sociated with the level of the real wage. A higher wage would lower the death rate, especially among infants, by allowing workers to consume a better standard of nutrition. A higher wage would also raise the birth rate, by encouraging earlier marriages.

As illustrated in Figure 4.3, the intersection of the death and birth rate schedules is a demographic equilibrium at which population would remain constant. Malthus assumed that labor supply would be closely related to population, so that a constant population would also mean a constant supply of labor. The level of the real wage at which birth and death rates equalize can be viewed as *subsistence*, since it is just high enough to reproduce the population and labor force without change. If the wage were to rise above subsistence, the population would grow, and the increased supply of labor would tend to force the wage downward. If the wage were to fall below subsistence, high infant mortality would lead the population to shrink, and the resulting decline in the supply of labor would tend to force the wage upward. Over a period of time long enough to allow for these changes in population, the wage in this model will tend to remain close to the subsistence level.

Marx criticized Malthus' theory on two grounds. First, Marx argued that the schedules of birth and death rates were themselves the product of specific social relations. Malthus' theory, in Marx's view, applied to early nineteenth-century capitalism, which lacked any regulation of the exploitation of labor and had no social "safety net" to protect workers from extreme poverty, but might not hold for different social relations (such as those of a socialist society). History has borne out this criticism of Malthus, since the modifications of capitalism to provide for the protection and education of workers have coincided with dramatic changes in fertility, and falsified Malthus' projections.

Marx also argued against Malthus' assumption that labor supply is proportional to population. Marx pointed out that capitalist production always coexists with noncapitalist production such as domestic labor and subsistence agriculture, and draws part of its labor supply from these noncapitalist sectors through migration and the mobilization of female and child labor. Marx viewed these noncapitalist sectors as *reserve armies of labor.* Thus the capitalist labor supply might not vary proportionally with population because of offsetting changes in these labor reserves.

Marx agreed, however, with Malthus' conclusion that the supply of labor was horizontal at a given real wage because the movement of labor from the reserve armies would increase the labor supply if the real wage rose. The real investment costs (transport, relocation, training, and so on) involved in migrating from backward sectors to industrial employment establish a *value of labor-power* which Marx viewed as determining the level of real wages. In Marx's view this was not a subsistence real wage in the sense of a biological minimum, but reflected social and historical factors affecting the cost of reproducing labor-power in different economies.

We will call these Classical and Marxian theories the *conventional wage model.* The supply of labor in the conventional wage model is horizontal at the exogenously given conventional wage, as shown in Figure 4.4.

Arthur Lewis explains the conventional wage model as reflecting a vision of economic development in which labor is drawn into a modern production sector from reserves that can support themselves by traditional production. In order to permit workers to move from the traditional sector to the modern sector, they must be supplied with the wherewithal to survive in that sector, because they cannot carry on their traditional production and work in the modern sector at the same time.

This vision of the process of labor supply is relevant to highly industrialized economies as well. In highly industrialized economies labor is supplied by migration from less developed countries or less developed regions within a given country, or by drawing workers from other pursuits (such as childcare and housework) into industrial production. The

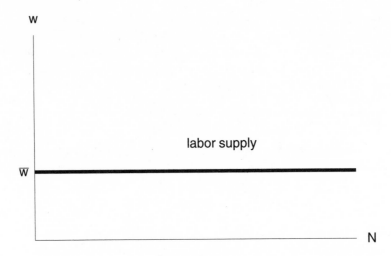

Figure 4.4: In the conventional wage model the supply of labor in each period is horizontal at an exogenously given real wage determined by the costs of reproducing labor-power.

Classical model assumes that these reserves of labor are practically limitless and that the subsistence wage necessary to attract labor to the modern sector is given in each period.

If there is only one technique of production, the conventional wage model determines the wage, and the accumulated capital stock determines output and employment, as in Figure 4.5.

When there is a spectrum of techniques, the conventional wage determines the wage level, and also determines the profit rate-maximizing technique of production. The capital stock, together with the profit rate-maximizing technique of production, determines the level of employment and output, as shown in Figure 4.6.

The conventional wage model thus can add one further condition to the growth model, by determining the real wage as an exogenous parameter. The real wage-profit rate schedule then determines the profit rate and the technique of production, leaving social consumption per worker and the growth rate of the capital stock still to be explained. The conventional wage assumption can be written algebraically as:

$$w = \bar{w} \tag{4.1}$$

Here $\bar{w}$ is the exogenously given conventional level of the real wage.

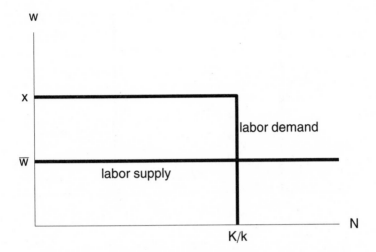

Figure 4.5: When there is only one technique, the conventional wage determines the wage, and the technique together with the accumulated capital determine the level of employment and output.

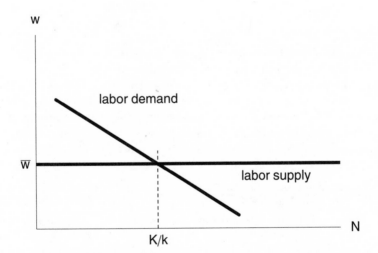

Figure 4.6: When there is a spectrum of techniques, the conventional wage determines the profit rate-maximizing technique, which, together with the accumulated capital stock, determines the level of output and employment.

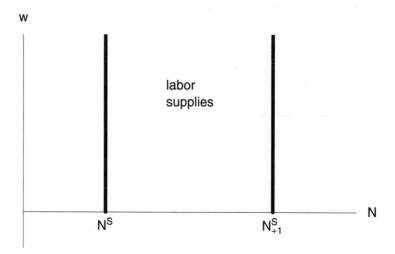

Figure 4.7: Neoclassical growth models assume an inelastically given supply of labor at any real wage. The shift from
N^s to N^s_{+1} represents the exogenous growth of the labor
force from one period to the next.

4.4   The Neoclassical Full Employment Model

At the opposite extreme from the conventional wage model is the assumption made in neoclassical growth models that the supply of labor
in any period is exogenously given. Neoclassical models allow for a shift
in the labor supply over time as the result of population growth, but
view the rate of population growth, n, as an exogenous parameter. This
approach views labor as an inelastically supplied input to production
like land, though it allows for the exogenous increase in the quantity of
labor supplied.

Neoclassical labor economists view the supply of labor in any period
as depending on the real wage, due to the possible disutility of labor,
with the supply of labor at any real wage determined by the population.
In the context of economic growth theory the inclusion of the wage
elasticity of the supply of labor in each period complicates the analysis
without adding important new insights. Neoclassical growth models
therefore typically abstract from labor supply responses to the real wage,
and assume that households supply labor inelastically. In these models
the supply of labor is a vertical line at the level given by the population,
as illustrated in Figure 4.7.

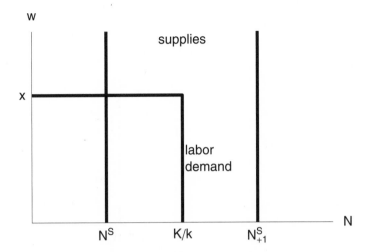

Figure 4.8: When there is only one technique of production, and a fixed supply of labor, either there will be a shortage of labor which will drive the wage up to x, and the profit rate down to 0, or there will be a surplus of labor, which will drive the wage down to zero, and the profit rate up to ρ.

When there is only one technique of production, the demand for labor is determined by the accumulated capital stock. If the supply of labor is smaller than this demand for labor, the real wage will rise to x, the productivity of labor, and the profit rate will fall to 0. If, on the other hand, the supply of labor is larger than the demand, the real wage will fall to zero, and the profit rate will rise to its maximum value, ρ, as shown in Figure 4.8.

Since neither of these outcomes is compatible with steady growth, the full employment assumption requires that the demand for labor and the supply of labor be matched in every period. Since the supply of labor is assumed to grow at the exogenously given rate n, this requires the demand for labor determined by the capital stock to grow at the same rate. If there is no change in the capital-labor ratio over time, this implies that the growth rate of the capital stock must also be equal to n. Thus the full employment assumption also adds one determining equation to the growth model, the requirement that the growth rate of the capital stock be equal to the exogenously given growth rate of the population. This assumption can be written

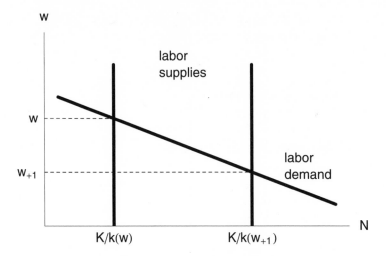

Figure 4.9: Wage flexibility can in theory achieve full employment by inducing entrepreneurs to change the technique of production. Here a rise in the supply of labor is accommodated by a move to a less capital intensive technique mediated by a fall in the wage.

$$\frac{N^d_{+1}}{N^d} = \frac{\frac{K_{+1}}{k_{+1}}}{\frac{K}{k}} = \frac{N^s_{+1}}{N^s} = 1 + n$$

or, if $k_{+1} = k$,

$$1 + g_K \equiv \frac{K_{+1}}{K} = 1 + n \qquad (4.2)$$

In the case where there is a spectrum of techniques and an exogenously fixed supply of labor, it is possible for a change in the technique in use to allow full employment. The way this would work is that if the wage were to fall in response to an excess supply of labor, entrepreneurs would shift to a less capital-intensive technique, thereby increasing the demand for labor. If this process could take place smoothly and rapidly in a single period of production, equilibrium could be reached in the labor market as in Figure 4.9.

The great difficulty in applying the neoclassical model of full employment through flexible wages and changes in technique to real economies is that it can take a long time in real economies for the wage and the technique of production to adjust. Thus there may be considerable periods of time when the labor market fails to reach full-employment equilibrium.

The neoclassical defense of the model is that it should work on average over time, and since the purpose of a growth model is to analyze the long-run behavior of the economy, the assumption of full employment is a permissible abstraction from real frictions. The Classical economists might respond that it is precisely over longer time periods that it makes sense to consider the labor supply itself as endogenously adjusting to the wage.

The idea that full employment could be achieved in the short run through changes in the technique of production in response to changes in the wage misleads some economists into thinking that the marginal product of labor determines the wage. As we have seen, however, the equality of the marginal product of labor (when it can be defined) to the wage is the result of profit maximization by entrepreneurs. A more accurate way to understand labor market equilibrium under the full employment assumption is that the wage determines the marginal product of labor (through the profit rate-maximizing decisions of entrepreneurs) and the supply of and demand for labor determine the wage so as to clear the labor market. Under these assumptions, the capital intensity of the technique in use has to change in each period to maintain full employment.

The full employment assumption can add one relation to an economic growth model: the wage rate is determined in each period so as to provide full employment of the exogenously given labor force. The growth rate and the level of consumption per worker still remain undetermined, even with the addition of the full employment assumption.

The full employment assumption can be written algebraically as:

$$\frac{K}{k(w)} = \bar{N} \tag{4.3}$$

Here $\bar{N}$ is the exogenously given labor supply.

4.5 Toward a Model of Economic Growth

A theory of the labor market adds one more determining relation to the growth-distribution schedule, but a full growth model still requires one more theoretical relation to determine the four endogenous variables, g_K, c, v, and w. As we have seen, the conventional wage model takes the real wage as given exogenously and thus determines the profit rate (and the profit rate-maximizing technique of production), but leaves the growth rate of the capital stock and social consumption per worker unexplained. The full employment model with no choice of technique forces the growth rate of the capital stock to be equal to the exogenously determined growth rate of the labor force, and thus through the social consumption-growth rate schedule also determines the level of social consumption per worker, but leaves the profit rate and the real wage unexplained. The Classical conventional wage model sees the labor market as determining distribution, but leaves growth to be determined elsewhere. The full employment model without choice of technique sees the labor market as determining growth, but leaves distribution to be determined elsewhere.

In the full employment model with choice of technique, the structure of the model is different in the short run and the long run. In the short run, the full employment condition determines the wage and the profit rate-maximizing technique, but leaves the growth rate and social consumption per worker unexplained. On a long-run steady state growth path on which the wage is constant, however, the capital stock must grow at the same rate as the labor force. In this time frame the full employment assumption determines the growth rate of the capital stock and social consumption per worker, leaving the wage and the profit rate unexplained.

4.6   Growth in Real Economies

In the theoretical models, the exogenous parameters are assumed to be constant or growing in some orderly way, such as a constant rate of Harrod-neutral technical change. In real economies, this rarely happens. We turn once again to the six countries that we have been following through the phases of growth identified by Angus Maddison. Table 4.1 focuses on the growth of output, capital and employment. The measure of employment in this table is total labor hours, which is the product of the number of workers and the annual hours worked by the average worker.

The volume of output and the capital stock have grown more or less continuously during the nearly two century stretch of time. There are no negative entries, and only a few growth rates below one percent per year. If this sounds small, consider that a sum of money invested at one percent compound interest will double in value in only 70 years.

As was true with labor productivity, the growth of output and capital has an irregular, stop-go character. Again, the period right after World War II (1950-1973) contrasts vividly with the most recent period (1973-1992). Because of the high rate of growth in the former period, it is sometimes called the Golden Age of Capital Accumulation.

We need to be careful about the variations in the growth of employment since some of these variations are reflections of changes in the

Table 4.1:
**Growth Rates of Output, Employment and Capital (%/year) for
Six Countries in Selected Periods from 1820-1992.**

	1820– 1870	1870– 1913	1913– 1950	1950– 1973	1973– 1992
U.S.					
Output, X	4.22	3.94	2.84	3.92	2.39
Employment, N	3.09	2.02	0.35	1.15	1.27
Capital Stock, K	5.46	5.53	2.01	3.27	3.13
France					
Output, X	1.27	1.63	1.15	5.02	2.26
Employment, N		-0.10	-0.75	0.01	-0.46
Capital Stock, K				4.80	4.30
Germany					
Output, X	2.00	2.81	1.06	5.99	2.30
Employment, N		0.92	0.45	0.00	-0.38
Capital Stock, K				5.93	3.37
Netherlands					
Output, X	1.93	2.20	2.43	4.74	2.14
Employment, N		0.92	1.10	-0.04	-0.07
Capital Stock, K				4.55	3.07
U.K.					
Output, X	2.04	1.90	1.19	2.96	1.59
Employment, N	0.86	0.76	-0.46	-0.15	-0.57
Capital Stock, K	2.61	1.73	1.09	5.17	3.32
Japan					
Output, X	0.31	2.34	2.24	9.25	3.76
Employment, N	0.21	0.45	0.40	1.44	0.61
Capital Stock, K		3.49	4.17	9.18	6.81

Source: [Maddison, 1995b, Table 2-6].

average number of hours worked per worker, and some are due to changes in the number of workers. The variations in the growth of employment can be interpreted through the different models in very different ways. Models which assume full employment of an exogenously given labor supply would treat these variations as exogenous changes in the supply of labor. The classical conventional wage model would interpret these variations as changes in the demand for labor caused by variation in the rate of capital accumulation. In either case, we might need to superimpose some exogenous technical change in order to make sense out of the real data. In models that assume a spectrum of techniques, we might seek evidence of changes in the technique chosen, in response to changes in the real wage that clears the labor market.

4.7   Suggested Readings

The Classical doctrine on labor supply originated with Malthus [1986], Ricardo [1951] and Marx [1977], and an influential modern view is given by Lewis [1954]. The distinction that Marx draws between labor and labor-power is elaborated in Marglin [1974] and Bowles [1985]; this distinction plays a major role in the theory of economic development and capital-labor relations presented in Gordon et al. [1982]. Goodwin [1967] studies the cyclical dynamics that can arise from variations in the Marxian reserve army of labor. The theoretical and applied literature on labor demand is surveyed from a neoclassical perspective in Hamermesh [1993]; for a view of the evidence which is skeptical of the neoclassical theory, see Michl [1987]. The Golden Age of Capital Accumulation is profiled in Armstrong et al. [1991] and theoretically evaluated in Marglin and Schor [1990].

Chapter 5

Models of Consumption and Saving

In order to close a model of economic growth, even given one of the labor market theories, we need to add a theory that explains how the society divides its income between consumption and investment.

The Classical economists, Smith, Malthus, and Ricardo, assumed that workers as a class consumed their whole wage. From one point of view this idea is a tautology, since if workers as a class saved, they would have positive wealth and would no longer be purely workers.

The assumption that workers as a class do little or no saving does not, of course, rule out the possibility that *individual* worker households might save. For example, workers might save in their youth and middle age in order to finance their retirement, as in the life-cycle theory of saving. Workers might save in order to meet certain contingencies, like unemployment, or the need to pay for their children's education. But this saving by some households will be offset by dissaving (spending out of accumulated saving) by other worker households. While some households are saving for retirement, others are spending their life saving on retirement consumption. While some households are saving to finance their children's education, others are spending out of saving to pay for that education. The Classical view amounts to the assumption that for workers as a class the saving of some households is matched by the dissaving of others.

Throughout much of this book, we will make the Classical assumption that workers spend all their wage income as a class, and contribute nothing to social saving. From the Classical point of view social saving is the function of the capitalists who already own wealth.

The model we will use to explain and predict capitalist consumption and saving, however, is quite neoclassical. Neoclassical economic theory views consumption decisions as the result of a tradeoff between consuming in the present and saving in order to consume in the future, and we will rigorously adopt this point of view in modeling capitalist consumption and saving decisions. One great advantage of this modeling approach is that it forces us to make explicit the *intertemporal budget constraint* of the capitalists, which, in turn, is the key to understanding *portfolio decisions* when there is more than one asset in the economy, and the basic principles of *financial arbitrage*.

We will also use other models of consumption and saving when they are appropriate. In our discussion of the neoclassical growth model in Chapter 8, we will assume that all households, including worker households, save a fixed fraction of their income. In the *overlapping generations model* we analyze in Chapter 13, which focuses on the economic consequences of limited time horizons, workers are the sole source of saving.

The particular model of capitalist consumption and saving we will use adopts a particular intertemporal utility function, of the Cobb-Douglas form. The mathematical optimization model that arises from this utility function is particularly easy to solve, and the solution has a particularly simple form: the capitalist household consumes a constant fraction of its wealth at the end of each period, regardless of the net profit rates it anticipates in future periods. This simple behavior is traceable to the fact that in the Cobb-Douglas demand system the wealth and substitution effects of changes in future net profit rates exactly offset each other.

An important limitation of this model of intertemporal consumption is that it abstracts from *uncertainty*, which plays a major role in real economies. The analytical tools we develop could also be used to study consumption and saving under uncertainty, but uncertainty greatly complicates the mathematics involved. In our models the capitalist always knows current and future net profit rates with certainty.

The remainder of this chapter is devoted to working out the basic model of capitalist consumption and saving behavior in detail, as the basis for closing the model of economic growth.

5.1   A Two-Period Consumption-Saving Model

To begin with, let us start by working through an example used in many economic theory courses: the *two-period saving* model with *Cobb-*

Douglas utility function. A capitalist lives for two periods, 0 and 1. We measure her wealth, consumption, and saving in terms of real output. At the beginning of period 0 she has an endowment of wealth, K_0, which she can invest at a net profit rate r_0. The net profit rate represents the real return on her investment, and is thus comparable to an inflation-adjusted interest rate. At the end of the first period her wealth will have increased to $K_0 + r_0 K_0 = (1 + r_0)K_0$ which she can consume, C_0, or save, K_1, in order to consume at the end of the second period. In period 1 she again will invest at the net profit rate r_1, and at the end of the period will consume, C_1, her whole principal and return, $(1+r_1)K_1$. We can write the capitalist's budget constraint in two parts:

$$C_0 + K_1 \leq (1 + r_0)K_0$$

$$C_1 + K_2 \leq (1 + r_1)K_1 \leq (1 + r_1)((1 + r_0)K_0 - C_0) \qquad (5.1)$$

For completeness we have included the possibility that the capitalist might save something at the end of period 1 (K_2), in order to provide for a still more distant future either for herself or her heirs. If the capitalist does not care about the future after period 1, she will set $K_2 = 0$, and consume all her wealth at the end of period 1. We have also included the possibility that she might throw some wealth away (neither consuming nor saving it), though if the capitalist gets positive marginal utility from consumption she will never do this, and the inequality signs will always be equalities.

The Cobb-Douglas utility function is defined for a parameter β (the Greek letter *beta*, pronounced "bay′-ta"), which is called the *utility discount factor* and lies between 0 and 1, as the weighted average of the logarithms of consumption in the two periods, with a weight of $1 - \beta$ on the first period and β on the second period:

$$u(C_0, C_1) = \ln(C_0^{1-\beta} C_1^{\beta}) = (1 - \beta)\ln C_0 + \beta \ln C_1 \qquad (5.2)$$

The natural logarithm function here plays the role of a utility function for each period. The utility a capitalist gains from consuming C in a period is $\ln C$, and the marginal utility of consumption when the capitalist is consuming C is the derivative of the natural logarithm, $1/C$, so that the higher is the capitalist's consumption, the lower is her marginal utility: the logarithmic utility function displays the property of *diminishing marginal utility.*

The form of equation (5.2) implies that the capitalist gets no utility from consumption after period 1.

To choose the pattern of consumption that maximizes utility subject to the budget constraint, the capitalist has to solve the mathematical programming problem:

$$\max_{C_0,C_1 \geq 0} (1 - \beta) \ln C_0 + \beta \ln C_1$$

$$\text{subject to } C_0 + K_1 \leq (1 + r_0)K_0$$

$$C_1 + K_2 \leq (1 + r_1)K_1 \leq (1 + r_1)((1 + r_0)K_0 - C_0) \qquad (5.3)$$

$$\text{given } \beta, K_0, r_0, r_1$$

The solution to this problem, which we will work out in detail below, is:

$$C_0 = (1 - \beta)(1 + r_0)K_0$$

$$K_1 = \beta(1 + r_0)K_0 \qquad (5.4)$$

$$C_1 = (1 + r_1)K_1 = \beta(1 + r_1)(1 + r_0)K_0$$

The capitalist spends a fraction, $1 - \beta$, of her wealth at the end of the first period on consumption, regardless of what the net profit rate will be in the second period. As we will see, this feature of the solution carries over no matter how long the time horizon may be.

5.1.1   Solving the two-period consumption problem

A convenient and economically insightful way to solve maximization problems of this type is through the *Lagrangian technique*. We define two new variables, λ_0 and λ_1 (the Greek letter *lambda*, pronounced "lam'-da"), one for each constraint, called *shadow-prices* or *Lagrange multipliers*, and view them as penalties for violating the constraints. Then we form the *Lagrangian function*, which is the utility of the capitalist less penalties for violating the constraints:

$$L(C_0, C_1, K_1, K_2; \lambda_0, \lambda_1)$$

$$\equiv (1 - \beta) \ln C_0 + \beta \ln C_1$$

$$- \lambda_0(C_0 + K_1 - (1 + r_0)K_0)$$

$$- \lambda_1(C_1 + K_2 - (1 + r_1)K_1) \qquad (5.5)$$

It is convenient to refer to the first part of the Lagrangian as the *utility function* and the rest of the Lagrangian as the *penalty function*.

If we can choose C_0^* and $C_1^* \geq 0$ (and as a result K_1^* and K_2^*) and λ_0^* and $\lambda_1^* \geq 0$ so that C_0^*, C_1^*, K_1^*, and K_2^* *maximize* the Lagrangian holding λ_0^* and λ_1^* constant, and λ_0^* and λ_1^* *minimize* the Lagrangian holding C_0^*, C_1^*, K_1^*, and K_2^* constant, the resulting C_0^* and C_1^* will be the maximum for the original constrained problem. Such a combination $(C_0^*, C_1^*, K_1^*, K_2^*; \lambda_0^*, \lambda_1^*)$ is called a *saddle-point* of the Lagrangian function.

To see why a saddle-point of the Lagrangian must solve the original constrained maximization problem, notice first that C_0^*, C_1^*, K_1^*, and K_2^* must satisfy the constraints of the original problem. If they did not (if, for example, $C_0^* + K_1^* > (1 + r_0)K_0$), then it would always be possible to make the Lagrangian function smaller by taking λ_0 bigger, since λ_0 would be multiplied by a negative number in the Lagrangian expression. This would contradict the saddle-point property that λ_0^* and λ_1^* minimize the Lagrangian function holding C_0^*, C_1^*, K_1^*, and K_2^* constant. In fact, the penalty function must be zero at a saddle-point: either the constraint is exactly satisfied, so that the corresponding penalty term is zero, or the number multiplying the shadow-price is negative, so that the Lagrangian function will be minimized only if the corresponding shadow-price is zero.

Now suppose that there were some alternative C_0, C_1, K_1, and K_2 that satisfied the constraints and also gave a larger utility than C_0^* and C_1^*. At this alternative plan, the utility function would be larger than at the assumed saddle point. Since this alternative plan satisfies the constraints, λ_0^* and λ_1^* must be multiplied by negative or zero numbers in the Lagrangian function, so that the penalty function is also either positive or zero. But the penalty function for the saddle-point was exactly zero, so the value of the Lagrangian at the alternative plan would be larger than at the saddle-point. This contradicts the saddle-point property that C_0^*, C_1^*, K_1^*, and K_2^* maximize the Lagrangian function holding λ_0^* and λ_1^* constant. This argument shows that there can be no alternative plan that satisfies the constraints and gives a larger utility. But this means that C_0^* and C_1^* are the maximum solution to the original problem.

To find the saddle-point of the Lagrangian, we find its critical points by setting its derivatives with respect to $C_0, C_1, K_1, K_2, \lambda_0$, and λ_1 equal to zero and solve the resulting set of *first-order conditions*. (This is not always possible, but does work for the Cobb-Douglas utility function.)

$$\frac{\partial L}{\partial C_0} = \frac{1 - \beta}{C_0} - \lambda_0 \leq 0 \ (= 0 \text{ if } C_0 > 0)$$

$$\frac{\partial L}{\partial C_1} = \frac{\beta}{C_1} - \lambda_1 \leq 0 \ (= 0 \text{ if } C_1 > 0)$$

$$\frac{\partial L}{\partial K_1} = -\lambda_0 + (1 + r_1)\lambda_1 \leq 0 \ (\ = 0 \text{ if } K_1 > 0) \qquad (5.6)$$

$$\frac{\partial L}{\partial K_2} = -\lambda_1 \leq 0 \ (\ = 0 \text{ if } K_2 > 0)$$

$$\frac{\partial L}{\partial \lambda_0} = -(C_0 + K_1 - (1 + r_0)K_0) \geq 0 \ (\ = 0 \text{ if } \lambda_0 > 0)$$

$$\frac{\partial L}{\partial \lambda_1} = -(C_1 + K_2 - (1 + r_1)K_1) \geq 0 \ (\ = 0 \text{ if } \lambda_1 > 0)$$

The first-order condition for K_1, for example, says that the coefficient multiplying K_1 in the Lagrangian must be less than or equal to zero: if it were positive, we could increase the value of the Lagrangian without limit by choosing K_1 to be very large, and there would be no saddle-point. If K_1 is chosen positive, then this coefficient must be equal to zero, since if it were negative and K_1 were positive, we could increase the value of the Lagrangian by reducing K_1. This coefficient could be negative at the saddle-point only if K_1 were zero, since we cannot reduce K_1 below zero. Similar reasoning underlies the other first-order conditions.

The first two first-order conditions can be satisfied only if C_0 and $C_1 > 0$, which further implies that λ_0 and $\lambda_1 > 0$. The economic intuition behind this mathematical condition is that the marginal utility of the logarithmic utility function grows without bound as consumption becomes smaller and smaller, so that the capitalist will always consume something in each period. Since $\lambda_1 > 0$, we see that $K_2 = 0$ (which we figured out already above). Since the penalty function is zero at the saddle-point, we can see that:

$$\lambda_0 C_0 + \lambda_1 C_1 = K_1(-\lambda_0 + (1 + r_1)\lambda_1) - \lambda_1 K_2 + \lambda_0(1 + r_0)K_0.$$

But we can also see from the first-order conditions that

$$\lambda_0 C_0 + \lambda_1 C_1 = 1$$

$$K_1(-\lambda_0 + (1 + r_1)\lambda_1) = 0$$

$$\lambda_1 K_2 = 0$$

Solving these equations, we get the *Cobb-Douglas demand system*:

$$\lambda_0 = \frac{1}{(1 + r_0)K_0}$$

$$\lambda_1 = \frac{1}{(1 + r_1)(1 + r_0)K_0}$$

$$K_1 = \beta(1 + r_0)K_0 \qquad (5.7)$$

$$C_0 = (1 - \beta)(1 + r_0)K_0$$

$$C_1 = (1 + r_1)K_1 = \beta(1 + r_1)(1 + r_0)K_0$$

The Cobb-Douglas demand system has the peculiar feature that the wealth and substitution effects of a change in future net profit rates are equal and opposite in sign, so that the consumption in period zero does not depend on the net profit rate in the second period, r_1. This simplification is a great help in the types of growth models we will be studying. For example, the capitalist's saving, K_1 is just a constant fraction β of her wealth at the end of the period $(1 + r_0)K_0$.

Problem 5.1 *Write down the capitalist choice problem for a capitalist facing three periods. Indicate clearly the utility function and the budget constraints, and explain your notation.*

Problem 5.2 *Write down the Lagrangian function for the three-period capitalist choice problem, and find the first-order conditions characterizing its critical points. How many shadow prices will there be?*

Problem 5.3 *Solve the first-order conditions for the three-period capitalist choice problem, and show that the resulting demand system is given by the equations:*

$$C_0 = (1 - \beta)(1 + r_0)K_0$$

$$K_1 = \beta(1 + r_0)K_0$$

$$C_1 = (1 - \beta)(1 + r_1)K_1 = (1 - \beta)\beta(1 + r_1)(1 + r_0)K_0 \qquad (5.8)$$

$$K_2 = \beta(1 + r_1)K_1$$

$$C_2 = (1 + r_2)K_2$$

5.2   An Infinite-Horizon Model

Ricardo and the Classical economists argued that wealth-holders would take into account the interests of their descendants in making consumption and saving decisions. Thus they would act as if their planning horizon stretched infinitely far into the future, even though their individual lives would come to an end in a finite time. This dynastic hypothesis is called *Ricardian equivalence*.

It is, happily, possible to generalize the two-period Cobb-Douglas saving problem to a longer horizon.

To allow for an *infinite horizon*, we let $t = 0, 1, 2, \ldots$ without any ending point.

The capitalist begins period 0 with a stock of wealth K_0, just as in the two-period model. She can invest this at the net profit rate r_0, and at the end of the period will have $(1 + r_0)K_0$ to divide between consumption and saving for the next period, just as in the two-period model. In fact, the budget constraints for the infinite horizon model are just the same as in the two-period model, except that there is an infinite sequence of them:

$$C_0 + K_1 \leq (1 + r_0)K_0$$

$$C_1 + K_2 \leq (1 + r_1)K_1$$

$$\cdots \tag{5.9}$$

$$C_t + K_{t+1} \leq (1 + r_t)K_t$$

$$\cdots$$

The capitalist has to make a sequence of decisions of this kind in each period. As a result her consumption will be a series

$$\{C_0, C_1, C_2, \ldots, C_t, \ldots\} = \{C_t\}_{t=0}^{\infty}$$

extending from period zero to infinity.

We will assume that the typical capitalist ranks consumption paths $\{C_t\}_{t=0}^{\infty}$ by calculating the discounted logarithmic utility function:

$$u(\{C_t\}_{t=0}^{\infty}) = (1 - \beta)\Sigma_{t=0}^{\infty}\beta^t \ln C_t$$

$$= (1 - \beta) \ln C_0 + (1 - \beta)\beta \ln C_1 + (1 - \beta)\beta^2 \ln C_2 + \ldots \tag{5.10}$$

This utility function is a generalization of the Cobb-Douglas utility function we used in analyzing the two-period saving problem. It is a weighted average of the logarithms of consumption in each period. (Remember that the geometric sequence can be summed: $\Sigma_{t=0}^{\infty}\beta^t = 1/(1-\beta)$ so that $(1 - \beta)\Sigma_{t=0}^{\infty}\beta^t = 1$.) The effect of multiplying $\ln C_t$ by $(1 - \beta)\beta^t$ is to shrink down or *discount* the utility from consumption in period t. Utility farther in the future counts for less in the typical capitalist's calculations. We are assuming that the capitalist has *perfect foresight*, that is, that she correctly anticipates all future net profit rates. The capitalist thus has to solve a planning problem, which is to maximize her utility subject to the series of budget constraints in each period:

choose $\{C_t \geq 0, K_{t+1} \geq 0\}_{t=0}^{\infty}$

so as to maximize $(1 - \beta)\Sigma_{t=0}^{\infty}\beta^t \ln C_t$ \hfill (5.11)

subject to $C_t + K_{t+1} \leq (1 + r_t)K_t \qquad t = 0, 1, \ldots$

$K_0, \{r_t\}_{t=0}^{\infty}$ given

The solution to this problem, worked out below, is, as we would expect from the two-period problem, that the capitalist consumes a fraction $1 - \beta$ of her end-of-period wealth in every period:

$$C = (1 - \beta)(1 + r)K \qquad (5.12)$$

This implies that she also saves a fraction β of her wealth:

$$K_{+1} = \beta(1 + r)K \qquad (5.13)$$

The growth of her wealth in each period depends only on the discount rate, β and the net profit rate, r:

$$1 + g_K = \frac{K_{+1}}{K} = \beta(1 + r) \qquad (5.14)$$

In growth theory Equation 5.14 is called the *Cambridge equation*.

5.2.1 Solving the infinite-horizon problem

We can solve the infinite-horizon problem by the Lagrangian technique exactly as in the two-period model. We now have an infinite sequence of shadow prices $\{\lambda_t\}_{t=0}^{\infty}$, one for each period's budget constraint. The Lagrangian function for the capitalist's planning problem is:

$$L(\{C_t, K_{t+1}; \lambda_t\}_{t=0}^{\infty})$$

$$= (1 - \beta)\Sigma_{t=0}^{\infty}\beta^t \ln C_t - \Sigma_{t=0}^{\infty}\lambda_t(C_t + K_{t+1} - (1 + r_t)K_t)$$

$$= (1 - \beta)\Sigma_{t=0}^{\infty}\beta^t \ln C_t$$

$$-\Sigma_{t=0}^{\infty}\lambda_t C_t - \Sigma_{t=0}^{\infty}(\lambda_t - \lambda_{t+1}(1 + r_{t+1}))K_{t+1} + \lambda_0(1 + r_0)K_0$$

In order to find a saddle-point for the Lagrangian, which is a set of values $\{C_t^*, K_{t+1}^*; \lambda_t^*\}_{t=0}^{\infty} \geq 0$ that have the property that $\{C_t^*, K_{t+1}^*\}_{t=0}^{\infty}$ maximizes L taking $\{\lambda_t^*\}_{t=0}^{\infty}$ as given and that $\{\lambda_t^*\}_{t=0}^{\infty}$ minimizes L

taking $\{C_t^*, K_{t+1}^*\}_{t=0}^{\infty}$ as given, we find the first-order conditions corresponding to each of the variables. If we can find a saddle-point, for the same reasons as in the two-period case, the values $\{C_t^*, K_{t+1}^*\}_{t=0}^{\infty}$ must be the solution to the original problem (5.11). These first-order conditions, which are necessary and sufficient to solve the capitalist's planning problem (5.11) are:

$$\frac{\partial L}{\partial C_t} = \frac{(1-\beta)\beta^t}{C_t} - \lambda_t \le 0 \ (\ = 0 \text{ if } C_t > 0) \tag{5.15}$$

$$\frac{\partial L}{\partial K_{t+1}} = -\lambda_t + (1+r_{t+1})\lambda_{t+1} \le 0 \ (\ = 0 \text{ if } K_{t+1} > 0) \tag{5.16}$$

$$\frac{\partial L}{\partial \lambda_t} = -(C_t + K_{t+1} - (1+r_t)K_t) \ge 0 \ (\ = 0 \text{ if } \lambda_t > 0) \tag{5.17}$$

These first-order conditions have to be satisfied for all $t = 0, 1, \ldots, \infty$.

Equation (5.15) can be satisfied only if $\lambda_t > 0$ and $C_t > 0$. We can use the saddle-point conditions, as in the two-period example, to figure out the typical capitalist's consumption function. At the saddle-point the value of the penalty function must be zero. But then we have:

$$\Sigma_{t=0}^{\infty}\lambda_t C_t = (1-\beta)\Sigma_{t=0}^{\infty}\beta^t = 1$$

$$= \Sigma_{t=0}^{\infty}K_{t+1}(-\lambda_t + (1+r_{t+1})\lambda_{t+1}) + \lambda_0(1+r_0)K_0$$

According to the first-order conditions:

$$\Sigma_{t=0}^{\infty}K_{t+1}(-\lambda_t + (1+r_{t+1})\lambda_{t+1}) = 0,$$

so we have, as in the two-period case,

$$\lambda_0 = \frac{1}{(1+r_0)K_0}$$

Equation (5.15) for $t = 0$ implies that $C_0 = (1-\beta)/\lambda_0$, so we have

$$C_0 = (1-\beta)(1+r_0)K_0$$

Since every period is actually just like the first, a similar argument shows that the first-order conditions lead to the consumption function:

$$C = (1 - \beta)(1 + r)K \tag{5.18}$$

As we have seen, this leads to the formulas for the growth of the capitalist's wealth:

$$K_{+1} = \beta(1 + r)K \tag{5.19}$$

$$1 + g_K = \frac{K_{+1}}{K} = \beta(1 + r) \tag{5.20}$$

Problem 5.4 *In the infinite horizon Cobb-Douglas consumption model, prove (5.13), and express C_t in terms of K_{t+1}.*

Problem 5.5 *Show that along the optimal consumption path in the infinite horizon Cobb-Douglas consumption model the sum of realized consumption and the value of the capital at the shadow price, $\Sigma_{t=0}^{T} \lambda_t C_t + \lambda_T K_{T+1}$, remains constant over time and is equal to $\lambda_0(1 + r_0)K_0$.*

5.3 The Constant Saving Rate Model

In the neoclassical growth model gross investment is often assumed to be a constant fraction, s, of output:

$$I = sX$$

In the Classical saving model we have developed here, gross investment depends on the stock of wealth of the capitalists, which in this model consists only of capital, K. Remembering that $\rho K = X$ and $r = v - \delta$, we see that in the Classical model:

$$I = K_{+1} - K + \delta K = (\beta(1 + r) - (1 - \delta))K = \frac{\beta v - (1 - \beta)(1 - \delta)}{\rho} X$$

Thus the Classical saving model also predicts that investment will be a constant proportion of output as long as the profit rate, v, and the productivity of capital, ρ, do not change. Thus the two saving models differ only when the profit rate and productivity of capital are changing.

5.4   Saving Rates and Growth Rates

The *saving rate*, $s = I/X$, is often used by economists to indicate where a country lies on its social consumption-growth schedule. As its definition indicates, the saving rate is actually the proportion of gross investment in output. In a closed economy saving and investment are identical, but open economies may export or import capital, so that saving may exceed or fall short of investment. For the purposes of studying economic growth in a country, the key factor is gross investment, so we measure the saving rate as the ratio of gross investment to output. Countries with high saving rates are devoting more effort to growth and less to consumption. From its definition, we can see that:

$$s = \frac{I}{X} = \frac{X - C}{X} = 1 - \frac{C}{X} = 1 - \frac{c}{x}$$

By rearranging this equation, we can see the relationship of the saving rate to the social consumption-growth schedule:

$$c = (1 - s)x$$

It is possible to use $1 - s$ in place of c to express social consumption in the social consumption-growth rate schedule:

$$1 - s = 1 - \frac{g_K + \delta}{\rho} \tag{5.21}$$

or:

$$g_K + \delta = s\rho \tag{5.22}$$

An important question in economic growth analysis is whether high saving rates lead to more rapid economic growth. In some theories higher saving rates accelerate economic growth only temporarily, and in others, higher saving rates have a permanent positive effect on economic growth.

Maddison's data set measures the saving rates for the six countries included in Table 2.8. We compare saving rates to growth rates of the capital stock for these countries by sub-period over the last century in Table 5.1. If you study each country over time, you can see that increases in the saving rate are usually associated with increases in the growth rate. It also seems true that the high-saving countries (such as Japan) grow more rapidly than the low-saving countries. There are some

Table 5.1:
Rates of saving (I/X in %)
and Capital Accumulation (I/K in % per year)
for Six Countries for Selected Intervals from 1870-1987

	1870–1890	1890–1913	1913–1938	1938–1950	1950–1973	1973–1987	1981–1987
U.S.							
I/X	16.3	15.9	14.2	13.1	18.0	18.0	17.7
I/K	6.79	4.17	2.10	1.75	3.22	3.31	3.01
France							
I/X	12.8	13.9	16.1		21.2	21.7	20.2
I/K					4.68	4.47	3.44
Germany							
I/X			12.9		23.2	20.6	20.2
I/K				-1.09	6.11	3.37	2.91
Netherlands							
I/X			17.5		23.8	20.2	19.4
I/K					4.45	2.92	2.54
U.K.							
I/X	8.4	8.5	7.8	6.5	16.3	17.7	16.5
I/K	1.66	1.75	1.29	0.65	5.04	3.08	2.81
Japan							
I/X	12.6	14.4	16.2	18.6	28.3	30.4	29.2
I/K		3.43	4.71	2.78	8.79	6.70	5.40

Sources: [Maddison, 1995b, Table K-1] and [Maddison, 1995a, pp. 148–164 and p. 172].

exceptions to these generalizations, which must reflect differences in the parameters (such as x or ρ) of the social consumption-growth schedule.

The saving rate in the U.S. has remained fairly constant over the last century. Perhaps because the U.S. economy has been the main source of data for macroeconomists, they once believed that a good theory of consumption and saving should explain the "fact" that the saving rate is a constant that lacks any trend.

But the data from other countries support an idea associated with John Maynard Keynes: countries save a greater proportion of their income as they grow richer. For most countries, saving rates have increased over the course of this century. One major qualification is that during the 1980s, saving rates declined, as can be seen by comparing the last two columns in Table 5.1.

5.5   Suggested Readings

The dynamic model of optimal consumption originated with the English mathematician Frank Ramsey [1928]. John Maynard Keynes's view of the class structure of saving, essentially a defense of capitalism based on its ability to deliver a high rate of capital accumulation, can be found in Keynes [1920]. His view that the saving rate tends to rise with income is elaborated in Keynes [1936]. The two-class assumption plays a major role in the work of Kaldor [1956] and Pasinetti [1974], and was an object of debate [Samuelson and Modigliani, 1966, for example] during the Cambridge capital controversy. Luigi Pasinetti's discovery that the Cambridge equation, linking accumulation to capitalist saving alone, remains valid even (paradoxically) when workers save remains of interest; see Fazi and Salvadori [1985] for a careful discussion of the conditions under which it holds. Stephen Marglin [1984] devotes considerable attention to the comparison between neoclassical and Classical theories of saving.

Chapter 6

Classical Models of Economic Growth

A particular theory of the labor market, a particular theory of consumption and saving, and the growth-distribution schedule constitute a *growth model*. The *Classical growth models* we will analyze in this chapter combine the infinite horizon model of capitalist consumption with either the assumption of a conventional wage or full employment in the labor market.

6.1 The Classical Conventional Wage Model

As we have seen, a key idea in the Classical approach to growth theory developed by Smith, Ricardo, and used as a base for Marx's critique of the capitalist economy, is that labor-power is elastically supplied at a given conventional wage. The Classical model thus assumes that the supply of labor is a horizontal line at a given real wage $\bar{w}$. This determines one (w) of the four variables, v, w, g_K and c:

$$w = \bar{w} \tag{6.1}$$

As we have seen in Chapter 5, in the Classical view social saving is the result of decisions of capitalists not to consume their wealth. We assume that there are many identical capitalists, all of whom begin with the same initial wealth K. If the number of capitalists stays the same over time, the decisions of the typical capitalist summarize what happens to the whole economy.

We have seen that in the one-sector model the typical capitalist receives the profit rate v on each unit of capital she rents to entrepreneurs. This is the residual profit per unit of capital after the entrepreneur has paid the wage bill, or, equivalently, the profit share in output times the output-capital ratio:

$$v = \frac{x - w}{k} = (1 - \frac{w}{x})\rho = \pi\rho \tag{6.2}$$

At the end of the period the typical capitalist has to divide her wealth, which consists of the profit she has received on her capital and her depreciated capital, between her consumption, C^c, and accumulation of capital for the next period:

$$C^c + K_{+1} = (1 - \delta)K + vK \tag{6.3}$$

As we have seen in Chapter 5, assuming that the typical capitalist maximizes a discounted logarithmic utility function, she will choose to consume a constant fraction $(1 - \beta)$ of her end-of-period wealth:

$$C^c = (1 - \beta)(1 + r)K \tag{6.4}$$

and, as a consequence:

$$K_{+1} = \beta(1 + r)K$$

$$1 + g_K \equiv \frac{K_{+1}}{K} = \beta(1 + r) \tag{6.5}$$

This relation between the capital growth factor $1 + g_K$, the discount factor or saving propensity of capitalists, β, and the net profit rate $1 + r$ plays an important role in many modern models of growth, and is often called the *Cambridge equation*. It will hold whenever workers spend all their wages and capitalists save a fraction β of their end-of-period wealth.

We can also express the Cambridge equation as a relation between the $g_K + \delta$, and the gross profit rate, v:

$$g_K + \delta = \beta v - (1 - \beta)(1 - \delta) \tag{6.6}$$

The Classical theories of the labor market and of capitalist consumption give us two equations to add to the real wage-profit rate relation and the social consumption-growth rate relation to make a complete model that will determine all four endogenous variables: social consumption, c, the growth rate of capital, g_K, the wage, w, and the profit rate v.

Table 6.1:

The Classical Conventional Wage Model

Endogenous variables: w, v, c, g_K

Exogenous Parameters: $k, x, \delta, \beta, \bar{w}$

$$w = x - vk \qquad (6.7)$$

$$c = x - (g_K + \delta)k \qquad (6.8)$$

$$\delta + g_K = \beta v - (1 - \beta)(1 - \delta) \qquad (6.9)$$

$$w = \bar{w} \qquad (6.10)$$

Exogenous parameters: $\rho, x, \delta, \beta, \bar{w}$

$$w = x\left(1 - \frac{v}{\rho}\right) \qquad (6.11)$$

$$c = x\left(1 - \frac{g_K + \delta}{\rho}\right) \qquad (6.12)$$

$$\delta + g_K = \beta v - (1 - \beta)(1 - \delta) \qquad (6.13)$$

$$w = \bar{w} \qquad (6.14)$$

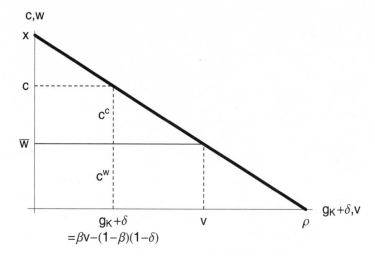

Figure 6.1: The addition of the Classical assumptions of
a conventional real wage and capitalist consumption which
is a constant fraction of wealth closes the growth model,
determining g_K, w, r, and c, given the real wage-profit rate
and social consumption-growth rate schedules.

We can write the four relations that make up the Classical model in
terms of the parameters x, δ, β, and $\bar{w}$, and either k or ρ, depending on
which we use to describe the technology as in Table 6.1.

We can also find capitalist consumption per worker, c^c, from the
fact that social consumption equals capitalist consumption plus workers'
consumption, and workers' consumption is equal to the wage:

$$c = c^c + c^w = c^c + w$$

We can visualize the full determination of the Classical system as in
Figure 6.1.

The Classical model has a straightforward explanatory structure.
The conventional real wage determines the profit rate, given the real
wage-profit rate relation determined by the production coefficients, and
also workers' consumption, given the assumption that workers as a class
consume the entire real wage. The profit rate then determines the
growth rate through the Classical profit rate-growth rate relation (the
Cambridge equation), and the growth rate in turn determines social
consumption, divided into capitalists' consumption and workers' consumption.

The Classical conventional wage model can be applied to real economies. For example, we can use the data in Tables 2.1 and 2.2, to

determine the appropriate parameters for the U.S. economy in 1989. We can read k, x, δ, and $\bar{w}$ directly from these tables. To calculate β, we need first to find $g_K = ((i/k) - \delta) = (.196-.091)/\text{yr} = .105$ %/yr. $\beta = (1 + g_K)/(1 + v - \delta) = 1.105/1.16 = .953$.

Problem 6.1 *If the real wage in Ricardia (see Problem 2.1) is 20 bu/worker-year and $\beta = .5$, find the growth rate of capital, social consumption per worker and capitalist consumption per worker.*

Problem 6.2 *If the real wage in Industria (see Problem 2.2) is \$10/hr., workers work 2000 hours per year, and $\beta = .97$, find the growth rate of capital, social consumption per worker, and capitalist consumption per worker.*

6.2 Comparative Dynamics in the Conventional Wage Model

A model explains changes in the endogenous variables as the result of changes in the exogenous parameters. In order to carry out this kind of analysis, we need to figure out what the effect of a change in the various parameters of the model will be on the endogenous variables.

In the Classical model the endogenous variables are the real wage, w, the profit rate, v, social consumption, c (divided into workers' consumption $c^w = w$ and capitalists' consumption c^c, both measured per worker), and the growth rate of capital, g_K. The parameters are the capital-labor ratio, k, or capital productivity, ρ, output per worker, x, the depreciation rate, δ, the capitalists' utility discount factor, β, and the conventional wage, $\bar{w}$. A typical comparative dynamic exercise is to work out the effect of an increase in labor productivity, x, holding capital productivity, ρ, constant, on the endogenous variables, w, v, c and $g_K + \delta$. In doing this type of comparative exercise, it is important to be very clear about which parameters are changing, and which are remaining constant. In this case, ρ, δ, β, and $\bar{w}$ remain the same: *only* x and $k = x/\rho$ change.

We can work this problem out either on the basis of the equations that define the equilibrium, or by looking at the graphical representation of the solution. The equilibrium conditions are Equations (6.11)–(6.14).

Since we are assuming that $\bar{w}$ does not change when we change x, the wage will remain the same when x increases. Then we can see from Equation (6.11) that the profit rate v will rise (since x increases and ρ stays constant). According to Equation (6.13), the Cambridge equation,

Table 6.2:
**The Comparative Dynamics of the
Classical Conventional Wage Model**

Parameter changes					Effects				
ρ	k	x	β	$\bar{w}$	v	w	g_K	c	c^c
same	up	up	same	same	up	same	up	up	up
down	up	same	same	same	down	same	down	up	up
same	same	same	up	same					
same	same	same	same	up					

a rise in v will increase $g_K + \delta$. Since both x and $g_K + \delta$ increase in Equation (6.12), it is not immediately possible to conclude whether c rises or falls. We can, however, look back at the capitalist's consumption function, which tells us that:

$$c^c = (1 - \beta)(1 + r)\frac{x}{\rho}$$

We know that $r = v - \delta$ and x increase, while by assumption β and ρ remain constant, so that capitalist consumption per worker, c^c, must increase. Workers' consumption is just equal to the real wage, which is held constant by assumption, so that total social consumption per worker must rise. We summarize this experiment in Table 6.2.

The same conclusions could be reached by studying the graphical representation of the equilibrium. For variety, let us work out another comparative statics exercise graphically, for example, an increase in the capital-labor ratio, k, holding constant x, δ, β, and $\bar{w}$. (Since $\rho = x/k$, this experiment also lowers the productivity of capital ρ.) As we can see in Figure 6.2, the growth-distribution schedule becomes steeper, rotating around the intercept $(0, x)$. With an unchanging real wage the profit rate and growth rate of capital must fall. It is also possible to conclude from the capitalist's consumption function that capitalist consumption per worker rises.

Problem 6.3 *Analyze the effect of an increase in β on the endogenous variables in the Classical conventional wage model.*

Problem 6.4 *Analyze the effect of an increase in the conventional real wage $\bar{w}$ on the endogenous variables in the Classical conventional wage model.*

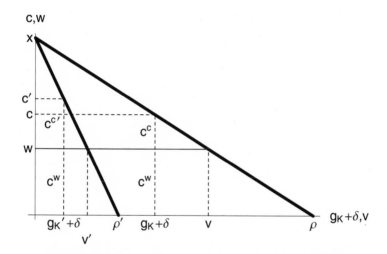

Figure 6.2: An increase in k, holding x, δ, β, and $\bar{w}$ constant (but lowering $\rho = x/k$), to k', makes the growth-distribution schedule steeper. Since the wage does not change, the profit rate must fall, which, given a constant β, leads to a fall in the rate of growth of capital, g_K. Since $c^c = (1 - \beta)(1 + r)k = (1 - \beta)(1 + v - \delta)k = (1 - \beta)((1 - \delta)k + vk)$, and $vk = x - w$ is constant, capitalist consumption per worker and social consumption per worker both rise.

6.3 Labor-Saving Technical Change in the Classical Model

The Classical conventional wage model can explain continuing economic growth, since with constant capital productivity the growth rate of output, g_X, will equal the growth rate of capital, g_K. But the conventional wage model cannot explain the increases in labor productivity and the wage observed in historical capitalist economies, since it assumes that x and $\bar{w}$ are constant over time.

The simplest way to modify the Classical model to accommodate increasing labor productivity is to add exogenous labor-saving technical change. If labor productivity steadily rises and the wage remains constant, however, the wage share, w/x, will fall steadily toward zero. In real capitalist economies the wage share, despite considerable fluctuation, does not tend to zero, but remains roughly constant. This suggests modifying the Classical model by assuming a conventional wage *share* rather than a conventional wage. These two modifications together yield a *Classical conventional wage share model* which is a good first approximation to observed patterns of capitalist economic growth.

The assumption that labor productivity grows steadily translates into the algebraic formula

$$x_t = x_0(1+\gamma)^t,$$

where x_0 is the labor productivity in some arbitrarily chosen base year, and γ is the exogenously given rate of growth of labor productivity. Since labor-saving technical change leaves capital productivity, ρ, constant, capital intensity,

$$k_t = x_t/\rho = (x_0/\rho)(1+\gamma)^t = k_0(1+\gamma)^t$$

where $k_0 \equiv x_0/\rho$ is the capital intensity in the base year, also grows steadily at the rate γ. The assumption that the wage share is given translates into

$$w_t = (1-\bar{\pi})x_t = (1-\bar{\pi})x_0(1+\gamma)^t = w_0(1+\gamma)^t$$

where $1-\bar{\pi}$ is the conventionally given wage share (and $\bar{\pi}$ is the corresponding profit share) and $w_0 \equiv (1-\bar{\pi})x_0$ is the wage in the base year, so that the wage will also be increasing steadily at the rate γ. Thus we could write the real wage-profit rate schedule as:

$$w_t = w_0(1+\gamma)^t = x_t - vk_t = x_0(1+\gamma)^t - vk_0(1+\gamma)^t$$

Table 6.3:

The Classical Conventional Wage Share Model

Endogenous variables: $\tilde{w}, v, \tilde{c}, g_K$

Exogenous parameters: $\tilde{k}, \tilde{x}, \delta, \beta, \bar{\pi}$

$$\tilde{w} = \tilde{x} - v\tilde{k} \qquad (6.15)$$

$$\tilde{c} = \tilde{x} - (g_K + \delta)\tilde{k} \qquad (6.16)$$

$$\delta + g_K = \beta v - (1 - \beta)(1 - \delta) \qquad (6.17)$$

$$\tilde{w} = (1 - \bar{\pi})\tilde{x} \qquad (6.18)$$

Exogenous parameters: $\rho, \tilde{x}, \delta, \beta, \bar{\pi}$

$$\tilde{w} = \tilde{x}\left(1 - \frac{v}{\rho}\right) \qquad (6.19)$$

$$\tilde{c} = \tilde{x}\left(1 - \frac{g_K + \delta}{\rho}\right) \qquad (6.20)$$

$$\delta + g_K = \beta v - (1 - \beta)(1 - \delta) \qquad (6.21)$$

$$\tilde{w} = (1 - \bar{\pi})\tilde{x} \qquad (6.22)$$

If we divide both sides of this equation through by $(1 + \gamma)^t$, it becomes:

$$w_0 = x_0 - vk_0$$

which is just the same as the real wage-profit relation for the Classical conventional wage model. This observation suggests that it would be easier to analyze the model in terms of a new set of variables, $\tilde{x} = x/(1+\gamma)^t$, $\tilde{k} = k/(1+\gamma)^t$, $\tilde{w} = w/(1+\gamma)^t$, and $\tilde{c} = c/(1+\gamma)^t$, which will remain constant over time. In these variables, the Classical conventional wage share model can be expressed algebraically as in Table 6.3.

If we compare these equations with Equations (6.7)–(6.13), we see that the Classical conventional wage share model has exactly the same mathematical form as the Classical conventional wage model, with "~" variables taking the places of the corresponding variables in the original

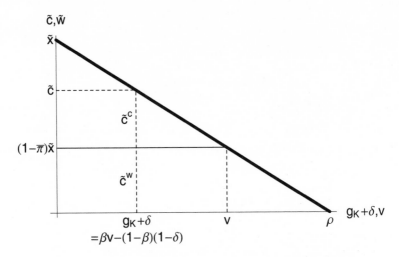

Figure 6.3: The Classical conventional wage share model with pure labor-saving technical change is mathematically identical to the Classical conventional wage model, substituting the effective labor units $\tilde{x}$, $\tilde{k}$, $\tilde{w}$, and $\tilde{c}$ for x, k, w, and c.

model. Thus all the comparative dynamics results from the conventional wage model carry over to the conventional wage share model with the appropriate change in interpretation.

One way to think about the change in variables to the "~" form is to recognize that labor-saving technical change effectively makes each employed worker in year t the productive equivalent of $(1 + \gamma)^t$ workers in the base year. Thus dividing through output variables by $(1 + \gamma)^t$ expresses them in terms of *effective workers*. In effective worker units, then, the Classical conventional wage share model is mathematically identical to the Classical conventional wage model expressed in terms of real workers.

Figure 6.3, which, except for the relabeling of the vertical axis, is the same as Figure 6.1, shows the Classical conventional wage share model in effective labor units.

The convenience of working in effective labor units comes at the price of having to reinterpret the predictions of the model to apply them to real economies. For example, a Classical conventional wage share economy with labor-saving technical change at rate γ will have constant output per effective worker, $\tilde{x}$, but output per real worker will be growing at the steady rate γ. The same reinterpretation has to be applied to the constant wage per effective worker, $\tilde{w}$, and the constant social

Table 6.4:

The Classical Conventional Wage Share Model in Share Variables

---

Endogenous variables: π, v, s, g_K

Exogenous parameters: $\rho, \delta, \beta, \bar{\pi}$

$$v = \pi\rho \tag{6.23}$$

$$g_K + \delta = s\rho \tag{6.24}$$

$$g_K + \delta = \beta v - (1-\beta)(1-\delta) \tag{6.25}$$

$$\pi = \bar{\pi} \tag{6.26}$$

---

consumption per effective worker, $\tilde{c}$, since the wage per real worker and social consumption per real worker will be growing steadily at the rate γ. This is roughly the pattern observed over long periods of time in real capitalist economies, so the Classical conventional wage share model is at least a first approximation to a workable theory of economic growth.

We can take a further step in simplifying the mathematical form of the Classical conventional wage share model by shifting to using the profit share, $\pi = 1 - (w/x) = z/x$, to measure the division of the value of output between wages and profits, and the saving rate, $s = 1 - (c/x) = i/x$, to measure the division of output between consumption and investment. In these variables, the Classical conventional wage share model has the form of Table 6.4.

In this form, the model determines the basic ratios of the economic growth process. In order to calibrate it to a real economy, we need to know both the base year output per worker, x_0, and the growth rate of labor productivity, γ. Then in any year we can calculate $x_t = x_0(1+\gamma)^t$, $w_t = (1-\pi)x_t$, and $c_t = (1-s)x_t$ from the solution of the model.

Figure 6.4 presents the Classical conventional wage share model graphically in share variables.

If γ is zero, the Classical conventional wage share model reduces exactly to the conventional wage model. From this point on, we will analyze only the more general conventional wage share model with labor-saving technical change, since the conclusions can be translated into the conventional wage model simply by setting $\gamma = 0$.

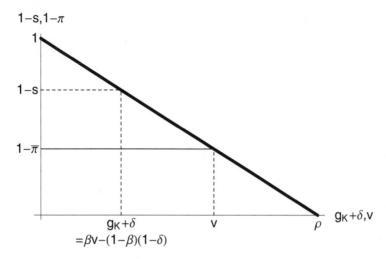

Figure 6.4: In terms of share variables, π and s, the growth-distribution schedule has vertical intercept 1, and horizontal intercept ρ. The exogenous wage share, $1 - \pi$, determines the profit rate, v, and the growth rate of capital, $g_K + \delta = \beta v - (1 - \beta)(1 - \delta)$ determines the consumption rate $1 - s$.

Growth in the Classical conventional wage share model is endogenous, since it is determined by the saving behavior of capitalists. If the saving propensity of capitalists, β, rises, the growth rates of capital and output will rise as well, because capital will be accumulated more rapidly. The labor force and its growth rate are also endogenous, adapting to the accumulation of capital.

Problem 6.5 *Analyze the effect of an increase in β on the endogenous variables in the Classical conventional wage share model.*

Problem 6.6 *Analyze the effect of an increase in the effective wage on the endogenous variables in the Classical conventional wage share model.*

6.4   Choice of Technique in the Classical Model

We have been analyzing the Classical conventional wage share model on the assumption that the technology consists of a single technique, so that it could be described by a Leontief production function. What if the technology consists of a continuum of techniques described by a smooth production function? In this case the assumption of labor-saving technical change must be translated into the assumption of pure labor-augmenting (Harrod-neutral) technical change that affects all the techniques of production uniformly. In this case the production function in year t can be written as:

$$X_t = F_t(K, N) = F_0(K, (1 + \gamma)^t N)$$

where $F_0(K, N)$ describes the technology in a base year. Dividing through by effective labor, $(1 + \gamma)^t N$, we see that the intensive production function is constant in effective labor units:

$$\tilde{x}_t = F_t(\tilde{k}_t, 1) = F_0(\tilde{k}_t, 1)$$

Thus we can define the effective labor intensive production function:

$$\tilde{x} = f(\tilde{k}) \equiv F_0(\tilde{k}, 1)$$

A technique can be characterized in effective labor terms by its effective capital intensity, $\tilde{k}$, or, equivalently, by its capital productivity $\rho = \tilde{x}/\tilde{k} = x/k$, and its effective labor productivity $\tilde{x}$. Each technique of production in effective labor terms corresponds to an effective real wage-profit rate schedule:

$$\tilde{w} = \tilde{x} - v\tilde{k}$$

Thus we can translate the whole growth-distribution schedule analysis, including the efficiency frontier, into effective labor terms by simply replacing the output, wage, and social consumption variables by their effective labor equivalents, as Figure 6.5, which is equivalent to Figure 3.4, illustrates.

For any effective wage, $\tilde{w}$, there will be a profit-maximizing technique, $(\tilde{k}(\tilde{w}), \tilde{x}(\tilde{w}))$, which determines the effective growth-distribution schedule for the economy, including the effective labor productivity $\tilde{x}$. Thus the Classical conventional wage model behaves in the same way with or without a choice of technique from a technology defined by a smooth production function. Only one profit-maximizing technique is ever used, and the others are irrelevant unless the effective wage changes.

For most production functions, it is possible to determine the profit-maximizing technique from the wage share as well as from the effective wage, because there will be a one-to-one correspondence between the

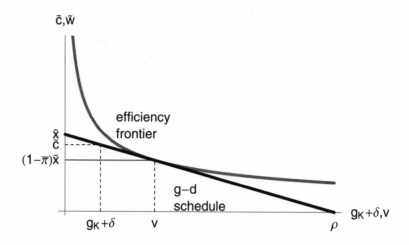

Figure 6.5: With pure labor-augmenting technical change the efficiency frontier defined in terms of the profit rate, v, and the effective wage, $\tilde{w}$, is constant over time. The effective wage, $\tilde{w}$, determines the profit-maximizing technique of production, and the effective growth-distribution schedule, including the effective labor productivity, $\tilde{x}$.

wage (or profit) share and the effective wage. In the Cobb-Douglas case, however, the wage share is equal to $1 - \alpha$ for any effective wage, so that in the Cobb-Douglas case it is necessary to specify the effective wage in order to close the model.

Problem 6.7 *Analyze the effect of an increase in the capitalists' propensity to save, β, on the choice of technique and endogenous variables in the Classical conventional wage share model with a technology described by the production function $\tilde{x} = \tilde{k}^{\alpha}$.*

Problem 6.8 *Analyze the effect of an increase in the conventional wage share, $1 - \tilde{\pi}$, on the choice of technique and endogenous variables in the Classical conventional-wage share model.*

6.5   A Classical Model of Growth with Full Employment

The alternative to the conventional wage share closure of the labor market is the *full-employment* assumption that the wage is determined in each period so as to equate the demand for labor to a given supply of labor, which grows at an exogenously given rate, n, independent of the wage. We will also assume pure labor-saving technical change at the rate γ, so that k and x both grow steadily at the rate γ, and $\tilde{k}$ and $\tilde{x}$ are constant. Thus the effective labor supply grows at the rate $n + \gamma$, which is called the *natural rate of growth*. We will assume that the depreciation rate, δ, is unchanging.

The Classical full-employment model, first analyzed by Luigi Pasinetti, has the same models of production and saving as the Classical conventional wage share model, but shares the full-employment model of the labor market with the neoclassical growth model we will analyze in later chapters. Thus the growth-distribution schedule and the Classical growth rate- profit rate relation (Cambridge equation), Equations (6.15)–(6.17), continue to hold in the Classical full-employment model.

The labor market equation, however, is different. The full employment theory of growth assumes that the supply of labor grows exogenously independently of the wage. In this case we must drop the assumption of a given conventional wage share, and substitute instead the assumption that the wage adjusts to employ the given labor force. The supply of labor in each year follows the path:

$$N_t^s = N_0(1 + n)^t$$

As we have seen in Chapter 4, it might not be possible for the economy to achieve full employment in any particular year, if there is only one technique of production, because the accumulated capital may not offer the right number of jobs. If the number of jobs offered by the accumulated capital is smaller than the labor force, there will be unemployment of labor. If, on the other hand, the number of workers required to employ the accumulated capital is larger than the labor force, some of the capital stock will be unemployed. If there is unemployment of labor, the wage in the period will fall to zero. If there is unemployment of capital, the real wage will rise to equal output per worker, x. Figure 4.8 illustrates the labor market equilibrium under these conditions.

If the economy manages to provide exactly the number of jobs necessary to reach full employment in one year, so that:

$$\frac{K_t}{k} = N_t^s$$

it will achieve full employment in the next year only if:

$$N_{+1}^s = (1 + n)N^s = (1 + n)\frac{K}{k} = \frac{K_{+1}}{k_{+1}} = \frac{(1 + g_K)K}{(1 + \gamma)k}$$

Table 6.5:
The Classical Full-Employment Model

Endogenous variables: $\tilde{w}, v, \tilde{c}, g_K$

Exogenous parameters: $\tilde{k}, \tilde{x}, \delta, \beta, n, \gamma$

$$\tilde{w} = \tilde{x} - v\tilde{k} \tag{6.28}$$

$$\tilde{c} = \tilde{x} - (g_K + \delta)\tilde{k} \tag{6.29}$$

$$g_K + \delta = \beta v - (1 - \beta)(1 - \delta) \tag{6.30}$$

$$1 + g_K = (1 + n)(1 + \gamma) \tag{6.31}$$

---

or, when n and γ are small, so that $n\gamma$ can be neglected:

$$1 + g_K = (1 + n)(1 + \gamma) \approx 1 + n + \gamma \tag{6.27}$$

The maintenance of full employment requires that the rate of growth of the capital stock equal the natural rate of growth, $n+\gamma$, the sum of the growth rates of the population and labor productivity, which supplies the fourth equation necessary to close the growth model.

The four equations that make up the Classical model with full employment are summarized in Table 6.5.

Figure 6.6 shows how the full-employment model works graphically. In this Figure output, wages and consumption are measured per *effective* worker.

A Classical full-employment economy reaches equilibrium through the impact of profits on the accumulation of capital. Suppose the wage were lower than the equilibrium level. Then profits would be higher, and the capital stock would grow more rapidly than the labor force, creating an upward pressure on the wage. Similarly if the wage were higher than the equilibrium level, capitalist saving out of profits would lead to a growth of capital that fell short of the growth of the labor force, and unemployment would emerge, pushing down the wage. Thus full employment in the labor market indirectly determines the profit rate and the real wage in this type of model.

In the Classical full-employment model the growth rate of the capital stock and of output are determined by the exogenously given natural rate

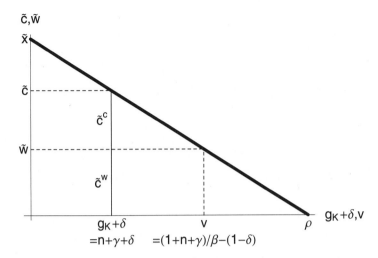

Figure 6.6: In the Classical full-employment model the capital growth rate, g_K, is equal to the natural rate of growth $n + \gamma$. The Cambridge equation then determines the profit rate, and the growth-distribution schedule determines the wage and social consumption per effective worker.

of growth. The growth of the labor force, rather than being endogenously determined, as in the Classical conventional wage share model, poses an external limit to the capital accumulation process. Growth, rather than being endogenous, as in the Classical conventional wage share model, is exogenous, ultimately imposed on the economy by independent demographic behavior. Thus changes in capitalist saving behavior cannot influence the rate of growth of the Classical full-employment model: such changes will be offset by changes in the wage, leaving the growth rate unaffected.

Problem 6.9 *Analyze the effect of an increase in the population growth rate, n, on the growth rate, profit rate, wage, social consumption and capitalist consumption per worker in the Classical full-employment model.*

Problem 6.10 *Analyze the effect of an increase in the capitalist propensity to save, β, on the growth rate, profit rate, wage, social consumption and capitalist consumption per worker in the Classical full-employment model.*

Problem 6.11 *Analyze the effect of a rise in the capital labor ratio, k, on the growth rate, profit rate, wage, social consumption and* *capitalist consumption per worker in the Classical full-employment model.*

Problem 6.12 *Analyze the effect of a rise in the productivity of effective labor, $\tilde{x}$, on the growth rate, profit rate, wage, social consumption and capitalist consumption per worker in the Classical full-employment model.*

6.6   Choice of Technique in the Classical Full-Employment Model

Suppose now that the technology provides a choice of techniques in the Classical full-employment model.

Since we continue to maintain the assumption that capitalists save a given fraction β of their end-of-period wealth, the Cambridge equation must hold, and if we assume full employment, we have the two relations:

$$(1+n)(1+\gamma) = 1 + g_K = \beta(1+r) = \beta(1+v-\delta)$$

Thus the rate of profit is still determined by the natural rate of growth and the capitalists' propensity to save. As we have seen, this rate of profit will correspond to a particular technique, which will be tangent to the efficiency frontier at the given rate of profit, as in Figure 6.7.

The fact that the chosen technique is on the efficiency frontier for the given rate of profit can also be expressed by saying that the marginal product of capital (if it exists) is equal to the profit rate at this point. But it is clear from the reasoning that it is the profit rate that determines the marginal product of capital in this model, not the other way around. Just as in the model with only one technique, changes in the wage will bring about an equilibrium, in this case through affecting both the choice of technique and the profit rate.

Problem 6.13 *If $n = .02$, $\gamma = 0$, $\delta = 0$, and $\beta = .9$, find the equilibrium real wage, profit rate, capitalist consumption and technique in use in a Classical full employment economy with a Cobb-Douglas production function, where the techniques satisfy $\tilde{x} = A\tilde{k}^{\alpha}$, where $\alpha = .2$ and $A = (\$10,000/worker)^{1-\alpha}$. What is the equilibrium marginal productivity of capital?*

Problem 6.14 *What effect does an increase in the population growth rate have on the technique in use and the profit rate in a Classical full-employment economy with choice of technique?*

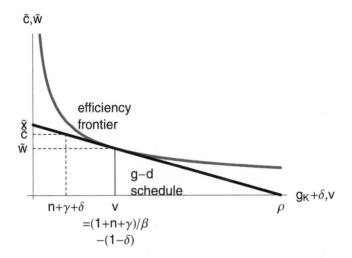

Figure 6.7: When there is a choice of technique in the full employment model, the natural rate of growth determines the rate of growth of capital, and hence the profit rate through the Cambridge equation. There will be one technique which maximizes real wages at this profit rate, and competition will force capitalists to choose it. Then the real wage is determined by the real wage-profit relation corresponding to the chosen technique.

6.7   The Classical Approach to Growth

Smith, Malthus, Ricardo, and Marx, the main thinkers who developed
the Classical approach to growth, saw class divisions between capitalists
and workers as the central drama of capitalist economies. Capitalist
accumulation, driven by competition, is the engine of growth. The consumption of workers poses limits to growth by restricting the proportion
of output available for accumulation. Capital accumulation increases the
demand for labor and induces population growth so that the population
itself is endogenous to the economic growth process. The growth rates of
capital and population are determined primarily by the class distribution
of income. The Classical conventional wage share model developed in
this chapter reflects the central preoccupations of the Classical political
economists.

The Classical full-employment model retains the class structure of
the Classical vision, but tames it considerably by regarding population
growth, rather than the class distribution of income, as the factor ultimately limiting growth. In this model, class distribution, rather than
population growth, adjusts to equilibrate the labor market, and becomes
endogenous.

The main empirical challenge to the Classical growth models is that
rates of growth and rates of profit often tend to decline over time in real
capitalist economies, while the Classical models in this chapter predict
constant growth and profit rates. To address this problem we have to
look more closely at the process of technical change.

6.8   Suggested Readings

The Classical model of growth has led a lively if somewhat subter-
ranean existence during this century in the writings of Marxian political
economists such as Luxemburg [1951] and Sweezy [1949]. For an introduction to Marxian political economy, consult Foley [1986]. The great
mathematician John von Neumann developed an essentially Classical
model, and although his seminal contribution [von Neumann, 1945] is
difficult, an accessible exposition of it (and the Classical model in general) can be found in Gram and Walsh [1980]. Richard Goodwin's pio-
neering growth cycle [Goodwin, 1967], another important contribution,
uses the mathematics of biological predator-prey systems to depict an
economy with a growing labor force whose unemployment rate cycles
around an average rate. Luigi Pasinetti has been a major force in extending the Classical approach; see Pasinetti [1977, 1974] for examples.

Chapter 7

Biased Technical Change in the Classical Model

7.1 The Classical Conventional Wage Share Model with Biased Technical Change

The Classical model can be extended so that it matches more of the qualitative features of real economies. The historical record presented earlier in Table 2.8 shows that although labor productivity has improved persistently over the last two centuries, Harrod-neutral technical change has not always prevailed. In the U.S., for example, the periods from 1820–1913 and 1973–1992 were characterized by declining capital productivity. Sandwiched in between these periods was a span of rising capital productivity. Similarly, Japan witnessed two long periods of declining capital productivity from 1870–1950 and 1973–1992, with a period of near-neutrality sandwiched in between. Declining capital productivity, together with a roughly constant wage share, reduces the rate of profit, which in turn can slow down the accumulation of capital and the growth of output. We can understand these periods of declining profitability and slowing growth through the Classical model with Marx-biased technical change.

Marx-biased technical change is a mix of capital-using and labor-saving change. The equations written out in Chapter 6 for purely labor-saving technical change remain valid for biased technical change, and we continue to maintain the conventional wage share assumption. The key difference is that with biased technical change, the economy never reaches a steady state because the net rate of profit changes over time,

Table 7.1:

The Classical Conventional Wage Share Model with Marx-Biased Technical Change

Endogenous variables x, ρ, w, v, c, g_K

Exogenous parameters: $x_0, \rho_0, \delta, \beta, \bar{\pi}, \gamma, \chi$

$$x = x_0(1 + \gamma)^t \qquad (7.1)$$

$$\rho = \rho_0(1 + \chi)^t \qquad (7.2)$$

$$w = x(1 - \frac{v}{\rho}) \qquad (7.3)$$

$$c = x(1 - \frac{g_K + \delta}{\rho}) \qquad (7.4)$$

$$\delta + g_K = \beta v - (1 - \beta)(1 - \delta) \qquad (7.5)$$

$$w = (1 - \bar{\pi})x \qquad (7.6)$$

generating changes in the rates of capital accumulation and growth. We return to accounting in real workers rather than effective workers in order to emphasize the relation of the model to real-world growth-distribution schedules, and write the equations for the Classical conventional wage share model with biased technical change as in Table 7.1.

We can visualize the path of the economy under these assumptions in Figure 7.1 which shows the growth-distribution schedules for two adjacent time periods, t and $t + 1$. The biased nature of technical change rotates the growth-distribution schedules around the switchpoint between the techniques. For clarity, Figure 7.1 omits social consumption and the growth rate of capital in order to focus attention on the profit rate and the wage rate. We can see that the profit rate has declined, and it is easy to show that this must be true, if the wage rises proportionately to the productivity of labor: since the profit rate is equal to $\pi\rho$, as capital productivity declines, the rate of profit will also decline in the absence of offsetting rises in the profit share.

We can work out the paths of social consumption and the rate of capital accumulation from the Classical conventional wage share model equations. Since the net rate of profit, r, declines, the rate of capital accumulation, $g_K = \beta(1 + r) - 1$, will also decline. The rate of growth of output, g_X, is equal to $g_K + \chi$, and with χ constant it will decline as well. The level of social consumption per worker increases, since

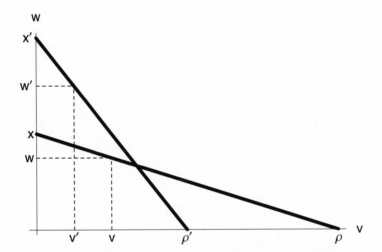

Figure 7.1: Marx-biased technical change raises labor productivity, x, lowers capital productivity, ρ, and hence rotates the growth-distribution schedule around a switchpoint in the positive quadrant. If the wage share, $1 - \pi$, remains constant, the wage, w, rises proportionately to labor productivity, and the profit rate, v, must fall.

workers' consumption, which is equal to the wage, has risen, and with some effort it can also be shown that capitalist consumption per worker has increased as well.

This pattern could not go on forever. Eventually, the rate of profit would fall so low that the economy would stop growing altogether. From the Cambridge equation, $1+g_K = \beta(1+r)$, we see that when the net rate of profit reaches $(1-\beta)/\beta$, capital accumulation halts completely. If the profit rate fell farther, the rate of capital accumulation would become negative, and the capitalists would eat up the capital stock until it was exhausted. Real economies have never reached this point because the episodes of capital-using bias which underly this pattern have not lasted indefinitely. As we have seen, periods of capital-using technical change in real capitalist economies eventually have given way to periods of stable or rising capital productivity.

Problem 7.1 *The Industrian economy (see Problem 2.2) now experiences biased technical change with $\gamma = 5\%$ per year and $\chi = -2\%$ per year. In the initial period, the wage is $20,000 per worker-year, labor productivity is $50,000 per worker-year, and capital productivity is 33 1/3 % per year. What will be the rate of profit and the wage rate (per worker-year) in the next period? Compare the rate of profit in the next period to the rate of profit in the base year.*

Problem 7.2 *Calculate the wage share and profit share in Industria. Show that the wage share did not change in the first year.*

Problem 7.3 *Find the level of consumption per worker and the growth rate of capital in the Industrian economy for the base year and the first year, assuming $\beta = .97$.*

Problem 7.4 *In how many years will the net rate of profit in Industria reach zero if there is no change in the rates of technical change? In how many years will the growth rate of capital reach zero?*

7.2   Viability of Technical Change

Why would entrepreneurs introduce technologies which lower the rate of profit?

Individual entrepreneurs can choose their own technologies, but they cannot control the social forces that technological change sets in motion that result in increases in real wages. Each entrepreneur acts under competitive pressure to be the first to adopt a profit rate-increasing technology. Marx argues that this fact lies behind the technologically progressive character of capitalist production. As individual entrepreneurs race to adopt more profitable technologies, they raise labor productivity in the society as a whole, and set in motion forces that raise wages as well (in the conventional wage share model). The net result, if technical change takes a Marx-biased form, is a fall in the rate of profit. But capitalist entrepreneurs could avoid this outcome only through an agreement not to pursue their individual self-interests by pursuing profit-increasing technical changes. Such an agreement is impossible to enforce in advanced, highly competitive, capitalist economies.

Each individual entrepreneur decides whether to adopt a new technique based only on the private rate of profit that she anticipates. Techniques that raise the rate of profit at the current level of wages and prices are called *viable*. It generally takes some time before competitors catch up with an innovator, so that entrepreneurs are motivated to adopt viable techniques by the prospect of reaping temporary above-normal profits before other firms have time to catch up.

The fate of the average profit rate for the whole economy, however, depends on what happens to wages as labor productivity rises. Because the Classical tradition sees the conventional wage, rather than the supply of labor, as the exogenously given factor in the labor market, it can embrace the possibility that institutional and political factors contribute to determining wage levels. Trade unions and legislated changes in the minimum wage, for example, keep upward pressure on the wage during periods of rising labor productivity. The conventional wage share assumption implies that wages increase proportionately with labor productivity. Thus a rise in wages is a predictable indirect effect of the widespread adoption of techniques of production that raise labor productivity, but is not under the control of any single entrepreneur.

When all the entrepreneurs act on their perception that a new technique will increase their rate of profit, the increase in the productivity of labor creates the conditions for institutional factors to enforce a proportionate increase in the wage. At the end of the day the entrepreneurs will have to raise pay by the same amount as labor productivity. The average rate of profit declines because the entrepreneurs have fallen victim to the *fallacy of composition*: actions that appear to be advantageous to individual capitalists are not always advantageous when all capitalists take them.

The expectation of increasing wages as a result of social patterns of technical change only increases the pressure on individual entrepreneurs to adopt labor-saving techniques in an effort to protect their rate of profit from erosion by higher wages. Each entrepreneur may understand quite well that the falling rate of profit is the result of the general adoption of labor-saving techniques, and still see it as in her own best interest to adopt precisely such techniques.

In judging the viability of a new technique, (ρ', x'), entrepreneurs focus on the rate of profit they would get if they adopted it while paying the existing wage, w. Let us call the private rate of profit expected by the typical entrepreneur, $v^e = (1 - w/x')\rho'$. We can simplify this equation by substituting the equations which describe technical change:

$$x' = (1 + \gamma)x$$

$$\rho' = (1 + \chi)\rho$$

Remembering the definition of the wage share, $w = (1 - \pi)x$, the expected rate of profit can be written:

$$v^e = \frac{\rho(1 + \chi)(\gamma + \pi)}{1 + \gamma}$$

The entrepreneurs compare this expected rate of profit with the prevailing rate of profit, $v = \pi\rho$. The condition for a technical change to be considered viable by the entrepreneurs is that its expected rate of profit should exceed the prevailing rate of profit, or $v^e > v$. This *viability condition* can be expressed in terms of the profit share:

$$\pi < \frac{\gamma(1 + \chi)}{\gamma - \chi} \tag{7.7}$$

The economic intuition behind this condition is that a technical change that saves on labor but requires more capital will be profitable if labor costs are a sufficiently large proportion of total costs. The viability condition plays an important role in implementing the Classical model empirically, and in distinguishing the Classical theory from the neoclassical theory.

Entrepreneurs who anticipate a rising wage will have that much more incentive to adopt viable new techniques, because a labor-saving technique that is viable at a given wage is also viable at any higher wage. Equation (7.7) reflects this fact, since a higher wage will correspond to a lower profit share, making the inequality even stronger.

Problem 7.5 *In Industria (see Problem 7.1) in the base year, calculate the private rate of profit that entrepreneurs perceive they would receive in the next year if they adopt the new technique. Would this technical change be considered viable?*

Problem 7.6 *Show that the viability condition is met in Industria (see Problem 7.1).*

Problem 7.7 *Show that if entrepreneurs expect the wage to increase at the same rate as labor productivity, γ, they will still adopt new labor-saving techniques that satisfy the viability condition. For simplicity, assume that δ is zero. (Hint: show that at the new wage, w', the rate of profit will be higher using the new technique, $\{\rho', x'\}$, than with the old technique, $\{\rho, x\}$, if the viability condition is satisfied.)*

7.3 Biased Technical Change and the Fossil Production Function

The Classical model with Marx-biased technical change and a conventional wage share provides a way of understanding capital-labor substitution that is alternative to the neoclassical production function. A history of Marx-biased technical change leaves behind a trail of evidence that is hard to distinguish from movement along a pre-existing production function. In fact, if the rates of capital-using ($\chi < 0$) and labor-saving ($\gamma > 0$) are constant, the historical path of labor and capital productivities left behind by technical change will exactly resemble a Cobb-Douglas production function.

To see this, consider an economy undergoing Marx-biased technical change with constant $\gamma > 0$ and $\chi < 0$. First, the measured rate of labor productivity growth will be:

$$g_x = \gamma,$$

and the growth rate of the capital-labor ratio will be:

$$g_k = \frac{1+\gamma}{1+\chi} - 1 = \frac{\gamma - \chi}{1+\chi}$$

Dividing the latter equation into the former and rearranging, we obtain the following expression linking labor productivity growth to the rate of growth of the capital-labor ratio:

$$g_x = \frac{\gamma(1+\chi)}{\gamma-\chi} g_k = \omega g_k \tag{7.8}$$

where the coefficient $\omega \equiv \gamma(1+\chi)/(\gamma-\chi)$ is a positive fraction less than unity since $\gamma > 0$ and $\chi < 0$. Notice that ω appears in the viability condition as the profit share at which the new techniques will just be viable.

Now consider an economy moving along a Cobb-Douglas production function, $X = K^\alpha N^{1-\alpha}$, or $x = k^\alpha$. Then in successive periods:

$$\frac{x_{+1}}{x} = (\frac{k_{+1}}{k})^\alpha$$

or, taking logarithms of both sides:

$$\ln(x_{+1}) - \ln(x) = \alpha(\ln(k_{+1}) - \ln(k))$$

The first difference of the natural logarithm of a dated variable is equal to its exponential compound growth rate, which in turn is very close to the growth rate formula that we are using here, as we saw in Chapter 2. In other words, the Cobb-Douglas economy will have a measured growth of labor productivity:

$$g_x \approx \ln(x_{+1}) - \ln(x) = \alpha(\ln(k_{+1}) - \ln(k)) = \alpha g_k \tag{7.9}$$

Comparing equations (7.8) and (7.9), we see that they are identical when we substitute ω for α. A history of Marx-biased technical change at a constant rate is indistinguishable from movement along a Cobb-Douglas production function, since the Cobb-Douglas growth path has the same mathematical form as the biased technical change growth path.

In the Classical conventional wage share economy with Marx-biased technical change, the historical path of labor and capital productivity creates a *fossil production function*. The history of past techniques appears to trace out a production function, but is in fact just the fossil record of past technology.

This similarity in form between the Classical fossil record and the neoclassical production function invites us to ask what the substantive difference between the Classical conventional wage model with biased technical change and the neoclassical model with a Cobb-Douglas production function actually is. At issue in the contest between the Classical and neoclassical theories are some of the deepest questions in political economy. The Classical theory regards capital as a social relationship between two classes: the owners of wealth (the actual capital goods) and the direct producers, workers. It regards profit as the form of the social surplus appropriated by capitalists through the capitalist property relations. The neoclassical theory, with its essentially harmonious vision of the economy, imputes a definite productive contribution to capital as well as to labor. It explains profit and wage income symmetrically, as the equilibrium of supply and demand in the capital and labor markets. The neoclassical theory attaches great significance to equality between the wage (profit rate) and the marginal product of labor (capital). Modern Classical economists criticize the neoclassical theorists for misrepresenting social reality by reifying capital and treating a social relationship as if it were a thing.

It would be useful to be able to distinguish empirically between hypotheses generated by these competing theories. As we saw in Chapter 3, neoclassical theory assumes a smooth production function like the Cobb-Douglas, and assumes that the economy is always operating at a switchpoint on the efficiency frontier of the production function. By contrast, in the Classical model the best practice technique will generally be chosen over a range of wage rates. The Classical theory, therefore, allows the economy to operate at a wage higher than the switchpoint; only in the limiting case is the wage at the switchpoint. In the economy represented in Figure 7.1, for example, the initial wage is greater than the wage at the switchpoint. Since, as we saw in Chapter 3, the assumption that the wage is equal to the marginal product of labor is just another way of saying that the economy is at a switchpoint, we can also say that in the Classical conventional wage share model the wage may be higher than the apparent marginal product of labor.

The distance between the actual wage and the wage at the switchpoint is given in terms of the profit share by $\omega - \pi$. When $\pi = \omega$, the viability condition is satisfied as an equality and the economy operates at a switchpoint. When $\pi < \omega$, the viability condition is satisfied as a strict inequality and the economy operates above the switchpoint. Therefore, we can use the viability condition to evaluate competing hypotheses generated by the neoclassical and Classical theories. An implication of neoclassical theory's insistence that the wage is equal to the marginal product of labor is that the viability condition will be satisfied as an equality, while the Classical theory allows it to be satisfied as a strict inequality. Note that finding the viability condition to be an equality does not falsify the Classical theory that apparent capital-labor substitution is a result of a historical pattern of technical change but finding it to be a strict inequality does falsify the neoclassical theory that the wage is equal to the marginal product of labor.

We have assembled statistics to evaluate the viability condition in

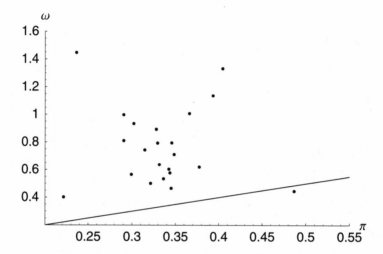

Figure 7.2: Average ω and π for 22 countries from 1965–95 plotted against each other reveal an overwhelming tendency for $\omega > \pi$, or in other words, for advanced capitalist economies to operate at a wage above the apparent marginal product of labor. Source: Authors' calculations from OECD [1997].

Figure 7.2. Profit shares and the growth rates of x and ρ (measuring γ and χ) have been calculated from 1965–1995 in the business sectors of the 22 countries* for which the OECD provides sufficient data. These data have been used to calculate the viability condition, which is displayed visually in the figure. The 45-degree line divides the figure, with the viable region lying above the diagonal. The neoclassical theory predicts that the data points should lie along the diagonal (or at least close to it). The Classical theory allows for the possibility that the data points should lie above the diagonal, which they clearly do. In fact, the average value of ω is .77 while the average profit share, π, is .33. The neoclassical theory of distribution appears from this test to be off by a factor of more than 100 per cent. We will see in Chapter 9 that neoclassical theorists have had to make auxiliary assumptions in order to explain these basic discrepancies between their predictions and real observations.

Problem 7.8 *In a classical model with biased technical change and a wage share $1 - \pi = 0.8$, $1 + \gamma = 1.02$/year and $1 + \chi = 0.99$/year, find the relationship between the growth rates of x and k. If you were able to estimate this relationship without knowing how the data had been generated, would you accept or reject the hypothesis that there is a Cobb-Douglas production function with perfectly competitive markets?*

Problem 7.9 *Use the data in Tables 2.4 and 2.8 to check whether technical change from 1973-1992 in the six countries satisfied the viability condition. (Use the value of the profit share during the 1980s.) Do the values you compute satisfy the predictions of the neoclassical theory?*

7.4 Convergence and the Classical Model

One of the most striking features of capitalism on the world scale is *uneven development*: advanced industrial capitalist economies with high labor productivity and standards of living coexist with poor, low labor productivity economies. An important question for growth theory is whether the process of economic growth tends to reproduce these differences, or to narrow them.

The answer to this question depends on whether economies that have relatively low labor productivity at one point in time tend to have faster

---

*U.S., Japan, Germany, France, Italy, U.K., Canada, Australia, Austria, Belgium, Denmark, Finland, Greece, Iceland, Ireland, Netherlands, New Zealand, Norway, Portugal, Spain, Sweden, and Switzerland.

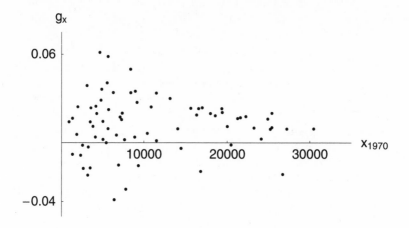

Figure 7.3: The growth of labor productivity over the period 1970–90, g_x, is plotted against 1970 levels of labor productivity, x_{1970}, for 73 economies at all levels of capital intensity from the EPWT dataset. No strong negative correlation is apparent.

labor productivity growth. If this were true, the differences in labor productivity would tend to narrow over time, as low productivity economies
catch up with higher productivity economies. In this case there would be
convergence in labor productivity levels among the world's economies.
The historical evidence on convergence is mixed. If we look, as in Figure
7.3, at a broad sample of economies at all levels of labor productivity,
there appears to be no strong correlation between initial levels of labor productivity and the growth of labor productivity in the succeeding
period.

On the other hand, if we look at a sample of economies which begin with relatively high capital intensity, and therefore tend to have
relatively high labor productivity, as in Figure 7.4, a strong negative
correlation between the growth rate of labor productivity and its initial
level appears.

The empirical data suggest, in other words, that there are tendencies
toward convergence of economies already at a relatively advanced level of
development, but that the pressures to convergence are much weaker in
economies which have not experienced much economic growth to begin
with.

The Classical model sees the evolution of labor productivity as the

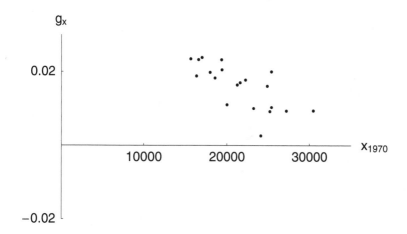

Figure 7.4: The growth of labor productivity over the period 1970–90, g_x, is plotted against 1970 levels of labor productivity, x_{1970}, for 21 economies with 1970 capital intensity above \$25,000 per worker, from the EPWT dataset. A
strong negative correlation is apparent.

reflection of a process of historical change in technology. This change can
come about in two ways: through the discovery of previously unknown
methods of production, or through the new adoption of methods already
in use in some other economy. A country can either invent new technology, or transfer existing technology from other countries. The transfer
of technology is costly, because it requires the import of the appropriate
equipment, the reeducation of the labor force, and a period of learning
how to operate the new technology, but it is reasonable to suppose that
transfer is easier than the discovery of completely new technologies.

The Classical model would explain convergence through the hypothesis that less developed countries have higher rates of labor productivity
growth because of technology transfer from more developed countries.
Because technology is not a pure public good, and firms that discover
new methods are seeking above-normal profits before the innovations diffuse, it takes time for technology to diffuse through the world economy.
But the speed of diffusion will depend on how big the gap between existing technology and the best available technology is. Firms in economies
that are lagging will typically get more out of borrowing from the world's
technological leaders than firms in economies that have already largely
caught up.

The model of biased technical change thus applies to technologically leading economies. Technological change in lagging economies will depend more on the diffusion of existing technology than on independent discovery. For illustrative purposes, let us use the U.S. to represent the technological leader and Japan to represent a country catching up. We focus on the behavior of labor productivity, but what we have to say can also be applied to capital productivity.

The *pure time delay hypothesis* of technological diffusion is that the follower country, Japan, receives a stream of technical changes from the leader, the U.S., that arrive with a constant time delay of d years. Then the productivity of each economy would be given by the following equations:

$$x_{US} = x_0(1 + \gamma)^t$$

$$x_J = x_0(1 + \gamma)^{t-d}$$

We can use these equations to calculate the apparent size of the time delay. For instance, Maddison's data tell us that U.S. output per worker grew around 1.11 per cent per year from 1973 to 1992. The level of labor productivity in the Japanese economy in 1992 was 68.8 per cent of the level in the U.S., so the ratio $x_J/x_{US} = .688$. Substituting these values into the equations above and solving for d (by taking logarithms of both sides) we find an implied delay of 34 years. The pure time delay hypothesis implies that the Japanese are working with technologies that were first introduced in the U.S. over three decades ago. This procedure, however, may overestimate the delay in technology transfer. Technological knowledge does not consist only of recipes or machine designs that can be bought and sold; practical knowledge is subtly embedded in institutions and organizations. While Japanese firms may be working with technologies that were introduced fairly recently in the U.S., they may not have fully absorbed them into their business organizations. Studies of industrial productivity show that two factories located in different countries but using the same technology often have widely different levels of productivity. In addition, the availability of cheaper natural resources may raise labor productivity even with the same technology.

The pure time delay theory implies that the relative productivity gap between economies will not change over time, because labor productivity in the follower country will grow at the same rate as in the leader. Thus the pure time delay model is incompatible with convergence. From 1973 to 1992, for example, Japanese labor productivity grew by 3.13 per cent per year, almost three times the rate of the U.S., shrinking the productivity gap.

The *catching-up hypothesis* of technological diffusion argues that the farther behind follower countries are, the greater their benefit from transferring technology from the leaders. This hypothesis views the process of technology transfer like prospecting for oil. Economies that are far behind have many possible technologies (all those either in use or recently discarded in leading economies) to use as examples from which to learn. They are much more likely to strike oil by finding transferable models. As they close the gap, however, the number of more advanced technologies from which to learn falls, and the chances of striking oil decline.

We can implement the catching-up hypothesis by making the growth rate of labor productivity in a follower country, say, Japan, depend on the relative level of productivity through the following equation for γ_J, the growth rate of Japanese labor productivity:

$$\gamma_J = \gamma_{US} + \psi\left(\frac{x_{US} - x_J}{x_J}\right)$$

where the parameter ψ reflects the catching-up effect. If ψ is not so large that overshooting becomes possible, but large enough to ensure actual catching up, this equation predicts that the growth rate of the follower's labor productivity will decelerate as it approaches the leader's labor productivity. Once Japan converges with the U.S., their growth rates of labor productivity will be equal and the apparent time delay will have vanished. In this implementation the catching-up hypothesis predicts absolute convergence in levels of labor productivity.

This approach to convergence could be broadened to include capital productivity. Again we must be careful to avoid interpreting the model too rigidly, because the same basic designs and factory plans will not have the same economic results in every country. For one thing, the availability of other inputs such as natural resources may differ between economies. This is perhaps why convergence has not been symmetric with respect to capital productivity. Maddison's data in Table 2.7 show that capital productivity has converged from above on U.S. levels (as would be expected), but not at the same rate as labor productivity. Figure 7.5 shows that the tendency for convergence of capital productivity even in the "convergence club" of relatively advanced economies is much weaker than the convergence of labor productivity. There is, however, as Figure 7.6 shows, a strong tendency to convergence in capital intensity among the advanced economies.

To explain the failure of many less developed countries to join the convergence club requires some additional explanation. We can borrow

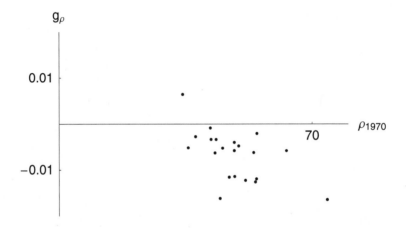

Figure 7.5: The growth of capital productivity over the
period 1970–90, g_ρ, is plotted against 1970 levels of capital
intensity, ρ_{1970}, for 21 economies with 1970 capital intensity
above \$25,000 per worker, from the EPWT dataset. The
negative correlation is much less strong than for labor productivity or capital intensity.

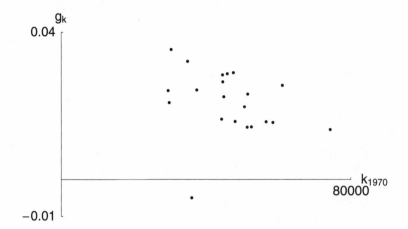

Figure 7.6: The growth of capital intensity over the period 1970–90, g_k, is plotted against 1970 levels of capital
intensity, k_{1970}, for 21 economies with 1970 capital intensity above \$25,000 per worker, from the EPWT dataset. A
strong negative correlation is apparent.

from the technology gap literature by making ψ a function of the effort a
country makes to catch up through spending on education or investment
in new capital goods that embody the latest technology. Economists
who accept the technology gap framework point out that substantial
effort on the part of a national economy is required to import technical knowledge and exploit it commercially. The ability to appropriate
technological advances depends on an educated workforce that can read
manuals and technical journals. The ability to take advantage of much
new technology requires the physical presence of the capital goods in
which the technology is embodied. These considerations suggest that
catching-up is contingent on the effort of the follower country, represented by the extent to which resources are devoted to education and
investment. A country with a weak commitment to education, for example, would suffer a small value of ψ due to the difficulty of borrowing
modern technical ideas with a poorly educated work force. A country
with $\psi = 0$ would be a follower country with a constant time delay,
growing at the same rate as the leader but remaining indefinitely at a
lower relative productivity level. A country with $\psi < 0$ would be falling
behind the leader. Thus, the technology gap approach accommodates
the reproduction of unevenness at the global level.

7.5   One Vision of Economic Growth

The Classical conventional wage share model with Marx-biased technical change represents one vision of the process of capitalist economic growth. This Classical vision sees world capitalist development as an historically unique event shaped by specific social factors. The fundamental driving force of capitalist development is the class division it induces in society. The tendency of class conflict to maintain a high wage share in income creates strong incentives for labor-saving innovations, which accounts for the technologically progressive character of capitalism. The resulting bias toward capital-using technical change, however, poses an obstacle to capitalist growth because it depresses rates of profit and growth. Periodic bursts of capital-saving innovation have so far sufficed to restore capital productivity and profitability. The future of capitalism in this vision is open and undetermined, hanging on many historical contingencies. Continuing rises in labor productivity and standards of living, for example, depend on the maintenance of a high wage share in the technologically leading economies. Within this framework the ultimate fate of capitalism is a genuine intellectual, moral, and historical problem.

The Classical vision, however, is not the only way economists have tried to put together the complex aspects of economic growth in a coherent gestalt. Neoclassical growth theory, to which we now turn, offers an alternative perspective from which many of the same empirical facts appear in a quite different light.

7.6   Suggested Readings

The first significant reference to the phenomenon of mechanization is probably David Ricardo's speculation [Ricardo, 1951, Ch. 31, "On Machinery"] that machinery could generate what today would be called technological unemployment. Karl Marx discusses the underlying causes and forms of capitalist technical change extensively in the first volume of *Capital* [Marx, 1977]. For a modern continuation of this investigation, see Lazonick [1990]. Marx's law of the tendency for the rate of profit to fall has been the object of considerable controversy, which was reopened by Okishio [1961]; for an overview, consult Foley [1986]. The model in this chapter is basically an extension of Okishio's approach; for further elaboration of the model, see Michl [1999]. It has also been influenced by the work of Gérard Duménil and Dominique Lévy, particularly Duménil and Lévy [1994].

For more insight into the issues separating neoclassical and Classical economic theory, see Nell [1967]. In an early empirical critique of the Cobb-Douglas production function, Shaikh [1974] argues that when the profit share is constant, the Cobb-Douglas form is an accounting identity that will fit almost any underlying data, including some artificially constructed to spell out the word "humbug."

The literature on convergence is now enormous. A good survey which has influenced this chapter considerably is given by Fagerberg [1994]. The catching-up hypothesis traces back to the iconoclastic Thorstein Veblen [1915] or, more recently, Alexander Gerschenkron [1962].

Chapter 8

The Neoclassical Growth Model

8.1　The Solow–Swan Model

During the 1940s and 1950s, economists debated the Keynesian proposition that unemployment tends to persist indefinitely unless special actions are taken by the government. Roy Harrod, a follower of Keynes, and Evsey Domar, a student of socialist planned economies, argued that only by accident would a capitalist economy's *warranted* growth rate (at which planned saving would equal planned investment) equal its *natural* growth rate (the growth needed to create jobs to employ a growing population in the presence of labor-augmenting technical change). Robert Solow and T. W. Swan independently developed a neoclassical model of growth to show that full employment is compatible with steady-state growth. The Solow–Swan model assumes, like the Classical model, that planned investment and planned saving are identical, so that it does not directly address the problem of the stability of the actual growth path. (We will study explicit models of the warranted rate of growth in Chapter 10.) The Solow–Swan model is now a standard theoretical explanation of why some countries grow faster than others, and it plays an important role in many policy discussions related to the long run significance of saving and investment.

The Solow–Swan growth model reaches closure by assuming full employment. This is achieved by the choice of the appropriate technique of production from a production function, guided by changes in the real wage. The Solow–Swan model also assumes that there is one representative type of household which saves and invests a constant fraction of its gross income.

8.2 The Intensive Production Function

Constant returns to scale in production means that a proportional increase in all inputs makes it possible to increase output in the same proportion. If we can produce one ton of corn using one bushel of seed corn and one worker, we ought to be able to replicate that result by hiring one more worker and buying one more bushel of seed, and producing two tons of corn. This replication argument makes constant returns an attractive assumption. There is strong evidence, however, that real production is subject to *increasing returns to scale*, because it is possible to adopt new techniques of production involving a more detailed division of labor at a larger scale.

As we saw in Chapter 3, constant returns to scale permits us to work with the intensive production function, $x = f(k)$, which in the Cobb-Douglas case is $x = Ak^\alpha$. The graph of this function, shown in Figure 8.1, has an inverted dish shape. Economically, the intensive production function exhibits a *diminishing marginal product of capital*: increasing the amount of capital per worker raises output per worker, but by progressively smaller increments. Mathematicians describe such functions as *concave*.

The neoclassical production function in general, and the Cobb-Douglas function in particular, can be viewed as the result of increasing the number of techniques available, until there is an infinite continuum of techniques. Therefore, each point on the Cobb-Douglas represents a single technique (ρ, x). One feasible technique has been highlighted by the thin lines in Figure 8.1. The slope of the thin line up to the capital intensity k represents the output-capital ratio, ρ, for that technique. With that technique, adding more capital per worker above k will yield no further output, so the thin line representing the technique becomes horizontal to the right of k.

While the Classical theory of technical change sees more capital intensive techniques as coming into being historically as the result of technical innovation, the neoclassical production function implies that a broad spectrum of techniques of every capital intensity have already been invented and are available in any historical period.

An important corollary of the assumption of diminishing marginal productivity of capital is that the productivity of capital, the output-capital ratio, ρ, will be a decreasing function of the capital-labor ratio, k. This point can be seen geometrically in Figure 8.1: the ray through

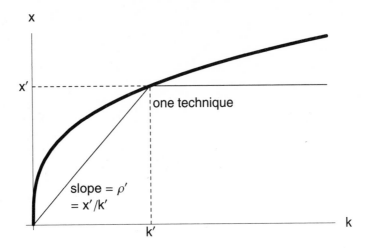

Figure 8.1: The intensive production function.

the origin representing the productivity of capital declines in slope as k rises. In the Cobb-Douglas case, the relation between the productivity of capital and the capital intensity is described by the function $\rho = Ak^{\alpha-1}$, which is a decreasing function when $\alpha < 1$.

Problem 8.1 *Write the Leontief production function in intensive form.*

Problem 8.2 *Find the value of x and ρ for the Cobb-Douglas production function $X = AK^\alpha N^{1-\alpha}$, when $k = \$14,000/worker$, $A = 1,000$, and $\alpha = .2$.*

Problem 8.3 *Show that the Cobb-Douglas production function implies that $\rho = Ak^{\alpha-1}$.*

8.3   Saving, Population, and Steady State Growth

The Solow–Swan growth model assumes that the economy saves a constant, exogenously given, fraction of its income, and that the population and labor force grow at a constant, exogenously given, rate. Note that the Solow–Swan model, in assuming that households save the same proportion of profit and wage income, abstracts from the distinction between workers and capitalists that is central to the Classical model.

Furthermore, unlike later neoclassical growth theory, the Solow–Swan model does not base the saving equation on the household's utility maximizing problem as we did in Chapter 5. The Solow–Swan model simply assumes that gross saving is a constant fraction of gross output:

$$S = sX$$

Here S represents the flow of gross saving and s is the fraction of gross income which is saved, the saving ratio, also called the *saving propensity*. Notice that saving in the Solow–Swan model is a constant fraction of the *flow of output*, rather than being a constant fraction of the *stock of wealth*, as in the model of Chapter 5.

The Solow–Swan model assumes, like the Classical model, that saving is identical to investment, which implies that the change in the capital stock per period is the excess of saving over depreciation:

$$K_{+1} - K = sX - \delta K$$

Dividing both sides of this equation by K, we obtain an equation for the rate of capital accumulation, g_K:

$$g_K = \frac{sX}{K} - \delta = s\rho - \delta \tag{8.1}$$

When we recall that the output-capital ratio, ρ, is an inverse function of the capital-labor ratio, we can see that this makes the rate of accumulation an inverse function of the capital-labor ratio too. In the Cobb-Douglas case, this function will be:

$$g_K = sAk^{\alpha-1} - \delta$$

which is shown in Figure 8.2.

The labor force is assumed to grow at a constant rate, n, which is an exogenous parameter of the model. The Solow–Swan model assumes that labor remains fully employed at all times. The mechanism which assures that any excess labor will be absorbed by the demand for labor in production is the constant adjustment of the wage, so that entrepreneurs' profit-maximizing choice of technique creates enough jobs to clear the labor market. If labor were to become unemployed, the wage would decline, leading entrepreneurs to choose more labor-intensive techniques, and create more jobs. The existence of techniques with arbitrarily high and low capital intensity, as is the case for the Cobb-Douglas production function, guarantees that there will always be a technique

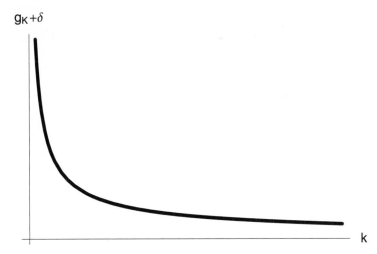

Figure 8.2: The rate of capital accumulation is a decreasing function of the capital-labor ratio under the assumptions of the Solow–Swan model.

that will provide full employment, no matter how much or how little capital has been inherited from the past.

In order to predict the direction of the choices of technique in a dynamic setting, we need to know whether the supply of capital or labor is growing faster. Mathematically, this amounts to solving an equation for the growth rate of the capital-labor ratio, g_k. Since $k = K/N$ is a ratio, its growth rate (like the growth rate of any ratio) can be expressed as the difference between the growth rates of its numerator and denominator:

$$g_k = \frac{\frac{K_{+1}}{N_{+1}} - \frac{K}{N}}{\frac{K}{N}} = \frac{1 + g_K}{1 + n} - 1 \approx g_K - n$$

The approximation holds when g_K and n are small. When we substitute the expression for g_K from Equation 8.1 into this equation, we arrive at the fundamental equation of the Solow–Swan growth model, (8.2):

$$g_k \approx (s\rho - \delta) - n \tag{8.2}$$

This equation tells us that when the rate of capital accumulation (which is the term bracketed on the right-hand side) exceeds the rate of population growth, the capital-labor ratio will be growing. As capital

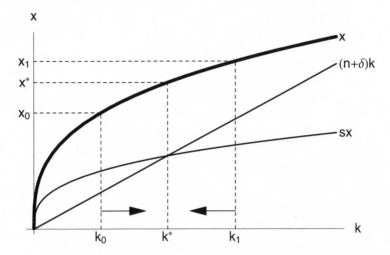

Figure 8.3: Steady state equilibrium in the Solow–Swan model.

increases faster than labor, the wage is bid up so that more capital-intensive techniques become the most profitable. Otherwise, there would be an excess demand for labor (overemployment). This path of increasing capital intensity is known as *capital deepening*.

In the converse situation, with labor growing faster than capital, the wage would be falling. This would cause firms to switch to more labor-intensive techniques to soak up the excess supply of labor.

We can visualize these cases better by specializing the Solow–Swan model to the case of the Cobb-Douglas production function. In this case, the fundamental equation becomes:

$$g_k = (sAk^{\alpha-1} - \delta) - n$$

Figure 8.3 graphs the saving per worker, sAk^{α}, with a Cobb-Douglas production function, and the investment per worker required to maintain the capital stock per worker, $(n + \delta)k$. When investment per worker is equal to $(n + \delta)k$, the capital-labor ratio will remain constant.

At the intersection of these saving and required investment curves, $g_K = n + \delta$. Here the economy has reached its *steady state equilibrium*, k^*, where there is no change in the capital-labor ratio ($g_k = 0$). The capital accumulation occurring in this state is called *capital widening*. By setting $g_k = 0$ in equation (8.2), we can see that output per worker and the capital intensity in the steady state must be related by the equation:

$$k^* = \frac{s}{n + \delta} x^*$$

The asterisk superscript identifies the steady state values of the capital-labor and output-labor ratios.

In the case of the Cobb-Douglas production function, we can derive an explicit or *closed-form* solution for the equilibrium capital-labor and output-labor ratios in terms of the parameters of the model:

$$k^* = \left(\frac{sA}{n + \delta} \right)^{\frac{1}{1-\alpha}}$$

$$x^* = Ak^{*\alpha}$$

The upper curve in Figure 8.3 shows output per worker along the Cobb-Douglas production function. The lower curves show saving per worker and the investment per worker required to maintain the capital stock for different levels of k. Their intersection determines the steady state capital intensity, k^*. Corresponding to the steady state capital-labor ratio will be the equilibrium level of output per worker, x^*. Using Figure 8.3, we can work out many of the important characteristics of the Solow–Swan model.

The steady state at (k^*, x^*) is stable because if the economy starts out at a low level of capital per worker, such as k_0 in Figure 8.3, the fundamental equation (8.2) tells us that capital will be growing faster than the labor force. The arrows on the k-axis indicate the direction of change of k over time. By the same token, starting with a high level of capital per worker at k_1 results in capital growing more slowly than the labor force. In the long run, the system converges on (k^*, x^*).

Problem 8.4 *Production in Solowia is described by a Cobb-Douglas production function with $A = 1000$, $\alpha = .2$. The saving rate is .15, the rate of depreciation, δ, is .1 per year, and the population growth rate, n, is .02 per year. What will the growth rates of capital and the capital-labor ratio be when the capital-labor ratio is $5,000 per worker?*

Problem 8.5 *Find the steady state equilibrium values of the capital-labor ratio, productivity of labor, and productivity of capital for Solowia (see Problem 8.4).*

8.4   The Solow–Swan Model and the Growth-Distribution Schedule

The Solow–Swan model can be analyzed by means of the growth-distribution diagram, as in Figures 8.4 and 8.5.

Recall that the efficiency frontier contains the same information as the intensive production function; each technique is represented by a growth-distribution schedule which contributes one point to the frontier. The profit-maximizing technique for any wage, w, is represented by the growth-distribution schedule tangent to the efficiency frontier at w, and the slope of the growth-distribution schedule is equal to the negative of the corresponding capital-labor ratio, k. In the Classical model, the wage is given exogenously and determines the technique in use and the capital intensity of production. In the Solow–Swan model, by contrast, the *capital intensity*, $\bar{k}$, is given exogenously in each period by the past growth of the population and the past accumulation of capital. If the efficiency frontier is concave toward the origin, as in Figure 8.4, there will be one tangent to the efficiency frontier whose slope is equal to $-\bar{k}$. This tangent is the growth-distribution schedule for the technique in use, and determines the wage and profit rate in the period. Consumption per worker is just $c = (1 - s)x$, and the growth rate of the capital stock is determined by the growth-distribution schedule.

Figure 8.4 also shows the growth of the labor force plus the depreciation rate, $n + \delta$. As the figure is drawn, the gross growth rate of the capital stock, $g_K + \delta$, exceeds $n + \delta$, so the capital intensity next period, k_{+1}, will be higher:

$$k_{+1} = k + \Delta k = (1 + g_K - n)k$$

Thus in the next period the economy will move to a point where the efficiency schedule is steeper, the profit rate lower, the real wage higher, and the growth rate of the capital stock lower. This process will continue until the economy reaches the *steady state capital intensity*, k^*. The steady state is represented in Figure 8.5, which shows the efficiency frontier and the growth-distribution schedule associated with the steady-state technique. The slope of this schedule equals the steady state capital-labor ratio, or $-k^*$. The vertical intercept equals the steady-state productivity of labor, x^*.

Once any technique has been chosen by entrepreneurs, its growth-distribution schedule determines the trade-off between social consumption per worker and growth. In the steady-state, the growth rate of capital will be the exogenously given rate of growth of the labor force,

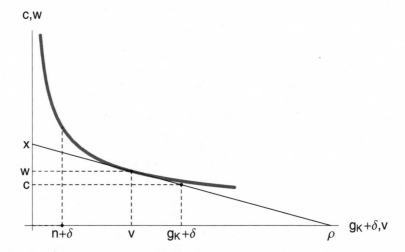

Figure 8.4: The Solow–Swan model takes the capital-labor
ratio in each period, $\bar{k}$, as exogenously determined by past
population growth and capital accumulation. The technique
in use, the wage, and the profit rate are determined by the
point on the efficiency schedule where the slope of the tangent is equal to $-\bar{k}$. The saving propensity, s, then determines consumption per worker and the growth rate of the
capital stock.

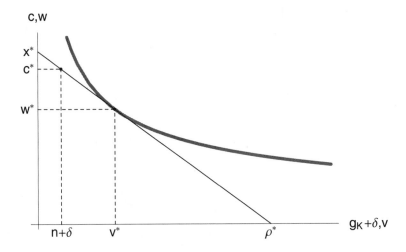

Figure 8.5: The Solow–Swan model reaches a steady state when the capital intensity rises to the point where saving finances just enough investment to offset depreciation and the growth of the labor force.

n. The rate of growth of output is $g_X = g_\rho + g_K$. Since capital productivity remains constant at its steady state value, $g_\rho = 0$, the rate of growth of output will also be equal to n.

8.5 The Complete Model

In the Classical conventional wage share model, each period is identical to the last except that all the aggregate variables, output, capital stock, and employment, have grown at the same rate. In the Solow–Swan model, however, outside of the steady state each period differs from the last because the capital intensity of production changes. Thus in the Classical model the analysis of equilibrium in a single period is the same as the analysis of the steady state, whereas in the Solow–Swan model it is necessary to consider equilibrium outside of the steady state separately from the analysis of the steady state.

We can summarize equilibrium in an arbitrary period in the Solow–Swan model in Table 8.1.

The accumulated capital stock and population determine the given capital stock per worker, $\bar{k}$, for the period, which in turn determines output per worker, x. The profit rate is equal to the marginal prod-

Table 8.1:

Short Run Equilibrium in the Solow–Swan Model

Endogenous variables: x, w, v, c, g_K, k_{+1}

Exogenous Parameters: $\bar{k}, \delta, s, n$

$$x = f(\bar{k})$$

$$v = f'(\bar{k})$$

$$c = (1 - s)x$$

$$w = x - v\bar{k}$$

$$g_K + \delta = \frac{sx}{\bar{k}}$$

$$k_{+1} = sf(\bar{k}) - (n + \delta)\bar{k}$$

---

uct of capital corresponding to $\bar{k}$, and consumption per worker is determined by the saving propensity and the output per worker. The growth-distribution schedule then determines the remaining variables, w and g_K.

With the Cobb-Douglas production function, we can solve these equations explicitly in terms of the parameters of the model in each period: $x = A\bar{k}^{\alpha}$, and $v = \alpha A\bar{k}^{\alpha-1}$, $c = (1 - s)x$, $w = (1 - \alpha)x$, $g_K = sA\bar{k}^{\alpha-1} - \delta$, and $k_{+1} = sA\bar{k}^{\alpha} - (n + \delta)\bar{k}$.

The steady state capital intensity of the Solow–Swan model, k^*, is defined by the condition $g_k = sf(k^*) - (n + \delta)k^* = 0$. The steady state conditions for a general production function are Table 8.2.

With the Cobb-Douglas production function, we can use these equations to solve for the steady state variables in terms of the exogenous parameters in Table 8.3.

8.6   Substitution and Distribution

During the convergence to a steady state, capital deepening will cause the wage to rise and the profit rate to fall. The effect a rising wage has on the distribution of income between wages and profits depends on the ease with which capital and labor can be substituted for one another.

Table 8.2:
Steady State in the Solow–Swan Model

Endogenous variables: k^*, x^*, w^*, v^*, c^*

Exogenous Parameters: $f(.), \delta, s, n$

$$sf(k^*) - (n+\delta)k^* = 0$$

$$x^* = f(k^*)$$

$$v^* = f'(k^*)$$

$$c^* = (1-s)x^*$$

$$w^* = x^* - v^*k^*$$

$$g_K^* = n$$

Table 8.3:
**Steady State in the Solow–Swan Model
with Cobb-Douglas Production Function**

Endogenous variables: k^*, x^*, w^*, v^*, c^*

Exogenous Parameters: A, α, δ, s, n

$$k^* = \left(\frac{sA}{n+\delta} \right)^{\frac{1}{1-\alpha}}$$

$$x^* = Ak^{*\alpha}$$

$$\rho^* = Ak^{*\alpha-1}$$

$$w^* = (1-\alpha)x^*$$

$$v^* = \alpha\rho^*$$

$$c^* = (1-s)x^*$$

$$g_K^* = n$$

If it is easy to substitute capital for labor, entrepreneurs will shift to much more capital intensive techniques in the face of a small increase in wages, and wages will become a smaller proportion of income. If it is very difficult to substitute capital for labor, large increases in the wage will be required to induce entrepreneurs to choose even slightly more capital intensive techniques. The ease of substitution between capital and labor implied by a particular production function at a particular capital intensity is measured by the *elasticity of substitution*, σ (the Greek letter *sigma,* pronounced "sig'-ma") between capital and labor, which is defined as the percentage change in the capital intensity induced by a one percent change in the ratio of the wage to the profit rate:

$$\sigma = \frac{\%\Delta(K/N)}{\%\Delta(w/v)}$$

To understand how the value of the elasticity of substitution affects the distribution of income, it is helpful to remember the following definitions of the wage share and the profit share of income:

$$1 - \pi = \frac{wN}{X}$$

$$\pi = \frac{vK}{X}$$

As the economy converges on its steady state capital intensity from below, the wage is rising and the profit rate is falling. This induces entrepreneurs to switch to more capital intensive technologies. If the elasticity of substitution is greater than one, entrepreneurs will increase the capital intensity more than proportionately to the change in the wage-profit rate ratio. Labor input per unit of output will fall more than proportionately to the increase in the wage, and capital input per unit of output will rise more than proportionately to the fall in the profit rate, so that the profit share of income will rise and the wage share will fall.

On the other hand, if the elasticity of substitution is less than one, the rise in the wage will cause the share of labor to rise and the share of capital to fall.

In general the elasticity of substitution may change with the technique in use, but for the production functions we have used in this book, the elasticity of substitution is constant. For example, the elasticity of substitution is zero for the Leontief production function, since it is impossible to substitute capital for labor in the Leontief technology.

If the elasticity of substitution is *exactly* one, the shares of wages and profit will not change during the convergence process. The rise in the wage as the economy moves toward the steady state capital intensity will be just offset by a proportionate fall in the amount of labor employed per unit of output, leaving the wage share constant. The Cobb-Douglas production function has a constant elasticity of substitution equal to one. (In fact, the Cobb-Douglas production function is the *only* production function with a constant elasticity of substitution equal to one.) In the Cobb-Douglas case, any changes in w and v on the growth path will be exactly canceled out by offsetting changes in N/X and K/X.

As we have seen, a constant wage share is a good first approximation to the behavior of real capitalist economies, and appears as a fundamental assumption in the Classical conventional wage share model. That model attributes the constant wage share to the behavior of labor supply: it assumes that historical, economic, political, and sociological forces will tend to make the wage rise roughly at the same rate as labor productivity. The neoclassical model explains the constant wage share as a property of a specific production function that happens to describe substitution possibilities between labor and capital, the Cobb-Douglas function. The explanation of the distribution of income between wages and profits is thus a central point of divergence between the neoclassical and Classical approaches.

8.7 Comparative Dynamics

As in the Classical model, it is useful to compare one steady state of the Solow–Swan model with another when only one parameter of the model has changed. This can be done by using the diagrams in Section 8.3 and the steady state equations for the Solow–Swan model with a Cobb-Douglas production function in Section 8.5.

For example, consider the effect of an increase in the saving rate from s to s'. An increase in the saving rate will increase the saving per worker for every level of the capital-labor ratio, as shown in Figure 8.6. The new steady state capital intensity will therefore be higher. With more capital per worker, the economy will enjoy more output per worker. The same conclusion emerges from examination of Table 8.3.

The increase in the saving rate will not affect the growth rate, which in the long run returns to the exogenously given rate of population growth, n. This somewhat disconcerting result is characteristic of *exogenous growth models*, in which the rate of growth is fixed by the exogenous growth of some input to production, such as labor or land. The increase in saving will result in a temporary increase in the rate of growth, as the system converges on its new equilibrium.

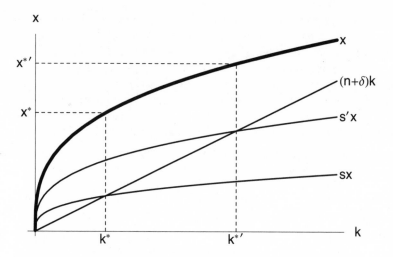

Figure 8.6: The effect of an increase in the saving rate on the steady state in the Solow–Swan model.

An increase in the saving rate has offsetting effects on steady state consumption per worker. Increasing labor productivity from a higher capital intensity raises consumption per worker, but the higher saving rate tends to reduce it. There is one steady state at which consumption per worker is maximized in the Solow–Swan model. At lower rates of saving (and therefore capital intensity), a small increase in the saving rate tends to increase consumption per worker because the productivity effect dominates. At higher rates of saving and capital intensity, the saving effect dominates any increase in productivity, so small increases in the saving rate will decrease consumption per worker.

Edmund Phelps called the equilibrium capital stock per worker at which consumption per worker is maximized the *Golden Rule* capital stock. The net profit rate, $r = v - \delta$, will equal the population growth rate, n, at the Golden Rule equilibrium.

Increasing the saving rate will always bring about an increase in the real wage and decrease in the profit rate. This can be seen by inspection of the last two equations in Table 8.2. Another way to see this is to recognize that increasing the saving rate will push the economy up along its efficiency frontier, to a point with a higher capital intensity.

Problem 8.6 *In a Solow-Swan model with a Cobb-Douglas production function, where $A = 1,000$, $\alpha = .2, \delta = .1$, and $n = .02/year$,* *what is the capital intensity, labor productivity, and consumption/worker at the original and new steady state when the saving rate rises from s = .15 to s' = .17? Show these two steady states on the efficiency frontier.*

Problem 8.7 *Find the Golden Rule values of $\hat{s}, \hat{k}, \hat{c}$ and $\hat{r}$ for the economy of Problem 8.5.*

Problem 8.8 *Analyze the comparative dynamics of an increase in the population growth rate, n, using the equations and the diagram for the Solow–Swan growth model. What effect would this change have on $k, x, c, g, r,$ and w?*

Problem 8.9 *Prove that $r = n$ at the Golden Rule steady state.*

8.8 Transitional Dynamics

If the economy starts out with less than the steady state level of capital per worker, it finds the capital stock growing more rapidly than the labor force, and the wage rising to clear the labor market. This would propel the economy along the efficiency frontier in the direction of the steady-state position since higher wages would lead to more capital-intensive techniques. This is the process of capital deepening we have already seen, during which the economy is in transit between disequilibrium and its steady-state. This process is the *transitional dynamics* of the Solow–Swan model.

The Solow–Swan model explains the growth of output per worker as the effect of the transitional dynamics of the economy while it converges on its steady state equilibrium. When an economy which saves a constant proportion of its income starts out with little capital per worker, it will have a high rate of capital accumulation because saving will be large relative to the investment required to offset depreciation and the growth of the labor force. As the capital-labor ratio increases, saving per unit of capital decreases owing to the operation of diminishing returns, while the investment per unit of capital required to maintain the capital per worker in the face of depreciation and labor force growth remains constant.

There is no guarantee, however, that diminishing returns will be strong enough to extinguish growth in the capital-labor ratio. With the Cobb-Douglas production function the system will always converge to a steady state, because the marginal productivity of capital approaches zero as k approaches infinity. This assumption has already been incorporated into the figures above.

For other production functions, however, no such guarantee can be made. For example, if we merely add a linear term to the Cobb-Douglas function:

$$X = BK + AK^\alpha N^{1-\alpha}$$

then the marginal productivity of capital will approach the parameter B as k approaches infinity. If $sB - \delta > n$, diminishing returns will not be strong enough to shut down growth in the capital-labor ratio, which will continue asymptotically forever at the rate $sB - \delta - n$, with capital accumulating at the rate $g_K = sB - \delta$. Here we have an example of *endogenous growth*, where the long run growth rate is affected by changes in s. The last decade has seen a revival of interest in models of endogenous growth. The Classical conventional wage share model, for example, is an endogenous growth model.

Most extensions of the Solow–Swan model, however, assume that diminishing returns are strong enough to extinguish growth in capital per worker, so that a steady state exists. In this case, the rate of growth will converge on n, the exogenously given rate of population growth, regardless of the saving ratio s.

Problem 8.10 *Consider a Solow–Swan model with the production function $X = K + 1000K^{.2}N^{.8}, s = .15, \delta = .1/year$, and $n = .02/year$. Derive the equation for the rate of accumulation as a function of k, and graph it as in Figure 8.2. Add a line showing the growth rate of the labor force to your figure. Why won't this economy ever achieve a steady state?*

8.9   Limitations of the Solow–Swan Model

Two limitations of the Solow–Swan model deserve mention, one pertaining to its internal consistency and the other to its ability to explain features of real economic growth.

First, economists working in the Classical tradition have put forward serious criticisms of the concept of the one-sector production function as a basis for the explanation of growth in real economies. These criticisms were the issues in *Cambridge Capital Controversy* debates in the 1960s and early 1970s. The Classical critics of the Solow–Swan model argue that it cannot be generalized rigorously to economies that have more than one produced output, where the efficiency frontier may not be concave to the origin. We have seen this possibility arise in Chapter 3. The difficulty is that when the efficiency frontier is not concave to the origin, there may be more than one point at which its slope is equal to any given value of capital per worker, pk. In this case the accumulated capital per worker is not sufficient information to determine the technique in use, or the wage and profit rate as the Solow–Swan approach requires. There may be several techniques, and several levels of the wage and profit rate that are consistent with a given value of capital per worker.

The Classical critics of the Solow–Swan model argue that this problem arises because *capital* cannot be defined independently of *capital goods*, and have pointed out numerous logical contradictions, paradoxes, and inconsistencies that arise from trying to reason purely in terms of the value of capital in economies where capital takes the form of many different commodities. These problems were discovered through Piero Sraffa's work studying the properties of the efficiency frontier in a model that allows capital to consist of a multiplicity of commodities.

Second, the Solow–Swan model makes several specific strong empirical predictions that appear inconsistent with the historical record of capitalist economic growth. It predicts that the wage and profit rate should be equal to the marginal products of labor and capital, yet we have already seen evidence that contradicts this prediction. In Chapter 7, we saw that the Cobb-Douglas production function that appears to fit the OECD economies has a parameter α that is roughly twice as large as the observed profit share. The Solow–Swan model predicts that the profit share should be equal to α. The Solow–Swan model also predicts that growth in labor productivity and the capital-labor ratio should eventually fade out under the operation of the law of diminishing returns. We have seen in Chapter 2, however, that there has been scarcely any sign in Maddison's data of productivity growth dying out over the last two centuries. In Chapter 9, we will see how the Solow–Swan model proposes to solve both these empirical problems with the auxiliary assumption of some form of exogenous neutral technical change.

8.10 Suggested Readings

The basic neoclassical growth model is called the Solow-Swan model in honor of its simultaneous discovery by Solow [1956] and Swan [1956]. (The sociologist Robert K. Merton points out that such twin scientific discoveries are surprisingly common.) The Keynesian growth model to which Solow and Swan were responding is due to Roy Harrod [1942] and Evsey Domar [1946].

On the Golden Rule, see Phelps [1966]. The Solow-Swan model raises the issue of whether modern economies might be saving too much (called dynamic inefficiency), which researchers such as Abel et al. [1989] have found not to be the case.

Finally, Piero Sraffa's difficult but rewarding little book [Sraffa, 1960] is a milestone in the ongoing Classical critique of neoclassical economic theory.

Chapter 9

Technical Change
in the Neoclassical Model

9.1 Technical Change and
the Production Function

The Solow–Swan model presented in Chapter 8 predicts that if the production function has strongly diminishing marginal productivity of capital, the growth of output per worker will ultimately cease altogether as the economy reaches a steady state. Since no advanced capitalist country shows signs of having reached this plateau, the Solow–Swan model needs to be extended to explain the growth in per capita output at or near the steady state. This can be done by assuming the presence of exogenous technical change.

Growth models with technical change will not converge on a steady state unless the technical change is Harrod-neutral, or purely labor-augmenting, with no effect on the productivity of capital associated with each technique. Hicks neutral technical change, which presumes proportional capital- and labor-saving effects on each technique, plays an important role in empirical studies of productivity growth, but not in theoretical growth models because it is not consistent with the existence of a steady state.

Harrod-neutral technical change is illustrated in Figure 9.1, where one technique has been highlighted. The point representing the technique has been projected along the ray through the origin whose slope measures the productivity of capital, ρ, which Harrod-neutral change leaves unchanged. All the other techniques have been projected in the

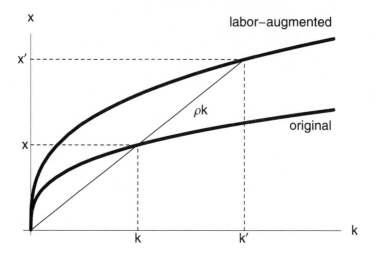

Figure 9.1: Harrod-neutral technical change with a smooth neoclassical production function.

same proportion. Hicks-neutral technical change, which preserves the capital-labor ratio for each technique, would project each point on the intensive production function vertically. Both types of neutral technical change shift the whole efficiency frontier to the northeast, since the frontier is made up of the growth-distribution schedules of all the techniques.

Harrod-neutral technical change in the Cobb-Douglas production function is described by the equation:

$$X = AK^{\alpha}((1 + \hat{\gamma})^t N)^{1-\alpha}$$

In the Cobb-Douglas case, Harrod-neutral technical change is also Hicks-neutral. We can see this since:

$$X = AK^{\alpha}((1 + \hat{\gamma})^t N)^{1-\alpha} = \left((1 + \hat{\gamma})^{1-\alpha}\right)^t (AK^{\alpha} N^{1-\alpha}).$$

This equivalence between Hicks and Harrod neutrality holds only for the Cobb-Douglas family of production functions.

As in Chapter 6, we will find it convenient to translate the Solow-Swan model with Harrod-neutral technical change into effective labor units. We continue to use a tilde ("~") over a variable when it is measured in effective labor terms. The mathematical form of the Solow–Swan model conveniently remains unchanged when we transform all the

per-worker variables to effective labor units. As in Chapter 6, in order
to recover variables such as x, w, and c in real labor units, we have
to multiply the effective labor variables by $(1 + \hat{\gamma})^t$. We can convert
growth rates from effective to real worker terms by adding $\hat{\gamma}$, as long
as the growth rates are small. For example, the growth rate of the real
capital intensity, k is given by $g_k \approx g_{\tilde{k}} + \hat{\gamma}$, and the growth rate of real
labor productivity by $g_x \approx g_{\tilde{x}} + \hat{\gamma}$. The *effective labor input*, $\tilde{N}$, is the
number of actual workers, N, multiplied by $(1+\hat{\gamma})^t$. The effective work-
force will therefore grow at a rate equal to $(\hat{\gamma} + n)$, which plays the role
of the natural rate of growth, n, in the basic model.

The intensive Cobb-Douglas production function with Harrod-neutral
technical change can be written as:

$$\tilde{x} = A\tilde{k}^\alpha$$

$$\rho(\tilde{k}) = A\tilde{k}^{\alpha-1}$$

The neoclassical model of neutral technical change differs conceptually from the Classical model with biased technical change. The neoclassical approach regards capital-labor substitution as a process of moving
along a static or timeless production function, while the Classical approach regards it a historical process of discovery of new techniques.
The neoclassical approach treats technical change as global in the sense
that it affects every technique, from the most to the least mechanized, in
exactly the same way. The Classical approach regards technical change
as a sequence of improvements, each slightly more capital intensive than
the last. Classical technical changes are localized since they have no
effect on old, less capital intensive fossil techniques. In Chapter 7, we
saw that some predictions of the Classical and neoclassical models of
capital-labor substitution could be tested against real economic data.
When the neoclassical theory is augmented to incorporate neutral technical change, however, it becomes difficult to devise a simple empirical
test of the two approaches.

Problem 9.1 *If the rate of Harrod-neutral technical change is 2% per
year, what is the rate of growth of the capital-labor ratio if the
ratio of capital per effective worker grows at 5% per year?*

Problem 9.2 *Suppose the production function is a Cobb-Douglas function with $A = 1000$ and $\alpha = 0.2$. If technical change is Harrod-
neutral at 2% per year and there is $14,000 per worker of capital
in the base year, find the value of output per effective worker and
per worker after two years, assuming that the capital stock grows
at the same rate as the labor force.*

9.2   The Solow–Swan Model with Harrod-Neutral Technical Change

If we retrace the steps we took in developing the equations for the Solow growth model by using the definitions for $\tilde{x}$ and $\tilde{k}$, we can derive the main equations for the Solow–Swan model with Harrod-neutral technical change. For example, substituting the definition for the growth rate of $\tilde{k}$ into the fundamental equation of the Solow growth model gives us the fundamental equation of a Solow growth model with Harrod-neutral technical change:

$$g_{\tilde{k}} = (s\rho - \delta) - (n + \hat{\gamma})$$

This looks just like the fundamental equation in the original Solow–Swan model, but with $(n + \hat{\gamma})$ replacing n. The similarity between these two fundamental equations suggests that it would be easy to extend most of the apparatus developed earlier, provided we redefine the variables in effective labor terms. As before, the fundamental equation predicts that the economy will converge on a steady state equilibrium $(\tilde{x}^*, \tilde{k}^*)$, as long as the production function exhibits a sufficiently diminishing marginal product of capital. The equilibrium effective capital intensity, $\tilde{k}^*$, and the equilibrium effective labor productivity, $\tilde{x}^*$, will be related by:

$$\tilde{k}^* = (\frac{s}{n + \hat{\gamma} + \delta})\tilde{x}^*$$

Specializing the Solow–Swan model to the Cobb-Douglas family of production functions lets us derive a closed-form solution for $\tilde{k}^*$ and $\tilde{x}^*$. Using the Cobb-Douglas function in effective labor terms, we find:

$$\tilde{k}^* = (\frac{sA}{n + \hat{\gamma} + \delta})^{\frac{1}{1-\alpha}}$$

$$\tilde{x}^* = A(\tilde{k}^*)^\alpha$$

This equilibrium is depicted in Figure 9.2, which shows that we can continue to use the same diagrammatic apparatus developed for the Solow–Swan model, provided we do our accounting in effective labor terms.

We know that in the steady state, output per effective worker, $\tilde{x}$, will be stationary. Output per worker, however, will be growing at the rate of technical change, $\hat{\gamma}$, since $g_x = g_{\tilde{x}} + \hat{\gamma}$. Similar reasoning shows that capital intensity also grows at the rate $\hat{\gamma}$. Output and capital expand at the natural rate of growth, $n + \hat{\gamma}$.

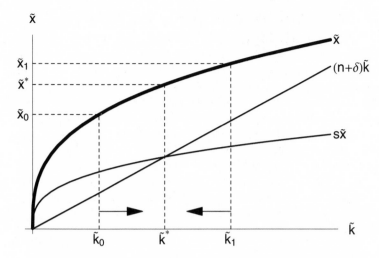

Figure 9.2: The Solow–Swan model with Harrod-neutral technical progress.

Problem 9.3 *Draw the growth-distribution schedules over two periods, t and $t+1$, for the technique that has been selected in the steady state equilibrium of the Solow model with neutral technical change. Identify the wage rate and profit rate, and growth rate and consumption per worker-year on the growth-distribution schedule in each year.*

Problem 9.4 *Let the Cobb-Douglas production function have $A = 1,000$ and $\alpha = .2$. Find the steady state values of $\tilde{x}, \tilde{k}$ and ρ when the saving propensity is 15%, depreciation, $\delta = 10\%/year$, the rate of population growth, $n = 1\%/year$, and the rate of Harrod-neutral technical change, $\hat{\gamma} = 2\%/year$.*

Problem 9.5 *In the economy described in Problem 9.4, what would be the growth rate of capital in the steady state? the capital-labor ratio?*

Problem 9.6 *If the economy described in Problem 9.4 began in its steady state in the base year, and remained there, what would be the value of output/worker after ten years?*

9.3   Growth Accounting

From the perspective of the neoclassical growth model, improvements
in living standards come about for two reasons: technical change and
increased capital per worker. Since economic policies to raise the level of
national savings operate through the latter channel, there is a need to develop an accounting system which separates these two sources of growth.
In general (no matter whether technical change is biased or neutral)
we can write the neoclassical production function as $X = F(K, N; T)$,
where technical change is represented as it occurs over time by the variable T. If we use the symbol F_K to represent the marginal product of
capital, F_N the marginal product of labor, and F_T the change in output
associated with a unit change in time owing to improved technology,
differencing this equation (and assuming $\Delta T = 1$) gives us:

$$\Delta X = F_K \Delta K + F_N \Delta N + F_T$$

Dividing both sides by X, and manipulating leads to:

$$\frac{\Delta X}{X} = \left(\frac{F_K K}{X}\right)\frac{\Delta K}{K} + \left(\frac{F_N N}{X}\right)\frac{\Delta N}{N} + \frac{F_T}{X}$$

or

$$g_X = \left(\frac{F_K K}{X}\right)g_K + \left(\frac{F_N N}{X}\right)g_N + \frac{F_T}{X} \tag{9.1}$$

The neoclassical theory assumes that the wage is equal to the marginal
productivity of labor, and the profit rate to the marginal productivity of
capital. Under this assumption, we can substitute the wage and profit
shares for the terms in brackets on the right hand side of this equation.
Since the wage and profit rate are observable from macroeconomic data,
while marginal products are not directly observable, this assumption
makes it operationally possible to decompose the growth of output into
a part due to the growth of resources (i.e., capital and labor) and a part
due purely to technical change. This decomposition, which is only possible under the neoclassical assumption of equality of factor prices and
marginal products, can be written:

$$g_X = \pi g_K + (1 - \pi)g_N + \frac{F_T}{X}$$

The first two terms on the right-hand side of this expression represent the part of output growth due to input growth, and the last term
represents the part of output growth due to technical change.

This method of allocating the sources of growth is often called *Solow decomposition*. The part of growth due to the increased availability of capital and human resources is easily understood. But the remainder, sometimes called the *Solow residual*, has been dubbed a "measure of our ignorance" because it is not clear how it is generated by economic activity. The Solow–Swan model attributes the part of output growth represented by the Solow residual to exogenous shifts in the production function, but the model has nothing to say about the origins of these shifts in economic reality.

Another concept of the residual associates it with *total factor productivity*, sometimes called *multi-factor productivity*. This is distinguished from *labor productivity* (X/N), because total factor productivity attempts to measure the output produced by a combination of *both* capital and labor inputs. Suppose that technical change takes the form of capital- and labor-augmenting technical change at rates $\hat{\chi}$ and $\hat{\gamma}$ respectively applied to an unchanging, constant returns to scale production function. Letting $\tilde{K}_t = (1 + \hat{\chi})^t K_t$ and $\tilde{N}_t = (1 + \hat{\gamma})^t N_t$ represent the effective capital and labor inputs, the production function can be written:

$$X_t = F(\tilde{K}, \tilde{N}) = F((1 + \hat{\chi})^t K, (1 + \hat{\gamma})^t N)$$

Applying equation (9.1) to this production function, we see that:

$$g_X = (\frac{F_{\tilde{K}}\tilde{K}}{X})g_{\tilde{K}} + (\frac{F_{\tilde{N}}\tilde{N}}{X})g_{\tilde{N}}$$

If we adopt the neoclassical assumption that the wage is equal to the marginal product of effective labor, and the profit rate equal to the marginal product of effective capital, we can express this decomposition in terms of the profit and wage shares:

$$g_X = \pi g_{\tilde{K}} + (1 - \pi)g_{\tilde{N}}$$

By definition, $g_{\tilde{K}} = g_K + \hat{\chi}$ and $g_{\tilde{N}} = g_N + \hat{\gamma}$, so that:

$$g_X = \pi g_K + (1 - \pi)g_N + \pi\hat{\chi} + (1 - \pi)\hat{\gamma}$$

In this decomposition the technical change term F_T/X appears as a weighted average of the rates of capital-augmenting and labor-augmenting technical change, $\pi\hat{\chi} + (1 - \pi)\hat{\gamma}$. But if we attempt to use this equation to measure technical change with macroeconomic data, the best we can

Table 9.1:
**Solow Decomposition of Four East Asian Economies,
1966-1990 (%/year)**

| | Country | | | |
	Hong Kong	Singapore	South Korea	Taiwan
g_X	7.3	8.7	10.3	8.9
g_K	8.0	11.5	13.7	12.3
g_N	3.2	5.7	6.4	4.9
$\pi g_K + (1 - \pi)g_N$	5.0	8.5	8.6	6.8
$\hat{\gamma}$	2.3	0.2	1.7	2.1
Memo item:				
$(1 - \pi)$ (%)	62.8	50.9	70.3	74.3

Source: Young [1995].

do is calculate the weighted average of capital- and labor-augmenting technical change:

$$\pi\hat{\chi} + (1 - \pi)\hat{\gamma} = g_X - (\pi g_K + (1 - \pi)g_N) \tag{9.2}$$

If we assume that technical change is Hicks-neutral, however, $\hat{\chi} = \hat{\gamma}$, so that $\pi\hat{\chi} + (1 - \pi)\hat{\gamma} = \hat{\gamma}$, and equation (9.2) becomes:

$$\hat{\gamma} = g_X - (\pi g_K + (1 - \pi)g_N) \tag{9.3}$$

Under the assumption of Hicks-neutral technical change, the total factor productivity approach becomes operational. Perhaps for this reason most studies of total factor productivity rely on the assumption of Hicks neutrality. If technical change is biased, on the other hand, it is not possible to measure total factor productivity unambiguously, because the residual determines only the weighted average of capital- and labor-augmenting rates of technical change.

Since the early 1980s the Bureau of Labor Statistics in the U.S. has compiled official statistics on multi-factor productivity based on the approach of equation (9.3).

This analytical framework has been used by Alwyn Young to investigate the growth of the celebrated "Four Dragons of East Asia," Hong Kong, Singapore, South Korea and Taiwan. Was their phenomenal growth from 1966 to 1990 due to an increase in the efficiency with which they used their resources (i.e., total factor productivity) or was it

Table 9.2:

Growth Decomposition of the U.S. Productivity Slowdown (%/year)

	1948-73	1973-90	Change
g_x	2.9	1.0	-1.9
g_k	2.8	2.4	-0.4
πg_k	0.9	0.7	-0.2
$\hat{\gamma}$	2.0	0.3	-1.7

Source: Bureau of Labor Statistics [1996].
Notes: Multifactor productivity growth is calculated according to the formula in the text, and differs slightly from the Bureau of Labor Statistics measure because the BLS also corrects for the skill composition of the labor force.

due to an increase in the resources themselves? Table 9.1 displays the Solow decomposition of data for these economies. Their GDP growth rates are extraordinary, ranging from 7.3 to 10.3% per year. But they also experienced very high rates of capital accumulation, from 8.0 to 13.7% per year, and growth in their labor forces. Thus, the Solow residual measuring total factor productivity growth is not nearly as large, which can be seen in the penultimate row. In fact, Young argues, the performance of these economies was not very different from the rest of the world when it is measured by total factor productivity.

We can also derive the following equation which decomposes the growth rate of labor productivity into a part attributable to increasing capital intensity, and a residual:

$$g_x = \pi g_k + \hat{\gamma} \tag{9.4}$$

This equation lets economists estimate the relative importance of technical change and capital deepening during selected historical periods. Table 9.2 shows data assembled by the Bureau of Labor Statistics for the non-farm private sector of the United States over the last four decades. Labor productivity growth declined abruptly after around 1973, from 2.9% per year to only 1.0%. But did this happen because of a shortage of capital formation or because of a slowing of technical progress? The rest of the table shows that while slower capital formation might have accounted for some of the observed productivity slowdown, the bulk was an exogenous decline in the rate of growth of total factor productivity.

The slowdown in productivity growth (which has also been observed in virtually every other country in the world for the period after around 1970) has been among the most intensively studied empirical phenomena in applied macroeconomics. The hypothesis that an exogenous decline in the rate of technical change accounts for most of the observed slowdown enjoys broad support. However, as technical change is not measured directly in growth accounting exercises but only as a residual, there is room for competing hypotheses.

Problem 9.7 *Use the data in Table 9.1 to determine what proportion of labor productivity growth in each country was caused by capital deepening.*

Problem 9.8 *Derive the formula for the Solow decomposition of labor productivity growth assuming that technical change is Harrod-neutral.*

9.4   Classical and Neoclassical Interpretations of the Residual

The Classical model dispenses with the need for a Solow residual to interpret macroeconomic data by attributing all the growth in labor productivity to technical change. In other words, the Classical model assumes that its technical change parameters, χ and γ, are identical to the measured increases in capital and labor productivity: $\chi = g_\rho$ and $\gamma = g_x$. In contrast, the neoclassical Hicks-neutral growth accounting scheme measures its technical change parameters, $\hat{\gamma}$ and $\hat{\chi}$, as $\hat{\gamma} = \hat{\chi} = g_x - \pi g_k$. From the Classical perspective, the Solow decomposition appears to be a device for explaining the discrepancy between the viability coefficient and the actual value of the profit share that we explored in Chapter 7.

We can see the relation between the Classical and neoclassical approaches by writing out the mathematical expression for total factor productivity growth as it would be measured by a neoclassical growth accountant in terms of the Classical parameters. Substituting for $g_x = \gamma$ and $g_k = (\gamma - \chi)/(1 + \chi)$ in equation (9.4), we have:

$$\hat{\gamma} = \gamma - \pi \frac{\gamma - \chi}{1 + \chi}$$

Multiplying through by $(1 + \chi)/(\gamma - \chi)$, we arrive at an expression connecting the viability condition to the Solow residual.

$$\gamma \frac{1+\chi}{\gamma - \chi} = \omega = \pi + \frac{1+\chi}{\gamma - \chi} \hat{\gamma} \qquad (9.5)$$

We can see from equation (9.5) that the Classical viability condition will *always* be an inequality, $(\omega > \pi)$, when there is a positive rate of total factor productivity growth, $\hat{\gamma}$, as measured by a neoclassical accountant. Conversely, when $(\omega > \pi)$, a neoclassical growth accountant will see an increase in total factor productivity. The neoclassical economist will thus be disinclined to take data showing $\omega > \pi$ as evidence that the wage is greater than the marginal product of labor. Instead, she will argue that some of the productivity growth used to calculate ω has been misclassified, and that when the viability condition is recalculated using the corrected values it will turn out to be satisfied as an equality. The Classical response is that the method for correcting the data— translating them into effective labor terms using the measured rate of technical change—is tautological since the accounting framework used to measure technical change rests on the assumption that the marginal productivity theory is true. Consequently, the Classical economist regards the Solow residual as an accounting device to explain the gap between the viability condition and actual profit shares.

9.5 Comparative Steady State Dynamics in the Solow–Swan Model

In analyzing the steady state of the Solow–Swan model with exogenous Harrod-neutral technical change, the endogenous variables are $\tilde{k}^*, \tilde{x}^*$, $v^*, \tilde{w}^*, g_K^*$, and $\tilde{c}^*$. The exogenous variables are the production function, $f(.), n, \hat{\gamma}, \delta$ and s. Comparative steady state analysis studies the question: what effect does a change in one of the exogenous variables have on the steady state endogenous variables? It does this by comparing the steady states before and after the change, either by working out the mathematical solution or by interpreting the relevant diagram. The equations for the steady state of the Solow–Swan model with Harrod-neutral technical change and a Cobb-Douglas production function are:

$$\tilde{k}^* = (\frac{sA}{n + \hat{\gamma} + \delta})^{\frac{1}{1-\alpha}}$$

$$\tilde{x}^* = A(\tilde{k}^*)^{\alpha}$$

$$\rho^* = A(\tilde{k}^*)^{\alpha - 1}$$

$$\tilde{w}^* = (1 - \alpha)\tilde{x}^*$$

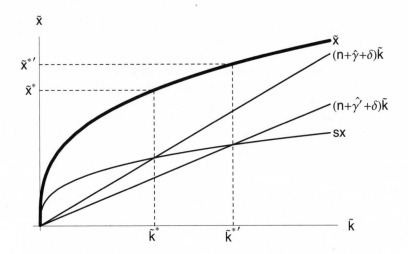

Figure 9.3: Productivity slowdown in the Solow–Swan model.

$$v^* = \alpha \rho^*$$

$$\tilde{c}^* = (1 - s)\tilde{x}^*$$

$$g_K{}^* = n + \hat{\gamma}$$

We saw earlier that a leading candidate to explain the decline in labor productivity growth in the U.S. (and other countries) after 1970 is a decline in the rate of labor-augmenting technical change. It is instructive to analyze the effects of a decline in the rate of technical change, $\hat{\gamma}$, on the steady state growth path of the Solow–Swan model.

In Figure 9.3 we have represented the old and new steady states associated with the old and new rates of technical change, $\hat{\gamma}$ and $\hat{\gamma}'$. Remember that the axes for this diagram are capital and output per effective worker. A reduced rate of Harrod-neutral technical change rotates the line representing required investment per effective worker downward. Thus, a lower $\hat{\gamma}$ will raise the steady state capital-effective labor ratio.

This increase in capital per effective worker will reduce the marginal product of capital and the profit rate, in conformity with the principle of diminishing marginal productivity. This change can also be visualized by means of the efficiency frontier for the economy. Figure 9.4 represents the efficiency frontier in effective labor terms.

We can see that the economy will be pushed up (to the northwest) along its efficiency frontier, and the effective wage will rise. This leads to

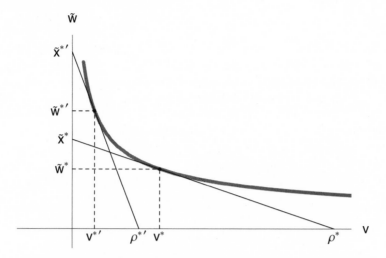

Figure 9.4: The steady state effective worker wage rises with a productivity slowdown.

the paradoxical situation that the wage received by each actual worker began to grow more slowly after 1970 (since it grows at the rate $\hat{\gamma}$), while the wage per effective worker must have increased. Similarly, output per worker grew more slowly after 1970, though output per effective worker increased. These conclusions underline the need to distinguish between comparative dynamics effects on the endogenous variables measured in effective and actual labor units.

Martin Neil Baily and Charles L. Schultze, Brookings Institution economists, have estimated a version of this model for the nonfarm business sector of the U.S. economy. They assume a production function slightly different from the Cobb-Douglas. Their main conclusions are presented in Table 9.3. As the model predicts, they found that the capital-effective labor ratio rose after 1973. They thus explain the decline in the net rate of profit during the 1970s and 1980s as the result of capital deepening. Furthermore, they note that the shares of income were very stable over this period, which from the neoclassical perspective implies an elasticity of substitution close to unity. The last column in the table shows the elasticity of substitution in each of the sub-periods, calculated by using the definition of σ given in Chapter 8. While there is some variation over time, these sub-period estimates average 1.1. Over the whole period the Cobb-Douglas production function, which has an elasticity of substitution equal to unity, would have fit the data to a close approximation.

Table 9.3:

The Effect of Slower Productivity Growth on the U.S. Economy

Year	$\tilde{k}$	π	r	σ
1948	1.00	0.684	0.136	—
1968	0.86	0.680	0.153	0.89
1973	0.92	0.702	0.136	0.40
1979	1.02	0.698	0.128	1.20
1987	1.13	0.686	0.123	1.91

Source: Baily and Schultze [1990].

Note: The elasticity of substitution has been calculated over each sub-interval, using the formula in Chapter 8.

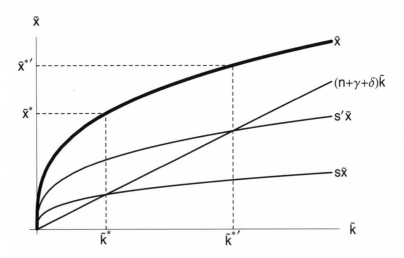

Figure 9.5: Effects of an increase in the saving rate on the steady state of the Solow–Swan model.

Policy makers in the U.S. have used the Solow–Swan model to evaluate proposals to reduce the government's budget deficit. Our model does not contain an explicit government sector, but one possible assumption is that an increase in government saving (i.e., reduction in the budget deficit) would raise the national saving rate. Analytically, an increase in the parameter s will shift up the savings function, as shown in Figure 9.5. The new steady state will therefore have more capital per effective worker and more capital per real worker. This increase in capital per worker will imply a higher level of output per worker. If the economy starts out below its Golden Rule capital-labor ratio, the increased productivity of labor will also permit more consumption per effective worker.

As in Chapter 8, an increase in the saving rate has no effect on the long run growth rate of the economy. During the transition to the new equilibrium, of course, there will be a temporary increase in capital accumulation and in output growth. However, at the new steady state, the growth rate of output will settle down to its natural rate, $(n + \hat{\gamma})$, and the growth rate of output per worker and capital per worker will return to the rate of technical progress, $\hat{\gamma}$.

In the 1994 Economic Report of the President, the Council of Economic Advisors calibrated the Solow–Swan model to fit the U.S. economy in an effort to estimate the long run benefits of reducing the budget deficit. They used a Cobb-Douglas production function with $\alpha = 1/3$: as we saw above, this is approximately the value of the profit share in the U.S. They assumed that $n + \hat{\gamma} = 2.5\%/\text{year}$, $\delta = 9\ \%/\text{year}$, and that the deficit-reduction package then being contemplated would raise the national saving rate from 13 to 14% of GDP. With these parameters, they calculate that it will take about 50 years to reach a new steady state. At the new steady state they predict that the capital stock (per effective worker) will increase by nearly 12% and that this increase will drive down the rate of profit by about 2 percentage points. It will also raise wages and productivity by about 3.75%, and consumption by more than 2.5 %. Estimates derived from implementations of the Solow–Swan model play an important role in policy debates.

Problem 9.9 *Analyze the effects of an increase in the rate of population growth on the steady state in the Solow–Swan model with Harrod-neutral technical change. Explain your results in terms of both the figure and the equations representing the model.*

Problem 9.10 *Use the figures given in the text to check the calculations of the Council of Economic Advisors. Assume that the scale parameter in the production function, $A = 750$, the rate of* population growth $n = 1.5\%/year$ and the rate of Harrod-neutral technical change $\hat{\gamma} = 1\%/year$. Calculate the old and new values of $\tilde{k}^*, \tilde{x}^*$ and $\tilde{c}^*$.

Problem 9.11 *Assuming it takes 50 years to reach the new equilibrium, by how much will the increase in national savings considered by the Council of Economic Advisors succeed in raising consumption/worker (not /effective worker)?*

Problem 9.12 *Calculate the profit rate before and after the increase in national saving using the same Council of Economic Advisors assumptions.*

9.6   Transitional Dynamics in the Solow–Swan Model

The fact that the Council of Economic Advisors predicts that it would take fifty years to reach a new steady state after a major change in the national saving rate underlines the importance of transitional dynamics in the Solow growth model. An economy that is not in its steady state can undergo a lengthy process of adjustment during the transition to a new steady state. Is it possible that the enormous disparities in levels of development of economies we observe in the world could be the result of such long processes of adjustment? If this were true, economic growth would gradually equalize levels of development through a process of *convergence.*

A tendency for countries to converge on the same level of labor productivity is called *absolute convergence.* Absolute convergence implies that economies that are farther behind the leader will have faster labor productivity growth. We have seen in Chapter 7 that there is evidence for absolute convergence among already advanced economies, but not for all economies. Large differences in the growth rates of output and productivity among some economies persist over time. If these economies are assumed to be on their individual steady state growth paths, then differences in rates of labor productivity growth can be explained within the Solow–Swan model only by differences in the exogenous rate of technical change. But the model itself does not explain the exogenous rate of technical change, so the persistence of differences in rates of labor productivity growth among economies is a challenge to the neoclassical model. One way the neoclassical model can be defended is to assume that most countries are undergoing a process of adjustment toward their long run steady states, and to attribute differences in rates of labor productivity growth to capital deepening.

In this context, the Solow–Swan model makes three predictions about economic growth. First, it predicts that among economies that share access to the same technology, have similar population growth and similar saving behavior, there will be a tendency for productivity to converge over long enough periods of time. This would explain the prevalence of absolute convergence among the advanced economies.

Second, the neoclassical model predicts that among economies that share access to the same technology but have different population growth rates and saving behaviors, there will still be a tendency for economies that are far behind to grow faster, but only after controlling for these differences in population growth and saving. This tendency is called *conditional convergence.* Economies tend to grow faster the farther they are from their *own* steady state. There is now widespread agreement that conditional convergence prevails at the global level, although its meaning remains open to alternative interpretations. The conditional convergence interpretation makes the Solow–Swan model consistent with the failure of absolute convergence to prevail globally. Thus, economic data can be regarded as qualitatively consistent with the predictions of the Solow–Swan model with respect to absolute and conditional convergence.

Third, the Solow–Swan model makes specific predictions about the *speed* of convergence, which can be checked against the empirical experience of actual economies. Most recent studies suggest that convergence among real capitalist economies is slower than the Solow–Swan model predicts it should be. In this respect, the predictions of the Solow–Swan model, at least in its basic form, are quantitatively inconsistent with economic data.

When the Solow–Swan economy reaches its steady state, output and capital per worker grow at the rate of technical change, $\hat{\gamma}$. But when the economy lies below its steady state level of capital intensity, the capital stock will grow faster than the labor force. The fundamental equation of the Solow–Swan model describes this rate of accumulation. With a Cobb-Douglas production function, the fundamental equation (in effective labor terms) is:

$$g_{\tilde{k}} = sA\tilde{k}^{\alpha-1} - (n + \hat{\gamma} + \delta)$$

This equation shows that the growth rate of capital per effective worker will be higher the less capital there is per effective worker (since α is less than 1). This higher rate of capital accumulation owes its existence to diminishing marginal productivity of capital, which makes the level of output per effective worker higher when there is less capital per worker.

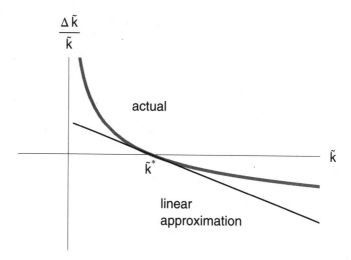

Figure 9.6: The linear approximation to the fundamental equation near the steady state.

If two economies share similar values of the parameters $s, n, \hat{\gamma}$, and δ, it follows that the poorer country (with the lower level of capital per worker) will grow faster, illustrating how absolute convergence works. This same equation shows that a poor country may not grow faster than a rich country if the poor country has a low enough saving rate or a high enough rate of population growth, illustrating how conditional convergence works.

If we had data on output and capital per worker for a large number of economies, we might be able to estimate the fundamental equation. In its present nonlinear form, however, it is a difficult equation to estimate so economists use a linear approximation that is regarded as reasonably accurate if economies are close enough to their steady state positions. The approximation is based on the mathematical technique of taking a first-order Taylor expansion of the fundamental equation around the steady state value of $\tilde{k}$ as illustrated in Figure 9.6. This figure shows the actual shape of the fundamental equation, and the linear approximation that provides a good fit for points near the steady state position.

In most applications, economists find it easier to work with a linear approximation of a version of the fundamental equation that is expressed in terms of the logarithm of output per effective worker. The details of the derivation are left to the Appendix. The logarithmic output convergence equation for the Solow growth model is:

$$\Delta \ln(\tilde{x}) = \phi(\ln(\tilde{x}^*) - \ln(\tilde{x}))$$

where

$$\phi = (n + \hat{\gamma} + \delta)(1 - \alpha)$$

There is now a large econometric literature estimating this convergence equation, and the value of ϕ is generally estimated to be near .02, which is too low to be consistent with observed profit shares of $1/4$ to $1/3$. For example, if we take the commonly used values $n = .02$, $\hat{\gamma} = .02$, and $\delta = .03$, we will find that $\phi = .02$ implies that $\alpha = .71$. Since the marginal productivity theory of distribution predicts that the profit share should be equal to α, there is a conflict between the neoclassical predicted and actual profit shares.

Some neoclassical economists, notably Gregory Mankiw, David Romer, and David Weil, explain this conflict by arguing that the relevant concept of capital in the Solow–Swan model needs to be broadened to include human capital as well as physical capital. They interpret the share of profits implied by the convergence coefficient to include both profits as normally understood and the returns to education. These returns show up in the higher wages that more skilled workers are able to earn. This would imply that about half the wages of workers are really returns to human capital. Under this hypothesis only about $1/3$ of the national income takes the form of labor income per se, while $1/3$ represents the return to human capital, and $1/3$ represents the return to physical capital. The Cobb-Douglas production function consistent with this hypothesis would add human capital, H, to the other two inputs, taking the form $X = AK^{1/3}N^{1/3}H^{1/3}$.

This effort to rescue the Solow–Swan model remains controversial. There is little dispute that education, particularly primary and secondary schooling, plays an important role in the growth process. The neoclassical interpretation is that the intellectual skills produced by education are a form of capital, so that increases in the amount of skill directly produce increases in output. The alternative interpretation coming from the technology gap literature is that intellectually skilled workers facilitate the transfer of technology, which speeds up the catching-up process. This suggests that a high level (rather than a high growth rate) of intellectual skills is associated with increases in output. If the alternative interpretation is correct, the conflict between the predicted and actual profit share may not be so easily resolved.

Problem 9.13 *Find the approximate rate of growth of labor productivity for an economy whose current level of labor productivity is 3/4 of its steady state value under the assumptions that the rate of Harrod-neutral technical change is 1%/year, the depreciation rate is 4%/year, population grows 2%/year, and the gross profit share is 1/3.*

Problem 9.14 *If population growth is 2%/year, Harrod-neutral technical change is 1%/year, and the depreciation rate is 4%/year, find the implicit gross profit share for a convergence coefficient $\phi = .02$.*

Problem 9.15 *If the gross profit share were 1/3, what should be the value of the convergence coefficient in Problem 9.14?*

9.7   Suggested Readings

The Solow decomposition appears in Solow [1957]. Opinion about the size of the residual ranges from Denison [1967] to Jorgenson [1995], with the latter arguing that more careful measurement reduces the residual considerably. A critical review of the whole growth accounting approach is given by Nelson [1973, 1981]. For the New Growth Theory approach, see Romer [1987a].

A modern defense of the extended Solow-Swan model appears in Mankiw [1995] and the article mentioned in the text, Mankiw et al. [1992]. While a full evaluation of this empirical work awaits completion, some important papers have already appeared. Cho and Graham [1996] point out that the Mankiw, Romer, Weil results carry the questionable implication that about half the world's countries, all of them poor, are converging on their own steady states *from above*. Benhabib and Spiegel [1994] find that intellectual skills do not affect growth significantly when treated as a form of capital (contradicting Mankiw, Romer, and Weil) but that they do affect growth through the transfer of technology discussed in the text. Finally, Islam [1995] supports the original findings, but only when each country is assumed to have a unique level of total factor productivity that remains outside the scope of the Solow-Swan model. For two different perspectives on intellectually skilled labor, consult Becker [1964] for the traditional treatment of human capital as an ordinary input and Nelson and Phelps [1966] for the idea that intellectually skilled labor chiefly facilitates the transfer of technology

The two sources cited in this chapter which apply the Solow-Swan model are Young [1995] and Baily and Schultze [1990].

Appendix: Deriving the Convergence Equation

First, using the fact that $g_k = \Delta k / k$, rearrange the fundamental equation as follows:

$$\Delta \tilde{k} = sf(\tilde{k}) - (n + \hat{\gamma} + \delta)\tilde{k}$$

Next, take a first-order Taylor expansion of the right hand side of this equation, around the steady state value of $\tilde{k}$:

$$\Delta \tilde{k} \approx sf'(\tilde{k}^*) - (n + \hat{\gamma} + \delta)(\tilde{k} - \tilde{k}^*)$$

At the steady state $s = (n + \hat{\gamma} + \delta)(\tilde{k}/\tilde{x})$, so that we can write:

$$\Delta \tilde{k} \approx \left(\frac{f'(\tilde{k}^*)\tilde{k}^*}{\tilde{x}^*} - 1 \right)(n + \hat{\gamma} + \delta)(\tilde{k} - \tilde{k}^*)$$

According to the neoclassical theory of distribution, the profit rate is equal to the marginal product of effective capital, $v = f'(\tilde{k}^*)$, and $f'(\tilde{k}^*)\tilde{k}^*/\tilde{x}^*$ is equal to the profit share, π. Now define $\phi \equiv (1 - \pi)(n + \hat{\gamma} + \delta)$ and collect terms to get:

$$\frac{\Delta \tilde{k}}{\tilde{k}} = \phi(\frac{\tilde{k}^*}{\tilde{k}} - 1)$$

Using the fact that $(\frac{\tilde{k}^*}{\tilde{k}} - 1) \approx \ln(\frac{\tilde{k}^*}{\tilde{k}})$ when $\tilde{k}$ is close to $\tilde{k}^*$, we can write this equation in the form of a convergence equation for effective capital intensity, $\tilde{k}$:

$$\frac{\Delta \tilde{k}}{\tilde{k}} \approx \phi \ln(\frac{\tilde{k}^*}{\tilde{k}})$$

If we assume a Cobb-Douglas production function, for simplicity::

$$\frac{\Delta \tilde{x}}{\tilde{x}} = \alpha \frac{\Delta \tilde{k}}{\tilde{k}}$$

$$\ln(\frac{\tilde{x}^*}{\tilde{x}}) = \alpha \ln(\frac{\tilde{k}^*}{\tilde{k}})$$

Substituting these expressions into the effective capital intensity convergence equation gives us a convergence equation in terms of effective labor productivity:

$$\frac{\Delta \tilde{x}}{\tilde{x}} = \phi \ln(\frac{\tilde{x}^*}{\tilde{x}}) = \phi(\ln(\tilde{x}^*) - \ln(\tilde{x}))$$

(It can be shown that this convergence equation holds for any constant returns to scale production function.)

Chapter 10

Investment Constrained Economic Growth

10.1 Saving, Investment, and Output

Entrepreneurs play a limited and passive role in the Classical and neo-classical models: their only functions are to translate capitalist saving decisions into investment, and to choose the profit-maximizing technique of production. Keynesian economic theory, however, insists on the importance of the distinction between decisions to save, taken by the capitalist wealth holder, and decisions to invest, taken by entrepreneurs. *Investment* in this context refers to decisions to purchase new capital goods, while *saving* refers to decisions to refrain from consuming a portion of income. Entrepreneurs' decisions to invest can play a pivotal role in determining the actual growth path of an economy. The Classical and neoclassical models implicitly abstract from this distinction by assuming that all savings are automatically invested in real capital.

In real capitalist economies, the relation between saving and investment is more complicated. Savers generally accumulate financial assets, such as money, stock certificates issued by firms, or bank deposits, which can provide potential financing for real investment, but are not directly purchases of real capital goods. To take the simplest example, households in a monetary economy can save by hoarding money, without any corresponding increase in the purchase of capital goods. In real economies the decisions of savers and entrepreneurs' decisions to invest are linked by complex financial mechanisms.

Keynes argued that, at least in the short run, it is the level of output that adjusts in order to equalize planned investment and saving. Changes in the short run level of output change the degree of *capacity utilization* of the economy. The "Keynesian cross" diagram found in most macroeconomics textbooks describes the multiplier process through which levels of output change to generate the saving required to match any level of planned investment.

Keynesian models of economic growth build on these insights. Like the Classical models, Keynesian growth models do not view growth as constrained by the availability of labor. When a Keynesian economy is operating at less than full capacity utilization, the existing capital stock cannot constrain output, either. In the Keynesian tradition the willingness of entrepreneurs to invest is the key constraint on output and the growth of capital.

Investment constrained growth models lead to two characteristic conclusions that appear paradoxical from a Classical or neoclassical perspective. The *paradox of thrift* shows that an increase in the propensity to save, holding the willingness to invest constant, results in slower growth of capital at lower levels of capacity utilization, because it reduces the demand for consumption goods. The paradox of thrift is at odds with the Classical conventional wage share model, in which an increase in the capitalists' propensity to save raises the rate of growth of capital. The *paradox of costs* shows that an increase in the wage, holding the willingness to invest constant, will increase capacity utilization (and perhaps the growth of capital), because it increases the demand for wage goods (consumption goods for workers). The paradox of costs is also at odds with the Classical conventional wage share model, which predicts that a rise in the wage, by lowering the profit rate, will reduce the growth rate through the Cambridge equation.

10.2 A Model of Investment Constrained Growth

We will develop a model of investment constrained growth in the Keynesian tradition keeping as close as possible to the familiar elements of the Classical conventional wage share model.

First, we continue to assume that capitalists save a constant fraction, β, of their end of period wealth. The Cambridge equation therefore continues to describe the accumulation of wealth. Since capitalists own the firms operated by entrepreneurs, they receive the profits that are distributed, in the form of monetary dividends or interest payments. We will use the superscript s to identify the growth rate of the capitalist's financial wealth:

$$1 + g_K^s = \beta(1 + r) = \beta(1 + v - \delta), \text{ or} \qquad (10.1)$$

$$g_K^s + \delta = \beta v - (1 - \beta)(1 - \delta)$$

The hallmark of a Keynesian model is the introduction of independent entrepreneurial decisions to invest. An investment equation proposed by Joan Robinson relates entrepreneurs' target rate of growth of capital to the expected rate of profit. The central idea is that if entrepreneurs expect a higher rate of profit, their *animal spirits* will be excited and they will be willing to take more gambles on investment projects whose uncertain returns lie far in the future.

This theory can be represented mathematically by an equation relating the target rate of growth of capital, g_K^i, to the actual rate of profit, v. We must be careful about the interpretation of the rate of profit in this equation. Robinson argued that the actual rate of profit would provide entrepreneurs with a forecast about the future only if it persisted at a stable level for some time. Thus, the Robinsonian investment equation is not meant to be true instantaneously, but only after the economy has been in a stable position for some time, so that the actual rate of profit accurately reflects the expected rate of profit. We write Robinson's investment equation $g_K^i + \delta$ proportional to v:

$$g_K^i + \delta = \eta v \qquad (10.2)$$

In this equation the parameter η (the Greek letter *eta*, pronounced "ay'-ta") represents the propensity to invest out of profits, the animal spirits of the entrepreneurs. If you have difficulty visualizing exactly how entrepreneurs formulate the investment decisions described by (10.2), you can take some comfort from the fact that Keynes himself regarded this decision as inherently resistant to economic theorizing or modeling.

In equilibrium, the actual rate of growth of the capital stock must be consistent both with entrepreneurs' investment plans and capitalists' saving plans:

$$g_K^i = g_K^s (= g_K) \qquad (10.3)$$

When we add equations such as (10.2) and (10.3) to the Classical conventional wage share model, we face the problem of *overdetermination*: since we have added two equations and only one additional endogenous variable (g_K^i, since g_K^s takes the place of g_K), we have too many equations for the number of endogenous variables. In order to avoid this dilemma, we have to add another variable as well.

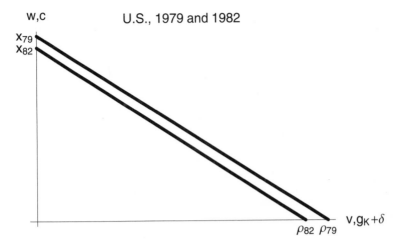

Figure 10.1: When the U.S. economy experienced a serious recession in the early 1980s, capacity utilization declined. The U.S. growth-distribution schedules for 1979 and 1982 illustrate the tendency for ρ and x to decline proportionately.

There is a natural resolution to this problem, which is to recognize that a Keynesian economy operates with some *excess capacity*, and add the *rate of capacity utilization*, u, to the list of endogenous variables. The rate of capacity utilization is a positive fraction between 0 and 1, indicating how much of the economy's productive potential is being realized.

The impact of changes in capacity utilization on the growth-distribution schedule depends on how entrepreneurs adjust inputs of labor and capital to fluctuations in demand. In periods of recession in real advanced capitalist economies, both labor and capital productivity fall close to proportionately. Figure 10.1, for example, shows the growth-distribution schedule for the U.S. in 1979, when capacity utilization was high, and in the recession year 1982, when capacity utilization was low. In other words, while entrepreneurs do not reduce their inputs of either labor or capital proportionately to the reduction in output, they do allow utilization of both labor and capital to decline in roughly the same proportions. Thus we will assume that measured labor and capital productivity are ux and $u\rho$ when the level of capacity utilization is u. As a result, capital intensity, $k = ux/u\rho$, the slope of the growth-distribution schedule, will not change as u varies.

As in the Classical conventional wage share model, we assume that labor will be elastically supplied at a conventional wage share. Because money and a well-developed financial system lie in the background of the Keynesian model, we should think of workers being paid in money and purchasing wage goods at the prevailing price level. Prices must adjust to changes in money wages to keep the wage share in income constant:

$$w = (1 - \bar{\pi})ux \tag{10.4}$$

When the rate of capacity utilization is less than 1, the real wage-profit rate equation and the social consumption-growth rate equation depend on the *actual* productivities of labor and capital, ux and $u\rho$, rather than on their potential productivities at full utilization, x and ρ. The slope of the growth-distribution schedule continues to be $-k$.

$$w = ux - vk = x\left(u - \frac{v}{\rho}\right) \tag{10.5}$$

$$c = ux - (g_K + \delta)k = x\left(u - \frac{g_K + \delta}{\rho}\right) \tag{10.6}$$

The growth-distribution schedule for the investment constrained Keynesian economy is illustrated in Figure 10.2 for a given rate of utilization, u. This needs to be distinguished from the *full capacity growth-distribution schedule* that applies only when $u = 1$. As long as utilization is below full capacity, the actual growth-distribution schedule lies inside the full capacity growth-distribution schedule. Changes in capacity utilization in this model are input-using, like Hicks-neutral technical change. Most of our attention will focus on the real wage and profit rate, so let us focus on equation (10.5), which describes the *actual real wage-profit rate schedule*.

Along the full capacity real wage-profit rate schedule, an increase in the profit rate is always associated with a decrease in the wage. But when the economy is below full capacity, an increase in the rate of capacity utilization creates the possibility (which did not exist before) of an increase in the profit rate with no change in the wage, or of an increase in the real wage with no change in the profit rate, because it shifts the actual growth-distribution schedule outward. It is even possible for the wage and profit rate to increase simultaneously when the rate of utilization rises.

The actual profit rate is the product of the rate of capacity utilization, the profit share and potential capital productivity according to equation (10.5).

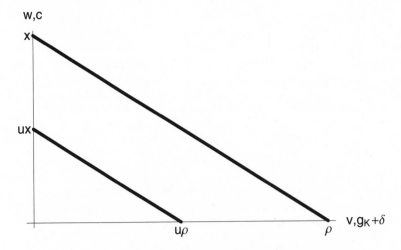

Figure 10.2: When capacity utilization is lower than 1, the growth-distribution schedule shifts inward parallel to itself, so that actual labor and capital productivity, ux and $u\rho$, fall proportionately, while capital intensity, k, remains constant.

$$v = \pi \rho u \tag{10.7}$$

We can substitute this into the investment equation, (10.2):

$$g_K^i = \eta u \pi \rho \tag{10.8}$$

Thus, the investment constrained model assumes that entrepreneurs forecast the rate of profit on the basis of the prevailing rate of capacity utilization and wage share.

Problem 10.1 *Kaldoria is an economy similar to Industria (see Problem 2.2), with $x = \$50,000/wkr\text{-}yr$, $k = \$150,000/wkr$, and $\delta = 1/15 = .0666 = 6.66\%$. The wage share in Kaldoria is 60%. Find labor productivity, capital productivity, and the profit rate when $u = 100\%$ and when $u = 85\%$.*

Problem 10.2 *Graph on the same diagram the full capacity growth and distribution schedule for Kaldoria and the actual growth and distribution schedule at 85% utilization. Identify the points on both schedules when the wage share is 60%.*

Table 10.1:

The Investment Constrained Model

Endogenous variables: u, v, w, g_K^i, g_K^s, c

Exogenous parameters: $k, x, \delta, \beta, \bar{\pi}, \eta$

$$w = ux - vk \tag{10.5}$$

$$c = ux - (g_K + \delta)k \tag{10.6}$$

$$g_K^s + \delta = \beta v - (1 - \beta)(1 - \delta) = \beta(1 + v - \delta) - (1 - \delta) \tag{10.1}$$

$$g_K^i + \delta = \eta v \tag{10.2}$$

$$g_K^s = g_K^i (= g_K) \tag{10.3}$$

$$w = (1 - \bar{\pi})ux \tag{10.4}$$

10.3 Equilibrium in the Investment Constrained Model

The six equations of the investment constrained model exactly determine the six endogenous variables, u, v, w, g_K^s, g_K^i, and c. The whole system is shown in Table 10.1. We will focus first on the sub-system of equations (10.1), (10.2), and (10.3). These equations can be solved for the equilibrium rate of profit, v:

$$v = \frac{(1-\beta)(1-\delta)}{\beta - \eta} \tag{10.9}$$

In order to avoid negative profit rates, we must assume that $\beta > \eta$. Once we have calculated the equilibrium profit rate, it is straightforward to find the equilibrium values of the other endogenous variables.

From equation (10.7) we can see that the equilibrium level of capacity utilization is just:

$$u = \frac{v}{\pi\rho} \tag{10.10}$$

The equilibrium level of the wage is then:

$$w = (1 - \bar{\pi})ux \tag{10.11}$$

From equation (10.2), we see that the equilibrium rate of growth of capital is:

$$g_K = \eta v \tag{10.12}$$

Finally, we can calculate the equilibrium level of social consumption per worker, c:

$$c = ux - (g_K + \delta)k = x(u(1 - \eta\pi) - \frac{\delta}{\rho}) \tag{10.13}$$

When the Cambridge equation and the Robinson investment function are plotted together, as in Figure 10.3, we see that when $\beta > \eta$ they determine a unique equilibrium level of the profit rate, and hence of capacity utilization. At profit rates below the equilibrium level, capitalists save too little to finance entrepreneurs' investment plans: the resulting excess demand will raise the capacity utilization rate and hence the profit rate. At profit rates above the equilibrium level, capitalist saving exceeds entrepreneurial investment, creating excess supply that will drive down the capacity utilization and profit rates. Thus this unique equilibrium is also stable when $\beta > \eta$.

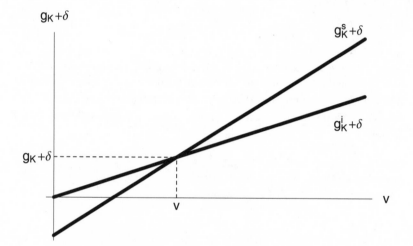

Figure 10.3: For each rate of profit the Cambridge equation determines the growth rate of capital consistent with capitalists' saving plans, and the Robinson investment function determines the growth rate of capital consistent with entrepreneurs' investment plans. Since the Cambridge equation has a lower intercept and higher slope than the Robinson investment function, under the assumption that $\beta > \eta$, there is a unique equilibrium level of the profit rate, v, and the gross growth rate of capital, $g_K + \delta$. The equilibrium capacity utilization rate is then $u = v/\pi\rho$.

Problem 10.3 *Entrepreneurs in Kaldoria (see Problem 10.1) have a Robinsonian investment function with $\eta = .7$. What is their desired gross rate of capital accumulation, $g_K^i + \delta$, when the rate of utilization, u, is .9?*

Problem 10.4 *Capitalist households in Kaldoria (see Problem 10.1) have a propensity to save out of wealth $\beta = .97$. What is their desired gross rate of wealth accumulation, $g_K^s + \delta$, when the rate of utilization, u, is .9?*

Problem 10.5 *If the entrepreneurs had expected the rate of utilization to be .7, and invested on the basis of the corresponding profit rate, what utilization rate would the Kaldorian economy achieve? Would the entrepreneurs find that they had chosen the right amount of investment? How will they respond?*

Problem 10.6 *Calculate the equilibrium rate of utilization, gross rate of growth of capital and rate of profit in Kaldoria.*

Problem 10.7 *Graph the saving and investment equations for Kaldoria, and identify the equilibrium. Where on your graph does the economy lie in Problem 10.3? Discuss the dynamics in this position.*

10.4 Comparative Dynamics in the Investment Constrained model

The investment constrained model gives rise to three comparative dynamic results which are characteristic of Keynesian models, but appear paradoxical from the point of view of the Classical or neoclassical tradition. First, there is a *paradox of thrift* in the investment constrained model. When the saving rate, β, increases, holding the investment propensity, η, constant, it shifts and rotates the savings schedule, equation (10.1), upward. The new equilibrium occurs at lower rates of profit, utilization and gross capital growth, as Figure 10.4 shows.

This paradox of thrift contrasts sharply with both the Classical and neoclassical theories, in which increases in saving generally increase growth, even if only in the short run. In the Keynesian model, in which investment demand can be held constant, less capitalist consumption leads to insufficient demand to maintain the original rate of utilization. The reduced rate of profit that results will induce less growth. Perhaps nothing illustrates the nature of an investment constrained economic system better than the paradox of thrift. It is easy to see why economists

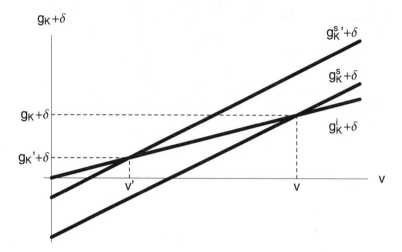

Figure 10.4: The paradox of thrift. When β rises, the savings schedule shifts and rotates upward, cutting the unchanged investment schedule at a lower rate of profit, v, and hence lower rates of capacity utilization and gross capital growth.

who view growth as investment constrained rarely join campaigns to raise national saving rates.

A second distinctive feature of Keynesian models is the *paradox of costs*. An increase in the conventional wage share, holding constant the investment propensity, has a positive effect on the rate of capacity utilization and level of output, despite the fact that each individual capitalist perceives it as increasing her costs. An increase in the conventional wage share lowers the profit share, π, but leaves the equilibrium rates of profit, $v = (1 - \beta)(1 - \delta)/(\beta - \eta)$, and gross growth of capital, $g_K + \delta = \eta v$, unchanged in Figure 10.3. But the equilibrium rate of capacity utilization, $u = v/\pi\rho$ rises with a fall in π.

When the wage share increases, the redistribution of income from capitalists to workers reduces the rate of growth of financial wealth, since workers consume all their income. Thus, a wage share increase reduces overall saving and raises effective demand at each rate of capacity utilization. As a result, the rate of capacity utilization rises to generate the savings needed to finance investment. In its emphasis on the adjustment of capacity utilization to accommodate an unchanging propensity to invest, the paradox of costs bears a noticeable family resemblance to the paradox of thrift.

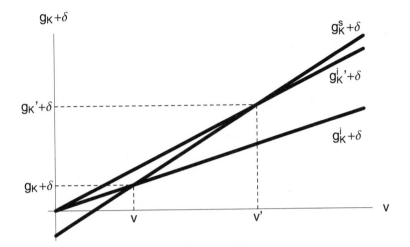

Figure 10.5: The Widow's Cruse. An increase in the entrepreneurial propensity to invest, η, rotates the investment schedule upward to intersect the unchanged saving schedule at a higher rate of profit, v, and gross growth rate of capital, $g_K + \delta$. The higher profits and saving are made possible by an increase in capacity utilization, $u = v/\pi\rho$.

The third characteristic comparative dynamics result in the investment constrained model arises from considering the impact of a rise in η, the propensity to invest. Keynes called the outcome of this experiment the *Widow's Cruse*. If entrepreneurs decide to spend more on investment, they will find that once they begin spending, the profits to finance the expenditure miraculously appear, just as in the Biblical tale of the widow whose jar (cruse) of oil would miraculously refill whenever it was drawn down. For example, a surge in animal spirits, represented by an upward shift in η, will rotate the investment schedule, equation (10.2) upward, increasing the rates of profit, gross growth of capital, and capacity utilization to provide entrepreneurs with enough capitalist saving to finance their projects, as Figure 10.5 shows. The equilibrium rate of profit, $v = (1-\beta)(1-\delta)/(\beta-\eta)$, rises with an increase in η, and the rate of capacity utilization, $u = v/\pi\rho$ and the gross growth rate of capital, $g_K + \delta = \eta v$, follow suit. The ability of entrepreneurs to invest profits before they have earned them in the Keynesian analysis relies critically on the existence of a financial system in the background that can advance funds to the entrepreneurs.

Problem 10.8 *Suppose the saving propensity in Kaldoria increased from .97 to .98. What are the new equilibrium rates of profit, gross growth of capital, and capacity utilization? Would an increased rate of saving benefit the Kaldorian economy?*

Problem 10.9 *Suppose the saving propensity in Kaldoria remained at .97, but the wage share increased to 65%. What are the new equilibrium rates of profit, gross growth of capital, and capacity utilization? Would an increased wage share benefit the Kaldorian economy?*

Problem 10.10 *Calculate social consumption per worker before and after the increase in the wage share in Problem 10.9. How has this change been divided between capitalists' consumption and workers' consumption?*

Problem 10.11 *Graph the real wage-profit rate and social consumption-growth rate schedules for Kaldoria before and after the wage share increases from 60% to 65%. Find the equilibrium wage-profit rate and social consumption-growth rate points on your graph before and after the change (four points in all).*

10.5   Profit-Led or Wage-Led Growth?

The Robinsonian investment function makes the entrepreneurs' target gross rate of investment, $g_K^i + \delta$, proportional to the profit rate, v. But the profit rate is itself the product of the profit share, π, the capacity utilization rate, u, and the productivity of capital, ρ. One way to generalize Robinson's idea, proposed by Stephen Marglin and Amit Bhaduri, is to allow each of these factors to have an independent influence on investment plans. The simplest way to do this is to make planned gross investment a linear function of the three components of the profit rate:

$$g_K^i + \delta = \eta_u u + \eta_\pi \pi + \eta_\rho \rho \tag{10.14}$$

Here $\eta_u > 0$ represents the impact of capacity utilization on investment plans, and analogously for $\eta_\pi > 0$ and $\eta_\rho > 0$.

This generalization adds some intriguing insights to the investment constrained model. The equilibrium of the generalized investment constrained model requires saving and investment plans to be consistent, which implies a level of capacity utilization:

$$u = \frac{\eta_\pi \pi + \eta_\rho \rho + (1 - \beta)(1 - \delta)}{\beta \pi \rho - \eta_u} \tag{10.15}$$

To keep the rate of capacity utilization positive, we must assume that $\beta\pi\rho > \eta_u$. This condition is analogous to the condition $\beta > \eta$ in the basic model, and implies that saving rises faster than investment as capacity utilization increases, which ensures the stability of the equilibrium.

As in the simpler version of the investment constrained model, the profit rate is proportional to the capacity utilization rate:

$$v = \pi\rho u \tag{10.16}$$

The gross rate of growth of capital can be calculated from the Cambridge equation:

$$g_K + \delta = \beta v - (1 - \beta)(1 - \delta) = \beta(1 + v - \delta) - (1 - \delta) \tag{10.17}$$

The paradox of thrift continues to hold in the generalized model: an increase in the capitalist saving propensity increases the denominator and reduces the numerator of equation (10.15), and thus lowers the rates of capacity utilization and profit. An increase in β has offsetting effects on the gross growth rate of capital, since β rises and v falls in equation (10.17). In the Appendix to the chapter we show, however, that the v effect predominates, and the gross growth rate of capital falls with an increase in β, as in the simple model.

The generalized investment constrained model, however, can respond to an increase in the wage share in more complex ways than the paradox of costs of the basic model. If the value of $\eta_\pi = 0$, for example, an increase in the wage share lowers the profit share, which lowers the denominator of equation (10.15), and thus raises the equilibrium level of capacity utilization. A rise in the wage share has offsetting effects on the profit rate, $v = \pi\rho u$, since u rises but π falls. It is possible to show that when $\eta_\pi = 0$ the rise in u prevails, and the profit rate rises. (See the Appendix.) In this case the gross growth rate of capital, $g_K + \delta$, also rises with a rise in the wage share, and the paradox of costs continues to hold. This case is called *wage-led growth*, since an increase in the wage share raises the rates of capacity utilization and growth. Wage-led growth occurs because the increase in workers' consumption demand has a positive feedback effect on investment, through raising the rate of utilization. Since $\eta_\pi = 0$, there is no dampening effect through changes in profitability from the wage share increase at all.

On the other hand, if $\eta_u = 0$, then $\eta_\pi\pi > \eta_u u$, and the profit rate will rise with a rise in the profit share, leading to an increase in the gross growth rate of capital. This case is sometimes called *profit-led growth*. Profit-led growth occurs because an increase in the profit share can have offsetting effects on demand: a higher profit share reduces consumption demand by redistributing income away from workers, but increases investment demand, through raising profitability. For profit-led growth to occur, the increase in investment demand must dominate the reduction in consumption demand.

As these two extremes suggest, and the Appendix shows, whether growth is wage-led or profit-led depends critically on the relative value of the parameters in the investment and saving equations. Real economies may alternate between periods in which one or the other regime prevails.

Problem 10.12 *Suppose the entrepreneurs in Kaldoria are behaving according to the following investment function: $g^i + \delta = .25\pi$, and the wage share is $.6 = 60\%$. Use the equations in the Appendix to this chapter to find the equilibrium rates of capacity utilization, profit, and gross growth of capital. What happens to the endogenous variables when the wage share rises to $.65 = 65\%$? Explain what has happened.*

Problem 10.13 *Suppose the entrepreneurs in Kaldoria shift to behaving according to the following investment function: $g^i + \delta = .1u$. Find the equilibrium rates of capacity utilization, profit and gross growth of capital when the wage share is $.6 = 60\%$, and when the wage share is $.5 = 50\%$. Explain what has happened.*

10.6   Long Run or Short Run?

Even among economists who accept Keynes' visions, opinions are divided about whether the conclusions we have reached with the investment constrained model are valid in the long run. The terms *long run* and *short run* can take on different meanings, depending on context, but generally economists assume that in the short run economic actors are out of equilibrium in some dimension while in the long run they are fully adjusted in all dimensions. There are some aspects of the investment constrained model which suggest that it might apply only when the economy is out of equilibrium along some dimension, that is, in the short run. In particular, the model assumes that entrepreneurs continue to invest in the face of excess capacity, which suggests that they have not fully adjusted to long run equilibrium.

The investment constrained model, however, can be seen as a long run model. In this interpretation, firms form expectations about the normal or desired rate of capacity utilization by looking back at the rates that have prevailed in the past, and thus come to accept excess capacity as a normal condition. Economists who see the investment constrained model in this light often describe themselves as *stagnationist* or *underconsumptionist*. They believe that mature capitalist economies have a tendency to stagnate because of inadequate growth of aggregate demand, and that this tendency can be overcome by policies to encourage wage-led growth. The stagnationist view resonates with the goals of trade unionists, who emphasize the beneficial demand effects of higher wages in capitalist economies.

Many economists, on the other hand, view the investment constrained model as a short run model. The relation between short and long run equilibrium in investment constrained models remains controversial.

One interpretation sees the investment function as the expression of financial constraints on entrepreneurs' plans to invest. (In this view the investment constrained model is actually a *finance constrained* model of growth.) Profits relieve entrepreneurs from the need to go to financial markets or banks to raise funds to finance investment. The profit rate thus could influence investment plans through changing entrepreneurs' ability to finance expenditures from their retained earnings. In this interpretation, entrepreneurs anticipate that the economy will gravitate toward full capacity utilization, and make investment decisions based on their forecast of the full capacity utilization rate of profit, in spite of the presence of excess capacity in the present.

If this interpretation is to be complete, it must explain how the economy gets to the long run position, where utilization is at its full capacity level. In our presentation of the investment constrained model, this adjustment to long run equilibrium would take place through shifts over time in the coefficients of the investment demand equation. Marx and Keynes have different views as to how these shifts arise.

Marx views excess capacity as the symptom of *crisis* in a capitalist economy, but argues that crises function to eliminate the short run obstacles to continuing capital accumulation. In the Marxian perspective, prolonged crisis raises unemployment and puts downward pressure on wages, thus raising the profit share, which can revive investment under conditions of profit-led growth. Furthermore, Marx argued, crises lead to the liquidation and consolidation of low-profit capital, thus increasing entrepreneurs' incentives to invest, and shifting up the planned investment schedule. Finally, structural change in technology may raise the productivity of capital, also raising the investment schedule. In Marx's view the capitalist economy constantly fluctuates between crisis and boom, so that the long run "normal" level of capacity utilization emerges only as a statistical average over time.

Keynes, on the other hand, saw shifts in the investment function as representing changes in financial constraints on investment spending.

Any forces tending to push the economy to a long run equilibrium level of capacity utilization must, in this perspective, operate through the financial system that lies in the background of the investment constrained model.

One familiar mechanism of financial adjustment is the *Keynes effect*, which is used in many intermediate macroeconomics textbooks to explain the existence of an "aggregate demand curve." The Keynes effect occurs when the price level falls during periods of excess capacity, but the nominal money supply remains constant. In this case, the real money supply will increase, which, according to the Keynesian theory of liquidity preference, reduces the interest rate on loans to entrepreneurs to finance investment. More generally, we get a Keynes effect when the rate of growth of prices (i.e., the inflation rate) drops below the rate of growth of the nominal money supply. The Keynes effect can lead to an upward shift in the investment function, through increases in η. Alternatively, a central bank, faced with widespread excess capacity, might inject liquidity into the banking system, making loans more readily available to firms. Again, the relaxation of financial constraints on investment could shift the investment function upward. If these shifts take place more slowly than the saving and investment decisions we have been examining, the investment constrained model would be valid in the short run, but the economy might gravitate toward a long run equilibrium of full capacity utilization.

The Keynesian equilibrating mechanisms work equally well (perhaps better) in a situation of over-utilization of capacity, when $u > 1$. (For this to occur, we must treat u as a fraction of a desired rate of capacity utilization which leaves some spare capacity to cover surges in demand, rather than as a strict technological limit.) When a surge in demand occurs, it will push the level of utilization closer to the technological limit. Inflationary forces in such an overheated economy would tend to increase the financial constraints on investment, either through the Keynes effect or through direct interventions on the part of the central bank, thus lowering the investment demand function.

In the long run, the economy would be attracted to the full utilization of capacity at $u = 1$, as illustrated by Figure 10.6. In this situation, the investment function becomes superfluous, replaced by the condition that $u = 1$. In the long run, then, the investment constrained model transforms itself into the Classical model with a conventional wage share. Economists sometimes say that the economy is Keynesian in the short run but Classical in the long run. This way of compartmentalizing macroeconomics into short and long runs comes naturally to a wide range of modern economists, even though they may disagree about which models are right in each instance.

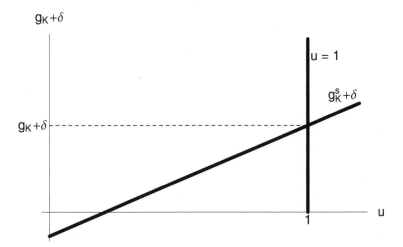

Figure 10.6: In long run equilibrium investment demand adjusts to saving, and the Cambridge equation again determines the rate of growth of capital.

10.7   The Keynesian Contribution to Growth Theory

The investment constrained model introduces fundamentally new considerations into the modeling of capitalist economic growth. Both Classical and neoclassical traditions see saving as the engine of capital accumulation and assume that saving decisions always lead to a corresponding decision to invest. In these models *Say's Law* holds, and there can be no discrepancy between aggregate demand and supply (though Say's Law does allow for disequilibrium between demand and supply in particular markets). The introduction of an independent investment demand function together with the rate of capacity utilization as an endogenous variable breaks the identity between saving and investment, and generates a class of Keynesian models in which Say's Law does not hold. As we have seen, the results of comparative dynamics experiments in investment constrained models are quite different from the parallel results in Classical and neoclassical models. Parametric changes, such as a rise in the saving propensity, or in the profit share, that raise the rate of growth of capital in Classical and neoclassical models can lower the rate of growth of capital in investment constrained models when the investment demand schedule is unchanged. These differences in comparative dynamics lead to different evaluations of policies toward growth, as well.

In the Classical and neoclassical perspective redistribution of income from profits to wages may be viewed as desirable in itself, but comes at a price in terms of slower capital accumulation. In the Keynesian models these tradeoffs are less painful or even nonexistent: redistribution can move the economy to a higher rate of capacity utilization and thus create a larger income to be divided between profits and wages, and a larger output to be used as consumption and investment.

The great policy debates in macroeconomics and growth economics of the last half of the twentieth century have concerned the limits of applicability of the Keynesian models. Many economists agree that Keynesian effects are important in the short run, but question whether Keynesian analysis can safely be used to guide long run economic policy toward economic growth. These debates should presumably be settled by looking at the empirical evidence as to how strong the tendencies moving capitalist economies toward full capacity utilization actually are. But econometric techniques for answering this question are themselves in dispute, and macroeconomic evidence is limited, so the policy dilemma remains unresolved.

10.8   Suggested Readings

Roy Harrod [1939] is probably most responsible for the birth of Keynesian growth theory, while Nicholas Kaldor [1956] and Luigi Pasinetti [1974] developed Keynesian/Classical models of full employment growth. The model in the text (which does not presume full employment) owes much to Joan Robinson [1964] and of course Amit Bhaduri and Stephen Marglin [Bhaduri and Marglin, 1990]. These economists in turn were influenced by Michal Kalecki [1971], who discovered the theory of the multiplier simultaneously with Keynes [1936]. There have been numerous recent contributions in this broad tradition, including Taylor [1983], Skott [1989], Dutt [1990], Palley [1996a], and Palley [1996b]. The original reference to the Widow's Cruse can be found in Keynes [1930].

Appendix: The Marglin-Bhaduri Model

We can solve the investment and savings demand equations for the equilibrium level of capacity utilization by equating planned saving and investment.

$$g_K^i + \delta = \eta_u u + \eta_\pi \pi + \eta_\rho \rho$$

$$g_K^s + \delta = \beta(1 + v - \delta) - (1 - \delta)$$

Using $v = \pi \rho u$, we get the equilibrium equation:

$$\beta \pi \rho u - (1 - \beta)(1 - \delta) = \eta_u u + \eta_\pi \pi + \eta_\rho \rho$$

which can be solved for equilibrium u:

$$u = \frac{\eta_\pi \pi + \eta_\rho \rho + (1 - \beta)(1 - \delta)}{\beta \pi \rho - \eta_u}$$

Differentiating the equilibrium conditions with respect to β, we see that:

$$\frac{du}{d\beta} = -\frac{1 + v - \delta}{\beta \pi \rho - \eta_u} < 0$$

$$\frac{dv}{d\beta} = \pi \rho \frac{du}{d\beta} < 0$$

$$\frac{d(g_K + \delta)}{d\beta} = -\frac{\eta_u(1 + v - \delta)}{\beta \pi \rho - \eta_u} < 0$$

Thus the paradox of thrift results continues to hold in the generalized investment constrained model.

Differentiating the equilibrium conditions with respect to π, however, yields:

$$\frac{du}{d\pi} = \frac{\eta_\pi - \beta \rho u}{\beta \pi \rho - \eta_u}$$

Thus the sign of $du/d\pi$ is the same as the sign of $\eta_\pi - \beta \rho u$, and will always be negative, as we can see from the equilibrium condition above. Similarly:

$$\frac{dv}{d\pi} = (\eta_\pi \pi - \eta_u u) \frac{\rho}{\beta \pi \rho - \eta_u}$$

Thus the sign of $dv/d\pi$ is the same as the sign of $\eta_\pi \pi - \eta_u u$, and will be positive when $\eta_\pi \pi > \eta_u u$.

$$\frac{d(g_K + \delta)}{d\pi} = \beta \frac{dv}{d\pi}$$

If $\eta_\pi = 0$, we see that:

$$\frac{dv}{d\pi} = -\eta_u u \frac{\rho}{\beta \pi \rho - \eta_u} < 0$$

If $\eta_u = 0$, on the other hand:

$$\frac{dv}{d\pi} = \frac{\eta_\pi}{\beta} > 0$$

Thus the impact of an increase in profit share on growth depends on the coefficients of the investment function, leading to the distinction between wage-led and profit-led growth regimes.

Chapter 11

Land-Limited Growth

11.1 Non-Reproducible Resources

In the Classical conventional wage model where labor-power is supplied elastically at a given wage, all inputs are reproducible. The economy can produce capital by itself, and, practically speaking, it can reproduce labor-power as well by paying the wage. In this type of model there are no resource limitations to growth. The growth rate of the economy is determined entirely by productivity and the propensity of capitalists to accumulate.

When labor-power is inelastically supplied and grows at an exogenously given rate, as in the Solow–Swan model, the forces determining the steady-state growth rate change sharply. The long run growth rate of the economy has to adjust to the given natural growth rate of the labor force. Input prices must vary to make this adjustment.

In this chapter we will study a Ricardian economy where there is a fixed and limited amount of land which is necessary for production. We will suppose that property rights in land exist, creating both a *rental market* for the productive use of land in each period, and a *land market* on which land can be bought and sold.

Capitalists' asset portfolios now include both capital and land, and their portfolio choices determine a price for land. Since capitalists can invest either in capital or in land, the returns from owning land and their expectations about the path of the future price of land play a central role in the economy. The introduction of this second asset raises issues of asset pricing that are fundamental to the modern theory of finance as well.

197

11.2   Ricardo's Stationary State

David Ricardo, a successful London stockbroker whose implacably logical analysis of economic growth and distribution was a major influence in the development of political economy, analyzed the growth of an
economy with limited land in his *Principles of Political Economy and
Taxation*.

Ricardo works with a *corn model* of production very similar to the
Classical model that we presented earlier. In this model he abstracts
from the real diversity of commodities and assumes that the only produced good is *corn* (the comprehensive English term for all food grains),
which we will take as the numéraire. Production of corn requires workers, whose wages must be paid during the production period between the
planting of the corn and its harvesting. These advanced wages, together
with the seed corn, constitute the capital required to carry on production. Ricardo follows Malthus in assuming that the wage (in terms of
corn) is fixed at a level where the birth and death rates of the population
are close to equal, as in Chapter 4. In our terms Ricardo's corn model
is a conventional wage model.

In Ricardo's world there are three classes: workers, capitalists, and
landowners. The capitalists rent land from the landowners and perform
the entrepreneurial function of organizing production, as well as the
capitalist function of owning and accumulating capital. The landowners
own the land and rent it to the capitalists.

The central economic idea of Ricardo's model is that different plots
of land have different natural fertilities. Conceptually we divide up all
the land in the economy into *plots* that require the same *dose* of capital
and labor to cultivate (though they may not all have the same actual
area). Each plot of land has a certain *yield*, the average harvest that
can be expected when the standard dose of labor and capital of standard
quality are applied to it. Ricardo imagines that we can rank all the land
in the economy according to its fertility, starting from the most fertile,
and proceeding to the least fertile. If we graph the plots of land along
the horizontal axis and the yield of each plot of land on the vertical
axis, as in Figure 11.1, we can visualize the *diminishing returns* that
are at the heart of Ricardo's thinking as a *marginal product schedule* of
capital and labor applied together in fixed proportions. Since each plot of
land requires the same amount of capital and labor, the distance along
the horizontal axis measures the labor force (which Ricardo takes as
proportional to population) and capital employed. The yield of the least
fertile land in cultivation (the *extensive margin* in Ricardo's language)
is the marginal product of capital and labor together, since the removal
of one dose of capital and labor would remove the marginal land from

cultivation and reduce the total output by its yield. The area under the marginal product schedule up to the extensive margin is the total corn output of the economy.

On this graph we can draw a horizontal line at the height of the real wage, determined so as to bring about a demographic equilibrium of births and deaths. This is the familiar conventional wage supply schedule of labor. The amount of capital accumulated in the past by capitalists can offer employment for a certain number of workers, and thus determines the population, as well as the amount of land in cultivation and the extensive margin, in Ricardo's framework. The area under the marginal product schedule above the real wage is the *surplus product* of the economy, since it represents the excess of production over what is necessary to keep the current population of workers alive.

This surplus is divided between landowners and capitalists as they bargain over the rents on the various plots of land. Ricardo argued that the owner of the marginal land in cultivation could charge only a nominal rent on her land, since other land almost as good is available and earning no rent at all. He also argued that competition among the capitalists would force the rent on any cultivated plot of land to the point where the capitalist's profit rate on that land after paying rent would just be equal to the profit rate on the marginal land that paid practically no rent. Thus in Figure 11.1 the horizontal line at the level of the yield of the marginal land divides the surplus into rent and profit. Profit is the rectangle between the wage line and the yield on the extensive margin, and rent is the area above the yield on the marginal land under the marginal product schedule.

Ricardo assumed, extrapolating the behavior he thought he observed in British society, that workers and landowners would spend all their income on consumption (workers on wages for subsistence, and landowners on staffing great houses with armies of liveried servants), and that capitalists would save all or most of their profit income, and accumulate it to expand production. As long as profits are positive, capital will be expanding, creating more jobs, supporting a larger population, and pushing the extensive margin into less fertile land. As this accumulation occurs, the wage remains constant, but the profit rate falls.

In the end, Ricardo predicts that capital accumulation and growth will stop when the extensive margin is pushed out to the point where the yield on the marginal land is just equal to the conventional wage. At this point the profit rate and total profits are zero, so there is no more capital accumulation, and all the surplus takes the form of rent. Ricardo called this situation the *stationary state*. At the stationary state most of a large population lives at the edge of subsistence, pressing on the limited resources of the earth, while a small wealthy class of landowners

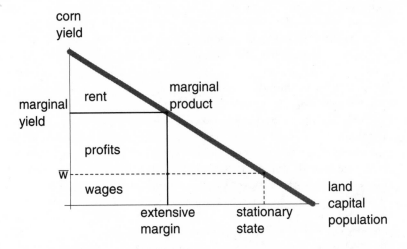

Figure 11.1: In Ricardo's model plots of land are graphed along the horizontal axis in order of diminishing fertility, and the yield of each plot constitutes the marginal product schedule for capital and labor. The extensive margin is the least fertile land in cultivation. The Malthusian conventional wage divides the yield of the marginal land between wages and profit, and determines the profit rate for the whole economy. Rents on more fertile land are equal to the excess of the output on that plot over the output on the marginal land. The stationary state is the point where the yield on the marginal land is just equal to the conventional wage: when capital accumulates and population grows to this point, the profit rate falls to zero and accumulation stops.

appropriate the social surplus product.

Ricardo's analysis of the stationary state has strong echoes in contemporary anxieties about resource depletion and environmental degradation as a result of economic growth. The diminishing returns that Ricardo modeled in terms of land could be seen as arising from the exhaustion of non-renewable resources and the destruction of the environment, and the stationary state as the unhappy fate awaiting an overcrowded humanity on a finite planet.

11.3 Production with Land

Let us consider the one-sector model of production, but with the added requirement that land is required as an input. In this chapter we will assume that the technology of production is unchanging over time. We will use the letters U and u for land and land per worker (since L is easy to confuse with labor). The technique of production then becomes:

$$1 \text{ labor } + k \text{ capital } + u \text{ land } \rightarrow$$
$$x \text{ output } + (1 - \delta)k \text{ capital } + u \text{ land}$$

In other words, in this model one worker equipped with k units of capital and u units of land can produce x units of output at the end of a year. Capital depreciates at the rate δ, but land does not depreciate at all. We are free to measure land in any units (acres or hectares, for example), and the coefficient u will change proportionately. In order to simplify the equations of the model, we will take as our unit of land the amount of land required per unit of capital, so that $u = k$. Thus we can measure land and capital directly on the same scale.

In any period there is a fixed amount of capital, K_t, inherited from the past, and a fixed amount of land U. Unlike Ricardo's model, all the land here is assumed to be of the same fertility. The quantity of capital will change from period to period because the economy can produce capital and capitalists can accumulate it. The quantity of land, on the other hand, can never change.

The idea that there is a fixed resource limitation of some kind (like land in this model) is very strongly rooted in human attitudes towards economic growth, but is perhaps not very well confirmed by human experience. First of all, all resources require some development. Agricultural land must be cleared, drained and plowed. Mineral resources must be discovered and developed (through the construction of mines, wells, and transportation facilities). Second, the process of technical change frequently renders resources obsolete before they are exhausted. The iron deposits in the Eastern United States that were the basis of

pre-Civil War industrial development have become economically irrelevant because of the emergence of larger-scale iron mines in the West
and in other countries. These deposits still exist, but it is unlikely that
they will play any important role in economic production. This way of
thinking suggests that we might best regard all resources as potentially
producible, though some may be producible only at a very high cost. If
this point of view is accurate, the model of land we are studying will be
misleading.

As before, there are entrepreneurs who actually organize production
by renting land and capital from capitalists and hiring labor. We suppose
that labor is available at the conventional wage $\bar{w}$. We denote the profit
rate on capital by v_{kt}, which is the amount of output the entrepreneur
has to pay for the use of capital for one period.

The use of land as an input in production leads to the emergence
of *land rent*. If entrepreneurs want to use all the land available in production, capitalists will be in a position as landowners to bargain for a
rent on land, which we will call v_{ut}. The payer of rent gets to use the
land in production for one period. The dimensions of v_{ut} are \$/unit of
land/year. Since our land unit is the amount of land required to employ
one dollar of capital, we could also express v_{ut} as \$/\$/year, or %/year,
like the profit rate. If the profit rate is 10%/year and the rent on land
5%/year, the entrepreneur has to pay 15%/year to rent capital and land
from capitalists.

The profit an entrepreneur makes on each worker employed will be
output per worker less the wage and rent on both capital and land.
Remembering that we are measuring land in units so that $u = k$, the
entrepreneurs' profit is:

$$x - w - v_{kt}k - v_{ut}k$$

The entrepreneur must make zero profit, for the same reasons as in
the one-input production model. If we reinterpret the profit share, π to
include rent on both land and capital, we can write this condition as:

$$v_{kt} + v_{ut} = \frac{1 - w}{k} = \pi\rho \qquad (11.1)$$

11.4   The Capitalist's Decision Problem with Land

We will attack the analysis of this economy with the same methods we
developed in Chapter 5. We will assume that there are a large number

of identical capitalist wealth-holders each of whom begin owning the same share of the total capital and land in the economy. We continue to assume that these capitalists maximize the discounted sum of the logarithm of their consumption of output.

The introduction of land into the picture adds a new dimension to the typical capitalist's decision. In the model of Chapter 5, the typical capitalist had to choose between holding capital and consuming at the end of each period. Now the typical capitalist has an additional choice: she has to choose how much of her wealth to invest in land and how much in capital.

Even though the amount of land in the whole economy is fixed, each individual capitalist could in principle own more or less land. Thus the *asset price of land* in terms of output (or capital), which we will call p_{ut}, must adjust in each period to make the capitalists willing to hold the existing stocks of capital and land. The asset price of land is quite different from rent. The renter gets to use the land only for one period, while the purchaser of the land itself gets to keep the land until she wants to sell it, and collect rent on the land in all the periods she owns it.

The typical capitalist starts each period holding some land, U_t, and some capital, K_t.

At the beginning of period $t+1$, then, the typical capitalist's source of funds will be the value of her depreciated capital together with the capital rent she has received, plus the value of her land together with the land rent she has received:

$$v_{kt}K_t + (1-\delta)K_t + (p_{ut+1} + v_{ut})U_t = K_t + (v_{kt} - \delta)K_t + (p_{ut+1} + v_{ut})U_t$$

$$= (1 + v_{kt} - \delta)K_t + (p_{ut+1} + v_{ut})U_t \qquad (11.2)$$

These funds must be divided between consumption, C_t, and holdings of capital and land in the next period, K_{+1} and $p_{ut+1}U_{t+1}$. The typical capitalist's budget constraint with land is thus:

$$K_{t+1} + p_{ut+1}U_{t+1} + C_t \leq (1 + v_{kt} - \delta)K_t + (p_{ut+1} + v_{ut})U_t \qquad (11.3)$$

This constraint defines the typical capitalist's utility maximization problem.

11.5　The Arbitrage Principle

The new element in the capitalist's utility maximization problem is the decision as to how much of her wealth to invest in land and how much

Capitalist's Utility Maximization with Land

$$\text{choose } \{C_t, K_{t+1}, U_{t+1}\}_{t=0}^{\infty} \geq 0 \qquad (11.4)$$

$$\text{so as to maximize } (1 - \beta) \sum_{t=0}^{\infty} \beta^t \ln(C_t)$$

$$\text{subject to}$$

$$K_{t+1} + p_{ut+1}U_{t+1} + C_t \leq (1 + v_{kt} - \delta)K_t + (p_{ut+1} + v_{ut})U_t \quad (11.3)$$

$$K_0, U_0, \{v_{kt}, p_{ut}, v_{ut}\}_{t=0}^{\infty} \text{ given} \qquad (11.5)$$

---

in capital in each period. We assume that the capitalist knows the paths of the price of land, the rental rate on land and the profit rate with certainty, which greatly simplifies this problem. In the real world the portfolio decision as to how to apportion wealth between competing assets, like equities and bonds, is highly dependent on the relative risk the wealth holder perceives in each choice. In our model, however, the issue of risk is absent. As a result the model's typical capitalist will choose between holding land and capital purely on the basis of which has the higher rate of return.

A capitalist who chooses to hold a unit of land during period t at the price p_{ut} will have $v_{ut} + p_{ut+1}$ at the end of the period, since she will collect the rent on the land and still have the land to sell. She could, alternatively, have invested the money in capital instead and had $(1 + v_{kt} - \delta)p_{u_t}$ at the end of the period. These two returns must be equal if the capitalist is to be willing to hold both land and capital in her portfolio. This is the *arbitrage principle*, which plays a central role in modern financial theory. Rational wealth holders will hold assets with equal risk only if their anticipated rates of return are equal. In our model the two assets are capital and land. They have the same (zero) risk, so capitalists will hold both only if they have the same rate of return. Furthermore, the capitalist is indifferent as to how much of her wealth she holds in capital and land as long as the rates of return on the two assets are identical. The mathematical expression of the arbitrage principle is:

$$1 + r_t \equiv 1 + v_{kt} - \delta = \frac{p_{ut+1} + v_{ut}}{p_{ut}} = 1 + g_{p_u t} + \frac{v_{ut}}{p_{ut}} \tag{11.6}$$

The arbitrage principle tells us immediately that the rate of return to capital and land in each period must be equal, establishing a single rate of return, r_t that applies to both assets. The rate of return to capital is the rental to capital, v_{kt} less the rate of depreciation, δ, and the rate of return to land is the rental to land, v_{ut} plus the capital gain or loss on land due to the change in its price, $g_{p_u t}$.

The arbitrage principle reduces the capitalist's utility maximization problem with land to the same form as the utility maximization problem with one asset, capital, that we have solved in Chapter 5. To see this, define the capitalist's total wealth in each period, $J_t = K_t + p_{ut}U_t$. The arbitrage principle assures us that she will get the same rate of return, r_t, whether she holds land or capital. Thus we can write the budget constraint as:

$$J_{t+1} + C_t \leq (1 + r_t)J_t \tag{11.7}$$

But this is exactly the budget constraint in Chapter 5, with wealth, J_t, substituted for capital, K_t. This makes sense, because in the earlier model the only form of wealth was capital. We already know the solution to this problem: the typical capitalist consumes a fraction $1 - \beta$ of her wealth at the end of the period:

$$C_t = (1 - \beta)(1 + r_t)J_t = (1 - \beta)(1 + r_t)(K_t + p_{ut}U_t) \tag{11.8}$$

The Cambridge equation now applies to the growth of total wealth:

$$J_{t+1} = \beta(1 + r_t)J_t \tag{11.9}$$

But the growth of capital itself is governed by the rule:

$$K_{t+1} = J_{t+1} - p_{ut+1}U_{t+1} = \beta(1 + r_t)J_t - p_{ut+1}U_{t+1}$$

$$= \beta(1 + r_t)(K_t + p_{ut}U_t) - p_{ut+1}U_{t+1} \tag{11.10}$$

The implications of capitalists' utility maximization in the model with land boil down to the arbitrage principle of equation (11.6) and the consumption function of equation (11.8).

Problem 11.1 *Write down the Lagrangian function for the capital-ist's utility maximization problem with land, and find the first-order conditions describing the saddle point. Use these conditions to derive the arbitrage principle and the consumption function.*

11.6   Equilibrium Conditions

The analysis of Section 11.5 tells us how the typical capitalist will behave if she is confronted with a given path of prices, rents, and profit rates $\{p_{ut+1}, v_{ut}, 1 + r_t\}_{t=0}^{\infty}$.

But the prices, rents and profit rates must be chosen so that the markets for capital, land rental and land owning clear in each period.

First consider the market for land as an asset. We have allowed the typical capitalist to make a free choice as to how much land she will own in each period. In equilibrium, however, she has to wind up owning her share of the actual amount of land in the economy U. So land market clearing requires:

$$U_t = U \qquad (t = 0, 1, \ldots, \infty) \tag{11.11}$$

But the rental land market has to clear as well. Entrepreneurs cannot plan to rent more land for production than exists. Furthermore, the rent on land will depend on whether entrepreneurs want to rent all the land or not. If there is so little capital in the economy that the entrepreneurs cannot use all the existing land, the land rent must be zero. If the land rent is positive, it must be the case that all the land is used. This turns out to be a key aspect of the growth path of this economy. Since we measure land in the same units as capital, rent will be zero if $K_t < U$, and can be positive only when $K_t = U$:

$$K_t \leq U (= \text{ if } v_{ut} > 0) \text{ or}$$

$$v_{ut} = 0 \text{ if } K_t < U \tag{11.12}$$

Thus we have two possible *regimes* in this economy. In the *abundant land regime* there isn't enough capital to cultivate all the land, so some land will remain uncultivated, and land rent will be zero. As far as production goes, the abundant land economy is exactly like the Classical conventional wage model of Chapter 6.

But if capital grows to the level $K^* = U$, the economy enters the *scarce land regime*. In this case the level of production is determined by the amount of land, not by the amount of capital.

Equilibrium in the Land Model

Exogenous Variables: $\rho, \delta, \beta, \bar{\pi}, U, K_t, J_t, p_{ut}$

Endogenous Variables: $v_{kt}, v_{ut}, r_t, p_{ut+1}, J_{t+1}, K_{t+1}$

$$v_{kt} + v_{ut} = \bar{\pi}\rho \qquad (11.13)$$

$$v_{ut} = 0 \text{ if } K_t < U \qquad (11.14)$$

$$r_t = v_{kt} - \delta \qquad (11.15)$$

$$p_{ut+1} + v_{ut} = (1 + r_t)p_{ut} \qquad (11.16)$$

$$J_{t+1} = \beta(1 + r_t)J_t \qquad (11.17)$$

$$K_{t+1} = J_{t+1} - p_{ut+1}U \qquad (11.18)$$

From equation (11.18) we see that the capital gains from land can soak up some of capitalist saving, and thereby reduce investment in capital. This can be an important factor in the development of capitalist economies where a large proportion of wealth is in the form of land.

11.7 The Abundant Land Regime

We can work out the pattern of growth in the abundant land regime from the general equilibrium conditions.

In the abundant land regime $K_t < U$, and the rent on land $v_{ut} = 0$. The only way that land can compete with capital for a place in portfolios, as equation (11.16) shows, is for the price of land to be rising at the net profit rate. Thus in the abundant land regime :

$$p_{ut+1} = (1 + r_t)p_{ut} \qquad (11.19)$$

Notice that the expectation of this price appreciation can justify a positive price for land, *even though the rental on land is zero*.

Now consider what is happening to the capital stock, by looking at equation (11.18). In the abundant land regime equation (11.19) holds, so the growth path of the capital stock follows the path:

$$K_{t+1} = \beta(1 + r_t)K_t + \beta(1 + r_t)p_{ut}U - p_{ut+1}U$$

$$= \beta(1 + r_t)K_t - (1 - \beta)(1 + r_t)p_{ut}U$$

Equilibrium in the Abundant Land Regime

$$v_{ut} = 0$$

$$r_t = v_{kt} - \delta = \bar{\pi}\rho - \delta$$

$$p_{ut+1} = (1 + r_t)p_{ut}$$

$$K_{t+1} = (1 + r_t)(\beta K_t - (1 - \beta)p_{ut}U)$$

If the price of land is low, there will be enough saving to allow the capital stock to grow.

In the abundant land regime both the price of land and the capital stock will rise, but as the price of land increases, capitalists will feel richer and richer and will consume a larger part of their resources, so that the growth of the capital stock will tend to slow down over time.

11.8   The Scarce Land Regime

Eventually the capital stock will grow to the point where $K_t = U$, and the economy will shift to the *scarce land regime*.

In the scarce land regime output is limited by the availability of land, and there is no point in accumulating capital, since without more land extra capital will be worthless in production. Thus in the scarce land regime we know that:

$$K_{t+1} = K_t = U = K^*$$

We also know that the net profit rate will be:

$$r_t = v_{kt} - \delta = \bar{\pi}\rho - v_{ut} - \delta$$

From equation (11.18) we can see that:

$$K_{t+1} = \beta(1 + r_t)K_t + \beta(1 + r_t)p_{ut}U - p_{ut+1}U$$

$$= K_t = K^* = U$$

Substituting for $1 + r_t$, and using equation (11.16), we have:

$$K_{t+1} = K^* = \beta(1 + \bar{\pi}\rho - \delta - v_{ut})K^* + \beta(p_{ut+1} + v_{ut})U - p_{ut+1}U$$

$$= \beta(1 + \bar{\pi}\rho - \delta)K^* + v_{ut}(U - K^*) - (1 - \beta)p_{ut+1}U$$

Since $K^* = U$, the rents disappear from this expression, leaving:

$$K^* = \beta(1 + \bar{\pi}\rho - \delta)K^* - (1 - \beta)p_{ut+1}U \qquad (11.20)$$

In the scarce land regime everything besides p_{ut+1} in equation (11.20) is unchanging, so the price of land must be unchanging as well, at some level p_u^*. Since the capital stock and price of land do not change from period to period in the scarce land regime, the wealth of the capitalists must not change either, so that:

$$J_{t+1} = J_t = J^* = \beta(1 + r^*)J^*$$

The requirement that wealth be constant in the scarce land regime thus implies that the profit factor $1 + r^*$ is equal to the inverse of the capitalist saving propensity or utility discount factor, β:

$$1 + r^* = \frac{1}{\beta}$$

Land rent, from equation (11.13), must satisfy:

$$v_u^* = \bar{\pi}\rho - \delta - r^*$$

From the land speculation condition, (11.16), we see that in the scarce land regime the price of land must be the present discounted value of future rents:

$$p_u^* = \frac{v_u^*}{r^*} \qquad (11.21)$$

The scarce land regime is very much like Ricardo's stationary state. The price of land is so high that capitalists consume all of their net income, and there is no growth. The profit rate after rent has fallen from its high level when land is abundant. Since the same capitalists own both land and capital, in this model there is saving and consumption out of both rents and profits, in contrast to Ricardo's assumption that all rents were consumed and all profits accumulated. Thus in the scarce land regime the net profit rate can be positive, rather than falling to zero, as Ricardo predicted for the stationary state.

Equilibrium in the Scarce Land Regime

$$K_{t+1} = K_t = K^* = U$$

$$1 + r_t = 1 + r^* = \frac{1}{\beta}$$

$$v_{ut} = v_u^* = \bar{\pi}\rho - \delta - r^*$$

$$p_{ut} = p_{ut+1} = p_u^* = \frac{v_u^*}{r^*}$$

11.9 From the Abundant to the Scarce Land Regime

How does the economy that grows rapidly in the abundant land regime hook up with the stationary economy of the scarce land regime? The key is the initial price of land. As we have seen, for any initial price of land we can predict the paths of the price of land and the capital stock in the abundant land regime. On this path the price of land is going to rise to its stationary state level p_u^*, in some period. If the capital stock in that same period has grown to its stationary state level, K^*, the two regimes will fit together and the expectations of the capitalists will be exactly fulfilled. In the same period that the price of land rises high enough to stop the growth of capital, the capital stock will be just large enough to raise the rent on land above zero. The expectations of rising land prices will turn out to have been correct, and when land prices stop rising, rents will become positive to make land competitive with capital in capitalists' portfolios. This is a *perfect foresight* equilibrium growth path. The price of land in the initial period is actually determined by the requirement that the two regimes fit together in this way.

If the price of land were too high in the first period, the capital stock would stop growing before it reached K^* level, and rents would never become positive. The price of land and wealth would have to continue rising indefinitely, and eventually on such a path the capitalists would eat up all the capital in consumption. If the price of land were too low in the first period, the capital stock would reach K^* while the price of land was still below p_u^*. Thus the capital stock would continue to grow, leading to unemployment of capital. Only when the market in the first period prices land as an asset at exactly the correct level will it be possible for the growth path to fulfill the expectations.

Example 11.1 Let $x = \$50,000/\text{worker}/\text{year}$, $\delta = 1/\text{year}$, $k = \$12,500/\text{worker}$, $\bar{w} = \$20,000/\text{worker}/\text{year}$, and $\beta = .5$. $\rho = x/k = 4/\text{year}$, and $\bar{\pi} = (1 - (w/x)) = .6$. Suppose one hectare of land can employ \$1,000 of capital, and there are 1 million hectares of land available. The unit of land that can employ \$1 of capital is $1/1000$ hectare, so there are 1 billion units of land. Find the scarce land regime equilibrium, and the growth path leading to it starting two periods before.

Answer: In the scarce land regime we have

$$K^* = U = \$1 \text{ billion}$$

$$1 + r^* = \frac{1}{\beta} = 2/\text{year, so}$$

$$r^* = 1/\text{year} = 100\%/\text{year.}$$

$$v_u^* = \bar{\pi}\rho - (r^* + \delta))$$

$$= (2.4 - 2)/\text{year} = \$.40/\text{unit of land}/\text{year} = \$400/\text{hectare}/\text{year}$$

$$p_u^* = \frac{v^*}{r^*} = \frac{\$.40}{1} = \$.40/\text{unit of land} = \$400/\text{hectare}$$

Thus in the scarce land regime the capital stock is worth \$1 billion and the land is worth \$.4 billion.

Suppose we take one step backward from the stationary state. In the abundant land regime we have

$$v_{ut} = 0$$

$$r_t = \bar{\pi}\rho - \delta = (.6)(4) - 1/\text{year} = 1.4/\text{year} = 140\%/\text{year}$$

$$(1 + r_t)p_{u-1} = p_u^*, \text{ so}$$

$$p_{u-1} = \$400/(2.4) = \$166.67/\text{hectare}$$

$$v_{u-1} = 0$$

$$K^* = (1 + r_t)(\beta K_{-1} - (1 - \beta)p_{u-1}U$$

$$\$1 \text{ billion} = (2.4/\text{year})(.5K_{-1} - .5(\$166.67(1 \text{ million hectares}))$$

and

$$K_{-1} = \$1 \text{ billion}$$

In the period in which the capital stock reaches its maximum level, the land rent is still zero and the price of land continues to rise one more period before reaching the scarce land regime level.

If we take one more step backward, we have:

$$(1 + r_t)p_{u-2} = p_{uu-1}, \text{ so}$$

$$p_{u-2} = \$166.67/(2.4) = \$69.44/\text{hectare}$$

$$v_{u-1} = 0$$

$$K_{-1} = (1 + r_t)(\beta K_{-2} - (1 - \beta)p_{u-2}U$$

$$\$1 \text{ billion} = (2.4/\text{year})(.5K_{-2} - .5(\$69.44(1 \text{ million hectares}))$$

$$K_{-2} = \$902.78 \text{ million}$$

Problem 11.2 *Suppose in Ricardia (see Problem 2.1) the production of 100 bushels of corn requires 1 acre of land, together with 20 bushels of seed corn and 1 worker-year. If there are 10,000 acres of land available, what is the maximum amount of seed corn capital that could be employed, and the maximum amount of corn output? If the wage rate is 20 bu/worker-year, what are the gross and net profit rates in the abundant land regime?*

Problem 11.3 *Find the land price, land rent, and gross and net profit rates in Ricardia (see Problem 11.3) in the scarce land regime when the wage is 20 bu/worker-year, and $\beta = 4/5$.*

Problem 11.4 *Make a spreadsheet program to calculate the growth path for Ricardia starting from the scarce land regime and working backward 20 years, calculating the asset price of land and the capital stock in each year.*

11.10   Lessons of the Land-Limited Model

The model of growth with an absolutely limited resource like land underlines several fundamental insights of economic analysis.

A long-lived asset can have a positive price even when it yields no current return, like land in the abundant land regime, where the price of land is positive and rising even though the rent on land is zero. The price of land in this model is determined by forward looking *speculative* forces. Capitalists will pay a positive price for land because they believe, correctly, that the rent on land will eventually become positive. Even before the rent becomes positive, landowners are rewarded at the average rate of return by the rising price of land.

Speculative pricing of assets is central to the operation of equity markets in capitalist economies. Equity claims on companies which pay no dividends and even have no earnings from which they might pay dividends can command a positive and rising price in speculative stock markets because asset-holders believe that the company may eventually become profitable. Even if the eventual profitability of a company is quite uncertain, and there is a significant probability in the minds of investors that it will never become profitable, its equity can still command a positive price because investors believe there is some probability that it will earn profits in the future. This effect, which the land model explains in a highly simplified setting, is the source of the *wealth-creating* powers of speculative asset markets. Hopes and dreams can be turned into hard cash, as long as enough speculators are convinced of the possibility that they will come to pass.

In the abundant land regime, the capital gains on land come to absorb a larger and larger part of the saving of capitalists, until at the moment land becomes scarce, the wealth represented by land is so large that capitalists stop saving altogether. This effect also occurs in real economies where wealth in land is very great. Wealthholders may believe themselves to be so rich that they stop saving, and make no funds available for investment in capital. The resulting economic stagnation has been a problem in some developing countries.

As Ricardo divined, a capitalist economy facing an absolute land constraint eventually reaches a stationary state where accumulation of capital ceases. In the limited land model the profit rate in the stationary state remains positive, in contrast to Ricardo's differential rent model. But the profit rate falls to the point where capitalists choose to consume all their net income, leaving nothing left over to finance new investment.

Ricardo disliked the idea of the stationary state, since he thought the accumulation of capital was the chief source of social change and improvement. He saw two factors that might, at least temporarily in his view, delay the stationary state. The first was international trade, and Ricardo's analysis became the bible of British free-trade advocates in the middle years of the nineteenth century. The effect of free trade, in Ricardo's eyes, was to incorporate all (or, at least, more) of the whole world's land in the economy, and thus to moderate the effects of diminishing returns. The extensive margin, instead of being confined to the narrow and rocky islands of Britain, could migrate to the fertile and empty prairies of North America, the pampas of Argentina, or the savannahs of east Africa.

The other factor Ricardo saw as delaying the stationary state was technical change, particularly land-augmenting technical change that would raise the marginal product schedule for capital and labor, and move the stationary state further away from the current extensive margin.

But Ricardo, like contemporary theorists of limited economic growth, viewed both free trade and technical change as only temporary stopgaps delaying, but not preventing, the arrival of the stationary state. He believed that the law of diminishing returns would sooner or later assert itself.

The world economy has seen dramatic increases in the scale and scope of foreign trade since Ricardo's time, and equally dramatic technical change in agricultural and other resource-intensive production. The stationary state seems no nearer today than it did when Ricardo wrote. But perhaps it equally seems no further off. The warnings of contemporary theorists of limited growth, who see human society threatened by the exhaustion of natural resources and the deterioration of the environment, are a reminder of the depth of Ricardo's vision.

11.11   Suggested Readings

The seminal work on the theory of rent is generally acknowledged to be [Ricardo, 1951, Ch. 2, "On Rent"]. The modern formalization of the Ricardian treatment by Pasinetti [1974] is highly recommended. For an in-depth discussion of land-rent and modern developments of the theory in the Classical tradition, see [Kurz and Salvadori, 1995, Ch. 10]. For treatment of land (and natural resources in general) in the basic Solow-Swan model, consult Meade [1961].

Chapter 12

Exhaustible Resources

12.1 Growth with an Exhaustible Resource

Land can neither be created nor used up in the model in Chapter 11. It is either abundant and has no immediate effect on production, or scarce, in which case it is an absolute limit on production.

Another important aspect of resource limitation is that some resources are *exhaustible*, in the sense that they get used up in production, and cannot be renewed. For example, certain mineral and oil resources exist as a quantity of ore or oil in deposits under the ground. As they are mined or pumped out they disappear. Once used, they cannot be replaced. We can use the same modeling approach as we used in the case of land to understand the fundamental economics of growth with exhaustible resources. This analysis is called the *Hotelling model* after Harold Hotelling, the economist who first solved this problem.

Just as it might make more sense to view land as ultimately producible than as absolutely fixed, it might make more sense to view mineral and oil resources as renewable rather than as non-renewable. First of all, new reserves of ores and oil can always be found by exploration and prospecting. In reality we do not know for sure exactly how large the ultimate reserves are; in practice it is possible at a cost to find new reserves. Second, the exploitation of mineral and oil reserves depends on the mining and drilling technology available. At any time there are known reserves that are too costly to exploit with existing technology. If society is willing to pay higher costs, more of these reserves become available. Furthermore, the technology is always changing, thus lowering the costs of exploiting known reserves. Oil companies now routinely drill wells that would have been impossibly deep 50 years ago. Some shallow reserves still have oil in them, but are not being pumped because the quantities are too small to justify the fixed cost required. Finally, technological innovation constantly turns up new alternatives to existing resources. The development of solar technology may make oil reserves economically irrelevant before they are physically exhausted.

Nonetheless, in this chapter we will assume that there is an exhaustible resource and an unchanging technology. We will investigate the economic forces that govern the pricing and utilization of this type of resource.

12.2   Production with an Exhaustible Resource

In order to introduce an exhaustible resource into the growth model, we begin with production. Suppose that oil is a source of energy that lowers costs of production. We will use the symbols Q and q for oil. The production technique (now assuming that there are no land limitations) is:

1 labor + k capital + x oil $\rightarrow$
x output + $(1 - \delta)k$ capital - x oil

Here we are again taking advantage of our freedom to choose the units in which we measure oil. This model of production assumes that to produce a unit of output you need to burn up one unit of oil. Thus at the end of the period, there are three results of the productive process: the x units of new output, the depreciation of capital, and the depletion of x units of oil. We are using the amount of oil required to produce one unit of output as our unit of measurement for oil.

Since the amount of oil available is finite, we have to have some theory of what happens when the oil runs out. If the only known production technology required oil, then we would have to assume that production would stop altogether when the oil reserves were exhausted. A more realistic modeling assumption is that there is another method of production (for example, one that depends on solar energy) that does not require oil:

1 labor + k capital $\rightarrow$ x' output + $(1 - \delta)k$ capital

For simplicity we assume that the alternative solar technology has the same capital intensity, k, and depreciation rate, δ, as the oil technology. If oil is an economically relevant resource, it must increase the productivity of other resources, such as labor and capital, so we assume that labor productivity is higher with the oil technology: $x > x'$. Under the assumption that the capital intensity is the same for the two

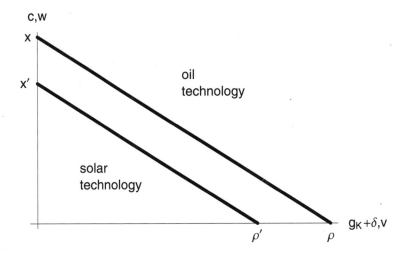

Figure 12.1: The real wage-profit rate relations for the oil
and solar technologies. The oil technology dominates the
solar technology, since it is more profitable at every real
wage. The slopes are the same, since we assume the two
technologies have the same capital-labor ratios: the use of
oil saves equal proportions of labor and capital.

technologies, the oil technology also raises the productivity of capital:
$\rho' = x'/k > x/k = \rho$.

Figure 12.1 shows the real wage-profit rate schedules for the two
techniques. The assumption that capital intensity, k, is the same in
the two technologies implies that oil saves labor and capital in equal
proportions. In other words, the use of oil is the equivalent of Hicks-
neutral technical progress. For a given wage, w, the wage share for
the oil technology is $1 - \pi = w/x$, while the wage share for the solar
technology is $1 - \pi' = w/x'$.

Since oil is a productive, scarce, and wasting resource, it will command a price in the market. If p_{qt} is the price of oil at the beginning of
period t, which is the end of period $t-1$, and entrepreneurs pay for their
oil, like wages, at the end of the period after they have sold their output,
the profit an entrepreneur using oil technology will make on each worker
employed is:

$$v_{qt}k = x - w - p_{qt+1}x = (1 - p_{qt+1})x - w$$

The profit per worker using solar technology is:

$$v_s k = x' - w$$

The corresponding profit rates for the two technologies are:

$$v_{qt} = (\pi - p_{qt+1})\rho$$

$$v_s = \pi'\rho'$$

The actual profit rate in any period will depend on whether the oil technology or the solar technology is the more profitable:

$$v_t = r_t + \delta = \max(v_{qt}, v_s) \tag{12.1}$$

There is a price of oil, p_q^*, at which the two technologies have the same profit rate for every real wage. If we set $w = 0$, we have $\pi' = \pi = 1$, so that:

$$\rho(1 - p_q^*) = \rho' \text{ or}$$

$$p_q^* = \frac{\rho - \rho'}{\rho}$$

The price of oil at which the two technologies have the same profit rates is equal to the proportion of capital (and labor) saved by oil, $(\rho - \rho')/\rho$. The price of oil cannot rise above p_q^*, because if it did the oil technology would have a lower profit rate than solar and no one would use it, so p_q^* is also the *maximum* price of oil. The more capital and labor oil saves, the higher will be its maximal price.

Problem 12.1 *Consider an economy with an oil technology where $x = \$50,000/worker/year$, $k = \$100,000/worker$, $\delta = 0/year$, and solar technology is 50% less productive, with the same rate of depreciation. Find the price of oil at which solar technology would just compete with oil.*

Problem 12.2 *For the economy described in 12.1, suppose that the capitalist $\beta = .95$ and that the wage is $\$10,000/worker/year$. Find the profit rate and the growth rate of the capital stock using solar technology.*

12.3 Saving and Portfolio Choice

The typical capitalist now has to choose how much oil reserves, Q_t, to hold as an asset in each period, and also how much oil to pump out of the reserves, ΔQ_t. If she pumps oil at the beginning of the period, she can sell it to entrepreneurs and receive p_{qt+1} at the end of the period, but in this case she will also have a smaller amount of oil reserves left at the end of the period.

The typical capitalist's budget constraint with oil in each period, given the net profit rate r_t, is thus:

$$K_{t+1}+C_t+p_{qt+1}Q_{t+1} \le (1+r_t)K_t+p_{qt+1}(Q_t-\Delta Q_t)+p_{qt+1}\Delta Q_t \quad (12.2)$$

We can also write the budget constraint as:

$$K_{t+1} + C_t + p_{qt+1}Q_{t+1} \le (1 + r_t)K_t + p_{qt+1}Q_t \quad (12.3)$$

The capitalist utility maximization problem is:

Capitalist's Utility Maximization Problem with Oil

---

choose $\{C_t, K_{t+1}, \Delta Q_t, Q_{t+1} \ge 0\}_{t=0}^{\infty}$ so as to maximize

$$(1 - \beta) \sum_{t=0}^{\infty} \beta^t \ln(C_t)$$

subject to

$$K_{t+1} + p_{qt+1}Q_{t+1} + C_t \le (1 + r_t)K_t + p_{qt+1}Q_t$$

$$\{p_{qt}, 1 + r_t\}_{t=0}^{\infty}, K_0, Q_0 \text{given}$$

A capitalist who chooses to hold a unit of oil reserves during period t at the price p_{qt} will have p_{qt+1} at the end of the period, due to the change in the price of oil over the period. She could, alternatively, invest the money in capital instead and receive $(1+r_t)p_{qt}$ at the end of the period. These two returns must be equal if the capitalist is to be willing to hold both oil reserves and capital in her portfolio. As Hotelling pointed out, the *arbitrage principle* of Chapter 11 applies to reserves of exhaustible resources like oil. Owners of reserves under conditions of competition must believe that the price of the reserves is rising at the same rate as the net profit rate on capital, since rational wealth holders will hold assets with equal risk only if their anticipated rates of return are equal. In this model the two assets are capital and oil reserves. They have the same (zero) risk, so capitalists will hold both only if they have the same rate of return. Furthermore, the capitalist is indifferent as to how much of her wealth she holds in capital and oil reserves as long as the rates of return on the two assets are identical. The mathematical expression of the arbitrage principle for the oil model is:

$$(1 + r_t)p_{qt} = p_{qt+1} \qquad (12.4)$$

This insight greatly simplifies the typical capitalist's budget constraint. Writing $J_t = K_t + p_{qt}Q_t$ for the capitalist's wealth at the beginning of period t, we can express the budget constraint as:

$$J_{t+1} + C_t \leq (1 + r_t)J_t$$

This is just the same as the budget constraint in Chapter 5, so we know that the solution to the utility maximization problem will be:

$$C_t = (1 - \beta)(1 + r_t)J_t, \text{ and}$$

$$J_{t+1} = (1 + r_t)J_t - C_t = \beta(1 + r_t)J_t$$

Thus wealth grows at the rate $\beta(1 + r_t)$.

Problem 12.3 *Write down the Lagrangian function for the capitalist's utility maximization problem with oil, and find the first-order conditions describing the saddle point. Use these conditions to derive the arbitrage principle and the consumption function.*

12.4   The Growth Path

The final piece of the puzzle is provided by recognizing that the amount of oil pumped, ΔQ_t, must be equal to X_t since each unit of output requires one unit of oil. Output, X_t, as in all Classical models where labor-power is elastically supplied, is determined by the amount of capital accumulated: $X_t = \rho K_t$. So we have:

$$\Delta Q_t = X_t = \rho K_t$$

But this allows us to trace the depletion of the oil reserves, since we know that:

$$Q_{t+1} = Q_t - \Delta Q_t = Q_t - \rho K_t$$

We can put all these relations together to see the laws governing the changes in market equilibrium prices and quantities in the oil model during periods while some oil reserves still remain. It turns out to be easier to express the quantities in terms of capitalist wealth $J = K + p_q Q$ and the remaining oil reserve, Q, rather than in terms of the capital stock K and Q, but if we know J, p_q, and Q in any period, we can easily find $K = J - p_q Q$.

Equilibrium in the Oil Model

$$r_t = (\pi - p_{qt+1})\rho - \delta \qquad (12.5)$$

$$p_{qt+1} = (1 + r_t)p_{qt} \qquad (12.6)$$

$$J_{t+1} = \beta(1 + r_t)J_t \qquad (12.7)$$

$$Q_{t+1} = Q_t - \rho(J_t - p_{qt}Q_t) \qquad (12.8)$$

Now we have a complete picture of the process of growth with the exhaustible resource. The price of oil rises steadily to provide capital gains on the oil reserves equal to the net profit rate, r_t. The net profit rate itself, r_t, declines in each period as oil becomes more expensive. Wealth grows through the saving of capitalists. Some part of this increase in wealth goes to increase the capital stock, thereby raising output and using up more oil.

There comes a time when the oil runs out. In this period the price of oil must rise to p_q^*, at which the solar technology is just competitive with the oil technology.

As in Chapter 11, the two regimes have to be fitted together by the correct speculative pricing of oil in the initial period. The price of oil in the initial period must be set by speculation in such a way that it reaches p_q^* in exactly the period that the oil reserves will be exhausted. Clearly this depends on the size of the oil reserves in the initial period in relation to the capital stock. If the oil price is too high, the resulting large oil wealth will induce the capitalists to consume at a high rate, and output and the capital stock will not grow fast enough to use up the oil reserves by the time the price of oil rises to its maximum level. If the oil price is set too low, on the other hand, the high rate of capitalist saving will exhaust oil reserves before the solar technology becomes competitive.

Forward-looking speculation attempts to find the initial price of oil that induces just the rate of growth of output and capital stock compatible with using up the oil reserves at the equilibrium rate.

The larger are initial reserves, the longer it will take to exhaust them, and the lower the initial equilibrium price of oil will be. The more efficient the alternative solar technology, the lower is the maximal price of oil (since it measures the efficiency advantage of oil over solar), and the lower will be the initial equilibrium price. Thus speculators in the oil market have to consider the size of known reserves, the likely rate of economic growth and demand for oil, and the rate at which alternative technologies are developing to form the equilibrium price.

Problem 12.4 *Explain what effect the following would have on oil prices, using the exhaustible resources model as a basis: (a) a discovery that would allow wells four times as deep as at present to be drilled at the same cost; (b) a drastic cheapening of solar cells; (c) an increase in the capitalist propensity to save.*

Problem 12.5 *Consider the economy described in Problem 12.2. Suppose that the economy has just exhausted its oil reserve. Work backward one period and find the price of oil and the profit rate in the period just before the oil reserve was exhausted.*

Problem 12.6 *Make a spreadsheet program to calculate the growth path for an oil economy starting from the period in which oil reserves are exhausted and working backward 20 years, calculating the price of oil in each year.*

12.5   Exhaustible Resources in the Real World

This model gives us some fundamental insights into the way a market capitalist economy will value reserves of exhaustible resources. The general outlines of the solution look plausible: profit rates and growth rates decline as the reserve is depleted, and the price of the exhaustible resource gradually rises until it makes the next best technology competitive.

In the real world, however, the prices of exhaustible resources do not always rise, and, in fact, sometimes fall dramatically and over a long period. These observations could mean that some assumption of the model is wrong. For example, the exhaustible resources in question might not be priced competitively in some periods. But a fall in the price of an

Example 12.1 *Let the oil technology have* $x = \$100,000/\text{-}$
worker/year, $\delta = 1/\text{year}$, $k = \$12,500/\text{worker}$, *and suppose that*
the alternative solar technology is half as productive, so that $x' =$
$\$50,000/\text{worker/year}$. $\rho = x/k = 8/\text{year}$ *and* $\rho' = x'/k = 4/\text{year}$.
The conventional wage, $\bar{w} = \$20,000/\text{worker/year}$. *Thus* $\pi =$
$1 - (w/x) = .8$ *and* $\pi\prime = 1 - (w/x') = .6$. *Find the maximum*
price of oil, and the price of oil and the net profit rate in the
period before oil reserves are exhausted.

Answer: The maximum price of oil is:

$$p_q^* = \frac{\rho - \rho'}{\rho} = .5$$

In each period before the oil reserves are exhausted we have

$$p_{qt+1} = (1 + r_t)p_{qt} = (v_{qt} + 1 - \delta)p_{qt}$$

$$= ((\pi - p_{qt+1})\rho + 1 - \delta)p_{qt}$$

This implies that

$$p_{qt} = \frac{p_{qt+1}}{\pi\rho + 1 - \delta - \rho p_{qt+1}}$$

Suppose we take one step backward from the period in which the oil
runs out.
The profit rate in the period before the oil runs out will be

$$v_{q-1} = (\pi - p_q^*)\rho = (.8 - .5)(8) = 2.4$$

Thus we have:

$$p_{q-1} = \frac{p_q^*}{\pi\rho + 1 - \delta - \rho p_q^*}$$

$$= \frac{.5}{(.8)(8) - (8)(.5)} = .5/2.4 = .21$$

or 21% of output.

exhaustible resource could also occur if new information about the size of reserves, or the costs of alternative technology, or the growth rate of the economy arrives. New information of this kind requires the owners of oil reserves to re-price them taking the information into account. Anticipated slower economic growth, or more rapid improvement in alternative technologies, or the discovery of new reserves can drive the price of the exhaustible resource down.

Thus the chief aspect of the real world the model leaves out is uncertainty about future technological developments, economic growth and resource discoveries. We have assumed that the initial oil reserve Q_0 is known, and that the solar costs, which determine p_q^*, are also known and unchanging. In the real world new information constantly changes the best estimates of the reserves and of the costs of competing technologies. This type of information is particularly important in the pricing of a speculative asset like oil reserves. To explain this rigorously would require a model where capitalists took account of the uncertainty of the relevant future developments.

12.6   Suggested Readings

The seminal work on the theory of optimal use of an exhaustible resource is Hotelling [1931]. For additional discussion of the model of oil and solar power developed in the text, see [Kurz and Salvadori, 1995, ch. 12] where an overview of the history of thought on the subject can also be found. Two sources which analyze the effects of the 1970s OPEC price increases on the wage-profit curve are Bruno and Sachs [1985], from a neoclassical perspective, and Michl [1991], from a Classical perspective.

Chapter 13

Government Debt and Social Security: The Overlapping Generations Model

13.1 Government Finance and Accumulation

In this chapter we will study the impact of government finance in the form of social security programs and deficit spending on the accumulation of capital. Social security benefits and government debt are an asset to private households, but do not necessarily correspond to any real investment on the part of the government. The key question is whether the existence of these government-created assets can reduce private saving and capital formation.

Government taxes and transfers can have effects on the allocation of resources if the taxes and transfers are linked to economic decision variables like saving or profit. This is because these taxes affect the rates of return perceived by decision makers, and will influence their decisions to save and invest by changing these rates of return. In this chapter, however, we are interested in whether government programs can divert private saving from the financing of real investment. In order to focus our attention on this particular impact of government fiscal policy, we will consider only programs financed by *lump-sum* taxes and transfers, which do not depend on agents' wealth or income, and thus do not change their economic incentives at the margin.

The effects of a social security system or a deficit spending policy of the government on household saving plans depend critically on whether we assume that each generation takes into account the welfare of future generations in making its spending plans. As Robert Barro has pointed out, if the welfare of future generations enters into the utility function of the current generation, then there will be no macroeconomic effects of deficits or social security plans. The assumption that the current generation takes the future generation's welfare into account in making its spending plans is called *Ricardian equivalence*. We have been using this assumption in all the models where saving decisions are made by a representative capitalist who maximizes utility over an infinite horizon.

It is not hard to see intuitively why the assumption of Ricardian equivalence implies that deficit spending by the government will have no real effects. Under these assumptions the typical household of the current generation can enforce whatever level of next generation consumption seems optimal by changing its bequest to the next generation and thus undo any effects of deficit spending or social security on social saving. In the next section we work through this problem rigorously by examining the budget constraints of the government and the typical capitalist household under the assumption of Ricardian equivalence.

In considering the importance of Ricardian equivalence in the real world, remember that from the economic point of view a bequest does not have to be an inheritance at the time of death of a member of the current generation. Ricardian equivalence holds as well if the current generation invests in the education of their children (since this investment is an intergenerational transfer, just like a bequest), or, indeed, if the children support their parents in retirement (which is like a negative bequest). If households are rational and forward-looking, the government social security policies and deficits will have an impact on social saving only if each generation acts selfishly.

13.2   Government and Private Budget Constraints

The difference between government revenues and outlays is the *fiscal surplus*. If outlays exceed revenues, the fiscal surplus is negative and is often referred to as a *fiscal deficit*. (It is crucial not to confuse the fiscal surplus and deficit with the *balance of payments surplus or deficit* of a country. The balance of payments surplus or deficit reflects the transactions of all sectors of an economy, private as well as public, with the rest of the world. The fiscal surplus reflects the transactions of the public sector with the private sector.) Revenues and outlays include interest payments received and made by governments. The difference between government revenues and outlays excluding interest payments is called the *primary fiscal surplus,* and measures the degree to which current non-interest revenues are financing current non-interest expenditures.

When governments spend more than their tax revenue, they must finance the resulting primary fiscal deficit by borrowing. In our models, where prices and profit rates are known with certainty, the government will have to pay the same real rate of interest as capitalists can get by investing their money in capital. In this chapter we will assume that the price level is constant, so that real and monetary quantities are the same. We will also assume that the only asset or liability held by the government is its own debt, B. The growth of the government debt under these assumptions will depend on the primary fiscal surplus, E, and its interest payments on the accumulated debt, rB:

$$B_{t+1} = B_t + r_t B_t - E_t = (1 + r_t)B_t - E_t \qquad (13.1)$$

From this series we can see that:

$$B_1 = (1 + r_0)B_0 - E_0$$

$$B_2 = (1 + r_1)B_1 - E_1 = (1 + r_1)(1 + r_0)B_0 - (E_1 + (1 + r_1)E_0)$$

$$\cdots$$

$$B_T = (1 + r_{T-1})(1 + r_{T-2})\ldots(1 + r_0)B_0$$
$$-(E_{T-1} + (1 + r_{T-1})E_{T-2} + (1 + r_{T-1})(1 + r_{T-2})E_{T-3}$$
$$\ldots + (1 + r_{T-1})(1 + r_{T-2})\ldots(1 + r_1)E_0)$$

The economic meaning of this way of looking at the government budget constraint is that the government effectively has to pay an opportunity cost for running a primary fiscal deficit $(-E)$ equal to all the future interest it would save if it financed the expenditures out of current taxes. If we define the *total return factor over the horizon T,* $R_T = (1 + r_{T-1})(1 + r_{T-2})\ldots(1 + r_0)$, we can divide through by R_T and write this equation as:

$$B_0 = \frac{B_T}{R_T} + \Sigma_{t=0}^{T-1}\frac{E_t}{R_{t+1}}$$

The value of the government debt in the current period is equal to the present discounted value of the primary fiscal surpluses over the horizon T plus the present discounted value of the debt at time T.

The government budget constraint depends on what we assume happens to B_T/R_T as $T \to \infty$. If we allow $\lim_{T \to \infty}(B_T/R_T) > 0$, we are assuming that the government can escape the intertemporal budget constraint by indefinitely paying the interest on its debt by new borrowing. Economists call such a path a *Ponzi game*, after a Boston financier who had temporary success with this creative financing method in the 1920s. The *conventional government budget constraint* requires that $\lim_{T \to \infty}(B_T/R_T) = 0$. Under the conventional budget constraint, taking the limit as $T \to \infty$:

$$B_0 = \Sigma_{t=0}^{\infty} \frac{E_t}{R_t}$$

The conventional government budget constraint implies that the value of the government debt in the current period is equal to the present discounted value of the primary fiscal surpluses over the whole future.

Lump-sum government tax and transfer programs that respect the conventional government budget constraint will have no macroeconomic effects in the Classical model where a representative capitalist makes consumption decisions over an infinite horizon. The reason is that the typical capitalist will take into account all the future tax payments and benefits involved in the government's programs, and adjust her own consumption accordingly. Since the government must abide by its budget constraint, the capitalist's consumption and savings decisions cannot be altered by anything the government does. This is the essence of Ricardian equivalence.

To see this point, return to the model of capitalist consumption where the capitalist earns a certain sequence of rates of return $\{r_t\}_{t=0}^{\infty}$ on her wealth in each period, J_t (which may consist of capital or a mixture of capital and other assets like land and government bonds). In each period the capitalist's budget constraint can be written:

$$J_{t+1} = (1 + r_t)J_t - C_t$$

This constraint is exactly the same as the government budget constraint, (13.1), with the capitalist's wealth, J_t, taking the place of the government debt, B_t, and the capitalist's consumption, C_t, taking the place of the primary fiscal deficit, $-E_t$. Thus we can draw the same conclusion:

$$J_0 = \Sigma_{t=0}^{\infty} \frac{C_t}{R_t} \tag{13.2}$$

Economically this means that we can summarize the capitalist's budget constraint as the requirement that the present discounted value of the capitalist's consumption over the infinite future must be equal to her initial wealth.

Now, suppose that the government, starting from a position where $B_0 = 0$, introduces a system of taxes and transfers that imply a series of primary fiscal surpluses (or deficits) $\{E_t\}_{t=0}^{\infty}$ that satisfy the conventional government budget constraint. Suppose for simplicity that the government invests any surpluses in real investment. The typical capitalist household's budget constraint in period t will now have to include these taxes and transfers:

$$J_{t+1} = (1 + r_t)J_t - C_t - E_t$$

So the capitalist can choose any consumption path that satisfies:

$$\Sigma_{t=0}^{\infty} \frac{C_t + E_t}{R_t} = J_0 \tag{13.3}$$

But if the government respects the conventional government budget constraint:

$$\Sigma_{t=0}^{\infty} \frac{E_t}{R_t} = 0$$

then (13.3) represents exactly the same constraints as (13.2), so the government tax and transfer policy has no effect whatsoever on the capitalist's consumption path.

In the types of models we are using, when the government runs a surplus and invests the resources in real capital, this government investment will just take the place of the reduction in saving of the capitalist households as they maintain their consumption plan in the face of higher taxes. (If the government provides consumption services, the capitalist households will take that into account and reduce their consumption accordingly, leaving the path of investment unchanged.) Similar reasoning applies to the periods in which the government runs a deficit: capitalist households will exactly offset the deficit to maintain the overall consumption and investment path unchanged.

13.3 Saving and Consumption with Selfish Households

In order to analyze real macroeconomic effects of social security programs and deficit spending we need a model in which households make saving decisions over a limited horizon, so that Ricardian equivalence does not hold. One influential model of this kind is the *overlapping generations* model, in which each generation lives a finite number (usually two) periods, and makes its savings and consumption decisions without regard to the future. In these models workers rather than capitalists save in order to finance their retirement consumption. We will look at a Classical version of the overlapping generation model, in which the growth rate of the population varies in order to keep the wage (or the wage share) constant. In this setting government finance decisions can affect the growth rate of the economy. Neoclassical economists have analyzed the overlapping generations model under the assumption of full employment of an exogenously growing labor force, so that the growth rate is determined in the labor market. Under this assumption government fiscal policy cannot have an impact on the growth rate itself, but can have impacts on saving and consumption decisions, wage and profit rates, and the average welfare of the agents in the society.

The overlapping generations model sees the source of social saving as worker households looking toward eventual retirement. The prospect of a period of life in which the household will not be able to earn money and still must live is a powerful motive for saving. This view of saving was developed by Franco Modigliani, and is often called the *life-cycle theory of saving*, because the motive for saving is to allow a steady stream of consumption over the whole life cycle, despite the fact that earnings from work are concentrated at one stage of the life cycle.

This approach differs from the model of capitalist consumption because households in the life-cycle theory plan for finite lifetimes, and therefore consume their whole wealth in retirement. The capitalist household, by contrast, considers the welfare of its whole posterity. Ricardian equivalence, which holds in the capitalist consumption model, does not hold in the life-cycle model.

In order to keep the model simple, we will make some other key assumptions: that households can borrow or lend freely at a single market rate of interest; that no one tries to cheat the system by dying in debt; and that all the funds lent by savers are borrowed by firms for investment, so that the rate of interest is equal to the rate of profit. We will also explain the model assuming that there is no inflation or deflation of money prices, so that all the transactions take place and are measured in terms of real output.

It is possible to analyze the overlapping generations model in two-dimensional diagrams if we assume that households live two periods, so that the only decision they have to make is how to divide their total lifetime income between consumption in their youth and in their retirement.

To begin with, consider a single household that lives two periods. Suppose that it is willing to supply one unit of labor-power to the market in its first (working) period at any positive wage, and will supply no labor-power at any wage in its second (retirement) period. Assume as well that the household leaves no bequests, so that it consumes all of its wealth and income in the retirement period. If we call the household's consumption when it is working c^w, its saving s^w, and its consumption in retirement c^r, we have the following budget constraints, writing $r = v - \delta$ for the net profit rate:

$$c^w + s^w = w$$

$$c^r = (1 + r_{+1})s^w$$

The households will receive the net profit rate on their saving in the second period of their lives, when they are retired. These two constraints can be combined into a single household budget constraint showing the consumption levels in the working and retirement periods the household can achieve:

$$c^w + \frac{c^r}{1 + r_{+1}} = w \qquad (13.4)$$

The neoclassical tradition explains household saving on the assumption that households have given *preferences* over different patterns of lifetime consumption. We can represent these patterns as *indifference curves* between consumption in the working period and consumption in the retirement period. These indifference curves reflect such factors as the household's *time preference*, that is, its relative valuation of consumption in the present and consumption in the future, and the different consumption possibilities and demands on the household in the working and retirement periods.

Given these indifference curves, the household will choose the point on its budget constraint that reaches the highest indifference curve. If the indifference curves are smooth and concave to the origin, this implies that the household will choose to consume at a point where the budget constraint is tangent to the indifference curve through that point.

This theory allows for a very wide range of responses of households to changes in wages and interest rates, depending on the relative size of wealth and substitution effects. A rise in the interest rate makes future consumption cheaper in terms of present consumption. A change in the price of future consumption affects present consumption (and saving) in the same ways that the change in the price of one good can affect the demand for another good in the general model of consumer demand. In particular, when interest rates increase, saving may either increase or decrease, depending on the exact shape of the indifference curves, which determines whether the substitution or wealth effect of an increase in interest rates predominates.

To make our analysis simpler, we will assume that the indifference curves of households arise from Cobb-Douglas utility functions:

$$U(c^w, c^r) = (1 - \beta) \ln(c^w) + \beta \ln(c^r)$$

Then we know that the household will spend a fraction $1 - \beta$ of its lifetime wealth on current consumption, and save a fraction β of its lifetime wealth. The consumption and saving functions are:

$$c^w(r, w) = (1 - \beta)w$$

$$s^w(r, w) = \beta w$$

$$c^r(r, w) = (1 + r_{+1})\beta w \tag{13.5}$$

The Cobb-Douglas assumption implies that current consumption and saving will both increase in a constant proportion to the wage rate and working period income. As we have seen in previous models, the substitution and wealth effects arising from a change in the interest rate exactly offset each other in the Cobb-Douglas case.

13.4   A Classical Overlapping Generations Growth Model

The overlapping generations saving model can be combined with the Classical conventional wage closure of the labor market to construct a model of economic growth.

In this Classical overlapping generations model all saving comes from workers who are looking forward to retirement. The capital stock is owned by retired workers, who save nothing at all because they do not care (by assumption) about future generations. Life-cycle saving theory thus explains social saving on the basis of the preferences of households as represented by their indifference curves, and on the demographics of the society, as represented by the ratio of retired to active workers. All saving comes from wages, in contrast to the capitalist consumption model, where all saving comes from accumulated capitalist wealth.

The technology is a Leontief system described by the parameters k, x, and δ, with no technical change. (It would be straightforward to incorporate pure labor-augmenting technical change.) Thus the demand for labor in each period depends on the amount of capital that exists in that period. The growth-distribution relations continue to hold:

$$w = x - vk \tag{13.6}$$

$$c = x - (g_K + \delta)k \tag{13.7}$$

Now let us make the Classical assumption that the wage is fixed at $\bar{w}$ because the labor force will grow if the wage is above $\bar{w}$ or decline if the wage is below $\bar{w}$, and the labor market clears at full employment in each period. Then the number of young, working households in period $t+1$ will be determined by the saving of working households in period t, since the number of jobs in period $t+1$ depends on the capital stock at the beginning of the period. Thus the growth rate of the population, n, on an equilibrium perfect-foresight path under these assumptions must be equal to the growth rate of the capital stock, g_K. The growth rate of output, g_X, will then also be equal to g_K.

The capital stock of the next generation must be financed entirely by the saving of the current working generation, since the current retired generation consumes all of its wealth and income. Thus the saving of the current generation, $s^w = \beta w$, has to buy back the undepreciated capital stock, $(1 - \delta)k$, from the retired generation, and finance gross investment, $(g_K + \delta)k$. Thus we have the overlapping generations *growth-wage relation*:

$$(1 - \delta)k + (g_K + \delta)k = (1 + g_K)k = \beta w = s^w \tag{13.8}$$

This savings-investment relation takes the place of the Cambridge equation to determine the growth rate of the capital stock in the Classical overlapping generations model. We can also write this as a relation between the wage, w, and the gross growth rate of the capital stock, $g_K + \delta$:

$$w = \frac{(1 - \delta + (g_K + \delta))k}{\beta} = \frac{(1 + g_K)k}{\beta} \tag{13.9}$$

The model is closed by assuming a conventional wage:

$$w = \bar{w} \tag{13.10}$$

In the Classical conventional wage overlapping generations model the wage, w, is equal to the conventional wage, $\bar{w}$, and the rate of profit, v, is determined from the wage through the real wage-profit rate relation. The wage also determines the growth rates of the capital stock, labor force, and output through equation (13.8). Social consumption, c, then follows from the growth-distribution schedule.

The social consumption per worker, c, is divided between the consumption of the current generation of workers, c^w, and the consumption of the retired generation, c^r. Since the labor force grew at the rate g_{K-1} in the last period, there are $1 + g_{K-1}$ active workers for every retired worker, and since each active worker supplies one unit of labor-power to the economy, the social consumption per active worker will be:

$$c = c^w + \frac{c^r_{-1}}{1 + g_{K-1}} \tag{13.11}$$

The retired generation consumes its saved principal and return:

$$c^r_{-1} = (1 - \delta + v)s^w_{-1} = (1 - \delta + v)(1 + g_{K-1})k \tag{13.12}$$

We can also find social saving per worker, which is just the difference between output and social consumption per worker:

$$x - c = w - c^w + vk - \frac{c^r_{-1}}{1 + g_{K-1}} = s^w - (1 - \delta)k \tag{13.13}$$

Social saving per worker, $x - c$, differs from the saving per working household, s^w, because retired households dissave the value of the undepreciated capital stock, $(1 - \delta)k$.

Figure 13.1 illustrates the Classical overlapping generations model.

Problem 13.1 *Find the Classical overlapping generations equilibrium for Industria (see Problem 2.2) when the wage is $30,000/worker-year and workers' households save 80% of the wage.*

Problem 13.2 *In the Classical overlapping generations model, what is the effect of an increase in the conventional real wage, $\bar{w}$ on w, v, g_K, c, c^w, and c^r?*

Problem 13.3 *In the Classical overlapping generations model, what is the effect of an increase in the saving propensity, β on w, v, g_K, c, c^w, and c^r?*

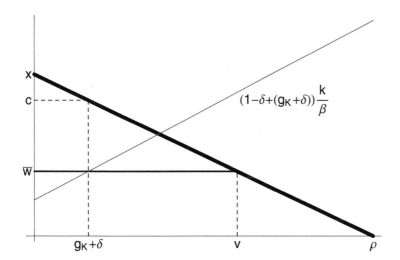

Figure 13.1: In the Classical overlapping generations model the conventional wage, $\bar{w}$, determines the profit rate, v, through the growth-distribution schedule, and the gross growth rate of capital through the growth-wage relation shown in gray, $w = (1-\delta+(g_K+\delta))k/\beta$. Social consumption per worker, c, is then determined by the growth-distribution schedule. Workers' consumption is $c^w = (1 - \beta)w$, and the consumption of the retired generation is $c^r = (1+g_{K-1})(1-\delta + v)k$.

Example 13.1 *Find the Classical overlapping generations equilibrium for Ricardia (see Problem 2.1) when the wage is 50 bushels of corn/worker-year and workers' households save 50% of the wage.*

Answer: In Ricardia: $x = 100$ bushels/worker-year; $\rho = 5$/year; $k = 20$ bushels/worker; and $\delta = 1$/year. Here we have $\bar{w} = 50$ bushels/worker-year, so the profit rate, $v = (x - w)/k = 2.5$/year. The gross growth rate of capital, $g_K + \delta = \beta w/k - (1 - \delta) = (.5)(50/20) = 1.25$/year, and the growth rate $g_K = .25$/year. Social consumption per worker is $c = x - (g_K + \delta)k = 100 - (1.25)(20) = 75$ bushels/worker-year. Worker consumption is $c^w = (1 - \beta)w = (.5)(50) = 25$ bushels/worker-year. Retired households consume $c^r = (1 - \delta + v)\beta w = (2.5)(.5)(50) = 62.5$ bushels/worker-year. We see that $c = c^w + (c^r/(1 + g_K))$ holds, since $c^w = 25$ bushels/worker-year and $c^r/(1 + g_K) = 62.5/1.25 = 50$ bushels/worker-year.

13.5   A Neoclassical Overlapping Generations Growth Model

The overlapping generations model can also be closed by assuming that the growth rate of the labor force, $\bar{n}$, is given exogenously, and that the wage, w, adjusts to assure the clearing of the labor market. As in the Classical version of the model, the rate of growth of the capital stock must be equal to the rate of growth of the labor force, $g_K = \bar{n}$, in order to assure full employment of the available labor.

The neoclassical overlapping generations model has the same growth-distribution and saving relations as the Classical overlapping generations model:

$$w = x - vk$$

$$c = x - (g_K + \delta)k$$

$$(1 + g_K)k = \beta w$$

The model is closed, however, by assuming a given growth rate of the labor force:

$$g_K = \bar{n} \tag{13.14}$$

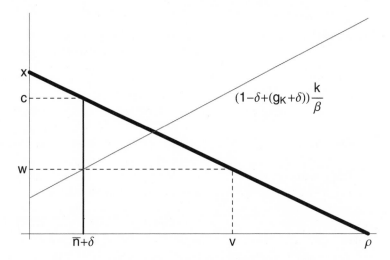

Figure 13.2: In the neoclassical overlapping generations model the growth rate of the labor force determines the growth rate of the capital stock directly, and the wage through the growth-wage relation, $w = (1 + \bar{n})(k/\beta)$. The growth rate of the capital stock determines social consumption per worker, c, and the wage determines the profit rate through the growth-distribution schedule.

The wage in the neoclassical overlapping generations model is determined by the requirement that the saving of the working generation finance enough investment to employ the next working generation completely:

$$\beta w = (1 + \bar{n})k \qquad (13.15)$$

Figure 13.2 illustrates the neoclassical overlapping generations model. The growth rate of capital is determined by the exogenously given growth rate of the labor force, $g_K = \bar{n}$, which determines social consumption, c. The wage is determined by the requirement that the saving of workers equal the whole capital stock necessary to employ the next generation, $w = (1 + \bar{n})(k/\beta)$.

There may be no equilibrium profit rate if β is small and $\bar{n}$ is large, because there may be no wage high enough to induce workers to save enough to employ the entire next generation of workers. We can read c^w from the graph as the distance from the efficiency schedule to the βw line. The consumption of the typical retired household, c^r, is equal

Example 13.2 *Find the neoclassical overlapping generations equilibrium for Ricardia (see Problem 2.1) when the growth rate of the labor force is .1/year and workers' households save 50% of the wage.*

Answer: In Ricardia: $x = 100$ bushels/worker-year; $k = 20$ bushels/worker; $\rho = 5$/year; and $\delta = 1$/year. Here we have $\bar{n} = g_K = .1$/year, so the wage, $w = (1 + \bar{n})(k/\beta) = 44$ bushels/worker-year, and the profit rate, $v = (x - w)/k = 2.8$/year. The gross growth rate of capital, $g_K + \delta = \beta w/k - (1 - \delta) = (.5)(44/20) = 1.1$/year, and the growth rate $g_K = .1$/year, which will just maintain full employment in the face of the growth of the labor force. Social consumption per worker is $c = x - (g_K + \delta)k = 100 - (1.1)(20) = 78$ bushels/worker-year. Worker consumption is $c^w = (1 - \beta)w = (.5)(44) = 22$ bushels/worker-year. Retired households consume $c^r = (1 - \delta + v)\beta w = (2.8)(.5)(44) = 61.6$ bushels/worker-year. We see that $c = c^w + (c^r/(1 + g_K))$ holds, since $c^w = 22$ bushels/worker-year and $c^r/(1 + g_K) = 61.6/1.1 = 56$ bushels/worker-year.

to $(1 - \delta + v)(1 + \bar{n})k$. Retired households consume the value of the undepreciated capital stock plus the profit, $(1 - \delta + v)k$, while working households consume a part of the real wage and save enough of the rest to buy the undepreciated capital stock from the retired workers and provide new capital to replace depreciation and create jobs for the next generation.

Problem 13.4 *Find the Classical overlapping generations equilibrium for Industria (see Problem 2.2) when the growth rate of the labor force is zero and workers' households save 80% of the wage.*

Problem 13.5 *Analyze the equilibrium of the overlapping generations model when there are several techniques available.*

Problem 13.6 *What is the effect of a rise in β on the equilibrium growth path of the overlapping generations model, in terms of v, w, g_K, c, c^w, and c^r?*

Problem 13.7 *What is the effect of an increase in the growth rate of the population on the equilibrium of the overlapping generations model, in terms of v, w, g_K, c, c^w, and c^r?*

13.6 Pareto-efficiency in the Overlapping Generations Model

An important idea in the history of economic thought is the claim, put forward vividly by Adam Smith, that free competition leads to a socially desirable use of resources. In the twentieth century economic theorists have worked to develop logical concepts to analyze this claim more precisely.

A key concept in this discussion is the notion of a *Pareto-efficient* allocation of resources. We imagine that, instead of having a market economy with private ownership and exchange, an economic dictator has the power to decide what will be produced, how it will be produced, and who will get the output. The dictator has control of exactly the same resources as exist in the market economy, and faces exactly the same production possibilities. The households in the market economy are imagined to have exactly the same preferences under the dictator as they do when there is exchange. An *allocation of resources* is a plan that specifies what will be produced, and what techniques of production will be used, and how the output will be distributed between the consumption of various generations and investment. An allocation is called *feasible* if it would actually be possible to carry it out with the existing resources and technology of the economy. The dictator is assumed to be so powerful that she can order any feasible allocation of resources that she wishes.

Now consider some particular feasible allocation, the *test allocation*. The test allocation could come about in any arbitrary way, but we are particularly interested in test allocations that are equilibrium paths of the overlapping generations model. To analyze the Pareto-efficiency of the test allocation, we consider whether there is another feasible allocation, the *alternative allocation*, that gives every household a consumption plan that it likes at least as well as its consumption under the test allocation, and gives at least one household a consumption plan that it prefers to the test allocation. This is the same thing as asking whether the dictator could rearrange production plans and distribution in such a way as to give at least one household something it likes better without forcing any household to accept something it likes worse than the test allocation. If an alternative allocation exists that does leave every household at least as well off and makes at least one household better off, the alternative allocation is said to be *Pareto-superior* to the test allocation, and the test allocation is *not* Pareto-efficient. If, on the other hand, there is *no* Pareto-superior alternative allocation, the test allocation is *Pareto-efficient*.

In order to prove that a test allocation is not Pareto-efficient, all
we have to do is to construct one Pareto-superior alternative allocation.
To prove that a test allocation is Pareto-efficient, on the other hand,
is logically much more difficult, because it requires us to show that *no*
alternative feasible allocation is Pareto-superior.

It is important to see why we use the term *Pareto-efficient* rather
than calling Pareto-efficient allocations *optimal*.   Optimal means *best*:
an optimal allocation is the best allocation under some method of ranking allocations. In particular, we can refer to an optimal allocation only
if we have a method of ranking every pair of allocations including cases
in which some households are better off and some worse off. But the
concept of Pareto-superiority does not allow us to compare *any* two allocations, and in particular cannot rank two allocations in which some
households are better off and some worse off. If we have two allocations, and the first makes some households better off and some worse
off, and the second makes some other households better off, and some
worse off, neither is Pareto-superior to the other. Thus it makes no
sense to say that one allocation was best, or optimal, using the logic of
Pareto-superiority. The fact that no allocation is Pareto-superior to a
Pareto-efficient allocation does *not* imply that a Pareto-efficient allocation is Pareto-superior to every other allocation.

Some economists have been tempted to think that Pareto-efficiency
is at least a part of full optimality and argue that an optimal allocation
chosen according to any reasonable method of ranking must be Pareto-
efficient. But this is not true. The reason is that the Pareto method
of comparison of allocation completely ignores the *relative levels* of consumption of different households. An allocation in which one household consumes almost everything and the rest consume almost nothing
can be Pareto-efficient because any change that would improve the lot
of low-consuming households would have to make the high-consuming
household worse off, for example. If the method of ranking we use to
decide which allocation is the best allocation includes some considera-
tion of the *distribution* of consumption among the households, it might
turn out under certain circumstances that the overall best, or optimal,
allocation of resources was not Pareto-efficient.

This is a difficult point for some people to follow. They reason as
follows: take the allocation you called the best allocation but is not
Pareto-efficient. Then there is by definition an alternative allocation that
makes some households better off without making any households worse
off. Surely that alternative allocation is better than the test allocation,
so that the test allocation could not be the best after all. The flaw in
this argument is that it might not be possible in reality to reach the
alternative allocation. For example, the alternative allocation might be

achievable in a real-world market economy only by using taxes that are unconstitutional in the country in question, or only by using private information that the government cannot collect. The only way to settle the question of whether an optimal allocation according to some ranking is Pareto-efficient is to specify exactly what the ranking criterion is, and what the institutional setting is within which allocations are going to be determined. Only with this information can we determine the optimal allocation in particular circumstances.

There is a famous economic argument, often called the *First Welfare Theorem*, that says that if an allocation arises as a market clearing equilibrium in an economy where all agents have full information about the qualities of commodities and the technology, where there are no external effects of one agent's economic activities on other agents, that is, effects that cannot be bought and sold for a price on a market, and where there is vigorous competition, so that each agent takes the market price as given, then that allocation will be Pareto-efficient. This theorem can be proved in an economy with a finite number of commodities by showing that if a test competitive allocation were not Pareto-efficient, the alternative allocation would be more profitable for some producer, or provide a higher level of satisfaction at the same income for some household than the test allocation, so that the test allocation could not in fact be an equilibrium allocation.

It is a striking fact that this theorem does not hold in the overlapping generations economy. It is possible to have a competitive equilibrium in the overlapping generations model that is not Pareto-efficient.

To see how this comes about, let us take for our test allocation a steady-state equilibrium of the overlapping generations model with a net profit rate $r = v - \delta$. Imagine that we are the dictator, and that we will try to make the retirees in the first period better off without making any of the later generations worse off.

First of all, in each period we have to assign enough output as investment so that the next generation will be fully employed. This requires us to set aside $(\delta + n)k$ units of output for every employed household, because, as we have seen, that will provide the next, larger, generation with just enough capital for all of them to work. As equation (13.7) shows, this means that the total consumption per active worker in each period on the alternative path ($c = x - (\delta + n)k$) will have to be the same as on the equilibrium path. The only freedom we have is to rearrange that consumption between the working generation and the retired generation.

If we want to make the first retired generation better off, we have to give them more consumption. But to do this, the first working generation will have to consume less. Is there any way to make them better off, despite the fact that they are consuming less in their working period? The only way would be to give them enough more consumption in their retirement so that they liked the alternative situation just as well.

Suppose for definiteness that we took a very small amount of consumption, Δc_1^w units of output, from each of the first generation of workers and gave it to the retirees in the first period. Clearly the first period retirees are better off, because they are consuming more. How much more must we give the first generation of workers when they are retired to keep them just as well off as under the original stationary equilibrium allocation? We know from the theory of saving that the marginal rate of substitution between working consumption and retirement consumption for every generation is $(1 + r)$, that is, that each household would view getting $(1 + r)\Delta c_1^w$ more units of consumption in its retirement as compensation for losing Δc_1^w units of consumption in its working period, as long as Δc_1^w is very small. In order to make the first generation of workers as well off in the alternative allocation, we have to have:

$$\Delta c_1^r = -(1 + r)\Delta c_1^w$$

Here Δc_1^r is the increase in household retirement consumption of the first generation in the second period (when the first generation of workers retire), and Δc_1^w is the decrease in consumption of the first generation in the first period, when they are working. But if we give the first generation more consumption in the second period, we have to take away consumption from the *second* generation while it is working. How much? We know that there are $(1 + n)$ households in the second generation for each household in the first generation, so:

$$\Delta c_2^w = -\frac{\Delta c_1^r}{1 + n} = \frac{1 + r}{1 + n}\Delta c_1^w$$

Now we are in exactly the same position with regard to the second generation as we were previously with respect to the first. The first generation of retirees is definitely better off, because they are consuming more. The first generation of workers is no worse off, because we have given them enough extra consumption in their retirement to compensate them for the loss when they were working. Now we have to compensate the second generation of workers in their retirement, by taking some away from the third generation of workers. We can see that following this plan will require:

$$\Delta c_t^w = \left(\frac{1 + r}{1 + n}\right)^{t-1}\Delta c_1^w$$

Is this plan going to work? If $1 + r > 1 + n$, it will not work, because we will have to take larger and larger amounts from each generation of workers to keep the last generation as well off as at the stationary equilibrium. But if $1 + r < 1 + n$ it will work, because the amount we have to take from each succeeding generation of workers will be getting smaller and smaller, and eventually will practically vanish. Thus if $1 + r < 1 + n$, that is, if the profit rate is smaller than the growth rate of the labor force, the competitive equilibrium is not Pareto-efficient. This example shows that the First Welfare Theorem does not hold in the overlapping generations model, despite the fact that all the assumptions of the Theorem are satisfied: the agents have full information, there are no externalities, and the households and firms take market prices as given.

Notice that in proving that the stationary equilibrium with $r < n$ is not Pareto-efficient, we did not compare it to an alternative *stationary* allocation: the alternative we constructed was not stationary because we allowed different generations to have different consumption plans (even though they were all required to save the same amount).

Problem 13.8 *Does the argument given above prove that if $r > n$ the stationary overlapping generations equilibrium is Pareto-efficient? Is the alternative path we constructed to show that the $r < n$ stationary equilibrium is not Pareto-efficient itself Pareto-efficient?*

Problem 13.9 *If you were a dictator in an overlapping generations economy, and you had to choose a stationary path for the economy, which one would you choose to maximize the utility of the representative household? (Hint: how much consumption do you have to allocate between workers and retirees in each period, after you have allowed for enough capital to permit steady growth to continue?) Is this path the one the market will choose?*

13.7 Analyzing Social Security and Budget Deficits

Under the assumptions of the overlapping generations model we can give some definite answers to questions often raised about the economic effects of social security programs and of deficit spending. A government runs a deficit when it spends more than it takes in currently in taxes and has to borrow to cover the difference. One important criticism of deficit spending as a policy is that it might impoverish future generations. A model like the overlapping generations model is a natural setting in which to examine this question.

Social security systems tax active workers and make benefit payments to retired workers. Within a model that distinguishes different generations we can trace through the effects of social security systems on saving, wages, profit rates, growth rates, and patterns of life-cycle consumption.

In the Classical overlapping generations model, social security systems and budget deficits can alter household saving decisions and change the growth rate of the capital stock and of population. Since the conventional wage is exogenously given, however, the wage and profit rate will not be affected by social security or budget deficits.

Since the neoclassical overlapping generations model is a full employment growth model, the growth rate in the model is determined by the exogenously given growth of the labor force and the rate of labor-augmenting technical progress. As a result, social security programs and government deficits can, by assumption, have no impact on the growth rate itself under the assumptions of the model, though they can have an impact on saving, investment, the wage, and the profit rate.

In the analysis that follows, it is important to keep in mind several limiting assumptions. First, the models we are studying do not distinguish different households in the same generation. In the real economy, social security taxes and benefits differ according to the wages earned by a particular household; income tax burdens also depend on the income level of the household. The models we examine because of this feature cannot say anything about the distributional or insurance effects of the policies within generations. They are limited to examining the effects of the policies between generations.

Second, both social security and income taxes have many economic effects. In the real world, for example, workers might react to high tax rates by cutting down the amount of hours they work, or by retiring earlier. In the model we study we assume that each household supplies exactly one unit of labor-power regardless of the after-tax wage in its first period of life, so that we assume away at the very beginning incentive effects of this kind. These are lump-sum taxes and benefits that have no effects on marginal incentives to work or consume. They do, however, have important wealth and income effects, which the model does reflect.

Third, because our model has no explicit treatment of money, our analysis will be carried out completely in real terms after correcting for inflation. Thus these models cannot tell us anything about the impact of government deficits or social security on inflation. We measure taxes, benefits, and government spending in terms of real output, and the interest rates we work with are real interest rates.

Finally, we will limit our discussions to comparisons of steady-state growth paths. The changes we see when we change some parameter of the system, like the social security tax level, correspond to the differences between two economies each of which has always had a constant social security tax at the two different levels. Thus we must be cautious in drawing conclusions from this analysis about what would happen in a real economy as it adjusted to a new level of social security benefits and taxes.

13.8 Social Security in the Overlapping Generations Model

We can model a social security system by assuming that the government taxes each working household an amount t and pays each retired household a benefit b, both measured in terms of real output. (The tax and benefit levels might in principle be different for different generations, to reflect changes in social security policies.) Then the budget constraint for the household facing the net profit rate $r = v - \delta$ is:

$$c^w + s^w = w - t$$

$$c^r = b + (1 + r_{+1})s^w, \text{ or}$$

$$c^w + \frac{c^r}{1 + r_{+1}} = w - (t - \frac{b}{1 + r_{+1}})$$

Because the taxes and benefits are lump-sum, the slope of the household's budget constraint is still $-(1 + r_{+1})$. The effect of the social security system is to reduce the household's lifetime wealth by the difference between its tax payment and discounted benefit $(t - \frac{b}{1+r_{+1}})$.

If the typical household maximizes a Cobb-Douglas utility function of consumption in the working and retired periods, the typical household demand functions are:

$$c^w = (1 - \beta)(w - (t - \frac{b}{1 + r_{+1}}))$$

$$s^w = w - t - c^w = \beta w - t + (1 - \beta)(t - \frac{b}{1 + r_{+1}})$$

$$c^r = (1 + r)s^w + b$$

As the social security system collects taxes and pays out benefits, it may accumulate a *reserve fund,* representing the excess of taxes over benefits. This reserve fund may become negative if benefits exceed taxes. We assume that the reserve fund is invested (or the deficit is financed by borrowing) at the net profit rate r. We will write f for the size of the reserve fund per worker. The reserve fund per worker will be depleted in each generation by the payment of benefits and the growth of the labor force, and replenished by the interest collected on it and taxes. Thus we have:

$$f = \frac{(1+r)f_{-1} - b_{-1}}{1 + g_{K-1}} + t \qquad (13.16)$$

Since the reserve fund is invested, it represents an additional source of finance for the capital stock. Thus the saving-investment condition must be modified to include the reserve fund:

$$(1 + g_K)k = s^w + f = \beta w - t + (1 - \beta)(t - \frac{b}{1 + r_{+1}}) + f \qquad (13.17)$$

The growth-distribution equations continue to hold when there is a social security system, providing two more determining conditions to the model, which can be closed either with the Classical assumption of a conventional wage, or the neoclassical assumption of an exogenous rate of growth of the labor force.

The impact of a social security system on the growth path of an overlapping generations economy depends on how much of the taxes are actually accumulated in a reserve fund.

13.8.1   Fully funded social security

In a *fully funded* social security system the government invests the taxes of each generation at the market rate of return by buying bonds or equity investments in enterprises. Thus at any moment in a funded social security system the government has a reserve equal to the taxes paid in that it has not yet paid out in benefits. The relation between the tax and benefit for a funded system is:

$$b = (1 + r_{+1})t \qquad (13.18)$$

The reserve of a fully funded system is $f = t$ (measured per working household). Thus the aggregate reserve of the fully funded system grows at the same rate as the labor force.

The existence of a fully funded social security system makes no difference whatsoever to the allocation of resources in the economy. Households will consume the same amount when they are working, and the same amount during retirement, regardless of the size of the social security system. To see this formally, notice that when $b = (1 + r_{+1})t$, the discounted lifetime income of the typical household in the budget constraint is exactly the same as when $b = t = 0$. Therefore the decision the household makes about working consumption is exactly the same.

We can see this point mathematically from equation (13.17), since:

$$(1 + g_K)k = \beta w + (f - t) + (1 - \beta)(t - \frac{b}{1 + r_{+1}}) = \beta w \qquad (13.19)$$

when $f = t$ and $b = (1 + r_{+1})t$.

In a fully funded social security system households save and invest collectively through the social security system on exactly the same terms they could save and invest individually. Some of their saving passes through the social security fund as taxes, but rational households will adjust their private saving exactly enough to compensate.

Most real-world social security systems, however, are *partially funded*. They hold reserves equal to only a fraction of the benefits they owe to retirees. In order to understand clearly the impact of partially funded systems on economic growth and distribution, let us look at the extreme case of an *unfunded* system.

13.8.2   Unfunded social security

In an *unfunded social security system* the government uses the taxes on current working households to pay benefits to the current generation of retired households. Thus it has no reserve fund at all. Each generation's contributions to the system are already consumed by the time that generation retires. The relation between the benefit level and the tax level for an unfunded social security system is:

$$b_{-1} = (1 + g_{K-1})t \qquad (13.20)$$

The benefit of each retired household, b_{-1}, is equal to the tax on each working household, t, adjusted by the difference in the number of working and retired households, $1 + g_{K-1}$. If $g_{K-1} > 0$ there are more working households in each period than retired households, so that a given tax on working households can support a proportionately larger benefit for each retired household.

The existence of an unfunded social security system does make a real difference to saving decisions, and hence to growth rates in the Classical overlapping generations model, and to the wage and profit rate in the neoclassical overlapping generation model. The budget constraint for the typical household under an unfunded social security system, taking account of the benefit-tax relationship (13.20), and assuming that the benefit level is constant over time, so that $b_{-1} = b$, is:

$$c^w + \frac{c^r}{1 + r_{+1}} = w - (t - \frac{b}{1 + r_{+1}})$$

$$= w - (\frac{b_{-1}}{1 + g_{K-1}} - \frac{b}{1 + r_{+1}}) = w - b(\frac{1}{1 + g_{K-1}} - \frac{1}{1 + r_{+1}})$$

$$= w - b\left(\frac{r_{+1} - g_{K-1}}{(1 + r_{+1})(1 + g_{K-1})}\right)$$

When $r_{+1} > g_{K-1}$, the unfunded system reduces the lifetime wealth of the typical household, while when $r_{+1} < g_{K-1}$, the unfunded system increases the wealth of the typical household. According to the Cobb-Douglas demand system, the working household will consume a fraction $1 - \beta$ of its lifetime resources:

$$c^w = (1 - \beta)\left(w - b\left(\frac{r_{+1} - g_{K-1}}{(1 + r_{+1})(1 + g_{K-1})}\right)\right)$$

$$= (1 - \beta)\left(w - b\left(\frac{1}{1 + g_{K-1}} - \frac{1}{1 + r_{+1}}\right)\right)$$

We can use this consumption function to see exactly what effects a change in the size of an unfunded system (corresponding to a change in the benefit of a typical working household, b) will have on the growth path of the economy. Saving per worker will be $w - c^w - t$, so with an unfunded social security system, and assuming that the benefit is constant, so that $b_{-1} = b$, we have:

$$s^w = w - c^w - t = \beta w - b\left(\frac{\beta}{1 + g_{K-1}} + \frac{1 - \beta}{1 + r_{+1}}\right)$$

Workers in an economy with an unfunded social security system save less than workers in an economy with no social security system for every wage rate. The effect of the social security system is to shift the growth-wage relation upward:

$$w = \frac{(1 - \delta + (g_K + \delta))k}{\beta} + b\left(\frac{1}{1 + g_{K-1}} + \frac{1 - \beta}{\beta(1 + r_{+1})}\right) \qquad (13.21)$$

In the Classical overlapping generations model the conventional wage, $\bar{w}$, determines the net profit rate, $r = v - \delta$, in all periods, so that $r_{+1} = r = (x - \bar{w})/k - \delta$. In this model the growth-wage relation relates the wage to the current period growth rate of capital, taking the last period growth rate of capital, g_{K-1}, as given by the history of the economy. In the neoclassical overlapping generations model, the growth rate of the labor force, $\bar{n}$, determines the growth rate of the capital stock in all periods, so that $g_{K-1} = g_K = \bar{n}$. In this model the growth-wage relation relates the current period wage to the growth rate of the capital stock, taking the next period's net profit rate, r_{+1}, (and wage) as given by expectations.

We can see through Figure 13.3 that with an unfunded social security system the growth rate will be lower for any conventional wage, $\bar{w}$, and last period growth rate, g_{K-1}, in the Classical overlapping generations model than with no social security system or a fully funded social security system. Exactly parallel reasoning shows that in the neoclassical overlapping generations model with an unfunded social security system the wage will be higher (and the profit rate lower) for any labor force growth rate, $\bar{n}$, and expected next period net profit rate, r_{+1}, than with no social security system or a fully funded social security system.

To find the steady state of the economy in the Classical overlapping generations model, we have to substitute the steady state growth rate, g_K^*, on both sides of the growth-wage relation, remembering that the net rate of profit, r, is constant over time:

$$\bar{w} = \frac{(1 + g_K^*)k}{\beta} + b \left(\frac{1}{1 + g_K^*} + \frac{1 - \beta}{\beta(1 + r)} \right) \qquad (13.22)$$

This is a quadratic equation in the steady state growth factor, $1 + g_K^*$.

We can see that when $b = 0$, corresponding to an economy with no social security system, the solution of (13.22) is just the steady-state growth rate for the Classical overlapping generations model without social security:

$$1 + g_K^* = \frac{\beta \bar{w}}{k}$$

We could use equation (13.22) to analyze the effect of a larger or smaller unfunded social security system on the growth rate, and hence on the division of social consumption between working and retired households. Since a change in b will change the equation, it is clear that an unfunded social security system has real effects on the economy that are reflected in changes in the steady-state growth rate.

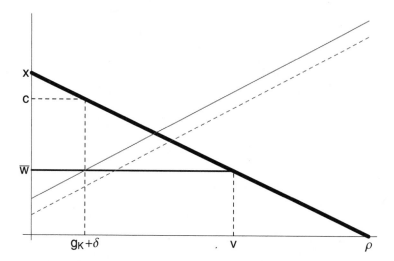

Figure 13.3: Workers in an economy with an unfunded social security system will save less at every wage. As a result
the growth-wage relation shifts upward (from the dashed to
the undashed gray line above). In the Classical overlapping
generations model, the growth rate is lower for any conventional wage and last period growth rate. In the neoclassical
overlapping generations model, the wage is higher for any
rate of growth of the labor force and anticipated next period profit rate.

Example 13.3 *Find the steady state equilibrium of the economy described in Example 13.1 with an unfunded social security system paying a benefit, b, of 5 bushels of corn/worker/year.*

Answer: In Ricardia: $x = 100$ bushels/worker-year; $k = 20$ bushels/worker; $\rho = 5$/year; and $\delta = 1$/year. Here we have $\bar{w} = 50$ bushels/worker-year, so the profit rate, $\delta + r = 1 + r = v = (x - w)/k = 2.5$/year. Simplifying equation (13.22) we get

$$(1 + g_K^*)^2 + (\frac{\beta}{k})(b\frac{1 - \beta}{\beta(1 + r)} - \bar{w})(1 + g_K^*) + \frac{\beta b}{k} = 0$$

or

$$(1 + g_K^*)^2 - 1.2(1 + g_K^*) + .125 = 0$$

The larger root is

$$(1 + g_K^*) = (\delta + g_K^*) = 1.173,$$

so the growth rate $g_K = .173$/year. Social consumption per worker is

$$c = x - (g_K + \delta)k = 100 - (1.173)(20) = 76.5 \text{ bushels/worker-year}$$

Worker consumption is

$$c^w = (1 - \beta)w - b(\frac{r - g_K^*}{(1 + r)(1 + g_K^*)})$$

$$= (.5)(50) - 5(1.5 - .173)/(2.5)(1.173) = 22.74 \text{ bushels/worker-year}$$

Retired households consume

$$c^r = (1 + g_K^*)(c - c^w) = (1.173)(76.5 - 22.74) = 63.1 \text{ bushels/worker-year}$$

Problem 13.10 *Consider an overlapping generations economy where the typical household has Cobb-Douglas utility with $\beta = .2$, the wage $\bar{w} = \$750,000/period$, $x = \$900,000/period$, $\delta = 1$, so that capital depreciates completely each period, and $k = \$100,000/worker$. Find the steady-state equilibrium profit rate, growth rate, and the pattern of consumption of the typical household in the absence of any social security system.*

Problem 13.11 *For the economy in Problem 13.10, find the steady-state equilibrium growth rate, and profit rate with a funded social security system where the benefit for a typical working household is $\$5,000/period$. Find the steady-state equilibrium growth rate, and profit rate for an unfunded social security system with the same social security benefit. What will the tax on working households be?*

Problem 13.12 *Consider a neoclassical overlapping generations economy where the typical household has Cobb-Douglas utility with $\beta = .2$, the population grows at $\bar{n} = .5/period$, $x = \$900,000/period$, $\delta = 1$, so that capital depreciates completely each period, and $k = \$100,000/worker$. Find the steady-state equilibrium real wage and profit rate, and the pattern of consumption of the typical household in the absence of any social security system.*

Problem 13.13 *For the economy in Problem 13.12, find the steady-state equilibrium wage and profit rate with a funded social security system where the benefit to a typical working household is $\$5,000/period$. Find the steady-state equilibrium wage and profit rate for an unfunded social security system with the same social security benefit level. What will the tax be?*

13.9 Government Debt in the Overlapping Generations Model

We can analyze the problem of government debt in the overlapping generations model with the same methods we used to analyze the social security problem. Suppose that the government continues to pay a retirement benefit, b, to each retired household, but that instead of financing it with a tax on workers' wages, as in the social security model, it finances it entirely through borrowing. With this policy the government will have a negative reserve fund, f, which will grow over time. In this case the government has two types of expenditures: the benefit, b, per retired household, and the interest on the outstanding government debt, $B = -f$.

With the Cobb-Douglas utility function, the demand of the workers for consumption, assuming $t = 0$, will be, using the results derived in the last section:

$$c^w = (1 - \beta)\left(w + \frac{b}{1 + r_{+1}}\right)$$

$$s^w = w - c^w = \beta w - (1 - \beta)\left(\frac{b}{1 + r_{+1}}\right)$$

$$c^r = (1 + r)s^w + b$$

As we saw in equation (13.16), the reserve fund debt will grow as a result of continued borrowing to finance the benefit:

$$f = \frac{(1 + r)f_{-1} - b}{1 + g_{K-1}} \tag{13.23}$$

The reserve fund deficit has to be financed by the saving of working households (who would hold it in the form of government bonds). Thus the saving-investment condition becomes:

$$(1 + g_K)k = s^w + f = \beta w - (1 - \beta)\left(\frac{b}{1 + r_{+1}}\right) + f \tag{13.24}$$

As a result the growth-wage relation in any period is:

$$w = \frac{1 - \delta + (g_K + \delta)k}{\beta} + b\left(\frac{1 - \beta}{\beta(1 + r_{+1})}\right) - f$$

Since $f < 0$ under the deficit-financed policy, the effect of the policy is to raise the growth-wage relation even more than the unfunded social security system. In the Classical overlapping generations model, the deficit financed social security system lowers the growth rate for any conventional wage and size of the government debt compared to either a fully funded or an unfunded social security system.

Can a Classical overlapping generations economy with a deficit financed social security reach a steady state? Writing f^* for the steady state debt per worker, this would require, according to equation (13.23):

$$f^* = \frac{(1 + r)f^* - b}{1 + g_K^*}$$

or:

$$f^* = -\frac{b}{g_K^* - r}$$

Since the social security benefit, b, is positive, and the steady state reserve fund f^* must be negative, a steady state is possible only if $g_K^* > r$. In this case the labor force will be growing fast enough to offset the constant growth in the debt from new borrowing and interest charges. If $g_K^* > r$, the government can violate the conventional government budget constraint and consistently run a Ponzi-game fiscal policy. Because the interest rate is lower than the rate of growth, the government debt will not explode in relation to GDP, even though the government is financing the interest payments on its accumulated debt entirely out of new borrowing.

Problem 13.14 *Show that the equilibrium profit rate is the same in the debt model when the debt is zero as in the social security model with no social security tax or benefit.*

13.10   The Lessons of the Overlapping-Generations Model

If households integrate their private consumption and savings decisions with the fiscal policy of the government, as they do in Ricardian equivalence models, government deficits and accumulated debt will have no effect on saving, investment, or the capital stock. Furthermore, even if households have foreshortened time horizons, as in the overlapping generations models, if the government itself matches its outstanding liabilities against real assets, as it does in operating a fully funded social security system, government finance will have no impact on saving and investment.

But in a world where households do not fully discount the future impact of government spending and taxation, there is room for viable government financial policies that households regard as real wealth, but result in no real accumulation of capital. Unfunded social security systems are an example. Households regard the guaranteed benefit in their retirement years as a real increment to their lifetime wealth, but the government does not invest contributions in real capital. As a result an unfunded social security system can influence social saving and investment, and the growth rate of the economy. In a similar fashion, government debt can appear to be real wealth to households which account for the impact of government taxation and spending over a limited time horizon, and as a result can displace capital from household port-folios.

In the real world, however, it is difficult to judge the degree to which households correctly anticipate the full, long-run impact of government financial policies, and try to optimize the inheritance of future gener-ations. Since we cannot independently observe the budget constraints or utility functions of households, it is difficult to construct indepen-dent tests of the hypothesis of Ricardian equivalence. If households do attempt to account correctly for the long-run effects of government fi-nancial policy, then changes in policy, whatever effects they may have on the distribution of income, will not make any difference to social saving, investment, and capital accumulation.

13.11 Suggested Readings

The overlapping generations model was introduced by Samuelson [1958] and Diamond [1965]. For a critical discussion of the neoclassical version of this model, including the specific criticism that its stability requires a high elasticity of substitution, see Marglin [1984]. Credit for reviving the Ricardian idea that government debt is neutral goes to Barro [1974]. There has been considerable debate about the relative importance of be-quests versus life-cycle saving, with Modigliani [1988] taking the position that life-cycle saving dominates while Kotlikoff [1988] takes the opposite position. Further discussion can be found in Kessler and Masson [1988]. For empirical evidence on the class structure of saving, Wolff [1981] sug-gests a three-class model, with the wealthy primarily engaged in bequest saving, a middle class engaged in life-cycle saving, and a working class which does no saving. The overlapping generations model is the inspi-ration for "generational accounting," an alternative method of treating government in national income accounts; see Kotlikoff [1992].

Chapter 14

Money and Economic Growth

14.1 Monetary Systems

In this chapter we will apply the principles of analysis developed in the earlier models to analyze economic growth in an economy where a particular produced commodity, gold, is the measure of value, or numéraire.

For considerable periods of time, the world capitalist system has operated on a gold standard, under which governments stand ready to convert their own currencies into gold at a fixed price. During the twentieth century national governments were unable to maintain the gold standard during the First World War, the Great Depression, and after the United States suspension of convertibility of the dollar into gold in 1971. In periods when the gold standard is suspended, each national currency is backed by the credit of its government, rather than by convertibility into gold. Under these circumstances the value of national currencies in relation to each other and to commodities fluctuates as a result of speculation over the future monetary and fiscal policies of their governments. The analytical tools we have developed in this book are insufficient to treat these complications adequately.

Nonetheless, there is considerable intellectual and historical interest in the functioning of the gold standard, and the study of gold standard principles sheds important light on problems in non-gold standard monetary systems as well.

14.2 The Gold Standard

Commodities are produced goods that are private property and distributed through exchange based on bargaining. Exchange establishes relative prices for commodities: a ton of iron exchanges for a thousand meters of cloth, for example. These relative prices allow us to add up the total value of a bundle of different commodities. A ton of iron together with a thousand meters of cloth is worth 2 tons of iron, or 2 thousand meters of cloth.

It is not hard to see that it is very convenient to have a single *measure of value* of commodities, some standard numéraire in which the value of commodities can be expressed. Economists often choose a numéraire to suit their purposes (as we have done in the previous chapters, where we took output as the numéraire and expressed the wage in terms of output). In commodity producing societies custom or law selects a particular numéraire. For example, the Europe-centered world market system of the nineteenth century established gold as the numéraire, through the institutions known as the *gold standard*. Values of commodities were expressed in terms of gold, and debt contracts were payable in particular quantities of gold. National currencies were defined as a certain quantity of gold (for example, the U.S. dollar was defined as one-twentieth of an ounce of pure gold—corresponding to a gold price of $20/ounce—from the original Congressional legislation setting up a monetary system in 1792 until President Franklin Roosevelt changed the value to one-thirty-fifth of an ounce of gold—corresponding to a gold price of $35/ounce—in 1933). National treasuries stood ready to buy or sell their own currencies at the stated price for gold, so that there was a close relationship between the value of currencies and gold.

If the government adheres to the gold standard, it promises to redeem its liabilities in gold, and thereby fixes the value of its liabilities in terms of gold. If the financial markets believe in the government's determination and ability to adhere to the gold standard, the conventional government budget constraint will be met because the market believes that the government will adjust receipts or expenditures in the future. But there are circumstances when a government's promise to redeem its liabilities in gold loses credibility. In this case the financial markets will try to exchange government liabilities for gold. If the government has issued paper currency ("One Dollar in Gold Payable to the Bearer at the Treasury"), the holders of the currency will exchange it for gold, leading to a run on the dollar, and a gold drain. If the government has issued long-maturity bonds, they will go to a discount against gold to reflect the doubts of the market about the ability of the government to maintain its promise to redeem the bonds eventually in gold. Ultimately the government may have to suspend payment of its liabilities in terms of gold. In this case the gold prices of commodities will not change, but the price of dollars in terms of gold will fall, because the price of gold in terms of dollars rises.

Even in the nineteenth century governments from time to time had difficulties in maintaining the gold standard, due to financial crises, depressions and wars. For example, in the U.S. both the Northern and the Southern governments suspended the gold standard during the Civil War, so that the greenback (the U.S. dollar) and the Confederate dollar floated against gold in financial markets. Military successes by one side or the other had a direct effect on the gold value of the dollar, because of changes in expectations about how long the war would last, and whether there was any chance that the Confederacy would survive.

Under gold standard institutions the prices of commodities can be thought of as gold prices. A price of \$40/ton for iron in 1880, for example, meant the same thing as 2 ounces of gold/ton. Since gold is produced within the commodity system, the gold prices of commodities depend on the relative cost of production (including profit) of gold on the one hand, and the commodity on the other.

14.3   Production with Gold

To model production with gold, suppose that there are just two products in the system, output other than gold, which we will call *commodities*, X, which can be used as capital or consumed, and gold, G. Take gold as the numéraire, and suppose that the national currency, say, the dollar, is convertible into gold at a fixed ratio, the *standard of price*. We will use the symbol p for the gold (or, equivalently, money) price of commodities.

We keep our basic model of the production of commodities:

1 labor + k_x capital $\rightarrow$ x commodities + $(1 - \delta)k_x$ capital

We can model the production of gold in a similar fashion:

1 labor + k_g capital $\rightarrow$ x_g gold + $(1 - \delta)k_g$ capital

In this model capital depreciates at the same rate in the gold and commodities sectors, and production in each sector takes one period of time. The capital-labor ratio in the production of commodities and gold, on the other hand, can be different.

If the real wage is w, the money wage paid at the end of the period will be $p_{+1}w$. The zero-profit conditions for entrepreneurs producing commodities and gold are:

$$p_{+1}x = p_{+1}w + vpk_x \qquad (14.1)$$

$$x_g = p_{+1}w + vpk_g \qquad (14.2)$$

Notice that we use the same wage and rental for capital in the two industries, since we assume that labor and capital are mobile between them.

We can eliminate the rental to capital from equations (14.2) and (14.1) and solve for the gold price of commodities in terms of the labor productivities and capital intensities in the two sectors, and the profit share in the commodities sector, π:

$$p_{+1} = \frac{x_g}{x}\frac{k_x}{\pi k_g + (1 - \pi)k_x} \qquad (14.3)$$

The first factor, x_g/x, is the ratio of labor productivity in gold to labor productivity in commodities, or, the ratio of the amount of labor required to produce a unit of commodities to the amount of labor required to produce a unit of gold. The denominator of the second factor is a weighted average of the capital-labor ratios in the two sectors, with weights equal to the wage and profit shares in the commodities sector. This second factor will be greater than or less than 1 depending on whether k_x is greater than or less than this weighted average, that is, on whether the commodities sector is more or less capital-intensive than the average of the two sectors. If $k_x = k_g$, so that the commodities sector has the same capital intensity as the average (a hypothesis Marx calls *equal organic compositions of capital* in the two sectors), we have simply:

$$p_{+1} = \frac{x_g}{x}$$

When the capital intensities of the two sectors are equal, the price of commodities is just the ratio of the labor required to produce a unit of commodities to the labor required to produce a unit of gold. Because it is much simpler to analyze the model when the capital intensities of the two sectors are equal, we will assume from this point on that $k_x = k_g = k$.

Problem 14.1 *If one worker can produce one ounce of gold in a year with 10 bushels of corn in Ricardia, where 1 worker can produce 100 bushels of corn from 20 bushels of seed corn in a year, and $1*

= 1/20th of an ounce of gold, find the price of corn and the money wage in Ricardia when the real wage is 20 bu corn/worker/year. Check by finding the rental rates for capital in the corn and gold industries.

14.4   Capitalist Consumption with Gold

In order to motivate the actual production of gold in this economy, let us suppose that the typical capitalist gains utility from holding gold in the form of treasure (which might include jewelry and coins). A simple way to extend the capitalist's utility function to include the holding of gold is:

$$(1 - \beta) \sum_{t=0}^{\infty} \beta^t ((1 - \mu) \ln(C_t) + \mu \ln(G_t))$$

The capitalist still maximizes the discounted sum of utilities in each period over the infinite future, but now her utility in each period is a weighted average of the logarithm of her consumption of commodities, C, and her holdings of gold, G. The parameter μ expresses the relative importance the capitalist gives to the consumption of commodities and gold. (If $\mu = 0$, this utility function reduces to the pure consumption case of Chapter 5.)

But gold is also an asset, since it does not wear out in a single period. (In fact, we will assume that gold doesn't depreciate at all.) Just as in the model of Chapter 11, the typical capitalist has to choose how much of her wealth to invest in gold and how much in capital.

Even though the amount of gold in the whole economy is fixed, each individual capitalist could in principle choose to hold more or less than the average share. (Since we assume all the capitalists are identical, they will wind up holding the same amount in equilibrium.)

The typical capitalist starts each period holding some gold, G, and some capital, K. A capitalist who rents out \$1 worth of capital to entrepreneurs will receive the profit rate v, and at the end of the period will have depreciated capital $(1-\delta)/p$, which will be worth $(1-\delta)(p_{+1}/p)$. Thus her net profit rate is defined by:

$$1 + r = v + \frac{p_{+1}}{p}(1 - \delta)$$

The capitalist's motive to hold gold is its consumption value. At the end of the period she has a total wealth of $(1 + r)K + G$ to divide between her next period portfolio of capital and gold, K_{+1} and G_{+1}, and consumption, $p_{+1}C$. Thus the budget constraint of the typical capitalist with gold is:

$$p_{+1}K_{+1} + G_{+1} + p_{+1}C = (1+r)pK + G \qquad (14.4)$$

The opportunity cost to the capitalist of holding gold is the loss of the net profit rate, r, since she could convert her gold into capital instead of holding it as treasure. We could rewrite the budget constraint, (14.4), to make this explicit, by adding rG to both sides:

$$p_{+1}K_{+1} + G_{+1} + rG + p_{+1}C = (1+r)(pK + G)$$

At the beginning of period 0, the typical capitalist has initial holdings of capital, $\bar{K}_0$, and gold, $\bar{G}_0$, which she can trade at the period 0 price of commodities, p_0. Thus her period 0 budget constraint is:

$$p_0 K_0 + G_0 = p_0 \bar{K}_0 + \bar{G}_0$$

The typical capitalist's utility maximization problem with gold is:

Capitalist's Utility Maximization with Gold

$$\text{choose } \{C_t, K_t, G_t\}_{t=0}^{\infty} \geq 0 \qquad (14.5)$$

$$\text{so as to maximize } (1-\beta) \sum_{t=0}^{\infty} \beta^t ((1-\mu)\ln(C_t) + \mu \ln(G_t))$$

subject to

$$K_{t+1} + G_{t+1} + rG_t + p_{t+1}C_t \leq (1 + v_t - \delta)(p_t K_t + G_t)$$

$$p_0 K_0 + G_0 = p_0 \bar{K}_0 + \bar{G}_0$$

$$\bar{K}_0, \bar{G}_0, \{v_t, p_t\}_{t=0}^{\infty} \text{ given} \qquad (14.6)$$

The solution to this problem follows from the familiar principles we have already derived in earlier chapters. In this case the capitalist's wealth is $J = pK + G$. The typical capitalist will spend a fraction $(1-\beta)$ of her end of period wealth, $(1+r)J$, on consumption of commodities and gold:

$$p_{+1}C + rG = (1 - \beta)(1 + r)J$$

As a result, the capitalist's accumulation of wealth follows the familiar Cambridge relation:

$$J_{+1} = \beta(1 + r)J$$

Since the utility function in each period is also of the Cobb-Douglas form, the capitalist will divide her consumption between commodities and gold in the proportions $1 - \mu$ and μ:

$$p_{+1}C = (1 - \mu)(1 - \beta)(1 + r)J$$

$$rG = \mu(1 - \beta)(1 + r)J \tag{14.7}$$

14.5   Steady State Growth

On a steady state growth path the capital and gold stocks are growing at the same rate, as is consumption of commodities, while the gold price of commodities is constant, so that $p_{+1} = p$.

The growth-distribution relations now have to treat gold and commodities separately. The real wage-profit rate relations in the two sectors are derived from equations (14.1) and (14.2), setting $p_{+1} = p$, and assuming $k_x = k_g = k$:

$$w = x - vk \tag{14.8}$$

$$w = \frac{x_g - vpk}{p} \tag{14.9}$$

From these equations we can immediately see that:

$$v = \frac{x - w}{k}$$

$$p = \frac{x_g}{x}$$

The social consumption-growth rate relations now have to take account of what proportion of the labor force is employed in producing commodities, n_x, and producing gold, $n_g = 1 - n_x$. The commodity output per worker in the whole economy is $n_x x$, so we have the social consumption-growth rate of capital relation:

$$c = n_x x - (g_K + \delta)k \tag{14.10}$$

Gold output per worker in the whole economy is $(1 - n_x)x_g$, and it is devoted entirely to the increase of the gold stock. Writing $a = G/N$ for the gold stock per worker:

$$g_G a = (1 - n_x)x_g \tag{14.11}$$

On a steady state growth path, the stocks of gold and capital must be growing at the same rate, and at the same rate as capitalist wealth, so we have the Cambridge equations for the two sectors:

$$1 + g_K = \beta(1 - \delta + v) \tag{14.12}$$

$$1 + g_G = \beta(1 - \delta + v) \tag{14.13}$$

From equation (14.7), we see that the gold stock per worker, a, is:

$$a = \left(\frac{\mu(1 - \beta)(1 + r)}{r - \mu(1 - \beta)(1 + r)} \right) pk \tag{14.14}$$

In the Classical model the conventional wage is given exogenously:

$$w = \bar{w} \tag{14.15}$$

Equations (14.8)–(14.15) determine the steady state path of the economy. The exogenous parameters are x, k, x_g, δ, β, μ, and $\bar{w}$. The endogenous variables are: p, v, n_x, g_K, g_G, c, and a.

One interesting aspect of this model is that the price level is determined by the relative productivities of labor in the gold and commodities sectors, $p^* = x_g/x$, and the quantity of gold is determined by the preferences of capitalist households. This is in sharp contrast to the quantity of money theory of prices, which sees the price level as determined by the quantity of money.

Problem 14.2 *In Aurea the production of $50,000 worth of commodities requires one worker-year of labor working with $150,000 worth of commodity capital. The same capital and labor can also produce 1000 ounces of gold. $1/10 = .1 = 10\%$ of the capital depreciates in each year and the real wage is $20,000/worker/year. If Aurean capitalists' propensity to save, $\beta = .97$, and capitalist households devote 90% of their consumption fund to commodities and 10% to holding gold, find the gold price of commodities, the profit rate, the net profit rate, the growth rates of the stocks of capital and gold, the stock of gold per worker, and the proportion of the labor force employed in the gold and commodities industries in the steady state.*

14.6   Unbalanced Technical Change

In a gold standard economy, inflation is the result of changes in the relative cost of production of gold and commodities, which lead to changes in the gold price of commodities. One simple way to model this type of change is to suppose that the gold sector experiences factor-augmenting technical change at the rate γ, while the commodities sector technology and the wage are constant. Under the assumption of equal capital-intensities in the two sectors, the gold price of commodities depends on the relative productivity of labor:

$$p_{+1} = \frac{x_g}{x}$$

Factor augmenting technical change in the gold sector increases x_g at the rate γ and leads to a steady rise in the gold price of commodities at the rate γ, that is, steady inflation.

From equation (14.1) we see that the gold profit rate will be increased above the commodities profit rate, $v_x = (x - \bar{w})/k$ by the inflation factor:

$$v = \frac{p_{+1}}{p}\left(\frac{x - \bar{w}}{k}\right) = (1 + \gamma)v_x$$

Similarly the gold net profit factor, $1 + r$ rises:

$$1 + r = v + \frac{p_{+1}}{p}(1 - \delta) = (1 + \gamma)(1 - \delta + v_x)$$

From the Cambridge equation, we see that the growth rate of the gold value of wealth rises, too. But the impact on the rate of increase in the stocks of gold and capital are different. On a steady state path the gold stock must grow at the same rate as the gold value of wealth:

$$1 + g_G = \beta(1 + r) = \beta(1 + \gamma)(1 - \delta + v_x)$$

The gold value of the capital stock, pk, must also grow at the same rate as the gold value of wealth. But the gold value of the capital stock will be changing both because the capital stock is growing and because the gold price of commodities is rising:

$$\frac{p_{+1}K_{+1}}{pK} = (1 + \gamma)(1 + g_K) = \beta(1 + r) = \beta(1 + \gamma)(1 - \delta + v_x)$$

Thus the capital stock itself grows at the same rate it would have without the inflation:

$$1 + g_K = \beta(1 - \delta + v_x)$$

The proportion of gold to capital on the steady state path, however, falls as a result of the inflation, which raises the net profit rate, which is the effective price of holding gold.

Unbalanced technical change thus gives rise to *unbalanced growth*, in which the output of one sector grows in relation to the output of other sectors. William Baumol has argued that this phenomenon can explain the inexorably rising price of commodities like higher education and artistic performances relative to other commodities. The premise of this argument is that it is difficult or impossible to increase labor productivity in education, which requires a certain minimum time engagement between teacher and student, or in string quartet performances. As a result increasing labor productivity in other sectors constantly lowers their relative cost and raises the relative price of the sectors in which productivity is stagnant.

Problem 14.3 *If labor productivity in the gold industry increases at the rate $\gamma = .01/year$ in Aurea (see Problem 14.2), find the profit rate, net profit rate, the growth rates of the stocks of capital and gold, and the ratio of the stock of gold to the value of the capital stock in the steady state.*

14.7 The Evolution of Credit Money

Even in a gold standard economy relatively few transactions are made in gold coin (or *specie*). Coin is cumbersome, risky to hold, and subject to constant loss of value through wear-and-tear and clipping. Most transactions between businesses in a gold standard system are accomplished by one or another form of credit, often a *bill of exchange.* A bill of exchange is a promissory note specifying payment in gold of a certain sum at a certain place and time drawn up by a business, and usually secured by produced goods being shipped to buyers. Since the goods securing the bill of exchange already exist, bills are a relatively safe investment. When a bill has been accepted by another business as payment, the acceptor endorses the bill by signing it. The endorsement commits the acceptor to pay the bill if for any reason the original drawer fails to pay. The acceptor takes the bill as payment for a smaller sum than the face value of the bill, so that the increase in the bill's value to maturity represents an interest payment for the funds borrowed by the drawer. The acceptor may in turn use the bill to pay a third party, who in turn accepts it. As the bill passes in this way through many hands, it accumulates many endorsements and payment becomes more and more certain.

Banks in the gold standard system also issued *banknotes,* promises to pay in small standard denominations, which circulated widely as a form of money. These banknotes, as opposed to bills of exchange, did not pay any interest, but convenience led people to hold them for day-to-day transactions anyway. The bank stood ready to exchange its banknotes for gold, but as a banknote moved away from its place of issue, the cost and risk of redeeming the banknote in coin meant that it would circulate at a discount against its face value.

The Federal government also issued bills, Treasury bills secured by future tax and custom receipts, and notes, which were promises to pay secured by the Treasury's gold reserve. These bills and notes played a role similar to that of private bills of exchange and private banknotes in the national circulation of money. It is important to realize that even in the gold standard system, the liabilities of the Federal government, both notes and bills, were secured, or backed not just by the gold reserve (which is part of the marketable assets held by the government) but by the present discounted value of future primary fiscal surpluses (the most important part of the nonmarketable assets of the government) as well.

Most European countries suspended the gold standard during the First World War, because they feared a run on their gold reserves, and wanted to preserve the gold to finance military and diplomatic operations. When this happened, day-to-day transactions were affected very little, because most transactions were carried out in terms of government bills and notes. The national currencies *floated* against gold in the sense that there was a market price for gold in each national currency established by market forces. Thus the value of national currencies could and did fluctuate in relation to gold and to each other.

After the First World War there was an attempt to restore the gold standard system, but it failed to survive the overwhelming financial-economic crises of the 1930s. During the 1930s most governments again suspended the gold standard. The United States did this in a complicated way in 1933, making it illegal for its citizens to hold gold coin, but maintaining a link between the dollar and gold at an official price of $35 per ounce (raised for the first time from the $20 per ounce price established in 1792). Again the effect on day-to-day transactions was minimal (though there was an important legal case in which the Supreme Court refused to enforce the clause in private contracts that provided for payment in gold).

After the Second World War the Bretton Woods system attempted to restore some elements of the gold standard. Under this *gold-exchange standard* the U.S. promised to buy or sell gold at the fixed standard of price of $35/ounce, and other countries fixed their exchange rates in terms of the dollar. This system broke down in 1971 when the U.S., facing huge dollar outflows because of the Vietnam War and massive capital exports to the rest of the world, suspended the convertibility of the dollar into gold.

These developments ushered in the contemporary world financial system, in which no national currency is tied to gold. Some countries fix their exchange rate in relation to the dollar or other reserve currencies like the Euro, Japanese yen, or British pound, but there is no agreed on system of fixed exchange rates among the reserve currencies, or between the reserve currencies and any produced commodity like gold.

14.8 Suggested Readings

Levine and Renelt [1992] study convergence with emphasis on the role of policy variables like monetary growth, inflation, and government spending and borrowing, concluding (surprisingly) that these do not have a very stable or clear statistical relationship to growth.

Baumol [1967] analyzes the patterns of growth in a two-sector economy with unequal rates of technical change.

Chapter 15

Approaches to Technical Change

15.1   The Origin of Technical Change

Technical change plays an indispensable role in bringing the models of growth considered so far in this book into alignment with the stylized facts of growth. In the Classical model, the biased nature of technical change frames the interpretation of the historical tendency toward greater mechanization evident in the process of economic development. The neoclassical model needs to be augmented by exogenous technical change, typically of a neutral variety, in order to escape from several key inconsistencies with the statistical and historical record. But what explains the origin of technical change? And why does it have a particular bias or (since there is nothing natural about neutrality) its total lack of bias? These questions have absorbed the interests of economists for generations, but they are currently at the center of some of the most intellectually exciting controversies in the field.

Macroeconomists have long debated whether it makes sense to treat technical change as *exogenous* or *endogenous*. Technical change is exogenous when it proceeds at a rate which is independent of economic behavior. A widely-used metaphor for exogenous technical change is that it falls on the economy like the manna that fell from heaven upon the Children of Israel. Technical change is endogenous when it occurs as the result, direct or indirect, of deliberate economic activity, in such a way that its rate or nature depends on economic behavior. There is general agreement that much technical change occurs because of activities like research and development (R&D) directed toward improving products and processes in pursuit of profit or fame. No one literally thinks technical change falls like manna from heaven. At issue is the value added by an economic model that incorporates these activities (or others that we will elaborate), compared to one that takes the rate of technical change as exogenous for all practical purposes.

If technical change is endogenous, it raises the question of whether behavioral changes (such as an increased saving rate or different income distribution) or policy changes (such as subsidies for R&D or incentives for saving) can permanently affect a nation's rate of technical progress. This chapter and the next consider some important examples of endogenous technical change.

15.2 The Technical Progress Function and the Embodiment Hypothesis

As we have seen, a key question facing growth theorists is whether it makes any sense to distinguish between shifts in the production function (technical change) and movements along the production function (capital-labor substitution). This separation is central to the neoclassical growth theories, whether they treat technical change as endogenous or exogenous. Critics of the neoclassical approach dismiss the idea that one can distinguish between movements along and shifts in the production function. Nicholas Kaldor articulated the problem in these words:

> The use of more capital per worker ... inevitably entails the introduction of superior techniques which require "inventiveness" of some kind, though these need not necessarily represent the application of basically new principles or ideas. On the other hand, most, though not all, technical innovations which are capable of raising the productivity of labor require the use of more capital per man — more elaborate equipment and/or more mechanical power ...
> It follows that any sharp or clear-cut distinction between the movement *along* a "production function" with a given state of knowledge and a *shift* in the "production function" caused by a change in the state of knowledge is arbitrary and artificial. [Kaldor, 1957, pp. 595–96]

Kaldor chose to overcome the difficulty identified in this quotation by means of the *technical progress function*. His technical progress function relates the rate of productivity growth on the most recent machines to the amount of gross investment per worker using the new machines.

Thus, this approach combines two separate ideas. First, it links the rate of technical change directly to the rate of capital accumulation. Second, by emphasizing growth in the amount of *new* capital per worker, it enlists the *embodiment hypothesis*.

Technical change frequently must be transmitted through a specific capital good, in which case it is said to be *embodied*. The discovery of the microprocessor does not help the typist who continues to use a manual typewriter. He needs a personal computer to enjoy the benefits of this advance in knowledge. Embodied technical change is transmitted through gross investment, since machines of the latest design replace the depreciated or worn-out capital stock. Technical change which requires no such transmission mechanism is said to be *disembodied*. An example of disembodied technical change might be *Taylorism*, the doctrine of the pioneer of management science, Frederick Taylor, which claims to improve the organization of work through methods like time and motion studies. (Critics point out that some of the improvement occurs by speeding up the workers, which is not technical progress.) It should be noted that the embodiment hypothesis can be incorporated into the neoclassical production function as well as into the technical progress function.

We can illustrate the technical progress function by abstracting from the embodiment hypothesis altogether, and writing it in linear form:

$$\gamma = a + bg_k$$

In this form, there will be one growth rate consistent with steady state growth. It can be found by observing that constancy of the output-capital ratio (a requirement for steady state growth) implies that

$$\gamma = \frac{a}{1 - b}$$

The technical progress function was an early attempt to formalize the idea of endogenous technical progress. However, the fact that the steady state growth rate is independent of economic behavior somewhat limits its interest for economists with a taste for steady state growth. Another alleged shortcoming of the technical progress function is that in the linear form written here, it is mathematically equivalent to a Cobb-Douglas production function with Harrod-neutral technical change, as can easily be seen by taking the integrals of both sides. However, when the technical progress function takes some more general form, it cannot ordinarily be integrated into a level production function of any kind.

Models of embodied technical change are often called *vintage models* because they include machines of different age or vintage. The vintage growth theorists left a legacy of useful nomenclature that clarifies the meaning of substitutions between capital and labor. When machines can be shaped to suit any technique of production (much like putty can be molded) both during construction and during use, capital is said to be *putty-putty*. When machines are malleable in the construction phase but once built (much like baked clay) cannot be altered, capital is said to be *putty-clay*. When machines are limited to one capital-labor ratio both during construction and in use, capital is said to be *clay-clay*.

The view that investment is the vehicle for technical change raises the question of whether an increase in saving can boost productivity by reducing the age of the capital stock, increasing the relative importance of more up-to-date machines. In the next two sections, we develop a simple vintage model under Classical assumptions to address this question. We then return to the technical progress function, in connection with the problem of biased technical change.

15.3 The Vintage Structure of Machines

We can illustrate the nature of vintage growth models by means of a simple clay-clay model with Harrod-neutral technical change. Let us assume that all the conditions of a Classical model with conventional wage share apply, with the exceptions that technical change is embodied and that capitalists save a constant share of their profits (rather than their wealth).

The capital stock now consists of machines of distinct vintage. We will label our variables with the subscript v, which identifies its vintage, and treat the time period as implicit. A variable with no subscript will be understood to refer to its aggregate level with the exception of ρ, which is the same for all vintages. The output using machines of vintage v is

$$X_v = \min\left(\rho K_v, x_v N_v\right)$$

In order to make any progress at all in describing the equilibrium, we will simply assume that the model is already on a steady state growth path. This means the amount of each vintage of machine will be a constant proportion, $1 + g_K$, of the previous vintage. The structure of such a balanced set of machines is mirrored in the structure of output produced by each vintage. Since these variables are all blown up together as time progresses, their ratios remain constant. Output grows at the same rate as capital in this model, allowing us to use g to refer to the growth rate of either. Each year is just an enlarged version of all the previous years, so we can restrict ourselves to describing the variables in one representative year, t.

We are free to choose the units in which we measure machines (100s, 1000s, etc.), so we choose units such that the price of a new machine is unity, measured in terms of units of output. It further simplifies matters to assume that ρ is unity: each "machine" produces one unit of output, and can be freely exchanged for one unit of output. With Harrod-neutral technical change, productivity improves by a constant proportion in each new vintage of machine, or $x_v = (1 + \gamma)x_{(v-1)}$.

Machines last forever, but they will become obsolescent after T years, when they begin generating losses. The *obsolescence condition* is

$$X_v - wN_v < 0$$

We are assuming a constant profit share, so the wage must be increasing at the same rate as labor productivity, or $w = w_0(1 + \gamma)^t$. As the wage rises, it squeezes down the profits on the old machines, until finally they cannot be used without incurring a loss. At this point, the machines are scrapped.

The service life of machines, T, can be found by substituting the wage equation into the obsolescence condition, presuming that the profit share on the most recent vintage is known to be π_t. We need to recognize that since we are dealing with discrete units of time, T must satisfy an integer constraint. Therefore, T will be the largest integer which satisfies the following inequality:

$$T \leq -\frac{\ln(1 - \pi_t)}{\ln(1 + \gamma)} \tag{15.1}$$

This inequality makes sense, because a faster rate of technical change will cause wages to rise more quickly, forcing old machines out of use more quickly, and a larger wage share on the most recent vintage will reduce the profits available for older machines, forcing them into retirement faster.

15.4   Steady State Growth in the Vintage Model

To characterize the equilibrium of the vintage model, we need to determine the rate of growth (which is the same as the rate of capital accumulation) and the profit share on the most recent machine. We economize on notation by simply assuming that the model is in its T-th year of operation (i.e., $t = T$), and that it has a balanced set of machines all the way back to vintage 0. The total output of all the vintages is

$$X = \sum_{v=0}^{T} X_0(1+g)^v = \frac{X_0}{g}((1+g)^{1+T} - 1)$$

The aggregate profit share can be conceived as the weighted sum of the profit shares on each of the vintages of machine in use. The weights are the shares of output from a given vintage in the total output. Mathematically, we could write

$$\pi = \sum_{v=0}^{T} \pi_v(X_v/X)$$

The share of profits in the output produced by any vintage of machine, π_v, depends on the productivity of that machine. With appropriate substitutions, it can be written in terms of π_T:

$$\pi_v = 1 - \frac{w}{x_v} = 1 - (1 - \pi_T)(1 + \gamma)^{T-v}$$

This expression and the equation for total output let us calculate the weighted sum of the profit shares. We are interested in the profit share on the latest vintage, π_t, which by assumption is equivalent to π_T. Resolving the summation, and solving for this profit share gives us:

$$\pi_t = \frac{(1+g)^{1+T}(\pi g + \gamma(1-\pi)) - g(1+\gamma)^{1+T} + (1-\pi)(g-\gamma)}{g((1+g)^{1+T} - (1+\gamma)^{1+T})}$$

$$(15.2)$$

We now have two useful expressions for T and π_t, but we have yet to determine the rate of growth, g. Our usual approach has been to assume that capitalists save a constant proportion of their wealth. In order to calculate the capitalists' wealth, we would need to evaluate the machines they own using the prices that would exist in a second-hand market. A shortcut which eliminates the need to carry out these calculations is to assume that capitalists save a constant fraction, s_p, of their profits. Saving out of profits in year T takes the form of the machines newly installed in period $T + 1$, which represent investment or the change in the capital stock. Taking advantage of the fact that $X = K$, we can express this mathematically as

$$K_{T+1} = s_p \pi X = s_p \pi K$$

When we divide both sides by K, the left-hand side becomes the growth rate, $g = g_K = K_{T+1}/K$, giving us a version of the Cambridge growth equation:

$$g = s_p \pi \tag{15.3}$$

The three numbered equations, (15.1), (15.2), and (15.3), uniquely determine the three unknown variables which characterize the steady state equilibrium: T, π_t, and g.

This model illustrates the important idea that when there is a productivity ordering of machines, the wage determines the productivity of the last machine on the list, which is sometimes called the *extensive margin*. This least productive machine plays a role reminiscent of the least fertile land in Ricardo's theory of rent.

The productivity ordering of machines returns us to the hope expressed earlier that an increase in the saving rate might be capable of improving productivity growth by reducing the average age of the capital stock. Aggregate productivity can be represented much like the aggregate profit share above, as the weighted sum of the productivity of each vintage of machine. The weights in this case would be each vintage's employment, expressed as a share of total employment. Mathematically, we express this as

$$X/N = \sum_{v=0}^{T} x_v (N_v/N)$$

In a steady state these employment weights do not change, and each year as new machines replace the oldest vintage, productivity increases by $1 + \gamma$. The immediate effect of an increase in investment would be to change the weights, raising the proportion of workers employed on the newest vintages. This would cause aggregate productivity to increase faster than γ through a composition effect, just as intuition suggests. However, when the new steady state is reached, the weights will have settled down to their new equilibrium values and this composition effect will expire. The rate of productivity growth will then return to the exogenous rate, γ, despite an increase in the rate of capital accumulation. The embodiment hypothesis thus has importance for predicting the medium-term effects of an increase in investment, but not for making long-term comparisons of steady state productivity growth rates.

Problem 15.1 *Consider a vintage model with a profit share equal to 1/3, a saving rate out of profits equal to 3/4, and a rate of Harrod-neutral technical change equal to 5% per year (.05 per year). Find* *the rate of growth, the profit share on the most recent vintage and the service life of machines. Use a graphing calculator or a spreadsheet to achieve a numerical solution.*

Problem 15.2 *Consider the model in Problem 15.1, but assume that the profit share has declined to 1/4. Find the new steady state value of the service life of machines, and explain why it is larger or smaller than it had been. Use a graphing calculator or a spreadsheet to achieve a numerical solution.*

15.5 Induced Technical Change

While it is possible that technical change takes a biased form more or less spontaneously, economists have long suspected that specific characteristics of capitalist society, such as the large share of wages in total costs, impart a labor-saving bias to technical change. Marx believed that by making labor more expensive, the nineteenth-century Factory Acts in Britain stimulated the discovery of labor-saving machinery. The theory of induced technical change constitutes yet another approach to the empirical phenomenon of capital-labor substitution.

A simple model which illustrates the basic idea of induced technical change begins by assuming that firms are presented with a menu of possible technical changes, which takes the form of a concave technical progress function (also known as the *invention possibility frontier*):

$$\gamma = f(\chi)$$

If, as seems reasonable, a greater saving on labor comes at the price of fewer savings on capital inputs (or even, at some point, an increase in capital inputs), this function will slope downward and have a negative derivative, written $f'(\chi) < 0$. If larger savings in labor require proportionately larger sacrifices of capital saving, then the function will be concave and have a negative second derivative, written $f'' < 0$. We assume that the technical progress function has both these mathematical properties in Figure 15.1.

It is not hard to imagine that some amount of labor-saving requires an actual increase in capital requirements, which would be the case with labor-saving, capital-using technical changes. In principle, it should also be possible to imagine capital-saving, labor-using technical changes.

The theory of induced technical change explains that the bias of technical change results from the response by capitalists to economic incentives. Each individual manager will seek to reduce the cost of producing one unit of output as fast as possible, taking as given the wage and rental rate of capital as in Chapter 7. This is just another way of saying that the manager seeks to maximize profits for the capitalists who own the firm. Costs consist of the wages paid to her workers, labor costs, and rents paid to the owners of the firm, capital costs. Since the firm operates in a competitive environment, it will always start out with a profit rate equal to the average profit rate, and as a result, the profit share represents the share of capital costs in total cost, and the wage share represents the share of labor costs in total costs. The rate of reduction of costs per unit is given by the expression $(1 - \pi)\gamma + \pi\chi$.

The planning problem for the entrepreneur-manager of the firm can thus be expressed as a one-period choice problem:

$$\max \ (1 - \pi)\gamma + \pi\chi$$

$$\text{subject to } \gamma = f(\chi)$$

$$\text{where } f' < 0, f'' < 0$$

$$\text{given } \pi$$

Substituting, we see that the entrepreneur wants to maximize:

$$(1 - \pi)f(\chi) + \pi\chi$$

The first-order condition for a maximum is:

$$(1 - \pi)f'(\chi) + \pi = 0$$

The solution value for χ clearly must satisfy:

$$f'(\chi) = -\frac{\pi}{(1 - \pi)}$$

We can visualize the solution by referring to Figure 15.1, which shows the first-order condition as the point where the tangent to the technical progress function has the slope $-\pi/(1-\pi)$. The solution value for γ can then be read off the vertical axis.

Under the conventional wage share assumption, this one-period solution would repeat itself over time. The increase in labor productivity

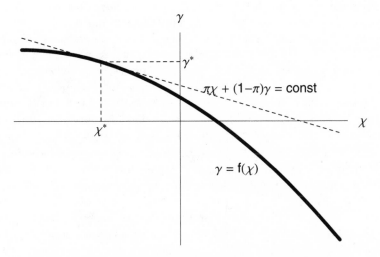

Figure 15.1: Given a technical progress function, $\gamma = f(\chi)$, represented by the heavy curve, profit-maximizing entrepreneurs will choose the pattern of technical change, (χ^*, γ^*) that leads to the largest reduction in costs, $\pi\chi + (1 - \pi)\gamma$. The profit-maximizing pattern occurs at the point where the technical progress function is tangent to the isocost-reducing locus, represented by the dashed line.

would lead to a corresponding increase in the real wage, so that the profit share remains constant. We can refer back to Chapter 7 to see how the economy would evolve. The key difference is that we now have an explanation for the biased character of technical change, which we previously had taken as exogenous.

The solution shown in Figure 15.1 represents an example of a labor-saving, capital-using or Marx-biased technical change, but there is nothing about this model that ensures this particular bias. The character of the solution reflects the response by the entrepreneurs to the structure of economic incentives. If the profit share were larger, that would create a greater incentive to save on capital and the solution value for χ would increase. At the profit share where $f'(\chi)$ crosses the vertical axis the value of χ will be zero, signifying Harrod-neutral technical change. For higher values of the profit share, entrepreneurs trying to economize on the most significant cost will choose capital-saving technical changes. This model would explain the existence of Marx-biased technical change as the joint result of the parameters of the technical progress function and the fact that wages constitute such a large share of costs.

The main weakness of this presentation of the theory of induced technical change is the absence of a counterpart to the technical progress function confronting firms in real economies. It seems more plausible to believe that the set of possible technical changes is stochastic or probabilistic. In this case, if we search for more labor-saving technical changes, the probability decreases of finding any that are not also more capital-using.

Problem 15.3 *Suppose that the technical progress function takes a quadratic form:* $\gamma = -\chi^2 - .52\chi + .0149$. *Find the optimum rate of capital-saving (or -using) technical change when the profit share is 1/3. Find the optimum rate when the profit share is 1/4. Compare your answers.*

Problem 15.4 *Using the data in Problem 15.3, find the rate of increase in the real wage under the conventional wage share assumption when the profit share is 1/3. Find the rate when the profit share is 1/4. Compare your answers.*

Problem 15.5 *Assume in an otherwise Classical model that full employment of the labor force is maintained through instantaneous changes in the profit share, and that the labor force is constant. Use the technical progress function in the previous problems. Characterize the steady state equilibrium with induced technical change by calculating the values of* γ, χ, g_K, g_X, *and* π.

15.6 Specialization and Imperfect Competition

Two themes in recent growth theory are that returns to scale promote imperfect competition and that greater specialization is a source of increasing returns. This idea is often represented mathematically by a special form of the Cobb-Douglas production function that takes into account the existence of many types of capital goods. In contrast to the vintage model, we assume that each type of good has the same intrinsic labor productivity as any other. The production function for final output is

$$X = N^{1-\alpha} \sum_{i=1}^{A} K_i^{\alpha}$$

The novelty of this function lies in A, the number of types or designs. Greater diversity of capital goods, i.e. greater specialization, increases the level of output, holding all else equal. It simplifies matters to treat A as a continuous variable.

To base a growth model on this production function, we will need to make some special assumptions. First, we will assume that the labor force is constant and fully employed. Second, the final goods sector is the only sector which hires workers, and it is competitive so the wage there will be equal to the marginal product of labor that clears the labor market. Third, the capital goods are used up in one period, and because of that we will call them circulating capital goods. Fourth, firms producing final output are able to pay for circulating capital goods and labor at the end of the period, so that interest is not a cost of production. Fifth, the capital goods are produced by monopolies in a separate sector using final goods as the input, giving this model a dual market structure. The circulating capital sector is monopolistic because each design is the private property of its inventor, who retains the ability to exclude anyone from producing it forever through a patent. The customers for circulating capital are the firms producing final goods. These firms will demand an amount of any particular good which maximizes profits: they will use the good at the level where its marginal product equals its price (measured in units of final output), P_i. (The same reasoning leads to the idea that the demand curve for labor is the marginal product of labor.) By differentiating the production function with respect to K_i and setting it equal to P_i, we can write the demand curve for the i-th capital good as

$$K_i^d = N(\alpha/P_i)^{\frac{1}{1-\alpha}}$$

The costs in the circulating capital sector consist of a fixed design cost, F, and a constant marginal cost, c, which represents the amount of final output that can somehow be transmuted into the particular capital good without using any labor. This kind of cost curve exhibits increasing returns to scale, because as output expands, the fixed design cost is spread over more units and this lowers unit costs.

The planning problem for a monopolist who has already sunk money into design is very simple. Given the demand curve above, she must choose the price which maximizes profits. Mathematically, this can be expressed as follows:

$$\max(P_i - c)N(\alpha/P_i)^{\frac{1}{1-\alpha}}$$

The solution is found by means of the first order condition. Setting the derivative of this expression with respect to P_i equal to zero, and solving for P_i^*, yields

$$P_i^* = \frac{1}{\alpha}c$$

Since α is less than one, the monopolist will charge a price which is a constant *markup* over marginal cost. Since the introduction of new designs does not affect the demand for existing capital goods, the monopolist will produce at the same level of output forever.

15.7   Endogenous Growth with Specialization

A capitalist thinking of allocating some wealth to the design process asks if the cost, F, is greater or less than the value of the monopoly as determined in an equity market in which monopolies are bought and sold. The monopolies are like consols: bonds which pay a fixed coupon forever. The rate of interest, r, is implicitly defined as the annual profit, $(P_i-c)K_i$, divided by the value of the monopoly, which in turn represents the present discounted value of all the future profits of the monopoly. If the value of the monopolies were to exceed the design cost, every capitalist would allocate all her wealth to design. In equilibrium, therefore, the value of the monopolies must be equal to the design cost. We can express these ideas mathematically as

$$F = \sum_0^\infty \frac{(P_i^* - c)K_i}{(1+r)^{1+t}} = \frac{(P_i^* - c)K_i}{r}$$

By substituting in K_i from the demand equation for the circulating capital good and P_i^* from the mark-up price equation, we can solve for the interest rate

$$r = \frac{1}{F}\left(N\alpha^{\frac{1}{1-\alpha}}(1-\alpha)(\frac{c}{\alpha})^{\frac{\alpha}{\alpha-1}}\right)$$

In a steady state equilibrium the capitalist planning problem consists of choosing to allocate her wealth, in the form of the value of the monopolies she holds, $(1+r)FA$, between consumption and design. This can be expressed in a familiar form:

$$\text{choose } \{C_t \geq 0, A_{t+1} \geq 0\}_0^\infty$$

$$\text{so as to maximize } (1-\beta)\Sigma_{t=0}^\infty \beta^t \ln C_t \qquad (15.4)$$

$$\text{subject to } C_t + FA_{t+1} \leq (1+r)FA_t \qquad t = 0, 1, \ldots$$

$$A_0 \text{ given}$$

We already know that the solution to this problem is to consume a constant fraction of wealth, or $C = (1-\beta)(1+r)FA$. Assuming that $r > (1-\beta)/\beta$, this implies that the growth rate of A takes the same form as the Cambridge equation, or

$$1 + g_A = \beta(1+r)$$

We are now in a position to describe the steady state equilibrium. Each monopoly will maintain a constant output of its circulating capital good since new arrivals do not disturb the demand for a capital good. Growth takes place entirely because new capital goods are brought into existence. This proliferation of designs increases the level of output and output per worker (recall the constant labor force), which grow continuously at the rate g_A. Thus, productivity growth is endogenous and takes place because of intentional activity on the part of profit-seeking by a class of capitalist-inventors. If the capitalists were to become more thrifty, the increase in β would increase the rate of productivity growth, because more effort would be devoted to increasing the diversity of circulating capital goods.

We are also in a position to see that if the labor force were permitted to grow, it would cause productivity to *accelerate* (grow at an ever increasing rate). In this sense the model seems very fragile. We can see this in the equation for the rate of interest, which contains the labor force, N. In effect, the growth of the market would continuously increase the monopoly profits and draw ever-increasing resources into design. This tendency for models to blow up because of scale effects is a central problem in the theory of endogenous technical change since we do not observe faster growth rates in more populous countries.

Problem 15.6 *Derive the equation for the equilibrium wage in the model of specialization. Show that the wage grows at the same rate as the number of designs.*

Problem 15.7 *Would the rate of growth in the model with specialization be greater or less than the rate of growth chosen by a benevolent dictator to maximize the utility of the capitalists?*

15.8   Cumulative Causation

The economist most responsible for recognizing the significance of specialization was Adam Smith, who entitled the third chapter of *The Wealth of Nations*, "the division of labor is limited by the extent of the market." A growing economy creates opportunities for increasing specialization among workers, firms and whole industries. Increasing specialization can give rise to economies of large scale production, which raise the productivity of inputs just as would a pure technical change. Smith's pin factory continues to serve as a handy example of the advantages of specialization among workers.

As we have seen, it is difficult to accommodate economies of scale without abandoning the assumption of perfect competition between firms in the product market. One alternative is to consider *external economies of scale* which are not present at the level of the firm but which do exist at higher levels of aggregation, such as the industry or even the whole economy. External economies of scale are consistent with perfect competition within an industry because no individual firm gains any special advantage when they are realized.

Smith's famous observation about the division of labor inspired the American economist Allyn Young to extend his argument to the whole economy. As the economy grows, Young pointed out, parts of individual industries spin off and form their own industry. An increase in the degree of specialization among industries raises the overall productivity of the economy for some of the same reasons specialization among pin workers raised their efficiency. In fact, some of the activities which were performed within Smith's pin factory, such as wire drawing, have evolved into separate industries.

Young's contribution lay dormant until the thought was picked up by Kaldor, who gave it a central role in his theory of *cumulative causation*. Cumulative causation grew out of Kaldor's disillusionment with his earlier models, which (like others of the time) saw the supply of resources as the basic constraint on growth. Cumulative causation puts at least as much emphasis on demand factors. The central idea is that the growth process consists of positive feedback loops of a progressive and cumulative nature between demand and supply factors. Increases in demand extend the market, providing opportunities for greater specialization. Increases in specialization generate growing incomes, which in turn lead to greater demand. Kaldor's approach rejects the notion of a steady state in which all the important variables grow at the same rate, and considers uneven development to be the natural condition of a growing economy.

In particular, Kaldor singles out the manufacturing sector as the engine of growth and safely confines the economies of scale to this sector. He was struck by the strong empirical relationship between the growth of labor productivity and the growth of output that seems to be found only across the secondary (manufacturing) sectors of regions or countries, but not across the primary (farming and mining) or tertiary (service) sectors. This empirical relationship has come to be called Verdoorn's Law after the Dutch economist who first noticed it. It plays the same role in the cumulative causation model that the technical progress function fills in Kaldor's earlier growth models. Most studies of Verdoorn's Law find that each one percentage point increase in the growth rate of manufacturing output is associated with around a 1/2 percentage point rise in the growth rate of labor productivity in manufacturing.

The cumulative causation model predicts that economic growth and stagnation tend to be self-reinforcing through a virtuous cycle of growth or a vicious cycle of stagnation. This dynamic would lead to divergence among countries' productivity levels. Thus, the cumulative causation model can be seen as a precursor of the endogenous growth models offered in the last decade, for which the lack of evidence of absolute convergence has been a major selling point.

15.9 Suggested Readings

A good place to start reading about technical change at the macroeconomic level is Fagerberg [1994], a survey of recent theoretical and empirical contributions to the field.

The literature on vintage growth models tends toward the difficult, but Allen [1968] offers a concise textbook presentation. The putty-clay metaphor was coined by Edmund Phelps [1963], while Salter [1969] is an important study taking a putty-clay approach. The impact on productivity of an increased rate of investment in a vintage model is explored by Nelson [1964].

For Kaldor's use of the technical progress function, compare Kaldor [1957] and Kaldor and Mirrlees [1962]. A recent example of work in this tradition is You [1994]. Those seeking more on cumulative causation will find the original Smith [1937], Young [1928] and Kaldor [1966, 1967] stimulating, and Ricoy [1987] an excellent overview. An empirical study of uneven development at the sectoral level is Rowthorn and Wells [1987]. Although it is not obviously linked to the cumulative causation approach, Jacobs [1984] is well worth reading for some insight into the regional dimensions of economic development.

The theory of induced technical change owes much to Kennedy [1964]. For a model in which technical change is treated as a stochastic process, see Duménil and Lévy [1995].

The model of specialization is based on Romer [1990], while the presentation in the text has been adapted from Barro and Sala-i-Martin [1995]. The production function with returns to specialization was introduced in Dixit and Stiglitz [1977], where it appears as a utility function for people who value variety. Related models that drop the assumption of permanent monopolies in favor of the idea that new designs displace old ones are called neo-Schumpeterian because they invoke the idea of "creative destruction" introduced in Schumpeter [1942]. An advanced textbook presentation can be found in Aghion and Howitt [1998]. The empirical problems with scale effects form the basis for an influential critique of neo-Schumpeterian models by Jones [1995a,b]. There is also an older tradition influenced by Schumpeter taking an evolutionary approach to technical change, to which Dosi et al. [1988] provides an overview and Nelson and Winter [1982] is an influential contribution.

Chapter 16

Endogenous Technical Change

16.1   Technical Change in a Capitalist Economy

Industrial capitalism is a powerful mechanism for the accumulation of wealth in the form of means of production. The concentration of social surplus production in the form of profits in the hands of private capitalists creates conditions for a massive increase in the quantity of factories, machines, and transportation facilities. This quantitative growth in the means of production leads to a qualitative change in the organization of production and in the productivity of labor. Competing capitalists seek out new methods of organizing production, new processes and new products in an attempt to achieve an advantage over their rivals. As a byproduct of this competitive struggle the productivity of labor rises. The steady increases in labor productivity in capitalist society are as important an influence on modern society as the accumulation of capital itself.

Attempts to make technical change endogenous in a model of economic growth generally fall into one of two broad categories. One approach treats technical change as a by-product of ordinary economic activity (sometimes called an *externality*). The second approach regards technical change as the output of a distinct research and development (R&D) sector. This chapter will consider examples of both categories.

16.2   Learning by Doing

Intel co-founder Gordon Moore once predicted that the capacity of silicon chips would double every eighteen months. "Moore's Law" has become an article of faith in the computer industry. In other industries, managers speak of the *learning curve* to describe improvements that result from experience. Kenneth Arrow calls this *learning by doing*.

The learning by doing of greatest interest to growth theorists creates knowledge which spills over to other firms and workers in the economy. The size of the region over which such spillovers occur is open to interpretation. It could be an industry, a country, a region, or the global economy. Arrow argues that learning by doing is most important in the production of new capital goods. When the knowledge that is gained is accessible to other producers through spillover effects, it can lead to self-sustaining technical change. Because the capital stock represents the accumulation of past investment, the stock of knowledge will depend on the stock of capital.

To demonstrate how learning by doing can be formalized as an external economy of scale, and hence compatible with a competitive equilibrium, we will need to distinguish between firm-level and economy-level variables. We do this by using a subscript to describe variables for the i-th firm. An unsubscripted variable refers by default to its aggregate value. Each firm is assumed to operate with a Leontief production function, or

$$X_i = \min(AK_i, x(K)N_i)$$

We will assume that technical change is Harrod-neutral, so capital productivity is constant. We will explain below why we have replaced the usual symbol ρ with A. The level of technology depends on the size of the aggregate capital stock through the function $x(K)$, which models the learning by doing effect. We are assuming that learning effects are too small to matter at the firm level. We can add a little structure by letting $x(K)$ take the convenient form of a power function, as in

$$x = K^a$$

The power function signifies that a one percent increase in K generates an a-percent change in x, with $a > 0$ to reflect labor-saving technical change.

In this model, firms take the technology as given, but as they collectively accumulate capital, they contribute to the discovery of new techniques. By aggregating (summing) over all the firms, we arrive at an aggregate production function which reveals the effects of these spillovers:

$$X = \min[AK, K^a N]$$

Ordinarily, firms will operate with no excess capital stock nor hire any excess labor, which means that both the constraints in the $\min(.,.)$ function will be satisfied as equalities. The labor constraint is in the Cobb-Douglas family of production functions, with increasing returns since $1 + a > 1$. This kind of scale effect, operating at an aggregate level, was one explanation put forward by Kaldor for Verdoorn's Law discussed in the previous chapter.

The capital constraint is in the form of a constant times capital. This production function is the basis for the "AK" family of growth models. We switched notation for capital productivity to make this connection clear. Obviously, the Classical model belongs to this family of models, even without the increasing returns to scale we are about to include in it.

To introduce learning by doing into our Classical model with a conventional wage share, let us continue to assume that the rate of capital accumulation depends on the rate of profit through the Cambridge equation. To economize on notation, assume that the rate of depreciation is zero. This makes the net rate of profit equal to the constant profit share times capital productivity, or $r = \pi A$. The rate of accumulation will thus be determined by

$$1 + g_K = \beta(1 + r) = \beta(1 + \pi A)$$

The rate of labor-saving technical change depends in a straightforward fashion on the rate of accumulation. From the definitions of γ and g_K we have

$$1 + \gamma = \frac{x_{t+1}}{x_t} = \frac{K^a_{t+1}}{K^a_t} = (1 + g_K)^a$$

This expression can be simplified further by using the mathematical fact that when a variable, z, is small in magnitude, $\ln(1 + z)$ is approximately equal to z. Taking logs of both sides, substituting from the Cambridge equation and applying this handy fact gives us

$$\gamma \approx a((\beta - 1) + \beta \pi A)$$

Thus, the rate of technical change depends on the rate of capital accumulation, since knowledge grows as an unintended consequence of investment. An increase in the propensity to save out of wealth will cause an increase in the rate of technical change, which might be one explanation for the observed correlation between saving and growth in per capita income across countries. An increase in the profit share (or the productivity of capital) will cause an increase in the rate of technical change. This means that an increase in the real wage, insofar as it squeezes down the profit share, will cause the rate of technical change to decline, which is at odds with what we concluded in the model of induced technical change.

Problem 16.1 *Derive an expression for the rate of growth of employment in the model with learning by doing. Must employment be increasing?*

Problem 16.2 *Suppose that learning by doing tends to lead to more mechanized technologies, so that $A = K^b$, where $b < 0$. Derive the expression that describes the rate of capital-using technical change, χ.*

16.3   R&D Investment in Technical Change

Another approach to understanding endogenous technical change focuses on the decisions of individual capitalists to invest in productivity increases through research and development spending. The resulting technological advances may then *spill over* to other producers as they are revealed in patents, publications, the products themselves, or the movement of technical workers from one firm to another.

To construct a model of endogenous technical change through R&D, assume that a typical capitalist starts each period with a stock of capital K, and that there is a socially available technology of production (x, k) which anyone can use. The rate of profit with this technology, assuming that the wage is w, is:

$$v = \frac{x - w}{k}$$

For simplicity we will assume that all technical change is Harrod-neutral, so that productivity $\rho = x/k$ and δ never change. But we will allow for changes in labor productivity, x. Remember that $w/x = 1 - \pi$ is the share of the gross product going to wages

Now suppose that the typical capitalist can use some of her capital to increase labor productivity above the socially given level x. Essentially the capitalist is in a position to buy technical progress. In order to make the model consistent with steady-state growth, assume that the *fraction* of the total capital allocated to improving productivity determines the amount of technical progress in the period. We could think of the improvement in technical progress as the result of teaching workers better methods of production. The larger a capitalist's stock of capital, the more workers she will employ, and the more resources it will take to educate the workers. Call the proportion of her capital spent on technical improvement rd. Then the capitalist can achieve the technology $(x/g(rd), k/g(rd))$ by spending a proportion rd of her capital on technical innovation.

To make sense of this picture, we have to assume that the capitalist cannot raise more capital by borrowing. If she could, the trade-off between the resources she puts into technical change and the resources she uses for production would not exist. In real capitalist economies firms can borrow, but there are limits to how much a firm can borrow in relation to its own equity (which corresponds to its capital in the model we are studying.) Thus the assumption that capitalists cannot borrow at all is not too inaccurate as a first approximation.

The function $g(.)$ expresses the productivity of resources in improving labor productivity. If the capitalist spends nothing on innovation, she will just use the average social technique (x, k); we reflect this by assuming that $g(0) = 1$. The more she spends on innovation, the higher will her workers' productivity, $x/g(rd)$, be. Thus we assume that the derivative $g'(rd)$ is negative. Because we are assuming that capital productivity remains constant, this implies that capital intensity, $k = x/\rho$ will also rise to $k/g(rd)$. As a particular example, assume that $g(rd) = (1 - rd)^\theta$, where θ is a parameter that measures how productive resources devoted to innovation are in raising labor productivity. Figure 16.1 illustrates $g(rd)$.

A capitalist who invests a proportion rd of her capital in innovation will have $(1 - rd)$ left for production. Thus her profit rate after paying wages will be:

$$\frac{(x/g(rd)) - w}{k/g(rd)}(1 - rd) = \frac{x - g(rd)w}{k}$$

Thus the effect of research and development from the point of view of the capitalist is the same as a reduction in the wage.

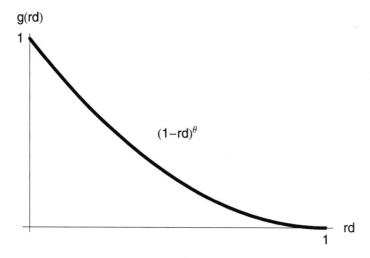

g(rd)

1

$(1-rd)^\theta$

rd

1

Figure 16.1:   A capitalist who invests a proportion rd of her capital in innovation can increase her labor productivity by a factor $1/g(rd)$ of the standard level. This graph is drawn on the assumption that $\theta > 1$.

The capitalist's net profit rate when she spends rd on innovation is:

$$r(rd) = \frac{x - wg(rd)}{k}(1 - rd) - \delta$$

$$= \frac{x - w(1 - rd)^\theta}{k}(1 - rd) - \delta$$

Her budget constraint, then, is:

$$K_{+1} + C = (1 + r(rd))K$$

$$= \left(\frac{x - wg(rd)}{k}(1 - rd) + (1 - \delta)\right)K \qquad (16.1)$$

We can write the typical capitalist's planning problem as:

$$\text{choose } \{C_t \geq 0, 0 \leq rd_t \leq 1\}_{t=0}^\infty$$

$$\text{so as to maximize } (1 - \beta) \sum_{t=0}^\infty \beta^t \ln(C_t)$$

$$\text{subject to}$$

$$K_{t+1} + C_t = (1 + r(rd_t))K_t \qquad t = 0, ..., \infty$$

$$\text{given } K_0, \{w/x\}_{t=0}^{\infty}$$

As we already know, a capitalist who maximizes a Cobb-Douglas intertemporal utility function spends a fraction $1 - \beta$ of her wealth at the end of the period on consumption.

$$C = (1 - \beta)(1 + r(rd))K \qquad (16.2)$$

What is new in this model is that the capitalist has to decide how much of her capital to devote to innovation in each period. Thus the capitalist's decision problem will be solved once we understand how she will choose rd_t. This also turns out to be the key to understanding the forces governing the growth of labor productivity.

16.4   How Much R&D?

The advantage in research and development spending from the point of view of the capitalist is that it raises her profit rate. The capitalist will choose the level of research and development spending that maximizes her profit rate. If she decides to invest in innovation at all, she should continue to invest until her net profit rate with respect to her R&D investment is maximized:

$$r'(rd) = \left(-\frac{w}{x}g'(rd)(1 - rd) - (1 - \frac{w}{x}g(rd))\right)\rho = 0, \text{ or}$$

$$g(rd) - g'(rd)(1 - rd_t) = \frac{x}{w} \qquad (16.3)$$

This first-order condition expresses the tradeoff the capitalist faces. She can determine her rate of profit

$$(1 + r(rd)) = \frac{x - wg(rd_t)}{k}(1 - rd) + (1 - \delta)$$

by choosing the level of innovative expenditure, rd. An increase in rd lowers her labor cost by raising labor productivity, which has a positive effect on profitability. But an increase in rd also leaves the capitalist with fewer resources to devote to production because of the $(1 - rd)$ term. If we graph the rate of profit as a function of rd, as in Figure 16.2, we can see that when $rd = 0$ the rate of profit is just the level available by taking the existing social technology, and when $rd = 1$, the rate of profit is zero. Somewhere in between is the maximal level, which is determined by equation (16.3).

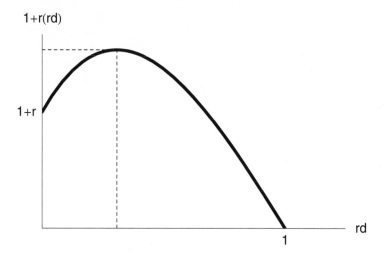

Figure 16.2: As the capitalist spends more on innovation her profit rate initially rises because of the effect of innovation on labor productivity, but eventually falls because she has so little capital left for actual production.

For the particular $g(rd) = (1 - rd)^\theta$, we can see that the profit rate for any level of rd will be:

$$1 + r(rd) = \frac{x - w(1 - rd_t)^\theta}{k}(1 - rd) + (1 - \delta)$$

In this case the first-order condition is satisfied when:

$$1 - rd^* = \left(\frac{1}{(1+\theta)(1-\pi)}\right)^{\frac{1}{\theta}} \qquad (16.4)$$

This expression makes sense only if $(1+\theta)(1-\pi) > 1$. If $(1+\theta)(1-\pi) \le 1$, the capitalist is better off not investing in innovation at all, because the profit rate is actually declining in rd even when $rd = 0$. Thus if innovation is very expensive (because θ is small) or if the wage share, $1 - \pi = w/x$ is small, there is no incentive for the capitalist to innovate.

If $(1+\theta)(1-\pi) > 1$, so that the capitalist does invest in innovation, the higher is the wage share in the gross product, the more resources the capitalist will find it profitable to devote to increasing the productivity of labor. This makes good sense, since if wage costs are only a small share of total costs, there isn't much point in trying to reduce them further, while if wage costs are a large share of total costs, an increase in labor productivity increases profits a lot.

We can also calculate the resulting labor requirement and wage share after the innovation since:

$$g(rd^*) = (1 - rd^*)^\theta = \frac{1}{(1+\theta)(1-\pi)}$$

$$(1 - \pi)g(rd^*) = \frac{1}{1+\theta} \tag{16.5}$$

As a result the profit rate for the capitalist after innovation will be:

$$r^* = \frac{\theta}{1+\theta}\left(\frac{1}{(1+\theta)(1-\pi)}\right)^{\frac{1}{\theta}}\rho - \delta$$

This expression shows the final effect of the induced technical change on the capitalist's profit rate.

Problem 16.3 In the model with $g(rd) = (1 - rd)^\theta$, if $w/x = .5$, and $\theta = 2$, find the proportion of capital a capitalist will devote to innovation, rd^*. What will the level of $g(rd^*)$ be? What will be her actual share of wages in costs? If $\rho = .333/year$ and $\delta = .05/year$, calculate her gross rate of profit when $rd = 0$ and at the optimum level of innovation.

Problem 16.4 Find the formula for the optimal rd^* if $g(rd) = 1 - \theta rd$.

16.5 Steady-State Growth with No Persistent Effects of R&D

We now have a model that explains what proportion of resources capitalists would devote to innovation, or training, or whatever activities increase the productivity of the labor force. What happens to the economy over time depends on what we assume about the effects of this innovative expenditure on labor productivity and wages in succeeding periods.

The simplest hypothesis is that the effects of the innovative expenditure wear off completely each period, putting the productivity of the labor back at a given level x, and that the conventional wage, $\bar{w}$, is constant. Under this assumption $1 - \bar{\pi} = \bar{w}/x$ in every period, so the capitalists will devote the same proportion of their resources, to innovation in each period. We have:

$$1 - rd^* = \left(\frac{1}{(1+\theta)(1-\bar{\pi})} \right)^{\frac{1}{\theta}} \text{ if } (1+\theta)(1-\bar{\pi}) > 1$$

$$rd^* = 0 \text{ if } (1+\theta)(1-\bar{\pi}) \leq 1$$

As a result of the innovative expenditure the actual labor productivity will be higher in every period. If $(1+\theta)(1-\bar{\pi}) > 1$:

$$g(rd^*) = (1 - rd^*)^\theta = \frac{1}{(1+\theta)(1-\bar{\pi})}$$

$$(w/x)g(rd^*) = \frac{1}{1+\theta}$$

$$\frac{x}{g(rd^*)} = w(1+\theta) \geq x \tag{16.6}$$

Thus labor productivity $x/g(rd^*)$ will be higher as a result of the innovative expenditure. The higher is the wage, the more resources the capitalists will be induced to put into innovation, and the higher will be the labor productivity in the steady-state.

The steady-state net profit rate in this economy will be:

$$r^* = \rho(1 - rd^*)(1 - \frac{\bar{w}}{x}g(rd^*)) - \delta \geq 1 + r = \rho(1 - \frac{\bar{w}}{x}) - \delta$$

Since the Cambridge equation holds for this economy, we have:

$$1 + g_K = \beta(1 + r^*) \geq \beta(1 + r)$$

Thus the steady-state growth rate for this economy will also be higher than if the capitalists did not innovate.

Problem 16.5 *Find the steady-state gross profit rate and gross growth rate for the economy described in Problem 16.3 under the assumption that there is no persistence to the improvement in labor productivity that results from innovative expenditure and that $\beta = .9$.*

Problem 16.6 *Can an increase in the wage raise the profit rate and growth rate in an economy where improvements in labor productivity from innovative expenditures do not persist?*

16.6 Steady-State Growth with Persistent Effects of R&D

In the last section we saw that innovative expenditure can raise the steady-state profit rate and growth rate of an economy, even if there are no persistent effects of innovation, so that the level of labor productivity is not increasing.

Innovative expenditure may have much more far-reaching effects, however. There may be *spillovers* from one capitalist's innovation to the average level of labor productivity in later periods. For example, if innovative expenditures raise the productivity of labor by training workers to be more efficient, in the next period there will be a larger pool of trained workers in the economy as a whole. In a competitive economy some of these workers will move to other firms. In this situation the effect of innovative expenditure in one period by all the capitalists is to raise the social level of labor productivity in the future.

In our model we assume that each individual capitalist takes the level of labor productivity in the system, x, as given in each period and beyond her control. She sees her innovative expenditure as helping her workers in one period improve over the social standard level. We also assume, however, that all the capitalists are exactly alike; whatever one of them does, they all will do, since they all face the same incentives. In this situation innovation is an *externality*: the innovative expenditures of one capitalist improve the productivity and profitability of the other capitalists in future periods, but because each capitalist makes her decision as to how much to spend on innovation taking future productivity as given, she does not take this external effect into account. In this circumstance the capitalists will spend too little on innovation, in the sense that they would all have higher utility if they agreed to increase innovative expenditure in each period, and thereby raised the whole path of labor productivities. When each makes this decision separately, she has no incentive to spend the increased amount.

In the case of persistent effects of innovation on labor productivity we have an additional equilibrium condition in the model, to take account of the effect of the average level of innovative expenditure on the future level of labor productivity. A simple (though somewhat extreme) assumption is to suppose that the level of social labor productivity (which will apply in the absence of any further innovative expenditure by the capitalists) in a period will equal the level of labor productivity actually achieved (including the effects of innovation) in the last period by the typical capitalist. Mathematically this amounts to the assumption:

$$x_{+1} = \frac{x}{g(rd^*)}$$

First let us assume that the wage is constant at $\bar{w}$. Then we know from (16.6) that after the first period

$$x_1 = \frac{x_0}{g(rd_0^*)} = (1 + \theta)\bar{w}$$

In this case we have $(\bar{w}/x_1) = \frac{1}{1+\theta}$, and $(1 + \theta)(1 - \pi_1) = 1$, so that after period 0 it will not pay any capitalist to innovate. Thus in this economy with persistent effects of innovation and a constant real wage the labor productivity, x, will immediately rise to the level $(1 + \theta)\bar{w}$, and at that point the wage share will be so small that there will be no further incentive for the typical capitalist to innovate. After period 0, $rd^* = 0$, and labor productivity will continue at its steady-state level.

The steady-state level of labor productivity will be the level where $rd = 0$, or where

$$1 + \theta = \frac{x}{\bar{w}}, \text{ or}$$

$$x = \bar{w}(1 + \theta)$$

But, as we have seen, this steady-state is not actually the best that the capitalists could achieve, since it would be to their collective advantage to lower the labor requirement even more, if they could make a group decision to do so.

Problem 16.7 *Find the steady-state level of labor productivity for the economy described in Problems 16.3 and 16.5 when there is complete persistence of the productivity enhancing effect of innovative expenditure and the wage is $\bar{w} = \$10,000/year$.*

16.7   Persistent Effects of R&D with a Conventional Wage Share

In real capitalist economies the wage tends to rise with labor productivity, so that the wage share does not decline as in the last example. The typical capitalist, of course, takes both the wage and the social level of

labor productivity as parameters in making her decisions about innovative expenditure. What happens if market forces beyond the capitalist's
control act to keep the labor share $1 - \pi$ constant at a given level, $1 - \bar{\pi}$,
but innovative expenditure has persistent effects on future levels of labor
productivity?

We know, since $\bar{\pi}$ is constant, that, if $(1 + \theta)(1 - \bar{\pi}) > 1$:

$$g(rd^*) = \frac{1}{(1 + \theta)(1 - \bar{\pi})}$$

Since improvements in labor productivity are persistent, if $(1+\theta)(1-\bar{\pi}) > 1$ we have:

$$x_{+1} = \frac{x}{g(rd^*)} = x(1 + \theta)(1 - \bar{\pi})$$

Thus the effect of a sufficiently high conventional wage share is to
induce an indefinitely continuing rise in labor productivity. The higher
is the wage share, the more resources the typical capitalist will put into
innovation, and the faster labor productivity will grow. This interaction
will give rise to Harrod-neutral technical progress at the rate:

$$1 + \gamma = \frac{x_{+1}}{x} = \frac{1}{g(rd^*)} = (1 + \theta)(1 - \bar{\pi})$$

What is happening here is that each capitalist, consulting her own
incentives to innovate to get ahead of the market, invests in innovation
that raises the labor productivity of the workers. This improvement
spills over into higher labor productivity in the next period. At the
same time, the wage is rising at the same rate as labor productivity, so
that the wage share is constant. This means the typical capitalist has
exactly the same incentive to spend on innovation in the next period. In
this situation labor productivity improvement is a kind of unintended
side-effect of the capitalists' pursuit of profit.

It is striking that the incentive for the capitalist to innovate rises
with the wage share. A high wage share economy, on these hypotheses,
tends to be an economy with rapidly rising labor productivity, other
things being equal, as was the case in the model of induced technical
change in Chapter 15.

It is also striking that the ability of a capitalist economy to sustain
high rates of labor productivity growth depends both on the costs of
innovation (represented by the parameter θ), and on the incentives to
innovate (represented by the labor share, $1 - \bar{\pi}$). A capitalist economy

whose labor share is low relative to the costs of innovation will settle into a stagnant regime where no capitalist puts resources into innovation and there is no productivity growth. This contrasts with the model of learning by doing, where a high profit share caused rapid accumulation and high productivity growth.

As with any abstract model, it is important to view the conclusions of this analysis with caution. Many assumptions are required to reach the conclusions, and some of them may not hold in any particular real economy.

Problem 16.8 *Find the growth rate of labor productivity for the economy described in Problem 16.3 under the assumption that labor productivity improvements are persistent and that the wage share is 60%.*

Problem 16.9 *What rd would lead to the maximum rate of growth of labor productivity in this model? Would it be a good idea to follow this policy? Explain why or why not.*

16.8   Suggested Readings

Learning by doing was elaborated by Arrow [1962]. The AK-models originated with Paul Romer [1986], which, along with Lucas [1988], is often credited with starting the New Endogenous Growth Theory.

Models which incorporate R&D also owe a debt to Romer, as in Romer [1987b] and Romer [1990]. For some insight into the larger controversy between proponents of the New Growth Theory and devotees of the Solow-Swan approach, Romer [1994] and Grossman and Helpman [1994] provide a New Growth perspective, rounded out on the other side by Solow [1994] and Mankiw [1995]. An influential study of the contribution of R&D is Coe and Helpman [1995]. Finally, don't overlook the often-cited Kremer [1993], which contemplates technical change from the Ice Age onward.

References

Andrew B. Abel, N. Gregory Mankiw, Lawrence H. Summers, and Richard J. Zeckhausen. Assessing dynamic efficiency: Theory and evidence. *Review of Economic Studies*, 56(1):1–19, 1989.

Moses Abramovitz. Catching up, forging ahead, and falling behind. *Journal of Economic History*, 46(2):385–406, 1986.

Philippe Aghion and Peter Howitt. *Endogenous Growth Theory*. MIT Press, Cambridge MA, 1998.

Roy George Douglas Allen. *Macroeconomic Theory: A Mathematical Treatment*. St. Martin's Press, New York, 1968.

Roy George Douglas Allen. *Index Numbers in Theory and Practice*. Aldine, Chicago, 1975.

Philip Armstrong, Andrew Glyn, and John Harrison. *Capitalism Since 1945*. Basil Blackwell, Cambridge MA, 1991.

Kenneth J. Arrow. The economic implications of learning by doing. *Review of Economic Studies*, 29(3):155–173, 1962.

David A. Aschauer. Is public expenditure productive? *Journal of Monetary Economics*, 23(2):177–200, 1989.

Martin N. Baily and Robert J. Gordon. The productivity slowdown, measurement issues, and the explosion of computer power. *Brookings Papers on Economic Activity*, (2):347–420, 1988.

Martin Neal Baily and Charles L. Schultze. The productivity of capital in a period of slower growth. *Brookings Papers on Economic Activity*, pages 369–406, 1990. Special Issue.

Robert J. Barro. Are government bonds net wealth? *Journal of Political Economy*, 81(6):1095–1117, 1974.

Robert J. Barro and Xavier Sala-i-Martin. *Economic Growth.* McGraw-Hill, New York, 1995.

William J. Baumol. Macroeconomics of unbalanced growth: The anatomy of urban crisis. *American Economic Review*, 67:1072–1085, 1967.

William J. Baumol, Sue Anne Batey Blackman, and Edward N. Wolff. *Productivity and American Leadership.* MIT Press, Cambridge MA, 1989.

Gary Becker. *Human Capital.* Columbia University Press, New York, 1964.

Jess Benhabib and Mark M. Spiegel. The role of human capital in economic development: Evidence from aggregate cross-country data. *Journal of Monetary Economics*, 34(2):143–173, 1994.

Amit Bhaduri and Stephen Marglin. Unemployment and the real wage: The economic basis for contesting political ideologies. *Cambridge Journal of Economics*, 14(4):375–393, 1990.

Samuel Bowles. The production process in a competitive economy: Walrasian, neo-Hobbesian, and Marxian models. *American Economic Review*, 75(1):16–36, 1985.

Elize Brezis, Paul Krugman, and Daniel Tsiddon. Leapfrogging in international competition: A theory of cycles in national technological leadership. *American Economic Review*, 85(5):1211–1219, 1993.

Michael Bruno and Jeffrey D. Sachs. *Economics of Worldwide Stagflation.* Harvard University Press, Cambridge MA, 1985.

Bureau of Labor Statistics. Multifactor productivity trends, 1994, 1996.

Dongchul Cho and Stephen Graham. The other side of convergence. *Economics Letters*, 50(2):285–290, 1996.

David T. Coe and Elhanan Helpman. International R&D spillovers. *European Economic Review*, 39(5):859–887, 1995.

Paul David. The computer and the dynamo: An historical perspective on the productivity paradox. *American Economic Review*, 80(2):355–361, 1990.

Frits DeJong. *Dimensional Analysis for Economists.* North Holland Publishing Company, Amsterdam, 1967.

Edward Denison. *Why Growth Rates Differ*. The Brookings Institution, Washington DC, 1967.

Peter Diamond. National debt in a neoclassical growth model. *American Economic Review*, 55(5):1126–1150, 1965.

Avinash Dixit and Joseph E. Stiglitz. Monopolistic competition and optimum product diversity. *American Economic Review*, 67(3):297–308, 1977.

Maurice Dobb. *Theories of Value and Distribution since Adam Smith*. Cambridge University Press, Cambridge UK, 1973.

Evsey D. Domar. Capital expansion, rate of growth, and employment. *Econometrica*, 14:137–147, 1946.

Giovanni Dosi, Christopher Freeman, Richard Nelson, Gerald Silverberg, and Luc Soete, editors. *Technical Change and Economic Theory*. Pinter Publishers, London, 1988.

Gérard Duménil and Dominique Lévy. *The Economics of the Profit Rate*. Edward Elgar Publishing Company, Aldershot, 1994.

Gérard Duménil and Dominique Lévy. A stochastic model of technical change: An application to the U.S. economy, 1869–1989. *Metroeconomica*, 46(3):213–245, 1995.

Amitava K. Dutt. *Growth, Distribution, and Uneven Development*. Cambridge University Press, New York, 1990.

Jan Fagerberg. Technology and international differences in growth rates. *Journal of Economic Literature*, 32(3):1147–1175, 1994.

Elido Fazi and Neri Salvadori. The existence of a two-class economy in a general Cambridge model of growth and distribution. *Cambridge Journal of Economics*, 9(2):55–164, 1985.

Duncan K. Foley. *Understanding Capital: Marx's Economic Theory*. Harvard University Press, Cambridge MA, 1986.

Pierangelo Garegnani. Heterogeneous capital, the production function, and the theory of distribution. *Review of Economic Studies*, 37:407–436, 1970.

Alexander Gerschenkron. *Economic Backwardness in Historical Perspective*. Harvard University Press, Cambridge MA, 1962.

Richard M. Goodwin. A growth cycle. In C. H. Feinstein, editor, *Socialism, Capitalism and Growth*. Cambridge University Press, Cambridge UK, 1967.

David M. Gordon, Richard Edwards, and Michael Reich. *Segmented Work, Divided Workers: The Historical Transformation of Labor in the United States*. Cambridge University Press, Cambridge UK, 1982.

Harvey Gram and Vivian Walsh. *Classical and Neoclassical Theories of General Equilibrium*. Oxford University Press, Oxford, 1980.

Gene M. Grossman and Elhanan Helpman. Endogenous innovation in the theory of growth. *Journal of Economic Perspectives*, 8(1):23–44, 1994.

Frank H. Hahn and Robin C.O. Matthews. The theory of economic growth: A survey. *Economic Journal*, 74(296):779–902, 1964.

Daniel S. Hamermesh. *Labor Demand*. Princeton University Press, Princeton, 1993.

Geoffrey C. Harcourt. *Some Cambridge Controversies in the Theory of Capital*. Cambridge University Press, Cambridge UK, 1972.

Donald J. Harris. *Capital Accumulation and Income Distribution*. Stanford University Press, Stanford, 1978.

Roy Harrod. An essay in dynamic theory. *Economic Journal*, 49(103): 14–33, 1939.

Roy Harrod. *Toward a Dynamic Economics*. Macmillan, London, 1942.

Harold Hotelling. The economics of exhaustible resources. *Journal of Political Economy*, 39(2):137–175, 1931.

Nazrul Islam. Growth empirics: A panel data approach. *Quarterly Journal of Economics*, 110(4):1127–1170, 1995.

Jane Jacobs. *Cities and the Wealth of Nations*. Random House, New York, 1984.

Charles I. Jones. R&D-Based models of economic growth. *Journal of Political Economy*, 103(4):759–784, 1995a.

Charles I. Jones. Time series tests of endogenous growth models. *Quarterly Journal of Economics*, 110(2):495–525, 1995b.

Charles I. Jones. *Introduction to Economic Growth*. W. W. Norton and Company, New York, 1998.

Hywel G. Jones. *An Introduction to Modern Theories of Growth.* Mc-Graw Hill, New York, 1976.

Dale W. Jorgenson. *Productivity.* MIT Press, Cambridge MA, 1995.

Nicholas Kaldor. Alternative theories of distribution. *Review of Economic Studies*, 23(2):83–100, 1956.

Nicholas Kaldor. A model of economic growth. *Economic Journal*, 68 (268):591–624, 1957.

Nicholas Kaldor. Capital accumulation and economic growth. In Friedrich A. Lutz and Douglas C. Hague, editors, *The Theory of Capital*, pages 177–222. Macmillan, London, 1965.

Nicholas Kaldor. *Causes of the Slow Rate of Economic Growth in the U.K.* Cambridge University Press, Cambridge UK, 1966.

Nicholas Kaldor. *Strategic Factors in Economic Development.* Cornell University Press, Ithaca, 1967.

Nicholas Kaldor and James A. Mirrlees. A new model of economic growth. *Review of Economic Studies*, 29:174–192, 1962.

Michal Kalecki. *Selected Essays on the Dynamics of the Capitalist Economy.* Cambridge University Press, Cambridge UK, 1971.

Charles Kennedy. Induced bias in innovation and the theory of distribution. *Economic Journal*, 74(295):541–547, 1964.

Denis Kessler and André Masson, editors. *Modelling the Accumulation and Distribution of Wealth.* Clarendon Press, Oxford, 1988.

John Maynard Keynes. *The Economic Consequences of the Peace.* Harcourt, Brace, and Howe, New York, 1920.

John Maynard Keynes. *A Treatise on Money.* Macmillan, London, 1930.

John Maynard Keynes. *The General Theory of Employment, Interest, and Money.* Macmillan, London, 1936.

Laurence J. Kotlikoff. Intergenerational transfers and savings. *Journal of Economic Perspectives*, 2(2):41–58, 1988.

Laurence J. Kotlikoff. *Generational Accounting: Knowing Who Pays, and When, for What We Spend.* Free Press, New York, 1992.

Michael Kremer. Population growth and technological change: One million B.C. to 1996. *Quarterly Journal of Economics*, 108(3):681–716, 1993.

Heinz-Dieter Kurz and Neri Salvadori. *Theory of Production: A Long-Period Analysis*. Cambridge University Press, Cambridge UK, 1995.

William Lazonick. *Competitive Advantage on the Shop Floor*. Harvard University Press, Cambridge MA, 1990.

Ross Levine and David Renelt. A sensitivity analysis of cross-country growth regressions. *American Economic Review*, 82(4):942–963, 1992.

William Arthur Lewis. Economic development with unlimited supplies of labor. *Manchester School of Economics and Social Studies*, 22: 139–191, 1954.

Robert E. Lucas. On the mechanics of economic development. *Journal of Monetary Economics*, 22(1):3–42, 1988.

Rosa Luxemburg. *The Accumulation of Capital*. Monthly Review Press, New York, 1951. [1913].

Angus Maddison. *Explaining the Economic Performance of Nations: Essays in Time and Space*. Edward Elgar Publishing Company, Aldershot, 1995a.

Angus Maddison. *Monitoring the World Economy: 1820–1992*. Organization for Economic Cooperation and Development, Paris, 1995b.

Jeffrey G. Madrick. *The End of Affluence: The Causes and Consequences of America's Economic Dilemma*. Random House, 1995.

Thomas R. Malthus. *An Essay on the Principle of Population*. W. Pickering, London, 1986. [1798].

N. Gregory Mankiw. The growth of nations. *Brookings Papers on Economic Activity*, (1):275–326, 1995.

N. Gregory Mankiw, David Romer, and David N. Weil. A contribution to the empirics of economic growth. *Quarterly Journal of Economics*, 107(2):407–437, 1992.

Stephen A. Marglin. What do bosses do? The origins and functions of hierarchy in capitalist production. *Review of Radical Political Economics*, 6(2):60–112, 1974.

Stephen A. Marglin. *Growth, Distribution, and Prices*. Harvard University Press, Cambridge MA, 1984.

Stephen A. Marglin and Juliet B. Schor, editors. *The Golden Age of Capitalism: Reinterpreting the Postwar Experience*. Oxford University Press, New York, 1990.

Karl Marx. *Capital: A Critique of Political Economy*, volume 1. Vintage Books, New York, 1977. [1867].

Robin C. O. Matthews, Charles H. Feinstein, and John C. Odling-Smee. *British Economic Growth, 1856-73*. Clarendon Press, Oxford, 1982.

McKinsey Global Institute. *Manufacturing Productivity*. McKinsey and Company, Inc., Washington DC, 1993.

McKinsey Global Institute. *Capital Productivity*. McKinsey and Company, Inc., Washington DC, 1996.

J. E. Meade. *A Neo-Classical Theory of Economic Growth*. George Allen & Unwin Ltd., London, 1961.

Thomas R. Michl. Is there evidence for a marginalist demand for labor? *Cambridge Journal of Economics*, 11(4):361–374, 1987.

Thomas R. Michl. Wage-profit curves in U.S. manufacturing. *Cambridge Journal of Economics*, 15(3):271–286, 1991.

Thomas R. Michl. Biased technical change and the aggregate production function. *International Review of Applied Economics*, 13, 1999.

Franco Modigliani. The role of intergenerational transfers and life cycle saving in the accumulation of wealth. *Journal of Economic Perspectives*, 2(2):15–40, 1988.

Edward J. Nell. Theories of growth and theories of value. *Economic Development and Cultural Change*, 16(1):15–26, 1967.

Richard R. Nelson. Aggregate production functions and medium range growth predictions. *American Economic Review*, 54(5):576–606, 1964.

Richard R. Nelson. Recent exercises in growth accounting: New understanding or dead end? *American Economic Review*, 63(3):462–468, 1973.

Richard R. Nelson. Research on productivity growth and productivity differences: Dead ends and new departures. *Journal of Economic Literature*, 19(3):1029–1064, 1981.

Richard R. Nelson and Edmund Phelps. Investment in humans, technological diffusion, and economic growth. *American Economic Review*, 56(2):69–75, 1966.

Richard R. Nelson and Sidney G. Winter. *An Evolutionary Theory of Economic Change*. Harvard University Press, Cambridge MA, 1982.

Richard R. Nelson and Gavin Wright. The rise and fall of American technological leadership: The postwar era in historical perspective. *Journal of Economic Literature*, 30(4):1931–1964, 1992.

Edward M. Ochoa. Values, prices, and the wage-profit curves in the U.S. economy. *Cambridge Journal of Economics*, 13(3):413–429, 1989.

OECD. *OECD Business Sector Data Base*. Organization for Economic Cooperation and Development, Paris, 1997.

Kasushi Ohkawa and Henry Rosovsky. *Japanese Economic Growth*. Stanford University Press, Stanford, 1973.

Nobuo Okishio. Technical changes and the rate of profit. *Kobe University Economic Review*, 7:86–99, 1961.

Thomas I. Palley. Growth theory in a Keynesian mode: Some Keynesian foundations for new endogenous growth theory. *Journal of Post Keynesian Economics*, 19(1):113–136, 1996a.

Thomas I. Palley. Old wine for new bottles: Putting old growth theory back in the new. *Australian Economic Papers*, 35(67):250–262, 1996b.

Luigi L. Pasinetti. *Growth and Income Distribution: Essays in Economic Theory*. Cambridge University Press, Cambridge UK, 1974.

Luigi L. Pasinetti. *Lectures on the Theory of Production*. Columbia University Press, New York, 1977.

Edmund S. Phelps. Substitution, fixed proportions, growth and distribution. *International Economic Review*, 4(3):265–288, 1963.

Edmund S. Phelps. *Golden Rules of Economic Growth*. Norton, New York, 1966.

Frank Ramsey. A mathematical theory of saving. *Economic Journal*, 38:543–559, 1928.

David Ricardo. *On the Principles of Political Economy and Taxation*. Cambridge University Press, Cambridge UK, 1951. [1817].

Carlos J. Ricoy. Cumulative causation. In John Eatwell, Murray Milgate, and Peter Newman, editors, *The New Palgrave: A Dictionary of Economics*, volume 1, pages 730–736. The Stockton Press, New York, 1987.

Joan Robinson. The production function and the theory of capital. *Review of Economic Studies*, 51:81–106, 1953.

Joan Robinson. *Essays in the Theory of Economic Growth*. St. Martin's Press, New York, 1964.

David Romer. *Advanced Macroeconomics*. McGraw Hill, New York, 1996.

Paul M. Romer. Increasing returns and long run growth. *Journal of Political Economy*, 94(5):1002–1037, 1986.

Paul M. Romer. Crazy explanations for the productivity slowdown. In Stanley Fischer, editor, *NBER Macroeconomics Annual*. MIT Press, Cambridge MA, 1987a.

Paul M. Romer. Growth based on increasing returns due to specialization. *American Economic Review*, 77(2):56–62, 1987b.

Paul M. Romer. Endogenous technical change. *Journal of Political Economy*, 98(5):S71–S102, 1990. Part 2.

Paul M. Romer. The origins of endogenous growth. *Journal of Political Economy*, 8(1):3–22, 1994.

Robert E. Rowthorn and John R. Wells. *De-industrialization and Foreign Trade*. Cambridge University Press, Cambridge UK, 1987.

Wilfred E. G. Salter. *Productivity and Technical Change*. Cambridge University Press, Cambridge UK, 1969.

Paul A. Samuelson. An exact consumption-loan model of interest with or without the social contrivance of money. *Journal of Political Economy*, 66(6):467–482, 1958.

Paul A. Samuelson. Parable and realism in capital theory: The surrogate production function. *Review of Economic Studies*, 29:193–206, 1962.

Paul A. Samuelson. A summing up. *Quarterly Journal of Economics*, 80(4):568–583, 1966.

Paul A. Samuelson and Franco Modigliani. The Pasinetti paradox in neoclassical and more general models. *Review of Economic Studies*, 33:269–301, 1966.

Joseph A. Schumpeter. *Capitalism, Socialism, and Democracy*. Harper and Brothers, New York, 1942.

Anwar Shaikh. Laws of production and laws of algebra: The humbug production function. *Review of Economics and Statistics*, 56(1):115–120, 1974.

Anwar Shaikh and Ertugrul Ahmet Tonak. *Measuring the Wealth of Nations: The Political Economy of National Accounts.* Cambridge University Press, Cambridge UK, 1994.

Peter Skott. *Conflict and Effective Demand in Economic Growth.* Cambridge University Press, Cambridge UK, 1989.

Adam Smith. *An Inquiry into the Nature and Causes of the Wealth of Nations.* Random House, New York, 1937. [1776].

Robert M. Solow. A contribution to the theory of economic growth. *Quarterly Journal of Economics*, 70(1):65–94, 1956.

Robert M. Solow. Technical change and the aggregate production function. *Review of Economics and Statistics*, 39(3):312–320, 1957.

Robert M. Solow. Perspectives on growth theory. *Journal of Economic Perspectives*, 8(1):23–44, 1994.

Luigi Spaventa. Rate of profit, rate of growth, and capital intensity in a simple production model. *Oxford Economic Papers*, 22:129–147, 1970.

Piero Sraffa. *Production of Commodities by Means of Commodities: Prelude to a Critique.* Cambridge University Press, Cambridge UK, 1960.

Joseph E. Stiglitz and Hirofumi Uzawa, editors. *Readings in the Modern Theory of Economic Growth.* MIT Press, Cambridge MA, 1969.

Robert Summers and Alan Heston. The Penn World Table (Mark 5): An expanded set of international comparisons. *Quarterly Journal of Economics*, 106(2):327–368, 1991.

T. W. Swan. Economic growth and capital accumulation. *Economic Record*, 32(63):334–361, 1956.

Paul M. Sweezy. *The Theory of Capitalist Development.* Monthly Review Press, New York, 1949.

Lance Taylor. *Structuralist Macroeconomics: Applicable Models for the Third World.* Basic Books, New York, 1983.

Thorstein Veblen. *Imperial Germany and the Industrial Revolution.* Macmillan, New York, 1915.

John von Neumann. A model of general economic equilibrium. *Review of Economic Studies*, 13(1):1–9, 1945.

Edward N. Wolff. The accumulaton of household wealth over the life cycle: A microdata analysis. *Review of Income and Wealth*, 27(2): 75–96, 1981.

Edward N. Wolff. *Growth, Accumulation, and Unproductive Activity: An Analysis of the Postwar U.S. Economy.* Cambridge University Press, Cambridge UK, 1987.

Jong-Il You. Macroeconomic structure, endogenous technical change, and growth. *Cambridge Journal of Economics*, 18(2):213–233, 1994.

Allyn Young. Increasing returns and economic progress. *Economic Journal*, 38(152):527–542, 1928.

Alwyn Young. The tyranny of numbers: Confronting the statistical realities of the East Asian growth experience. *Quarterly Journal of Economics*, 110(3):641–680, 1995.

Answers to Problems

Problems and Answers for Chapter 2

2.1 Ricardia is a corn economy, where the capital completely depreciates each year. Suppose that 20 bushels of seed corn can be planted by one worker to yield 100 bushels of harvest at the end of the year. Find x, k, ρ, δ, and y for Ricardia. How many workers and how much seed corn would be needed to grow a million bushels of corn?

Answer: $x = 100$ bushels/worker-year;
$k = 20$ bushels/worker;
$\rho = x/k = 100/20 = 5$/year $= 500\%$/year;
$\delta = 1$/year $= 100\%$/year;
$y = x - \delta k = 80$ bushels/worker-year.

To grow 1 million bushels of corn would require 10,000 workers and 200,000 bushels of seed corn.

2.2 In Industria \$50,000 worth of gross output requires one worker-year of labor working with \$150,000 worth of capital. If $1/15 = .0666 = 6.66\%$ of the capital depreciates in each year, what x, k, ρ, δ, and y would you choose to represent the Industrian production system? How much labor and capital would be needed to produce \$8 trillion in output in this economy? What would its net output be?

Answer: $x = \$50K$/worker-year;
$k = \$150K$/worker;
$\rho = x/k = \$50K$/worker-year/\$150K/worker $= .33$/year $= 33\%$/year;
$\delta = .0666$/year;
$y = x - \delta k = \$40K$/worker-year.

To produce \$8 trillion in gross output would require 160 million workers equipped with \$24 trillion worth of capital. Net output would be \$6.4 trillion.

2.3 Show the effect of an increase in labor productivity, holding the output-capital ratio and the depreciation rate constant, on the social consumption-growth rate schedule of an economy.

2.4 Show the effect of an increase in the output-capital ratio, holding labor productivity and the depreciation rate constant, on the social consumption-growth rate schedule of an economy.

2.5 Show the effect of an increase in the depreciation rate, holding labor productivity and the output-capital ratio constant, on the social consumption-growth rate schedule of an economy.

2.6 Draw the social consumption-growth rate schedule for the U.S. economy in 1990, using the data presented above.

2.7 Draw the social consumption-growth rate schedule for Ricardia (see Problem 2.1.) If the growth rate of the capital stock is 100%/year, how large is social consumption?

Answer: $c = y - g_K k$. For Ricardia $y = 80$ bu/worker-year, $k = 20$ bu/worker, so $c = 60$ bu/worker-year.

2.8 Draw the social consumption-growth rate schedule for Industria. If the growth rate of the capital stock is 10%/year, how large is social consumption?

Answer: $c = y - g_K k$.

For Industria, $y = \$40\text{K}$/worker-year, $k = \$150\text{K}$/worker, so $c = \$25\text{K}$/worker-year.

2.9 Draw the real wage-profit rate schedule for the U.S. economy in 1990, using the data presented above.

2.10 Draw the real wage-profit rate schedule for Ricardia (see Problem 2.1. If the real wage is 20 bushels of corn a year, what is the profit rate, and the cash flow/worker?

Answer: $r = (y - w)/k$. For Ricardia $y = 80$ bu/worker-year, $k = 20$ bu/worker, so $r = 300\%$/year. The cash flow/worker $z = x - w = 80$ bushels/worker-year.

2.11 Draw the real wage-profit rate schedule for Industria (see Problem 2.2). If the real wage is $10/hour and workers work 2000 hours each year, what is the profit rate and the cash flow/worker?

Answer: $r = (y - w)/k$. For Industria $y = \$40\text{K}$/worker-year, $k = \$150\text{K}$/worker, so $r = 2/15$/year $= 13.333\%$/year. The cash flow/worker $z = x - w = \$30\text{K}$/worker-year.

2.12 Graph the growth-distribution schedule for the U.S. economy in 1990.

2.13 Graph the growth-distribution schedule for Ricardia when the wage is 20 bu/worker-year and the growth rate of capital is 100%/year.

Answer: $r = 300\%$/year, $c = 60$ bu/worker-year, $c^c = 40$ bu/worker-year, $i = 40$ bu/worker/year.

2.14 Graph the growth-distribution schedule for Industria when the net profit rate is 13.333%/year and the growth rate of capital is 6.666%/year.

Answer: $w = \$20K/\text{worker-year}$, $c = \$30K/\text{worker-year}$, $c^c = \$10K/\text{worker-year}$, $i = \$20K/\text{worker year}$.

2.15 Graph on the same graph the new and old growth and distribution schedules for Ricardia if it experiences a 50% labor-saving and 0% capital-saving technical change.

Answer: $x' = 150$ bushels/worker-year; $k' = 30$ bushels/worker; $\rho' = \rho = x'/k' = 5/\text{year}$.

2.16 Graph on the same graph the new and old growth-distribution schedules for Industria if it experiences a 2% labor-saving and -2% capital-saving technical change.

Answer: $x' = (1.02)x = \$51K$ output/worker-year; $\rho' = (.98)\rho = .327/\text{years}$; $k' = x'/\rho' = \$156K/\text{worker}$.

2.17 Graph on the same graph the growth-distribution schedule for the U.S. in 1988 and 1989, using the data presented above.

Problems and Answers for Chapter 3

3.1 Draw the production isoquant (the combinations of capital and labor required to produce one unit of output), the real wage-profit rate schedule, and the intensive production function for the Leontief technology with $k = \$100,000/\text{worker}$ and $x = \$50,000/\text{worker-year}$. What is the marginal product of labor in the Leontief technology?

Answer: The production isoquant for the fixed coefficient production function is L-shaped, with the corner at (2 year, .0002 worker-year/\$), while the real wage-profit rate relation is a straight line with intercepts (0, \$50,000/worker-year) and (.5/year, 0). The marginal product of labor is not defined at the input proportions in the fixed coefficients production model, because the isoquant is not differentiable.

3.2 Draw the production isoquant (the combinations of capital and labor required to produce one unit of output), the real wage-profit rate schedule, and the intensive production function for the Cobb-Douglas technology with $A = \$10$ and $\alpha = .25$. What is the marginal product of labor in the Cobb-Douglas technology?

Answer: The production isoquant and aggregate consumption/worker-growth rate schedule for the C-D production function are both isoelastic curves with elasticity α. The marginal product of labor for the C-D is $(1 - \alpha)A(k)^{\alpha}$.

3.3 What technique of production will profit rate-maximizing entrepreneurs choose if they face a Cobb-Douglas production function and a given real wage, $\bar{w}$? What if they face a fixed coefficients production function and the same real wage?

Answer: With a C-D production function and a given real wage $\bar{w}$, capitalists will choose the profit-maximizing technique where the marginal product of labor is equal to the real wage. Thus $\bar{w} = (1 - \alpha)Ak^\alpha$, and from the production function $x = AK^\alpha$, so the chosen technique will have $x = 1 - \alpha/\bar{w}$, and $k = (x/A)^{1/\alpha}$. With fixed coefficients there is only one technique available, which is profit-maximizing at every real wage.

3.4 Show that the efficiency frontier expressing w as a function of v for the Cobb-Douglas production function has the same mathematical form as the unit isoquant expressing $1/x$ as a function of $1/\rho$.

Answer: Take $A = 1$ to simplify. Since $\rho = k^{\alpha-1}$, $\rho^{-1} = k^{-(\alpha-1)}$, and $k = (\rho^{-1})^{-1/(\alpha-1)}$. $x = k^\alpha$, so that $x^{-1} = k^{-\alpha} = (\rho^{-1})^{\alpha/(\alpha-1)}$ is the formula for the unit isoquant. Since $v = \alpha k^{\alpha-1}$, $k = (v/\alpha)^{1/(\alpha-1)}$. $w = (1 - \alpha)k^\alpha = (1 - \alpha)(v/\alpha)^{\alpha/(\alpha-1)}$ is the real wage-profit relation, which has the same form as the unit isoquant, substituting w for $1/x$ and (v/α) for $1/\rho$.

Problems and Answers for Chapter 5

5.1 Write down the consumer choice problem for a consumer facing three periods. Indicate clearly the utility function and the budget constraints, and explain your notation.

Answer: Over three periods the weights on the logarithms must be $(1 - \beta)$, $\beta(1 - \beta)$, and β^2, in order to keep the sum equal to 1. The consumer in this case must:

$$\max_{C_0, C_1, C_2 \geq 0} (1 - \beta)\ln C_0 + (1 - \beta)\beta\ln C_1 + \beta^2\ln C_2$$

$$\text{subject to } C_0 + K_1 \leq (1 + r_0)K_0 \qquad (16.7)$$

$$C_1 + K_2 \leq (1 + r_1)K_1$$

$$C_2 + K_3 \leq (1 + r_2)K_2$$

$$\text{given } \beta, K_0, r_0, r_1, r_2$$

5.2 Write down the Lagrangian for the three-period consumer choice problem, and find the first-order conditions characterizing its critical points. How many shadow prices will there be?

Answer: The Lagrangian becomes:

$$L(C_0, C_1, C_2, K_1, K_2, K_3; \lambda_0, \lambda_1, \lambda_2)$$

$$= (1 - \beta) \ln C_0 + (1 - \beta)\beta \ln C_1 + \beta^2 \ln C_2$$

$$- \lambda_0 (C_0 + K_1 - (1 + r_0)K_0) \tag{16.8}$$

$$- \lambda_1 (C_1 + K_2 - (1 + r_1)K_1)$$

$$- \lambda_2 (C_2 + K_3 - (1 + r_2)K_2)$$

The first order conditions are:

$$\frac{\partial L}{\partial C_0} = \frac{1 - \beta}{C_0} - \lambda_0 \leq 0 \ (\, = 0 \text{ if } C_0 > 0)$$

$$\frac{\partial L}{\partial C_1} = \frac{(1 - \beta)\beta}{C_1} - \lambda_1 \leq 0 \ (\, = 0 \text{ if } C_1 > 0)$$

$$\frac{\partial L}{\partial C_2} = \frac{\beta^2}{C_2} - \lambda_2 \leq 0 \ (\, = 0 \text{ if } C_2 > 0)$$

$$\frac{\partial L}{\partial K_1} = -\lambda_0 + (1 + r_1)\lambda_1 \leq 0 \ (\, = 0 \text{ if } K_1 > 0)$$

$$\frac{\partial L}{\partial K_2} = -\lambda_1 + (1 + r_2)\lambda_2 \leq 0 \ (\, = 0 \text{ if } K_2 > 0) \tag{16.9}$$

$$\frac{\partial L}{\partial K_3} = -\lambda_2 \leq 0 \ (\, = 0 \text{ if } K_3 > 0)$$

$$\frac{\partial L}{\partial \lambda_0} = -(C_0 + K_1 - (1 + r_0)K_0) \geq 0 \ (\, = 0 \text{ if } \lambda_0 > 0)$$

$$\frac{\partial L}{\partial \lambda_1} = -(C_1 + K_2 - (1 + r_1)K_1) \geq 0 \ (\, = 0 \text{ if } \lambda_1 > 0)$$

$$\frac{\partial L}{\partial \lambda_2} = -(C_2 + K_3 - (1 + r_2)K_2) \geq 0 \ (\, = 0 \text{ if } \lambda_2 > 0)$$

5.3 Solve the first-order conditions for the three-period consumer choice problem, and show that the resulting demand system is given by the equations:

$$C_0 = (1 - \beta)(1 + r_0)K_0$$

$$K_1 = \beta(1 + r_0)K_0$$

$$C_1 = (1 - \beta)(1 + r_1)K_1 = (1 - \beta)\beta(1 + r_1)(1 + r_0)K_0 \tag{16.10}$$

$$K_2 = \beta(1 + r_1)K_1$$
$$C_2 = (1 + r_2)K_2$$

Answer: Since the penalty function is zero at the saddle-point, we can see that:

$$\lambda_0 C_0 + \lambda_1 C_1 + \lambda_2 C_2$$

$$= K_1(-\lambda_0 + (1+r_1)\lambda_1) + K_2(-\lambda_1 + (1+r_2)\lambda_2) + K_3(-\lambda_2) + \lambda_0(1+r_0)K_0$$

But we can again see from the first-order conditions that:

$$\lambda_0 C_0 + \lambda_1 C_1 + \lambda_2 C_2 = 1$$

$$K_1(-\lambda_0 + (1+r_1)\lambda_1) = 0$$

$$K_2(-\lambda_1 + (1+r_2)\lambda_2) = 0$$

$$K_3(-\lambda_2) = 0$$

Thus we get the demand system

$$\lambda_0 = \frac{1}{(1 + r_0)K_0}$$

$$\lambda_1 = \frac{1}{(1 + r_1)(1 + r_0)K_0}$$

$$\lambda_2 = \frac{1}{(1 + r_2)(1 + r_1)(1 + r_0)K_0}$$

$$C_0 = (1 - \beta)(1 + r_0)K_0$$

$$K_1 = \beta(1 + r_0)K_0$$

$$C_1 = (1 - \beta)(1 + r_1)K_1 = (1 - \beta)\beta(1 + r_1)(1 + r_0)K_0$$

$$K_2 = \beta(1 + r_1)K_1$$

$$C_2 = (1 + r_2)K_2 \tag{16.11}$$

5.4 In the infinite horizon Cobb-Douglas consumption model, prove

$$K_{+1} = \beta(1 + r)K$$

and express C_t in terms of K_{t+1}.

Answer: $K_{t+1} + C_t = (1 + r_t)K_t$ and $C = (1 - \beta)(1 + r)K$ yield $K_{+1} = \beta(1 + r)K$. From these two results we get $C_t = \frac{1-\beta}{\beta}K_{t+1}$.

5.5 Show that along the optimal consumption path in the infinite horizon Cobb-Douglas consumption model the sum of realized consumption and the value of the capital at the shadow price, $\Sigma_{t=0}^{T}\lambda_t C_t + \lambda_T K_{T+1}$, remains constant over time and is equal to $\lambda_0(1+r_0)K_0$.

Answer: $\Sigma_{t=0}^{T}\lambda_t C_t + \lambda_T K_{T+1} - (\Sigma_{t=0}^{T-1}\lambda_t C_t + \lambda_{T-1}K_T) = \lambda_T C_T + \lambda_T K_{T+1} - \lambda_{T-1}K_T$. Multiply (4.20) by K_T and (4.21) by λ_T to prove this is zero. Evaluate $\Sigma_{t=0}^{T}\lambda_t C_t + \lambda_T K_{T+1}$ at $T=0$ to prove the final claim.

Problems and Answers for Chapter 6

6.1 If the real wage in Ricardia (see Problem 2.1) is 20 bu/worker-year and $\beta = .5$, find the growth rate of capital, social consumption/worker and capitalist consumption/worker.

Answer: $r = 300\%$/year (Problem 2.10), $v = 1+r = 4.0$/year, $1+g_K = .5(4.0$/year$) = 2.0$/year, $g_K = 1.0$/year $= 100\%$/year. $c^c = c - w = 60$ bu/worker-year (Problem 2.7) - 20 bu/worker- year $= 40$ bu/worker-year.

6.2 If the real wage in Industria (see Problem 2.2) is \$10/hour, workers work 2000 hours/year, and $\beta = .97$, find the growth rate of capital, social consumption/worker, and capitalist consumption/worker.

Answer: $r =13.33\%$/year (1.6.3), so $g_K = \beta(1+r) - 1 =.97(1.1333)$ - 1 = $.1$/year $= 10\%$/year. $c^c = c - w =\$25$K/worker-year (1.4.6) - \$20K/worker-year $= \$5$K/worker- year.

6.3 Analyze the effect of an increase in β on the endogenous variables in the Classical conventional-wage model.

6.4 Analyze the effect of an increase in the conventional real wage $\bar{w}$ on the endogenous variables in the Classical conventional-wage model.

Answers:

Parameter changes					Effects				
ρ	k	x	β	$\bar{w}$	v	w	g_K	c	c^c
same	up	up	same	same	up	same	up	up	up
down	up	same	same	same	down	same	down	up	up
same	same	same	up	same	same	same	up	down	down
same	same	same	same	up	down	up	down	up	down

6.5 Analyze the effect of an increase in β on the endogenous variables in the Classical conventional-wage share model.

6.6 Analyze the effect of an increase in the effective wage on the endogenous variables in the Classical conventional wage share model.

Answers: See the corresponding answers for 6.3 and 6.4.

6.7 Analyze the effect of an increase in the capitalists' propensity to save, β, on the choice of technique and endogenous variables in the Classical conventional-wage share model with a technology described by the production function $\tilde{x} = \tilde{k}^\alpha$.

Answer: Since the wage/effective worker stays constant, there will be no change in the profit-maximizing technique. The growth rate of the capital stock will rise, and social consumption/effective worker will fall.

6.8 Analyze the effect of an increase in the conventional wage share, $1-\bar{\pi}$, on the choice of technique and endogenous variables in the Classical conventional-wage share model.

Answer: If the elasticity of substitution is less than 1, at a higher conventional wage share the wage/effective worker will be higher for any technique of production and the profit rate lower, so entrepreneurs will choose a more capital-intensive technique, thus moving the economy to a steeper growth-distribution schedule. The wage/effective worker will rise, the profit rate will fall, the growth rate of capital will fall, social consumption/effective worker will rise, and capitalist consumption/effective worker will fall. When the elasticity of substitution is greater than 1, a higher conventional wage share corresponds to a lower wage/effective worker, and the effects are reversed.

6.9 Analyze the effect of an increase in the population growth rate, n, on the growth rate, profit rate, wage, social consumption and capitalist consumption/worker in the Classical full-employment model.

6.10 Analyze the effect of an increase in the capitalist propensity to save, β, on the growth rate, profit rate, wage, social consumption and capitalist consumption/worker in the Classical full-employment model.

6.11 Analyze the effect of a rise in the capital labor ratio, k, on the growth rate, profit rate, wage, social consumption and capitalist consumption/worker in the Classical full-employment model.

6.12 Analyze the effect of a rise in the productivity of effective labor, x, on the growth rate, profit rate, wage, social consumption and capitalist consumption/worker in the Classical full-employment model.

Answers:

Parameter changes					Effects				
ρ	k	x	β	$n+\gamma$	v	w	g_K	c	c^c
same	up	up	same	same	same	up	same	up	up
down	up	same	same	same	same	down	same	down	up
same	same	same	up	same	down	up	same	same	down
same	same	same	same	up	up	down	up	down	up

6.13 If $n = .02$, $\gamma = 0$, $\delta = 0$, and $\beta = .9$, find the equilibrium real wage, profit rate, capitalist consumption and technique in use in a Classical full employment economy with a Cobb-Douglas production function, where the techniques satisfy $\tilde{x} = A\tilde{k}^{\alpha}$, where $\alpha = .2$ and $A = (\$10,000/\text{worker})^{1-\alpha}$. What is the equilibrium marginal productivity of capital?

Answer: In equilibrium we have $1 + g_K = 1 + n + \gamma = 1.02/\text{year}$, and $\beta(1 + r) = 1 + g_K$, or $1 + r = \frac{1.02}{.9} = 1.1333/\text{year}$. Since $\delta = 0$, the profit rate, v, equals the net profit rate, r. When the profit rate is $.1333/\text{year}$, the technique that maximizes the real wage equates the marginal product of capital to the profit rate:

$$\alpha A k^{\alpha-1} = r$$

$$k = (\alpha A r)^{\frac{1}{1-\alpha}}$$

In this case we get:

$$k = (\frac{.2}{.1333})^{\frac{1}{.8}}(\frac{\$10,000}{\text{worker}}) = \frac{\$16,600}{\text{worker}}$$

Output/worker is:

$$x = A k^{\alpha} = \frac{\$11,067}{\text{worker-year}}$$

$$w = x - (\delta + r)k$$

$$= (\$11,067 - (.1333)(\$16,600))/\text{worker-year} = \$8,854/\text{worker-year}$$

$$c = x - (\delta + g)k$$

$$= (\$11,067 - (.02)(\$16,600))/\text{worker-year} = \$10,735/\text{worker-year}.$$

The marginal product of capital is equal to the profit rate, $13.33\%/\text{year}$.

6.14 What effect does an increase in the population growth rate have on the technique in use and the profit rate in a Classical full-employment economy with choice of technique?

Answer: An increase in the population growth rate raises the profit rate, through the Cambridge equation, and moves the economy to a less capital-intensive technique.

Problems and Answers for Chapter 7

7.1 The Industrian economy now experiences biased technical change with $\gamma = 5\%$ and $\chi = -2\%$. In the initial period 0, the wage is $20,000/worker-year, labor productivity is $50,000/worker-year, and capital productivity is 33 1/3 %/year. What will be the rate of profit and the wage rate (per worker-year) in the next period? Compare the rate of profit in the next period to the rate of profit in the base year.

Answer: In year 1, $k =$($50/effective worker-year)$/((.333)(.98)) =$ $153.060/effective worker-year, in units of $1,000. $r_1 = \frac{50-20}{153.06} - .0666 =$ .129 or 12.9 %/year. The rate of profit fell by $13.3\% - 12.9\% = 0.4$ percentage points.

7.2 Calculate the wage share and profit share in Industria. Show that the wage share did not change in the first year.

Answer: $\frac{w_0}{x_0} = \frac{\$20}{\$50} = .4$ or 40 %. $\frac{w_1}{x_1} = \frac{\$21}{\$52.5} = .4$.

7.3 Find the level of consumption/effective worker and the growth rate in the Industrian economy for the base year and the first year, assuming $\beta = .97$.

Answer: $g_1 = .97(1.129) - 1 = .095$ or 9.5 %/year. $g_0 = 0.099$ or 9.9 %/year. $c_1 = \$50 - (.095 + .066)\$153.06 = \$25.35$/effective worker. $c_0 = \$25.15$/effective worker.

7.4 In how many years will the rate of profit in Industria reach zero if there is no change in the rates of technical change? In how many years will the growth rate reach zero?

Answer: To reach $r = 0, (.6)(.33)(.98)^T - .066 = 0$, or $.98^T = .066/((.6)(.33)) = .33$, or $T = \ln(.33)/\ln(.98) = 54.3$ years. To reach $g = 0, r = 1/.97 - 1 = .0309$ so $(.6)(.33)(.98)^T - .066 = .0309$. $T = \ln(.488)/\ln(.98) = 35.5$ years.

7.5 In Industria (see Problem 7.1) in the base year, calculate the private rate of profit that entrepreneurs perceive they would receive in the next year if they adopt the new technique. Would this technical change be considered viable?

Answer: $v_{+1} = (1 - (20/(50(1.05))))(.33)(.98) = .2022$, or 20.22%, which is greater than 20%, so this technical change is viable.

7.6 Show that the viability condition is met in Industria (see Problem 7.1).

Answer: $\pi = (1 - .4) = .6 < \frac{\gamma(1+\chi)}{\gamma-\chi} = (.05(.98))/(.05 + .02) = .7$.

7.7 Show that if entrepreneurs expect the wage to increase at the same rate as labor productivity, γ, they will still adopt to adopt new techniques that satisfy the viability condition. For simplicity, assume that δ is zero. (Hint: show that at the new wage, w', the rate of profit will be higher using the new technique, $\{\rho', x'\}$ than with the old technique, $\{\rho, x\}$, if the viability condition is satisfied.)

Answer: Let v_{+1}^0 be the rate of profit in the next period with the old technology and v_{+1}^1 be the rate of profit in the next period with the new technology. Then $v_{+1}^1 > v_{+1}^0$ implies that $(x(1+\gamma) - w(1+\gamma))/(k(1+\gamma)/(1+\chi)) > (x - (1+\gamma)w)/k$. Solving gives $1 - (w/x) < \gamma/(\gamma - \chi)$, which is a close approximation to the viability condition for small values of χ.

7.8 In a classical model with biased technical change and a wage share $1 - \pi = 0.8$, $1 + \gamma = 1.02/\text{year}$ and $1 + \chi = 0.99/\text{year}$, find the relationship between the growth rates of x and k. If you were able to estimate this relationship without knowing how the data had been generated, would you accept or reject the hypothesis that there is a Cobb-Douglas production function with perfectly competitive markets?

Answer:

$$\frac{x_{+1}}{.x} - 1 = \frac{(1+\chi)\gamma}{\gamma - \chi}\frac{k_{+1}}{k} - 1$$

$$= \frac{(.99)(.02)}{.02 - (-.01)}(\frac{k_{+1}}{k} - 1)$$

$$\frac{x_{+1}}{x} - 1 = .66(\frac{k_{+1}}{k} - 1)$$

If you estimated this relationship based on the hypothesis of a Cobb-Douglas function, you would estimate that $\alpha = .66$, making the predicted value of the wage share .34. This conflicts with the actual value of the wage share, .8, so you would have to reject the hypothesis.

7.9 Use the data in Tables 2.4 and 2.8 to check whether technical change from 1973-1992 in the six countries satisfied the viability condition. (Use the value of the profit share during the 1980s.) Do the values you compute satisfy the predictions of the neoclassical theory of income distribution?

Answer:

USA viability condition: $.0111(1-.0072)/(.0111+.0072) = .602$ USA profit share: $.332 < .602$

Country	Profit Share	Viability Condition
USA	.332	.602
France	.322	.571
Germany	.315	.722
Netherlands	.358	.704
UK	.307	.557
Japan	.315	.508

In each case, the viability condition is satisfied. In no case is it satisfied as an equality, contradicting the neoclassical theory of income distribution.

Problems and Answers for Chapter 8

8.1 Write the Leontief production function in intensive form.

Answer:

The Leontief production function is:

$$X = \min(\rho K, x N)$$

Dividing through by N, we get:

$$x = \frac{X}{N} = \min(\frac{\rho K}{N}, \frac{x N}{N}) = \min(\rho k, x).$$

8.2 Find the value of x and ρ for the Cobb-Douglas production function $X = A K^\alpha N^{1-\alpha}$, when $k = \$14,000/\text{worker}$, $A = 1,000$, and $\alpha = .2$.

Answer:

$$x = A k^\alpha = 1,000(\$ \, 14,000/\text{worker-year})^{.2} = \$6,748.77/\text{worker-year}$$

$$\rho = \frac{x}{k} = \frac{\$6748.77/\text{worker- year}}{\$14,000/\text{worker}} = 0.482/\text{year}$$

8.3 Show that the Cobb-Douglas production function implies that $\rho = A k^{\alpha-1}$.

Answer:

$$\rho = \frac{x}{k} = \frac{A k^\alpha}{k} = A k^{\alpha-1}$$

8.4 Production in Solowia is described by a Cobb- Douglas production function with $A = 1000$, $\alpha = .2$. The saving rate is .15, the rate of depreciation, δ, is $.1$/year, and the population growth rate, n, is $.02$/year. What will the growth rates of capital and the capital-labor ratio be when the capital-labor ratio is $5,000/worker?

Answer:

$$g_K = s\rho - \delta = sAk^{(\alpha-1)} - \delta$$

$$= (.15)(\$1,000)(\$5,000)^{-0.8} - .1 = .06478/\text{year}$$

or 6.478 %/year.

$$\frac{\Delta k}{k} = g_K - n = .06478 - .02 = .04478/\text{year}$$

or 4.478 %/year.

8.5 Find the steady state equilibrium values of the capital-labor ratio, productivity of labor, and productivity of capital for Solowia (see Problem 8.4).

Answer:

$$k^* = (\frac{s}{n+\delta})^{\frac{1}{1-\alpha}} = (\frac{.15}{.02+.1})^{\frac{1}{.8}}$$

$$= \$7,432.54/\text{worker}$$

$$x^* = Ak^* = \$1,000(\$7,432.54).2 = \$5,946.04/\text{worker-year}$$

$$\rho^* = \frac{x^*}{k^*} = \frac{\$5,946.04}{\$7,432.54} = 0.48/\text{year}$$

8.6 In a Solow-Swan model with a Cobb-Douglas production function, where $A = 1,000$, $\alpha = .2, \delta = .1$, and $n = .02$/year, what is the capital intensity, labor productivity, and consumption/worker at the original and new steady state when the saving rate rises from $s = .15$ to $s' = .17$? Show these two steady states on the efficiency frontier.

Answer:

From Problem 8.5:

$$k^* = \$7,432.54/\text{worker}$$

$$x^* = \$5,946.04/\text{worker-year}$$

so that

$$c^* = (1-s)x^* = (1-.15)\$5946.03 = \$5,054.13/\text{worker-year}$$

When the saving rate rises to .17:

$$k^{*\prime} = (\frac{\$1000(.17)}{.02+.1})^{\frac{1}{.8}} = \$8,691.28/\text{worker}$$

$$x^{*\prime} = \$1,000(\$8,691.28)^{.2} = \$6,135.00/\text{worker- year}$$

$$c^{*\prime} = (1 - .17)(\$6,135) = \$5,092.05/\text{worker-year}$$

8.7 Find the Golden Rule values of $\hat{s}, \hat{k}, \hat{c}$ and $\hat{r}$ for the economy of Problem 8.5.

Answer: At the Golden Rule, $g_X = \hat{r} = n = .02$. Therefore $\hat{s}\rho - \delta = \alpha\rho - \delta$ and $\hat{s} = .2$. With $\hat{s} = .2$:

$$\hat{k} = (\frac{\$1000(.2)}{.2 + .1})^{\frac{1}{.8}} = \$10,649.05/\text{worker}$$

$$\hat{x} = \$1000(\$10,649.05)^{\alpha} = \$6,389.43/\text{worker-year}$$

$$\hat{c} = (.8)(\$6,389.43) = \$5,111.5/\text{worker-year}.$$

8.8 Analyze the comparative dynamics of an increase in the population growth rate, n, using the equations and the diagram for the Solow–Swan growth model. What effect would this change have on k, x, c, g, r, and w?

Answer: k down, x down, c down, g up, r up and w down.

8.10 Consider a Solow–Swan model with the production function $X = K + 1000K^{.2}N^{.8}, s = .15, \delta = .1/\text{year}$, and $n = .02/\text{year}$. Derive the equation for the rate of accumulation as a function of k, and graph it as in Figure 8.3. Add a line showing the growth rate of the labor force to your figure. Why won't this economy ever achieve a steady state?

Answer:

With this production function,

$$\rho = X/K = (K + 1000K^{.2}N^{.8})/K = 1 + 1000k^{-.8}$$

$$g_K = s\rho - \delta = .15(1 + 1000k^{-.8}) - .1$$

g_K is asymptotic to .05 as k increases, so the growth rate will never fall to the rate of growth of the labor force, $n = .02$, and the economy will never reach a steady state.

Problems and Answers for Chapter 9

9.1 If the rate of Harrod-neutral technical change is 2%/year, what is the rate of growth of the capital-labor ratio if the ratio of capital/effective worker grows at 5%/year?

Answer:

$$g_k = g_{\tilde{k}} + \hat{\gamma}$$

$$= 5\%/\text{year} + 2\%/\text{year} = 7\%/\text{year}$$

9.2 Suppose the production function is a Cobb-Douglas function with $A = 1000$ and $\alpha = 0.2$. If technical change is Harrod-neutral at 2%/year and there is \$14,000/worker of capital in the base year, find the value of output/effective worker and/worker after two years, assuming that the capital stock grows at the same rate as the labor force.

Answer:

By assumption, $k_{+2} = k_{+1} = k = \$14,000/\text{worker}$.

$$\tilde{k}_{+2} = \frac{k}{(1 + \hat{\gamma})^2} = \frac{\$14,000/\text{worker}}{1.0404 \text{ effective worker/worker}}$$

$$= \$13,456.30/\text{effective worker}$$

$$\tilde{x}_{+2} = A\tilde{k}_{+2}^{\alpha} = (1,000)(13,456.30)^{.2} = \$6,695.53/\text{effective worker}$$

$$x_{+2} = (1 + \hat{\gamma})^2\tilde{x} = (1.0404)(6,695.53) = \$6,966.03/\text{worker}$$

9.3 Draw the growth-distribution schedules over two periods, t and $t + 1$, for the technique that has been selected in the steady state equilibrium of the Solow model with neutral technical change. Identify the wage rate and profit rate, and growth rate and consumption/worker-year on the growth and distribution schedule in each year.

9.4 Let the Cobb-Douglas production function have $A = 1,000$ and $\alpha = .2$. Find the steady state values of $\tilde{x}, \tilde{k}$ and ρ when the saving propensity is 15%, depreciation, $\delta = 10\%/\text{year}$, the rate of population growth, $n = 1\%/\text{year}$, and the rate of Harrod-neutral technical change, $\hat{\gamma} = 2\%/\text{year}$.

Answer:

$$\tilde{k}^* = ((.15)(\$1000)/(.01 + .02 + .1))^{1.25} = \$6,724.88/\text{effective worker}.$$

$$\tilde{x}^* = \$1,000(6,724.88)^{.2} = \$5,828.23/\text{effective worker/year}.$$

$$\rho = \$5,828.23/\$6,724.88 = 0.866/\text{year}.$$

9.5 In the economy described in Problem 9.4, what would be the growth rate of capital in the steady state? the capital-labor ratio?

Answer: The steady-state condition is:

$$\frac{\Delta \tilde{k}}{\tilde{k}} = 0 = \frac{\Delta K}{K} - n - \delta$$

$$\frac{\Delta K}{K} = .01 + .02 = .03 = 3\%/\text{year}$$

$$\frac{\Delta k}{k} = \frac{\Delta K}{K} - n = .03 - .01 = .02 = 2\%/\text{year}$$

9.6 If the economy described in Problem 9.4 began in its steady state in the base year, and remained there, what would be the value of output/worker after ten years?

Answer:

$$x_{10} = (1.02)^{10}\tilde{x}^* = 1.21899(\$5, 828.23) = \$7, 104.70/\text{worker}/\text{year}.$$

9.7 Use the data in Table 9.1 to determine what proportion of labor productivity growth in each country was caused by capital deepening.

Answer:

$$(\frac{\pi_K \Delta k}{k})/(\frac{\Delta x}{x}) = ((1 - \pi_N)(\frac{\Delta K}{K} - \frac{\Delta N}{N})/(\frac{\Delta X}{X} - \frac{\Delta N}{N})$$

Hong Kong:

$$(1 - .628)(.08 - .032)/(.073 - .032) = .435 = 43.5\%$$

Singapore:

$$(1 - .509)(.115 - .057)/(.087 - .057) = .949 = 94.9\%$$

South Korea:

$$(1 - .703)(.137 - .064)/(.103 - .064) = .555 = 55.5\%$$

Taiwan:

$$(1 - .743)(.123 - .049)/(.089 - .049) = .475 = 47.5\%$$

9.8 Derive the formula for the Solow decomposition of labor productivity growth assuming that technical change is Harrod-neutral.

Answer:

$$\Delta X = F_K \Delta K + F_{\tilde{N}} \Delta \tilde{N}$$

$$g_X = \pi g_K + (1 - \pi) g_{\tilde{N}} = \pi g_K + (1 - \pi)(n + \hat{\gamma})$$

$$g_x = \pi g_k + (1 - \pi) \hat{\gamma}$$

9.9 Analyze the effects of an increase in the rate of population growth on the steady state in the Solow–Swan model with Harrod-neutral technical change. Explain your results in terms of both the figure and the equations representing the model.

9.10 Use the figures given in the text to check the calculations of the Council of Economic Advisors. Assume that the scale parameter in the production function, $A = 750$, the rate of population growth $n = 1.5\%$/year and the rate of Harrod-neutral technical change $\hat{\gamma} = 1\%$/year. Calculate the old and new values of $\tilde{k}^*, \tilde{x}^*$ and $\tilde{c}^*$.

Answer:

$\tilde{k}^* = ((.13)(\$750)/(.015+.01+.09))(3/2) = \$24,686.53/\text{effective worker}.$

$\tilde{k}^{*\prime} = ((.14)(\$750)/(.015+.01+.09))(3/2) = \$27,589.06/\text{effective worker}.$

% change $= (\$27,589.06 - \$24,686.53)/\$24,686.53 = .117 = 12\%$

$\tilde{x}^* = \$750(24,686.53)^{1/3} = \$21,838.09/\text{effective worker/year}.$

$\tilde{x}^{*\prime} = \$750(27,589.06)^{1/3} = \$22,662.45/\text{effective worker/year}.$

% change $= (\$22,662.45 - \$21,838.09)/\$21,838.09 = .0377 = 3.7\%$

$\tilde{c}^* = (1 - .13)(\$21,838.09) = \$18,999.14/\text{effective worker/year}.$

$\tilde{c}^{*\prime} = (1 - .14)(\$22,662.45) = \$19,489.71/\text{effective worker/year}.$

% change $= (\$19,489.71 - \$18,999.14)/\$18,999.14 = .0258 = 2.5\%$

9.11 Assuming it takes 50 years to reach the new equilibrium, by how much will the increase in national savings considered by the Council of Economic Advisors succeed in raising consumption/worker (*not* /effective worker)?

Answer:

$$c_{+50} = (1 + \hat{\gamma})^{50} \tilde{c}_{+50} = (1 + .01)^{50} \tilde{c}_{+50} = 1.645 \tilde{c}_{+50}.$$

Change in consumption/worker equals:

$$(1.644)(\$19,489.71 - \$18,999.14) = \$806.81/\text{worker}.$$

9.12 Calculate the profit rate before and after the increase in national savings using the same Council of Economic Advisors assumptions.

Answer:

$$\rho = \frac{x^*}{k^*} = \frac{\$21,838.09}{\$24,686.53} = .8846$$

$$v = \alpha\rho = (1/3)(.8846) = .2948$$

$$r = v - \delta = .2948 - .09 = .2049 = 20.49\%/\text{year}$$

$$\rho' = \$22,662.45/\$27,589.06 = .8214$$

$$v' = (1/3)(.8214) = .2738$$

$$r' = .2738 - .09 = .1838 = 18.38\%/\text{year}.$$

9.13 Find the approximate rate of growth of labor productivity for an economy whose current level of labor productivity is $3/4$ of its steady state value under the assumptions that the rate of Harrod-neutral technical change is $1\%/\text{year}$, the depreciation rate is $4\%/\text{year}$, population grows $2\%/\text{year}$, and the gross profit share is $1/3$.

Answer:

$$\phi = (n + \hat{\gamma} + \delta)(1 - \alpha) = (.02 + .01 + .04)(1 - (1/3)) = .0466$$

$$\frac{\Delta\tilde{x}}{\tilde{x}} = .04666 \ln(1 - .75) = .01343/\text{year} = 1.3\%/\text{year}$$

$$\frac{\Delta x}{x} = .01343 + .01 = .02343 = 2.34\%/\text{year}.$$

9.14 If population growth is $2\%/\text{year}$, Harrod-neutral technical change is $1\%/\text{year}$, and the depreciation rate is $4\%/\text{year}$, find the implicit gross profit share for a convergence coefficient $\phi = .02$.

Answer:

$$\phi = (1 - \alpha)(n + \gamma + \delta) \text{ so } \alpha = 1 - \frac{\phi}{n + \gamma + \delta}$$

$$\alpha = 1 - \frac{.02}{.02 + .01 + .04} = .71428 = 71.43\%$$

9.15 If the gross profit share were $1/3$, what should be the value of the convergence coefficient in Problem 9.14?

Answer:

$$\phi = (1 - 1/3)(.07) = .04666.$$

Problems and Answers to Chapter 10

10.1 Kaldoria is an economy similar to Industria (see Problem 2.2), with $x = \$50,000/\text{worker-year}$, $k = \$150,000/\text{worker}$, and $\delta = 1/15 = .0666 = 6.66\%$. The wage share in Kaldoria is 60%. Find labor productivity, capital productivity, and the profit rate at when $u = 100\%$ and when $u = 85\%$.

Answer:

$\rho = x/k = (\$50 \text{ K/worker-year})/(\$150 \text{ K/worker-year}) = 1/3$ or 33.33%/year. Labor and capital productivity are ux and $u\rho$, and the profit rate is $v = u\pi\rho$. When $u = 1$, $ux = \$150\text{K/worker-year}$, $u\rho = 33.33\%/\text{year}$, and $v = (.4)(.3333/\text{year}) = .133/\text{year} = 13.3\%/\text{year}$. When $u = .85$, $ux = (.85)(\$150\text{K/worker-year}) = \$127.5\text{K/worker-year}$, $u\rho = (.85)(.3333/\text{year}) = .283/\text{year}$, and $v = (.85)(.4)(.3333/\text{year}) = .1133/\text{year} = 11.3\%/\text{year}$.

10.2 Graph on the same diagram the full capacity growth and distribution schedule for Kaldoria and the actual growth and distribution schedule at 85% utilization. Identify the points on both schedules when the wage share is 60%.

10.3 Entrepreneurs in Kaldoria (see Problem 10.1) have a Robinson-ian investment function with $\eta = .7$. What is their desired gross rate of capital accumulation, $g^i_K + \delta$, when the rate of utilization, u, is .9?

Answer: $g^i_K + \delta = \eta v = \eta\pi\rho u = (.7)(.4)(.333)(.9) = .084/\text{year}$, or 8.4%/year.

10.4 Capitalist households in Kaldoria (see Problem 10.1) have a propensity to save out of wealth $\beta = .97$. What is their desired gross rate of wealth accumulation, $g^s_K + \delta$, when the rate of utilization, u, is .9?

Answer: $g^s_K + \delta = \beta v - (1 - \beta)(1 - \delta) = \beta\pi\rho u - (1 - \beta)(1 - \delta) = .97(.4)(.333)(.9)$ - $(.03)(.9333) = .088$ or 8.8%/year.

10.5 If the entrepreneurs had expected the rate of utilization to be .7, and invested on the basis of the corresponding profit rate, what utilization rate would the Kaldorian economy achieve? Would the entrepreneurs find that they had chosen the right amount of investment? How will they respond?

Answer: $g^i + \delta = \eta v = \eta\pi\rho u = (.7)(.4)(.333)(.7) = .065/\text{year}$ or 6.5%/year. The economy will achieve a temporary equilibrium where this amount of investment is equal to the amount of saving, or $\beta v - (1 - \beta)(1 - \delta) = g^s_K + \delta = g^i_K + \delta = .065/\text{year}$, which requires $v = (.065 + (.03)(.9333))/.97 = .096 = 9.6\%/\text{year}$, which implies $u = v/(\pi\rho) = .72$. The entrepreneurs will then discover that they were too pessimistic and increase their planned gross rate of investment to 6.7%/year.

10.6 Calculate the equilibrium rate of utilization, gross rate of growth of capital and rate of profit in Kaldoria.

Answer: $v = (1-\beta)(1-\delta)/(\beta-\eta) = (.03)(.9333)/(.97-.7) = .104/\text{year} = 10.4\%/\text{year}.$ $g_K + \delta = \eta v = (.7)(.104) = .0728/\text{year}$ or $7.2\%/\text{year}.$ $u = v/\pi\rho = .104/(.4)(.333) = .78 = 78\%.$

10.7 Graph the saving and investment equations for Kaldoria, and identify the equilibrium. Where on your graph does the economy lie in Problem 10.3? Discuss the dynamics in this position.

Answer: In Problem 10.3, Kaldoria is above its equilibrium rate of utilization. Entrepreneurs will be reducing the level of output until the equilibrium is reached.

10.8 Suppose the saving propensity in Kaldoria increased from .97 to .98. What are the new equilibrium rates of profit, gross growth of capital, and capacity utilization? Would an increased rate of saving benefit the Kaldorian economy?

Answer: $v = (1-\beta)(1-\delta)/(\beta-\eta) = (.02)(.933)/(.98-.7) = .067/\text{year} = 6.7\%/\text{year}.$ $u = v/\pi\rho = .067/(.4)(.333) = .5 = 50\%.$ $g_K + \delta = \eta v = (.7)(.067) = .047/\text{year} = 4.7\%/\text{year}.$ The Kaldorian economy is growing more slowly, with fewer jobs, because of increased thriftiness.

10.9 Suppose the saving propensity in Kaldoria remained at .97, but the wage share increased to 65%. What are the new equilibrium rates of profit, gross growth of capital, and capacity utilization? Would an increased wage share benefit the Kaldorian economy?

Answer: $v = (1-\beta)(1-\delta)/(\beta-\eta) = (.03)(.9333)/(.97-.7) = .104/\text{year} = 10.4\%/\text{year}$ is unchanged. $g_K + \delta = \eta v = (.7)(.104) = .0728/\text{year}$ or $7.2\%/\text{year}$ is also unchanged. $u = v/\pi\rho = .104/(.35)(.333) = .89 = 89\%.$ The Kaldorian economy is working at a higher rate of capacity utilization, with more employment, as a result of the increased wage share.

10.10 Calculate social consumption/worker before and after the increase in the wage share in Problem 10.9. How has this change been divided between capitalists' consumption and workers' consumption?

Answer:

$$c = x(u - ((g_K + \delta)/\rho))$$

$$= \$50\text{K}/\text{worker-year}(.78\text{-}(.0728/.333)) = \$28\text{K}/\text{worker-year}$$

when the wage share is 60%, and

$$\$50\text{K}/\text{worker-year}(.89\text{-}(.0728/.333)) = \$33.6\text{K}/\text{worker-year}$$

when the wage share is 65%. The wage is

$$w = (1 - \pi)ux = (.6)(.78)\$50\text{K}/\text{worker-year}$$

$$= \$23.4K/\text{worker-year}$$

when the wage share is 60%, and

$$(.65)(.89)\$50K/\text{worker-year} = \$28.9K/\text{worker-year}$$

when the wage share is 65%. Capitalist consumption/worker,

$$c^c = c - w,$$

rises from $4.6K/worker-year to $4.7K/worker-year.

10.11 Graph the real wage-profit rate and social consumption-growth rate schedules for Kaldoria before and after the wage share increases from 60% to 65%. Find the equilibrium wage-profit rate and social consumption-growth rate points on your graph before and after the change (four points in all).

10.12 Suppose the entrepreneurs in Kaldoria are behaving according to the following investment function: $g^i + \delta = .25\pi$, and the wage share is $.6 = 60\%$. Use the equations in the Appendix to this chapter to find the equilibrium rates of capacity utilization, profit, and gross growth of capital. What happens to the endogenous variables when the wage share rises to $.65 = 65\%$? Explain what has happened.

Answer: $\eta_u = \eta_\rho = 0$ and $\eta_\pi = .25$, so the equilibrium capacity utilization rate is $u = (\eta_\pi \pi + (1 - \beta)(1 - \delta))/(\beta \pi \rho) = ((.25)(.4)-(.03)(.933))/(.97)(.4)(.333) = .55$ or 55%. $v = \pi \rho u = (.4)(.333)(.55) = .073/\text{year} = 7.3\%/\text{year}$, and $g_K + \delta = \beta v - (1 - \beta)(1 - \delta) = (.97)(.073)-(.03)(.933) = .043/\text{year} = 4.3\%/\text{year}$. When the wage share rises to .65, the capacity utilization rate becomes

$$((.25)(.35) - (.03)(.933))/(.97)(.35)(.333) = .52 \text{ or } 52\%,$$

the profit rate falls to 6.1%/year, and the gross rate of growth of capital to 5.6%/year. The increase in the wage share has reduced the profit share and profitability, so that entrepreneurs invest less, causing decline in the rates of capacity utilization, profit, and gross growth of capital.

10.13 Suppose the entrepreneurs in Kaldoria shift to behaving according to the following investment function: $g^i + \delta = .1u$. Find the equilibrium rates of capacity utilization, profit and gross growth of capital when the wage share is $.6 = 60\%$, and when the wage share is $.5 = 50\%$. Explain what has happened.

Answer: Now $\eta_\pi = \eta_\rho = 0$, and $\eta_u = .1$, so the equilibrium capacity utilization rate is

$$u = (1 - \beta)(1 - \delta)/(\beta \pi \rho - \eta_u)$$

$$= (.03)(.933)/((.97)(.4)(.333) - .1) = .96 \text{ or } 96\%.$$

$$v = \pi\rho u = (.4)(.333)(.98) = .128/\text{year} = 12.8\%/\text{year},$$

and

$$g_K + \delta = \beta v - (1 - \beta)(1 - \delta)$$

$$= (.97)(.128) - (.03)(.933) = .096/\text{year} = 9.6\%/\text{year}.$$

When the wage share falls to .5, the capacity utilization rate becomes $(.03)(.933)/((.97)(.5)(.333)-.1) = .45$ or 45%, the profit rate falls to 7.6%/year, and the gross rate of growth of capital to 4.6%/year. The fall in the wage has raised the profit share, but this has not caused entrepreneurs to invest more. The decline in demand for consumption has lowered capacity utilization, which has caused entrepreneurs to invest less, depressed the profit rate and the gross rate of growth of capital.

Problems and Answers for Chapter 11

11.1 Write down the Lagrangian function for the capitalist's utility maximization problem with land, and find the first-order conditions describing the saddle point. Use these conditions to derive the arbitrage principle and the consumption function.

Answer: The Lagrangian is:

$$L(C_t, K_{t+1}, U_{t+1}; \lambda_t) =$$

$$(1 - \beta) \sum_{t=0}^{\infty} \beta^t \ln(C_t)$$

$$- \sum_{t=0}^{\infty} \lambda_t (K_{t+1} + p_{ut+1}U_{t+1} + C_t - (1 + r_t)K_t + (p_{ut+1} + v_{ut})U_t) \quad (16.12)$$

The first-order conditions are (for $t = 0, 1, \ldots, \infty$):

$$\frac{\partial L}{\partial C_t} = \frac{(1-\beta)\beta^t}{C_t} - \lambda_t \leq 0 \qquad (= 0 \text{ if } C_t > 0)$$

$$\frac{\partial L}{\partial K_{t+1}} = -\lambda_t + \lambda_{t+1}(1 + r_{t+1}) \leq 0 \qquad (= 0 \text{ if } K_{t+1} > 0) \quad (16.13)$$

$$\frac{\partial L}{\partial U_{t+1}} = -\lambda_t p_{ut+1} + \lambda_{t+1}(v_{ut+1} + p_{ut+2}) \leq 0 \qquad (= 0 \text{ if } U_{t+1} > 0)$$

$$(16.14)$$

$$\frac{\partial L}{\partial \lambda_t} = -(K_{t+1} + p_{ut+1}U_{t+1} + C_t - (1 + r_t)K_t + (p_{ut+1} + v_{ut})U_t) \geq 0$$

$$(= 0 \text{ if } \lambda_{t+1} > 0)$$

Equations 16.13 and 16.14 imply that:

$$p_{ut+1} + v_{ut} = (1 + r_t)p_{ut} \qquad (16.15)$$

Just as in the one-sector case, we can immediately conclude that $C_t > 0, \lambda_{t+1} > 0, K_{t+1} > 0$, and $U_{t+1} > 0$. We can also rearrange the penalty part of the Lagrangian to show that consumption will be proportional to the wealth the capitalist has at the end of the period:

$$C_t = (1 - \beta)((1 + r_t)J_t$$

11.2 Suppose in Ricardia (see Problem 2.1) the production of 100 bushels of corn requires 1 acre of land, together with 20 bushels of seed corn and 1 worker-year. If there are 10,000 acres of land available, what is the maximum amount of seed corn capital that could be employed, and the maximum amount of corn output? If the wage rate is 20 bu/worker-year, what are the gross and net profit rates in the abundant land regime?

Answer: The unit of land that employs one bushel of seed corn as capital is 1/20th of an acre, so there are $U = 200,000$ units of land available. In Ricardia $\rho = 5$/year. When $\bar{w} = 20$ bu/year, $\bar{\pi} = .8$. In Ricardia $\delta = 100\%$/year.

$$K^* = U = 200,000 \text{ bu}$$

$$X^* = \rho K^a st = (5)(200,000) = 1,000,000 \text{ bu/year}$$

In the abundant land regime, $v_{ut} = 0$, so:

$$v_{kt} = \bar{\pi}\rho = (.8)(5) = 400\%/\text{year}$$

The net profit rate in the abundant land regime, $r_t = v_{kt} - \delta = 300\%$/year.

11.3 Find the land price, land rent and gross and net profit rates in Ricardia (see Problem 11.2) in the scarce land regime when the wage is 20 bu/worker-year, and $\beta = 4/5$.

Answer:

$$1 + r^* = \frac{1}{\beta} = \frac{5}{4} \text{ so } r^* = 25\%/\text{year}.$$

$$v_u^* = \bar{\pi}\rho - \delta - r^* = (.8)(5) - 1 - .25$$

$$= 2.75 \text{ bu/unit of land/year} = 55 \text{ bu/acre/year}$$

$$p_u^* = \frac{v_u^*}{r^*}$$

$$= (55 \text{ bu/acre/year})/(.25/\text{year}) = 220 \text{ bu/acre}.$$

11.4 Make a spreadsheet program to calculate the growth path for Ricardia starting from the scarce land regime and working backward 20 years, calculating the asset price of land and the capital stock in each year.

Problems and Answers for Chapter 12

12.1 Consider an economy with an oil technology where $x = \$50,000$ /worker/year, $k = \$100,000$/worker, $\delta = 0$/year, and solar technology is 50% less productive, with the same rate of depreciation. Find the price of oil at which solar technology would just compete with oil.

Answer: $\rho = x/k = .5$/year, $x' = \$25,000$/worker/year, $k' = k = x/\rho = \$100,000$/worker, and $\rho' = x'/k' = .25$/year, $\delta' = \delta = 0$/year, so that

$$p_q^* = (\rho - \rho')/\rho = (4 - 2)/4 = .5 = \$.50/\text{unit of oil}$$

12.2 For the economy described in 12.1, suppose that the capitalist $\beta = .95$ and that the wage is $\$10,000$/worker/year. Find the profit rate and the growth rate of the capital stock using solar technology.

Answer:

$$\pi' = (1 - (w/x')) = (1 - (10/25)) = .6$$

$$v_s = \pi'\rho' = (.6)(.25) = .15/\text{year} = 15\%/\text{year}$$

$$r_s = v_s - \delta = 15\%/\text{year}$$

$$(1 + g_{Ks}) = \beta(1 + r_s) = (.95)(1.15) = 1.0925/\text{year}$$

so $g_{Ks} = 9.25\%$/year.

12.3 Write down the Lagrangian function for the capitalist's utility maximization problem with oil, and find the first-order conditions describing the saddle point. Use these conditions to derive the arbitrage principle and the consumption function.

Answer:

The Lagrangian and the first-order conditions for this problem are:

$$L(C_t, K_{t+1}, \Delta Q_t, Q_{t+1}, \lambda_t) =$$

$$(1 - \beta) \sum_{t=0}^{\infty} \beta^t \ln(C_t)$$

$$-\sum_{t=0}^{\infty} \lambda_t \{K_{t+1} + p_{qt+1}Q_{t+1} + C_t - (1 + r_t)K_t - p_{qt+1}Q_t\}$$

The first-order conditions are (for $t = 0, 1, \ldots, \infty$):

$$\frac{\partial L}{\partial C_t} = \frac{(1 - \beta)\beta^t}{C_t} - \lambda_t = 0$$

$$\frac{\partial L}{\partial K_{t+1}} = -\lambda_t + \lambda_{t+1}(1 + r_t) = 0$$

$$\frac{\partial L}{\partial Q_{t+1}} = -\lambda_t p_{qt+1} + \lambda_{t+1} p_{qt+2} = 0 (\leq \text{ if } Q_{t+1} = 0)$$

$$\frac{\partial L}{\partial \lambda_t}$$

$$= -(K_{t+1} + p_{qt+1}Q_{t+1} + C_t - (1 + r_t)(K_t + p_{qt}\Delta Q_t) - p_{qt+1}(Q_t - \Delta Q_t))$$

$$= 0$$

From the first-order condition on Q_{t+1} we can see that the price of oil must be rising each period to make capital gains on the oil left in the ground equal to the profit rate as well. The arbitrage principle thus takes the form:

$$p_{qt+1} = (1 + r_t)p_{qt}$$

Just as in the other capitalist consumption problems with this utility function, we can show that consumption is a fixed proportion of the capitalist's wealth at the end of the period:

$$C_t = (1 - \beta)((1 + r_t)K_t + p_{qt+1}Q_t)$$

12.4 Explain what effect the following would have on oil prices, using the exhaustible resources model as a basis: (a) a discovery that would allow wells four times as deep as at present to be drilled at the same cost; (b) a drastic cheapening of solar cells; (c) an increase in the capitalist propensity to save.

12.5 Consider the economy described in Problem 12.2. Suppose that the economy has just exhausted its oil reserve. Work backward one period and find the price of oil and the profit rate in the period just before the oil reserve was exhausted.

Answer: In the last period before the oil reserve is exhausted, the profit rate will be determined by the oil technology, and will be:

$$v_{q-1} = (\pi - p_q^*)\rho = (.8 - .5)(.5) = .15/\text{year}$$

According to the arbitrage condition, we must have:

$$p_q^* = (1 + r_{-1})p_{q-1}$$

$$p_{q-1} = p_q^*/(1 + r_{-1}) = .5/1.15 = .43/\text{unit of oil}$$

Problems and Answers for Chapter 13

13.1 Find the Classical overlapping generations equilibrium for Industria (see Problem 2.2) when the wage is \$30,000/worker-year and workers' households save 80% of the wage.

Answer: In Industria: $x = \$50\text{K}/\text{worker-year}$; $k = \$150\text{K}/\text{worker}$; $\rho = .33/\text{year}$; $\delta = .067/\text{year}$. Here we have $\bar{w} = \$30\text{K}/\text{worker-year}$, so the profit rate, $v = (x - w)/k = .133/\text{year}$. The gross growth rate of capital, $g_K + \delta = \beta w/k - (1 - \delta) = (.8)(30/150) - .933 = -.7733/\text{year}$, and the growth rate $g_K = -.84/\text{year}$. Industrian production is so capital intensive that life-cycle savings cannot sustain a positive growth rate of capital and the labor force even at very high wages and with a very high saving propensity. Social consumption per worker is $c = x - (g_K + \delta)k = 50 - (-.7733)(150) = \$166\text{K}/\text{worker-year}$. Worker consumption is $c^w = (1 - \beta)w = (.2)(30) = \$6\text{K}/\text{worker-year}$. Retired households consume $c^r = (1 - \delta + v)\beta w = (1.067)(.8)(30) = \$25.6\text{K}/\text{worker-year}$. We see that $c = c^w + (c^r/(1 + g_K))$ holds, since $c^w = \$6\text{K}/\text{worker-year}$ and $c^r/(1 + g_K) = 25.6/.16 = \$160\text{K}/\text{worker-year}$.

13.2 What is the effect on w, v, $g_K + \delta$, c, c^w, s^w, and c^r of an increase in the conventional real wage, $\bar{w}$?

Answer: $w = \bar{w}$ rises, $v = (x - w)/k$ falls, $g_K + \delta = \beta(w/k) - (1 - \delta)$ rises, $c = x - (g_K + \delta)k$ falls, $c^w = (1 - \beta)w$ rises, and $s^w = \beta w$ rises. The effect on $c^r = (1 + g_K)(c - c^w) = (1 - \delta + v)s^w$ can be either positive or negative, depending on the parameters.

13.3 What is the effect on w, v, g_K, c, c^w, and c^r of an increase in the saving propensity, β?

Answer: $w = \bar{w}$ and $v = (x-w)/k$ are unchanged, $g_K + \delta = \beta(w/k) - (1 - \delta)$ rises, $c = x - (g_K + \delta)k$ falls, $c^w = (1 - \beta)w$ falls, $s^w = \beta w$ rises, and $c^r = (1 + g_K)(c - c^w) = (1 - \delta + v)s^w$ rises.

13.4 Find the Classical overlapping generations equilibrium for Industria (see Problem 2.2) when the growth rate of the labor force is zero and workers' households save 80% of the wage.

Answer: In Industria: $x = \$50\text{K}/\text{worker-year}$; $k = \$150\text{K}/\text{worker}$; $\rho = .33/\text{year}$; $\delta = .067/\text{year}$. Here we have $n = g_K = 0$, so that $w = (1 + n)(k/\beta) = \$187.5\text{K}/\text{worker-year}$, and the profit rate, $v = (x - w)/k = -.9167/\text{year}$. The gross growth rate of capital, $g_K + \delta = \beta w/k - (1 - \delta) = (.8)(187.5/150) - .933 = .0667/\text{year}$, and the growth rate $g_K = 0/\text{year}$. Industrian production is so capital intensive that life-cycle savings cannot maintain the capital stock except at a wage so high that the profit rate is negative. Social consumption per worker is $c = x - (g_K + \delta)k = 50 - (.0667)(150) = \$40\text{K}/\text{worker-year}$. Worker consumption is $c^w = (1 - \beta)w = (.2)(187.5) = \$37.5\text{K}/\text{worker-year}$. Retired households consume $c^r = (1 - \delta + v)\beta w = (.0167)(.8)(187.5) = \$2.5\text{K}/\text{worker-year}$. We see that $c = c^w + (c^r/(1+g_K))$ holds, since $c^w = \$37.5\text{K}/\text{worker-year}$ and $c^r/(1 + g_K) = 2.5/1 = \$2.5\text{K}/\text{worker-year}$.

13.5 Analyze the equilibrium of the overlapping generations model when there are several techniques available.

Answer: The saving of active workers is still βw, so that this curve is the efficiency frontier projected downward by the factor β. The equilibrium profit rate, if it exists, lies at the intersection of this curve and the capital requirements line $(1 + n)k$.

13.6 What is the effect of a rise in β on the equilibrium growth path of the overlapping generations model, in terms of v, w, g_K, c, c^w, and c^r?

Answer: A rise in β leaves n, and therefore g_K and the capital requirements $(1+n)k$ unchanged. Since workers will save more for every level of the wage, the wage must fall and the profit rate rise. Social consumption will remain constant, since g_K has not changed, but c^r will rise and c^w will fall.

13.7 What is the effect of an increase in the growth rate of the population on the equilibrium of the overlapping generations model, in terms of v, w, g_K, c, c^w, and c^r?

Answer: An increase in n raises g_K, and the capital requirements $(1+n)k$, and thus increases the real wage, while lowering the profit rate. At the higher g_K social consumption/worker is lower. $c^w = (1 - \beta)w$, so the higher wage raises c^w. The impact on c^r depends on the exact parameters of the model.

13.8 Does the argument given above prove that if $r > n$ the stationary overlapping generations equilibrium is Pareto-efficient? Is the alternative path we constructed to show that the $r < n$ stationary equilibrium is not Pareto-efficient itself Pareto-efficient?

Answer: The argument does not prove that the stationary equilibrium is efficient because there might be some other way to construct a Pareto-superior path even though this way doesn't work when $r > n$. The alternative path we constructed may not be Pareto-efficient.

13.9 If you were a dictator in an overlapping generations economy, and you had to choose a stationary path for the economy, which one would you choose to maximize the utility of the representative household? (Hint: how much consumption do you have to allocate between workers and retirees in each period, after you have allowed for enough capital to permit steady growth to continue?) Is this path the one the market will choose?

Answer: The dictator will maximize the utility of the typical agent, $(1-\beta)\ln(c^w)+\beta\ln(c^r)$ subject to the constraint that social saving equal $(1+n)k$:

$$\text{choose } (c^w, c^r) \text{ to max } (1-\beta)\ln(c^w) + \beta\ln(c^r)$$

$$\text{subject to } c^w + \frac{c^r}{1+n} + (1+n)k = x - \delta k$$

This will be the same as the typical workers' problem when $r = n$, so the allocation will be the same as the competitive allocation when $r = n$. But the market real interest rate will not equal the population growth rate unless β has a particular value.

13.10 Consider an overlapping generations economy where the typical household has Cobb-Douglas utility with $\beta = .2$, the wage $\bar{w} = \$750,000/\text{period}$, $x = \$900,000/\text{period}$, $\delta = 1$, so that capital depreciates completely each period, and $k = \$100,000/\text{worker}$. Find the steady-state equilibrium profit rate, growth rate, and the pattern of consumption of the typical household in the absence of any social security system.

Answer: We have $r + \delta = v = (x - \bar{w})/k = (900 -750)/100 = 1.5$, so that $r = .5/\text{year}$. The gross growth rate of capital, $(g_K^* + \delta) = \beta w/k = .2(750)/100 = 1.5/\text{year}$, so that $g_K^* = .5/\text{year}$. The typical household will consume

$$(1-\beta)w = .8w = .8(\$750K)/\text{worker- period}$$

$$= \$600K/\text{worker-period}$$

in its working period, and

$$\beta(1+r)w = .2(1.5)(\$750K /\text{worker-period})$$

$$= \$225K \text{ /worker-period}$$

in retirement.

13.11 For the economy in problem 13.10, find the steady-state equilibrium growth rate, and profit rate with a funded social security system where the benefit for a typical working household is \$5,000/period. Find the steady-state equilibrium growth rate, and profit rate for an unfunded social security system with the same social security benefit. What will the tax on working households be?

Answer: A funded social security system will lead to the same equilibrium as no social security system.

For the unfunded system we have

$$(1 + g_K^*)^2 + (\frac{\beta}{k})(b\frac{1 - \beta}{\beta(1 + r)} - \bar{w})(1 + g_K^*) + \frac{\beta b}{k} = 0$$

or

$$(1 + g_K^*)^2 - 1.495(1 + g_K^*) + .01 = 0$$

which gives $1 + g_K^* = 1.488$/period. The tax will be $t = b/(1 + g_K^*) = \$3,360$/worker/year.

13.12 Consider a neoclassical overlapping generations economy where the typical household has Cobb-Douglas utility with $\beta = .2$, the population grows at $\bar{n} = .5$/period, $x = \$900,000$/period, $\delta = 1$, so that capital depreciates completely each period, and $k = \$100,000$/worker. Find the steady-state equilibrium real wage and profit rate, and the pattern of consumption of the typical household in the absence of any social security system.

Answer: We have $w = x - (r + \delta)k$ =\$900K/worker-period - $(1 + r$/period)(\$100K/worker), and the equilibrium condition $\beta w = .2w = (1 + n)k$ =(1.5/period)(\$100K/worker), so that $w = \$750K$ /worker-period, rk =\$50K/worker-period, and $r = .5$/period $= 50\%$/period. The typical household will consume $(1 - \beta)w = .8w =.8(\$750K)$/worker-period $= \$600K$/worker-period in its working period, and $\beta(1 + r)w = .2(1.5)(\$750K$ /worker-period) $= \$225K$ /worker-period in retirement.

13.13 For the economy in problem 13.12, find the steady-state equilibrium wage and profit rate with a funded social security system where the benefit to a typical working household is \$5,000/period. Find the steady-state equilibrium wage and profit rate for an unfunded social security system with the same social security benefit level. What will the tax be?

Answer: A funded social security system will lead to the same equilibrium as no social security system.

For the unfunded system we have

$$(1+r^*)^2+((x/k)-(1-\delta)-b/k(1+\bar{n})-(1+\bar{n})/\beta)(1+r^*)-(b/k)(1-\beta)/\beta = 0$$

or

$$(1 + r^*)^2 + 1.467(1 + r^*) - .2 = 0$$

The larger root is $(1 + r^*) = 1.315$/year, or $r = .315$/year. The wage will be $w = x - (r + \delta)k = 900 - (1.315)(100) = \$768.5K$/year. The tax will be $t = b/(1 + \bar{n}) = 5/(1.5) = \$3,333$/worker/year.

13.14 Show that the equilibrium profit rate is the same in the debt model when the debt is zero as in the social security model with no social security tax or benefit.

Problems and Answers for Chapter 14

14.1 If one worker can produce one ounce of gold in a year with 10 bushels of corn in Ricardia, where 1 worker can produce 100 bushels of corn from 20 bushels of seed corn in a year, and $\$1 = 1/20$th of an ounce of gold, find the price of corn and the money wage in Ricardia when the real wage is 20 bu corn/worker/year. Check by finding the rental rates for capital in the corn and gold industries.

Answer: $x_g = 1$ ounce of gold/worker/year $= \$20$/worker/year, and $k_g = 10$ bu corn/worker. We have $x = 100$ bu/worker/year, $k_x = 20$ bu/worker, $k_g = 10$ bu/worker, $1 - \pi = \bar{w}/x = (20$ bu/worker-year)(1 worker-year/100 bu$) = .2$, and $\pi = .8$, so the average capital-labor ratio is $\pi k_g + (1 - \pi)k_x = 10$ bu/worker$(.8) + 20$ bu/worker$(.2) = 12$ bu/worker.

The price of a bushel of corn is

$$p_{+1} = \frac{1 \text{ ounce of gold/worker/year}}{100 \text{ bu/worker/year}} \frac{20 \text{ bu/worker}}{12 \text{ bu/worker}}$$

$$= \frac{5/3 \text{ oz gold}}{100 \text{ bu}} = \$(1/3)/\text{bu}$$

The gold wage is $p_{+1}w = \$(20/3)$/worker/year. To check, the profit rate in corn production is $(x - w)/k_x = (80/20) = 4$ /year. The profit rate in gold production is

$$\frac{x_g - p_{+1}w}{pk_g} = (\$20 - \$(1/3)(20))/(\$1/3)(10)) = 4/\text{year}$$

14.2 In Aurea the production of $\$50,000$ worth of commodities requires one worker-year of labor working with $\$150,000$ worth of commodity capital. The same capital and labor can also produce 1000 ounces of gold. $1/10 = .1 = 10\%$ of the capital depreciates in each year and the real wage is \$20,000/worker/year. If Aurean capitalists' propensity to save, $\beta = .97$, and capitalist households devote 90% of their consumption fund to commodities and 10% to holding gold, find the gold price of commodities, the profit rate, the net profit rate, the growth rates of the stocks of capital and gold, the stock of gold per worker, and the proportion of the labor force employed in the gold and commodities industries in the steady state.

Answer: Here $x = \$50,000$/worker/year, $k = \$150,000$/worker, $x_g = 1000$ oz of gold/worker/year, $\delta = .1$/year, $\bar{w} = \$20,000$/worker/year, $\beta = .97$, and $\mu = .1$.

We have:

$$p = \frac{x_g}{x} = (1000/50000) = .02 \text{ oz of gold/\$}$$

$$v = \frac{x - \bar{w}}{k} = 30000/150000 = .2/\text{year}$$

$$1 + r = 1 - \delta + v = 1.1/\text{year}$$

$$g_G = g_K = \beta(1 + r) - 1 = .97(1.1) - 1 = .067/\text{year}$$

$$a = \left(\frac{\mu(1 - \beta)(1 + r)}{r - \mu(1 - \beta)(1 + r)} \right) pk$$

$$= ((.1)(.03)(1.1)/(.1 - .0033))(.02)(150000)$$

$$= 102.4 \text{ oz of gold/worker}$$

$$n_g = 1 - n_x = \frac{g_G a}{x_g} = (.067)(102.4)/1000 = .007$$

14.3 If labor productivity in the gold industry increases at the rate $\gamma = .01$/year in Aurea (see Problem 14.2), find the profit rate, net profit rate, the growth rates of the stocks of capital and gold, and the ratio of the stock of gold to the value of the capital stock in the steady state..

Answer: Here $v_x = .2$/year from Problem 14.2, and $\gamma = .01$/year. We have:

$$v = (1 + \gamma)v_x = (1.01)(.2) = .202/\text{year}$$

$$1 + r = (1 + \gamma)(1 - \delta + v_x) = (1.01)(1.1) = 1.111/\text{year}$$

$$g_G = \beta(1 + r) - 1 = .078/\text{year}$$

$$g_K = \beta(1 - \delta + v_x) - 1 = .97(1.1) - 1 = .067/\text{year}$$

$$a/pk = \left(\frac{\mu(1 - \beta)(1 + r)}{r - \mu(1 - \beta)(1 + r)} \right)$$

$$= ((.1)(.03)(1.111)/(.111 - .00333))(.02)(150000) = .031$$

Problems and Answers for Chapter 15

15.1 Consider a vintage model with a profit share equal to 1/3, a saving rate out of profits equal to 3/4, and a rate of Harrod-neutral technical change equal to 5% per year (.05 per year). Find the rate of growth, the profit share on the most recent vintage, and the service life of machines. Use a graphing calculator or a spreadsheet to achieve a numerical solution.

Answer: $g = s_p \pi = (3/4)(1/3) = .25$

$$T < 11.6 \rightarrow T = 11$$

$$\pi_t = .433$$

15.2 Consider the model in Problem 15.1, but assume that the profit share has declined to 1/4. Find the new steady state value of the service life of machines, and explain why it is larger or smaller than it had been. Use a graphing calculator or a spreadsheet to achieve a numerical solution.

Answer:
$$T < 9.2 \rightarrow T = 9$$

$$\pi_t = .355$$

The increased wage share reduces the profit available for older vintages, forcing earlier retirement of equipment.

15.3 Suppose that the technical progress function takes a quadratic form: $\gamma = -\chi^2 - .52\chi + .0149$. Find the optimum rate of capital-saving (or -using) technical change when the profit share is 1/3. Find the optimum rate when the profit share is 1/4. Compare your answers. *Answer:*

$$f' = -2\chi - .52 = \pi/(\pi - 1) = 1/3/(-2/3) = -.5 \rightarrow \chi = -.01$$

$$f' = -2\chi - .52 = 1/4/(-3/4) = -.33 \rightarrow \chi = -.093$$

A decrease in the profit share reduces the importance of capital costs, and induces a decrease in the rate of capital-saving technical change.

15.4 Using the data in Problem 15.3, find the rate of increase in the real wage under the conventional wage share assumption when the profit share is $1/3$. Find the rate when the profit share is $1/4$. Compare your answers.

Answer: When $\pi = 1/3$,

$$\gamma = -(.01)^2 - .52(.01) + .0149 = .02 \rightarrow g_w = .02$$

When $\pi = 1/4$,

$$\gamma = -(.093)^2 - .52(.093) + .0149 = .055 \rightarrow g_w = .055$$

An increase in the wage share increases the importance of labor costs, and induces an increase in the rate of labor-saving technical change. The real wage grows at the same rate as labor productivity under the conventional wage share assumption, so a higher wage share implies a faster rate of growth of wages as well.

15.5 Assume in an otherwise Classical model that full employment of the labor force is maintained through instantaneous changes in the profit share, and that the labor force is constant. Use the technical progress function in the previous problems. Characterize the steady state equilibrium with induced technical change by calculating the values of γ, χ, g_K, g_X, and π.

Answer:

Since $g_N = 0$, $g_X = \gamma$. The steady state equilibrium requires that $\chi = 0$. Therefore, $g_X = g_K = \gamma = f(0) = .0149$. To find π, use the first order condition

$$\pi/(\pi - 1) = f'(0) = -.52 \rightarrow \pi = .342$$

When full employment is assumed rather than a conventional wage share, this model produces an equilibrium with Harrod-neutral technical change and an endogenous profit share.

15.6 Derive the equation for the equilibrium wage in the model of specialization. Show that the wage grows at the same rate as the number of designs.

Answer:

The wage will be equal to the marginal product of the given labor force, N, or

$$w = \frac{\partial X}{\partial N} = (1 - \alpha)N^{-\alpha} \sum_{i=1}^{A} K_i^{\alpha}$$

Multiplying both sides by (N/N), this simplifies to:

$$w = (1 - \alpha)X/N$$

Since we already know that X/N grows at the rate g_A, it is clear that the wage does so as well. Workers receive a constant share of a steadily growing product.

15.7 Would the rate of growth in the model with specialization be greater or less than the rate of growth which maximizes the utility of the capitalists?

Answer:

The rate of growth which maximizes the utility of capitalists would be greater than the rate of growth that the capitalists choose through their own individual decisions. The capitalists, in consulting only their self-interest, do not take into account the externalities which benefit all future generations of inventors, and thus they underinvest in research.

Problems and Answers for Chapter 16

16.1 Derive an expression for the rate of growth of employment in the model with learning by doing. Must employment be increasing?

Answer:

$$g_N = g_X - \gamma = g_K - \gamma \approx g_K - ag_K = (1 - a)g_K$$

Assuming $g_K > 0$, employment will be increasing if $a < 1$ and decreasing if $a > 1$.

16.2 Suppose that learning by doing tends to lead to more mechanized technologies, so that $A = K^b$, where $b < 0$. Derive the expression that describes the rate of capital-using technical change, χ.

Answer:

$$\frac{\rho_{+1}}{\rho} = 1 + \chi = \frac{K_{+1}^b}{K^b} = (1 + g_K)^b$$

$$\chi \approx bg_K$$

Note that we cannot go any further since with biased technical change there will be no steady state rate of profit or capital accumulation.

16.3 In the model with $g(rd) = (1 - rd)^\theta$, if $w/x = .5$, and $\theta = 2$, find the proportion of capital a capitalist will devote to innovation, rd^*. What will the level of $g(rd^*)$ be? What will be her actual share of wages in costs? If $\rho = .333$/year and $\delta = .05$/year, calculate her gross rate of profit when $rd = 0$ and at the optimum level of innovation.

Answer: $1 - rd^* = (\frac{1}{(1+\theta)(1-\pi)})^{\frac{1}{\theta}} = (\frac{1}{3(.5)})^{\frac{1}{2}} = .82$. The capitalist will invest 18% of her capital in R&D, and 82% in production.

$g(rd^*) = (1 - rd^*)^\theta = (.82)^2 = .67$, so that the labor requirement is reduced by 33%.

At the optimum,

$$r^* = (1 - (1 - \pi)g(rd^*))\rho - \delta = (1 - (.5)(.67))(.333) - .05 = .17 \text{ /year}$$

The net profit rate without technical change is $r = \pi\rho - \delta = (.5)(.333) - .05 = .117$

16.4 Find the formula for the optimal rd if $g(rd) = 1 - \theta rd$.

16.5 Find the steady-state gross profit rate and gross growth rate for the economy described in Problem 16.3 under the assumption that there is no persistence to the improvement in labor productivity that results from innovative expenditure and that $\beta = .9$.

Answer: $r^* = .17$ in each period. $1 + g_K = \beta(1 + r^*) = .9(1.17) = 1.053$.

16.6 Can an increase in the wage raise the profit rate and growth rate in an economy where improvements in labor productivity from innovative expenditures do not persist?

16.7 Find the steady-state level of labor productivity for the economy described in Problems 16.3 and 16.5 when there is complete persistence of the productivity enhancing effect of innovative expenditure and the wage is $\bar{w} = \$10,000$/year.

Answer: The steady state level of productivity, x^* satisfies $x^* = (1 + \theta)\bar{w} = (1 + 2)(10,000 = \$30,000$/worker/year.

16.8 Find the growth rate of labor productivity for the economy described in Problem 16.3 under the assumption that labor productivity improvements are persistent and that the wage share is 60%.

Answer: $1 + \gamma = (1 + \theta)(1 - \bar{\pi}) = (1 + 2)(.6) = 1.8$, or $\gamma = 80\%$/period.

16.9 What rd would lead to the maximum rate of growth of labor productivity in this model? Would it be a good idea to follow this policy? Explain why or why not.

Answer: Since $1 + \gamma = \frac{1}{g(rd)}$, the maximal rate of labor productivity growth is achieved at the lowest $g(rd)$, which occurs when $rd = 1$. This policy, unfortunately, invests everything in innovation and nothing in production, so that the economy would have zero output.

Index